C-4396   CAREER EXAMINATION SERIES

*This is your
PASSBOOK for...*

# California Highway Patrol Officer (CHP)

*Test Preparation Study Guide
Questions & Answers*

# COPYRIGHT NOTICE

This book is SOLELY intended for, is sold ONLY to, and its use is RESTRICTED to individual, bona fide applicants or candidates who qualify by virtue of having seriously filed applications for appropriate license, certificate, professional and/or promotional advancement, higher school matriculation, scholarship, or other legitimate requirements of education and/or governmental authorities.

This book is NOT intended for use, class instruction, tutoring, training, duplication, copying, reprinting, excerption, or adaptation, etc., by:

1) Other publishers
2) Proprietors and/or Instructors of "Coaching" and/or Preparatory Courses
3) Personnel and/or Training Divisions of commercial, industrial, and governmental organizations
4) Schools, colleges, or universities and/or their departments and staffs, including teachers and other personnel
5) Testing Agencies or Bureaus
6) Study groups which seek by the purchase of a single volume to copy and/or duplicate and/or adapt this material for use by the group as a whole without having purchased individual volumes for each of the members of the group
7) Et al.

Such persons would be in violation of appropriate Federal and State statutes.

PROVISION OF LICENSING AGREEMENTS – Recognized educational, commercial, industrial, and governmental institutions and organizations, and others legitimately engaged in educational pursuits, including training, testing, and measurement activities, may address request for a licensing agreement to the copyright owners, who will determine whether, and under what conditions, including fees and charges, the materials in this book may be used them. In other words, a licensing facility exists for the legitimate use of the material in this book on other than an individual basis. However, it is asseverated and affirmed here that the material in this book CANNOT be used without the receipt of the express permission of such a licensing agreement from the Publishers. Inquiries re licensing should be addressed to the company, attention rights and permissions department.

All rights reserved, including the right of reproduction in whole or in part, in any form or by any means, electronic or mechanical, including photocopying, recording, or by any information storage and retrieval system, without permission in writing from the Publisher.

Copyright © 2024 by
## National Learning Corporation

212 Michael Drive, Syosset, NY 11791
(516) 921-8888 • www.passbooks.com
E-mail: info@passbooks.com

# PASSBOOK® SERIES

THE *PASSBOOK® SERIES* has been created to prepare applicants and candidates for the ultimate academic battlefield – the examination room.

At some time in our lives, each and every one of us may be required to take an examination – for validation, matriculation, admission, qualification, registration, certification, or licensure.

Based on the assumption that every applicant or candidate has met the basic formal educational standards, has taken the required number of courses, and read the necessary texts, the *PASSBOOK® SERIES* furnishes the one special preparation which may assure passing with confidence, instead of failing with insecurity. Examination questions – together with answers – are furnished as the basic vehicle for study so that the mysteries of the examination and its compounding difficulties may be eliminated or diminished by a sure method.

This book is meant to help you pass your examination provided that you qualify and are serious in your objective.

The entire field is reviewed through the huge store of content information which is succinctly presented through a provocative and challenging approach – the question-and-answer method.

A climate of success is established by furnishing the correct answers at the end of each test.

You soon learn to recognize types of questions, forms of questions, and patterns of questioning. You may even begin to anticipate expected outcomes.

You perceive that many questions are repeated or adapted so that you can gain acute insights, which may enable you to score many sure points.

You learn how to confront new questions, or types of questions, and to attack them confidently and work out the correct answers.

You note objectives and emphases, and recognize pitfalls and dangers, so that you may make positive educational adjustments.

Moreover, you are kept fully informed in relation to new concepts, methods, practices, and directions in the field.

You discover that you are actually taking the examination all the time: you are preparing for the examination by "taking" an examination, not by reading extraneous and/or supererogatory textbooks.

In short, this PASSBOOK®, used directedly, should be an important factor in helping you to pass your test.

# HOW TO PREPARE GUIDE FOR CALIFORNIA HIGHWAY PATROL

# WRITTEN EXAMINATION

## TABLE OF CONTENTS

**CHAPTER 1 – CALIFORNIA HIGHWAY PATROL (CHP)**
- GENERAL INFORMATION .................................................................. 1-1
- HISTORY OF THE CHP ....................................................................... 1-2
- CHP GEOGRAPHICAL JURISDICTION/ORGANIZATION ................... 1-2
- FULL PEACE OFFICER POWER ........................................................ 1-3
- THE CHP ACADEMY ........................................................................... 1-3

**CHAPTER 2 – SELECTION PROCESS**
- MINIMUM REQUIREMENTS FOR ELIGIBILITY FOR THE EXAM ....... 2-1
- PHYSICAL CONDITION ...................................................................... 2-1
- APPLICATION ..................................................................................... 2-2
- WRITTEN EXAMINATION ................................................................... 2-2
- SAMPLE WRITTEN TEST ................................................................... 2-C-1

**CHAPER 3 – PHYSICAL ABILITY TEST (PAT)**
- PHYSICAL ABILITY TEST (PAT) ......................................................... 3-1
- WRITTEN PSYCHOLOGICAL TEST (WPT) ........................................ 3-3

**CHAPTER 4 – QUALIFICATIONS APPRAISAL PANEL INTERVIEW (QAP)**
- QUALIFICATIONS APPRAISAL PANEL INTERVIEW (QAP) ............... 4-1
- YOU AND YOUR INTERVIEW ............................................................. 4-A-1

**CHAPER 5 – BACKGROUND INVESTIGATION, MEDICAL EVALUATION, PSYCHOLOGICAL EVALUATION, ACADEMY INVITATION**
- BACKGROUND INVESTIGATION ....................................................... 5-1
- MEDICAL EVALUATION ..................................................................... 5-2
- PSYCHOLOGICAL INTERVIEW .......................................................... 5-2
- ACADEMY INVITATION ...................................................................... 5-2

**CHAPTER 6 – LIFE AT THE ACADEMY**
- REPORTING TO THE ACADEMY ....................................................... 6-1
- ACADEMY LIFESTYLE ....................................................................... 6-2
- ACADEMY TRAINING ......................................................................... 6-3

**CHAPTER 7 – CADET FIELD ASSIGNMENT PROTOCOL**
- ASSIGNMENT/GRADUATION ............................................................. 7-1
- FIELD TRAINING AND PROBATION .................................................. 7-1

# CHAPTER 1

# CALIFORNIA HIGHWAY PATROL

1. **GENERAL INFORMATION**

    a. **Mission**: The mission of the California Highway Patrol (CHP) is to provide the highest level of safety, service, and security to the people of California. This is accomplished through five departmental goals:

    - **Prevent Loss of Life, Injuries, and Property Damage:** To minimize the loss of life, personal injury, and property damage resulting from traffic collisions through enforcement, education, and engineering. To enforce the provisions of the California Vehicle Code and other laws to prevent crime.

    - **Maximize Service to the Public and Assistance to Allied Agencies.** To maximize service to the public in need of aid or information, and to assist other public agencies when appropriate.

    - **Manage Traffic and Emergency Incidents.** To promote the safe and efficient movement of people and goods throughout California, and to minimize exposure of the public to unsafe conditions resulting from emergency incidents and highway impediments.

    - **Protect Public and State Assets.** To protect the public, their property, state employees, and the state's infrastructure. To collaborate with local, state, and federal public safety agencies to protect California.

    - **Improve Departmental Efficiency.** To continuously look for ways to increase the efficiency and/or effectiveness of departmental operations.

    b. **Organizational Values:** To accomplish our mission, we are committed to the following organizational values as the foundation of our pledge to public safety and service:

    - Respect for others
    - Fairness
    - Ethical practices
    - Equitable treatment for all

    c. **Rank Structure:** Commissioner, Deputy Commissioner, Assistant Commissioner, Chief, Assistant Chief, Captain, Lieutenant, Sergeant, Officer.

2. **HISTORY OF THE CHP**

   The first automobile appeared in California in 1896. California's love affair with the automobile had begun. With the increase of automobiles, particularly in populated cities and counties, traffic accidents increased also. The first automobile-related fatality was recorded in 1902. The need for traffic control services became apparent.

   Cities and counties began by regulating motor vehicle operations within their own jurisdictions. As each jurisdiction passed its own regulations, the differences from one area to another created a new set of problems. Therefore, in 1905 the California Legislature responded by providing the first in a series of laws related to traffic regulation. As the need for uniform motor vehicle regulations continued to grow, the "California Vehicle Act of 1915" was enacted, a forerunner of today's California Vehicle Code.

   By 1923, the Legislature authorized the appointment of State Inspectors and Traffic Officers. They were paid and employed by the state to enforce motor vehicle laws. These appointees were assigned to work in a specific county under a system known as "Dual Control." The problem with "Dual Control" was that the Traffic Officers were controlled by the counties. California still lacked statewide uniformity in traffic law enforcement. Therefore, on August 4, 1929, the Legislature created the California Highway Patrol. This new agency had statewide authority to enforce traffic laws on county and state highways, responsibilities that are still the Department's primary mission.

   Over the years, the CHP has continued to grow and change, and has assumed many more responsibilities. Today the organization includes a diverse group of men and women that ensures that the responsibilities of the Department are carried out professionally and efficiently.

3. **CHP GEOGRAPHICAL JURISDICTION/ORGANIZATION**

   Since California is comprised of 158,693 square miles from Oregon to the Mexico Border, the terrain, weather conditions, ad roadways are extremely diverse (Annex 1-A). The CHP patrols all state freeways in the 58 counties, including those within city boundaries. These freeways include interstate routes, U.S. routes, and state routes. The Department has traffic jurisdiction on all public streets and highways in unincorporated areas under state and county control. In all, there are more than 98,000 miles of roadway within the CHP's jurisdiction.

   The CHP is divided into eight geographical Divisions covering the entire State of California (Annex 1-B-1). Personnel ranking from chief to officer, with the support of civilian personnel, staff each Division. These ranking officials command, manage, and support operations in Area offices, communication centers, and commercial vehicle inspection and scale facilities posted throughout their geographical jurisdiction. Together these posts provide services to ensure public safety and security, as well as to ensure lawful and efficient use of the highway transportation system. To oversee the CHP Divisions, CHP Headquarters in Sacramento provides general support to the various CHP programs, disseminates policy and procedure, and provides training to run these programs.

4. **FULL PEACE OFFICER POWER**

   **Authorities**. Section 830.2 of the California Penal Code identifies the uniformed employees of the CHP as peace officers whose authority extends statewide. According to the Penal Code, their primary duty is the enforcement of any law relating to the use or operation of vehicles upon the highways, or laws pertaining to the provision of police services for the protection of state officers, state properties, and the occupants of state properties, or both, as set forth in the Vehicle Code and Government Code.

   Division 2 of the California Vehicle Code further defines CHP function and powers, including authorities for accident investigations, CHP issued licenses, and emergency vehicle permits.

   The Department's primary purpose is to ensure public safety and provide responsive services to the residents of California. The Department's mission is met through the management of traffic on California's highways, roadways, and assigned surface streets. Traffic management consists of various responsibilities that include accident prevention, emergency traffic and/or incident management, law enforcement duties, and assistance to allied agencies and the public. Additionally, the CHP has the responsibility for investigation of all crimes that occur on state property, and protection of state buildings, state supreme court justices, and appellate court justices. The following is a list of some of the diverse positions necessary to accomplish and maintain these services.

   | | | |
   |---|---|---|
   | • Motorcycle Officer | • Air Operations | • Academy Instructor |
   | • Recruiting Officer | Pilot/Observer | Staff Officer |
   | • Commercial Vehicle Enforcement Officer | • Drug Recognition Expert | • Safety Services Program Officer |
   | • Weapons Training Officer | • Court Officer | • Equestrian Patrol |
   | • Evidence Officer | • Multi-disciplinary Accident Investigation Team | • Bicycle Patrol |
   | • Advanced Accident Investigation Officer | • Background Investigator | • Capitol Protective Services |
   | • Field Training Officer | • Auto Theft Investigator | • Court Services |
   | • Canine Officer | • Training Coordinator | • Community Services Officer |
   | • Public Affairs Officer | • Dignitary Protection | |

5. **THE CHP ACADEMY**

   The CHP Academy is one of the most modern and complete law enforcement training facilities in the United States and is recognized as one of the finest law enforcement training institutions in the world. The facility is located on 456 acres in West Sacramento. The primary function of the Academy is to provide basic training for newly appointed CHP cadets. The Academy can accommodate over 300 cadets at any particular time. Its secondary function is to provide specialized in-service refresher training and other related training for CHP employees are allied agencies. These courses include specialized classes such as traffic accident reconstruction training, emergency vehicle operations training, tactical riot training, general law enforcement training, and motorcycle enforcement training. Providing the best training available using modern methods is a trademark of the CHP Academy.

The dining facility seats 400 persons and food is served cafeteria style, three times daily. A recreation room is available for students' use during their leisure hours. The Staff Office is located in the recreation building and is staffed by an officer 24 hours a day.

The multi-purpose room serves as a gymnasium and an auditorium for graduation ceremonies. It has a full-length basketball court, exercise machines, weight training equipment, and a whirlpool bath. A large water safety tank is used to teach water safety and underwater rescue training for air operations personnel and allied agencies. The underwater viewing room allows students and instructors to observe rescue techniques. Additional physical training facilities consist of a quarter-mile running track; a 442-foot long obstacle course; 2.5, 3.2, and 4.2 mile running trails; and a softball field.

There are thirteen Academy classrooms. Each classroom is equipped with a video projector, audio-visual equipment, and connecting cables for computer generated classroom presentations.

In addition to learning agency specific policies and procedures, cadets are academically responsible for 67 "learning domains" mandated by the Commission on Peace Officer Standards and Training (POST) in addition to CHP-specific policies and procedures. POST training was established by the Legislature to set minimum selection and training standards for California law enforcement. During the 27-week program, cadets receive over 1,255 hours of training.

The Emergency Vehicle Operations Course (EVOC) is famous throughout the world as the finest law enforcement driver training program available. The facility consists of a 2.3-mile, high performance driving track, two skid recovery practice areas, and a defensive driving complex. Additional driving facilities are provided for motorcycle enforcement training.

The Weapons Training Unit has both an indoor and outdoor range, each equipped with 30 electronically controlled moving targets. Each area has lighting which can be controlled to simulate different environmental conditions or to allow training during hours of darkness.

# CHAPTER 2

## SELECTION PROCESS
## CADET, CALIFORNIA HIGHWAY PATROL

Cadet, California Highway Patrol (CHP) is the entry level training classification for qualified persons to learn the duties of a CHP officer. All CHP officers begin their careers at this classification. Applications for Cadet, CHP, are accepted on a continuous basis. Examinations are conducted statewide, four times a year in each field Division.

There are seven separate test phases in the Cadet selection process. With the exception of the Qualifications Appraisal Panel (QAP) interview, all tests are scored on a pass/fail basis. Typically, the testing process requires an average of six months to one year to complete. The sequence is listed below:

- Application
- Written Examination
- Physical Ability Test (PAT), Written Psychological Test
- Qualifications Appraisal Panel (QAP) Interview
- Psychological Evaluation
- Background Investigation
- Medical Evaluation

1. **MINIMUM REQUIREMENTS FOR ELIGIBILITY FOR THE EXAMINATION**

    a. **Age.** 20 to 35 years of age. By state law, the maximum age for examination is 35 years. Successful applicants must be at least 21 years of age at the time of appointment to the Academy.

    b. **Education.** High school diploma from a United States (U.S.) institution or a general equivalency diploma (GED).

    c. **Citizenship.** An application for U.S. Citizenship must already be in process before you can begin the testing process. You must be a U.S. citizen at time of appointment to the CHP Academy.

    d. **Character.** No felony convictions.

2. **PHYSICAL CONDITION**

    a. Good health, sound physical condition.

    b. Normal hearing.

    c. Freedom from any physical or mental condition that would interfere with the full performance of the essential duties of an Officer, CHP.

d.  Vision. The applicant must read from a standard eye test chart. If eyeglasses or hard contact lenses are worn, uncorrected vision must be no less than 20/40 in each eye and corrected to 20/20 in each eye. Applicants who have successfully worn soft contact lenses for the past 12 months are not required to meet an uncorrected standard as long as their corrected vision is 20/20 in each eye. At least four quarterly checks for vision stabilization are required for applicants who have had any eye surgery. Normal color vision is required as assessed by the Farnsworth-D-15 test. An X-Chrom Lens is prohibited.

3. **APPLICATION**

Each applicant must submit a State of California, California Highway Patrol Cadet Application, CHP 678, designed to process electronically, and the State of California Examination and/or Employment Application (STD 678), which will be accepted for this examination prior to the QAP interview. Applications can be obtained from any CHP office, by calling a CHP recruiter at 1-888-4ACHPJOB (888-422-4756), by requesting an application online at www.ch.ca.gov, or via e-mail at Recruiting@chp.ca.gov.

4. **WRITTEN EXAMINATION**

The written examination was developed by CHP and POST to determine if the applicant possesses the **minimum** reading and writing proficiency needed to successfully perform the duties of a CHP officer. **This is not a test of law enforcement or knowledge of the CHP**.

a.  **The Written Examination.** The written examination consists of multiple choice and fill-in-the-blank. There are approximately 125 questions covering spelling, vocabulary, grammar, and reading comprehension. You have approximately 2 hours and 30 minutes to complete this portion of the test. See Annex C for a sample written test.

b.  **Written Examination Preparation.** Applicants often ask how they can prepare for the written examination phase of the cadet testing process. There are several options you may wish to consider.

   1) Study books that review reading comprehension skills, and English composition, including grammar and spelling.

   2) Study books that pertain to taking law enforcement examinations.

   3) Enroll in college or an adult education course that emphasizes English, reading comprehension, and writing skills.

   4) Develop a self-improvement writing program.

c. **Reading and Writing Self Improvement Books.** Whereas we may suggest books and guides, we do not require the purchase of, nor endorse, any publication to applicants. Since skills vary from applicant to applicant, it would be inappropriate to arbitrarily select books for an individual. If an applicant's skills/abilities are significantly below the 12$^{th}$ grade level, it is doubtful that any book would be enough to ensure success on the written examination.

There are many publications available at local libraries and bookstores that provide instruction on improving reading and writing skills. Select publications comprehensive to reading and writing skills at or beyond the 12$^{th}$ grade level.

d. **Law Enforcement Examination Books.** Also available at libraries and bookstores are books pertaining to civil service or law enforcement examinations. These may be helpful for applicants who believe their skills are sufficient to pass the written examination but want to become familiar with civil service/law enforcement examination questions.

e. **Preparatory Course.** If an applicant has not written in essay form for some time, or if he/she feels their knowledge of grammar is inadequate, it might be useful to take a writing course at a local college. A number of grammar handbooks exist, which can be located at almost any bookstore. One very popular handbook is called Easy Access: The Reference Handbook for Writers, by Katherine Adams and Michael Keene (McGraw-Hill Publishing). This text includes a section on English as a second language. One caution: the study of grammar without writing practice seldom improves writing.

Perhaps the most effective option is for an applicant to take college or adult education courses on English composition and writing. This ensures that the applicant is receiving professional instruction on correct and effective writing from staff with proper credentials. The instructors are able to determine the skill level of the students, and recommend the appropriate remediation necessary for proficiency.

As a complement to this instruction, the applicant should also consider speech courses. Most speech instructors include lessons on logical thought processes and topic organization. This training would also enhance the applicant's competitiveness at the QAP.

f. **Personal Self-Improvement.**

1) Some applicants may not have the time and/or the financial assets to consider the preceding options. Another suggestion an applicant may consider is to start a diary or journal.

a) The applicant should write one or two pages on what he/she accomplished that day, or record his/her daily personal thoughts.

b) The applicant should have access to a dictionary and thesaurus for help with spelling and vocabulary improvement.

- c) After writing out his/her activities or thoughts, the applicant should read the daily entries aloud.

- d) This exercise allows the applicant to hear what he/she has written. Oftentimes, what is written on paper sounds completely different when read aloud. By repeating this exercise daily, applicants can improve their reading, writing, and verbal skills.

2) Applicants must decide what course of study will be their best option. Ultimately, having a $12^{th}$ grade reading and writing skill level is the key to passing the written examination phase for the Cadet, CHP.

2-C-1

## SAMPLE WRITTEN TEST

(Answer key follows test)

**MULTIPLE CHOICE TEST**

A. Sentence Clarity (15 questions)

DIRECTIONS: Identify the sentence(s) that is most clearly written.

1. A. Even though they have spiked hair, wear leather, and roar through town on noisy motorcycles whenever they get bored. The group has bank accounts that make it respectable in Ruralia.
   B. Even though they have spiked hair, wear leather, and roar through town on noisy motorcycles whenever they get bored, the group has bank accounts that make it respectable in Ruralia.

   1.____

2. A. David buffed the fingerprint away. With his new cashmere sweater. Absent-mindedly.
   B. Absent-mindedly, David buffed the fingerprint away with his new cashmere sweater.

   2.____

3. A. David came untangled from the lotus position, he balanced his buckets and basket in his hands.
   B. As David came untangled from the lotus position, he balanced his buckets and basket in his hands.

   3.____

4. A. The price they paid for the car is a well kept secret speculation is that it was about the same as Coach Rhodes' recruiting budget.
   B. Although the price they paid for the car is a well kept secret, speculation is that it was about the same as Coach Rhodes' recruiting budget.

   4.____

5. A. David's whole life now revolved around his Sting Ray he could think of nothing else.
   B. David's whole life now revolved around his Sting Ray; he could think of nothing else.

   5.____

B. Vocabulary (15 Questions)

DIRECTIONS: Choose the word or phrase that most clearly means the same as the underlined word.

6. The man told his wife that she was confused about his identity while she was in the hospital.
   A. unclear         B. misinterpreted
   C. misconceived    D. doubtful

   6.____

ANNEX C

7. The peculiar noises prompted the officer to inspect the trunk of the vehicle.    7.____
   A. funny    B. familiar    C. strange    D. different

8. The supervisor disapproved of the employee's foul comment.    8.____
   A. hated    B. disliked    C. praised    D. tolerated

C. Spelling  (15 Questions)

DIRECTIONS: Choose the correct spelling of the missing word.

9. After taking a deep _____ he was able to relax.    9.____
   A. breeth    B. breathe    C. breath    D. breith

10. The _____ asked the Sergeant to prepare a written summary of the incident.    10.____
    A. Leiutenant    B. Leuitenant
    C. Lieutenant    D. Lewtenant

11. The strange _____ caused much suspicion amongst the people in the neighborhood.    11.____
    A. ocurrence    B. ocrurence
    C. occurrence    D. occurance

12. The _____ instructor administered a fairly easy final exam.    12.____
    A. Pshychology    B. Psychology
    C. Pyschology    D. Sychology

13. There is no _____ that everyone who takes the test will pass the exam.    13.____
    A. guarantee    B. gaurantee
    C. guarantee    D. garentee

D. Reading Comprehension

DIRECTIONS: Questions 14 and 15 are to be answered on the basis of the following passage.

From time to time, a police officer may have to appear in court as a witness in a criminal case. The content of his/her statement is very important. The way he/she gives his/her testimony may create a favorable or unfavorable impression in court. He/she should be able to talk about the kind of evidence he/she has seen and where the evidence came from. Otherwise, cross-examination may confuse him/her and reduce the value of what he/she has to say. If he/she reviews his/her facts before testifying, he/she will be prepared to carry out his/her assignment which is to provide accurate information in such a way that its meaning will be understood by the court.

ANNEX C

14. When testifying in court, the chief responsibility of a police officer is to   14.____
    A. prepare his/her case ahead of time
    B. make a favorable impression
    C. avoid becoming confused during cross-examination
    D. present factual evidence in a clear manner

15. Which one of the following statements regarding testimony by a police   15.____
    officer may be inferred from the passage?
    A. What he/she says in testimony should make the case stronger.
    B. Not only what he/she says in court is important, but also how he/she says it.
    C. He/she should memorize all the facts which he/she may be asked to give.
    D. How he/she gives his/her testimony is more important than what he/she says.

E. Reading Test (40 Questions)

DIRECTIONS:
1. Skim through the passage before attempting to give any answers.
2. Always guess if you do not know the answer.
3. You can miss many words and still do well.
4. Do not let your opinion about a statement influence your choice of words; choose words that are consistent.
5. Put only one letter in each blank space.
6. The word must make sense and fit in the spaces in order for you to receive full credit.

Dear California Motorist:

You are _____(1) at a compilation of statistics that describe in numerical terms the story of the motor vehicle _____(2) accidents that occurred in California in 2013. It is a disquieting story _____(3) of the tremendous amount of human _____(4) and economic loss that are the real substance of _____(5) compilation.

_____(6), it is a heartening story as _____(7) because it depicts the _____(8) chapter in what is now a four-year decline in the state mileage death_____(9).

A state's mileage death rate (MDR) is the _____(10) of traffic fatalities per one million miles of travel. In 2010, California's MDR _____(11) at 2.5. The following year it _____(12) to 2.4 and last year it was down to 2.2.

In 2013, _____(13) descended to 2.1 – once again the lowest in the State's driving _____(14). The most _____(15) single explanation for this four-year decline in the MDR is an increase in _____(16) belt use. At the beginning of 2010, when the State's safety belt law became _____(17), California's safety belt usage rate was around 25 _____(18). As of January 1, 2014, 70.3 percent of our vehicle occupants – passengers as _____(19) as drivers – were buckling up.

ANNEX C

That's an _____(20) of better than 45 percent. In human terms, it _____(21) that about 14 million more people _____(22) putting their safety _____(23) on when they get into a vehicle now than _____(24) them on four years ago. The consequence of this has been a dramatic _____(25) in the fatality and serious injury rates because of traffic _____(26).

If you are one of _____(27) currently buckling up, I urge _____(28) to continue doing so, _____(29) short the trip. If you are _____(30) those now traveling unprotected, I say _____(31) you: "Get smart; get it on." And I urge _____(32) of you to obey all the traffic _____(33) and not to drink and _____(34). If we all drive sensibly, we can help keep California's MDR heading in the _____(35) direction: down.

# KEY (CORRECT ANSWERS)

A. Sentence Clarity
1. B
2. B
3. B
4. B
5. B

B. Vocabulary
6. A
7. C
8. B

C. Spelling
9. C
10. C
11. C
12. B
13. C

D. Reading Comprehension
14. D
15. B

E. Reading Test

1. looking
2. traffic
3. because
4. suffering
5. this
6. But
7. well
8. latest
9. rate
10. number
11. stood
12. dropped
13. it
14. history
15. important
16. safety
17. effective
18. percent
19. well
20. increase
21. means
22. are
23. belts
24. put
25. reduction
26. crashes
27. those
28. you
29. however
30. among
31. to
32. all
33. laws
34. drive
35. right

ANNEX C

# CHAPTER 3

# PHYSICAL ABILITY TEST (PAT), WRITTEN PSYCHOLOGICAL TEST (WPT)

1. **PHYSICAL ABILITY TEST (PAT)**

   **NOTIFICATION**

   a. **The applicant will be scheduled to take the Physical Ability Test upon receiving notification of passing the written test.**

   > NOTE: In order to participate in this test phase, the applicant **MUST** bring the following forms which will be collected upon reporting to the PAT.
   > - A valid picture identification (i.e., driver's license, passport).
   > - State Employment Application (STD. 678) requires information about the applicant's education and employment history for the previous seven years.
   > - Cadet Arrest and Citation Questionnaire (CHP 446F) requires the applicant's traffic ticket(s) and arrest history.
   > - Completed Personal History Statement (CHP 446).
   >
   > (The applicant may want to organize this information early so it will be complete.)

   b. **Applicants should consider the following suggestions to assist in their performance in the PAT.**

      1) Applicants should not drink any alcoholic beverages for eight hours prior to the test.

      2) A minimum of three hours should have elapsed since your last meal.

      3) Applicants should not have engaged in any moderate to heavy physical or emotionally stressful work within two hours prior to the test.

      4) Applicants should attempt to have a minimum of six hours sleep the night prior to the test.

      5) If under the care of a physician or taking any prescribed medications, applicants should consult their physician and request approval to participate. Non-prescription medications should not be consumed 24 hours prior to the test.

      6) Applicants should wear loose-fitting clothing, preferably exercise clothing and athletic shoes.

c. **The Physical Ability Test** determines whether the applicant is able to perform the minimum physical standards required of a CHP officer. The PAT contains the following five sections:

   1) <u>100 Yard Sprint</u>. The applicant is required to run 100 yards in 20 seconds or less.

   2) <u>Upper Body Strength</u>. There are a total of three measurements.

      a) <u>Shoulder strength adduction</u> requires the applicant to hold a V-shaped device close to the chest with the forearms parallel to the floor and palms facing inward. The applicant pushes the handles of the device together with maximum effort.

      b) <u>Grip strength</u> requires the applicant to squeeze a grip strength tester with a maximum effort.

      c) <u>Dynamic arm</u>. If unable to achieve a minimum score in the shoulder and/or grip strength tests, the applicant is required to pedal a stationary bicycle with his/her arms at a workload of 2.5 kilopounds for up to one minute to reach minimum score.

   3) <u>Trunk Strength Flexion</u>. The applicant is required to exert 113 pounds of force by contracting the abdominal muscles. The applicant is strapped into a harness and is hooked to a device by a cable. The applicant then leans forward while tightening the stomach muscles and reaching for the ground in front of him/her. This motion puts tension on the cable and a gauge measures the applicant's strength. Some back muscle strength and flexion is involved.

   4) <u>Side Step</u>. There are three parallel lines – one center line with two outside lines positioned four feet from the center line. In a standing position, the applicant straddles the center line with feet parallel to lines. The applicant side steps to left of the center line until his/her foot touches the left outside line, then side steps to the right until his/her foot touches or crosses the right outside line. This activity is repeated as many times as possible in ten seconds. Crossing each line, including the center line, earns one point. The applicant must score thirteen points.

   5) <u>500-Yard Run</u>. The applicant is required to run 500 yards in two minutes or less.

d. **Each portion of the PAT test is pass/fail.** The applicant is notified of the score after each test. The applicant must pass all five portions to successfully complete the PAT.

e. **PAT Preparations.** Refer to information provided within the pamphlet titled "Physical Conditioning for the CHP Cadet Applicants." Engage in a physical fitness program, suited to your health and ability, designed to improve flexibility, muscular strength, and cardio-respiratory endurance.

## 2. WRITTEN PSYCHOLOGICAL TEST (WPT)

The WPT consists of a battery of three tests. It is a mandatory process required by state law for all prospective peace officers. These tests will be used in conjunction with your background investigation during a clinical interview with a psychologist to determine your suitability for a career in law enforcement.

Preparations:   This exam is based on your personal history and experiences; there are no study materials.

# CHAPTER 4

## QUALIFICATIONS APPRAISAL PANEL INTERVIEW (QAP)

1. **INTERVIEW**

    The applicant will be scheduled for an interview upon successful completion of the Physical Ability Test.

    a. Thirty to forty-five minutes should be allowed for the actual interview. Applicant should arrive at the interview site at least 15 minutes prior to the scheduled interview time. Note: Applicant must have a valid picture identification to be admitted into the interview.

    b. **Attire.** Applicant should wear clothing appropriate for a business interview. Dress should be conservative and color coordinated. For men, a suite, sport jacket and tie with dress slacks or a Class A military uniform for military personnel would be acceptable. Likewise for women, a business suit, dress, dress skirt/slacks and blouse or Class A military uniform for military personnel is appropriate.

    c. **Format.** The QAP interview determines the applicant's suitability for the position of Cadet, CHP. Questions asked by the panel do not require a law enforcement background. The interview panel has two members: Chairperson – a member trained by the State Personnel Board, and a State Service Representative, usually a CHP captain, lieutenant, or sergeant.

    d. Applicant will need to demonstrate the ability to speak clearly and concisely and display confidence. Applicant should be prepared to discuss their personal accomplishments, educational background, work history, and their driving and arrest record. Applicants must be open and absolutely honest with all information. The panel may also ask the applicant to respond to hypothetical scenarios. Applicants should be able to demonstrate knowledge of the duties and functions of the CHP officer and the California Highway Patrol; explain what they have to offer the CHP; and what they have done to prepare themselves for the position of Cadet, CHP. At the close of the interview, the panel will give the applicant an opportunity to ask questions and make a closing statement. NOTE: Applicants should review the following section entitled "You and Your Interview."

    e. **Additional Preparations.** In order to better prepare, applicants should study the CHP Cadet Bulletin (CHP 179D, blue sheet); review the CHP website at www.chp.ca.gov; talk to a recruiter; research the position; write out answers to obvious questions; participate in practice interview sessions with associates or family members; and/or use a tape recorder or videotape to study the quality of the presentation and consider asking others to view or listen to the tape for constructive criticism.

f. **Notification of Results.** The applicant will be notified of the results by mail in approximately four to five weeks following the QAP interview. Applicants who receive qualifying scores will be given a conditional offer of employment and will continue in the remaining selection phases. Applicants not selected to go forward in the process may re-apply if they still meet the minimum qualifications.

## YOU AND YOUR INTERVIEW

An oral interview can be a stressful situation. By familiarizing yourself with the "mechanics" of an interview and by preparing yourself, you can make your interview a successful experience.

1. **PREPARING FOR YOUR ORAL INTERVIEW**

    The oral interview evaluates intangible qualities of an applicant not easily measured. The oral interview scoring is on a sliding scale ranging from "not passable" to "outstanding." In fact, it is possible to achieve a relatively low score without a single "incorrect" answer, because of evident weaknesses (i.e., poor vocal delivery, lack of eye contact).

    a. **Before the Interview**

    1) Keep a copy of your application (STD 678) and review it carefully prior to the interview. This is one of the documents the oral panel reviews before your interview and often uses as a starting point of the interview. Know the sequence and dates of the experience and education you listed on the application. The panel may ask you to summarize the highlights of your education and experience. You should prepared, in advance, a brief oral summary of those aspects of your background that you think make you a more competitive candidate.

    2) Study the examination bulletin (CHP 179D). The bulletin explains the needed skills, knowledge, and abilities as well as personal characteristics considered important for the position. The bulletin also offers valuable clues about the oral interview. Never go into an oral interview without any knowledge of the duties and responsibilities of the classification. If possible, talk to CHP officers about the duties of a CHP officer, or participate in an approved ride-a-long with a CHP officer. This demonstrates your interest in becoming a CHP officer.

    3) Think through each qualification required. Imagine the types of questions you would ask if you were a member of the interview panel. How well can you answer those questions? Try especially to appraise your own knowledge and background in each area. In addition to identifying your strengths, identify areas which may be considered weaknesses. Be prepared to discuss your weaknesses with the interview panel, if they mention them, and what you have done or are doing to overcome those weaknesses.

    4) Consider setting up a mock interview using family or friends and have practice interview sessions. This would allow you to receive constructive criticism about your performance. Contact your local CHP Recruiter for information regarding upcoming oral interview seminars or "mock interviews" in your area.

    5) The night before your interview, get a good night's sleep and monitor your general health and mental attitude. You will want a clear head at the interview. Take care of a cold or other minor ailments. Do not take any stimulants or tranquilizers before your interview unless your doctor prescribes them and they will not affect your interview.

ANNEX A

b. **The Day of the Interview.**

   1) <u>Allow plenty of time to get to your destination.</u> Plan to arrive ahead of your scheduled time, particularly if your appointment is early. Should another applicant fail to appear, the oral interview panel may invite you to start your interview early. By late afternoon, the panel may be behind schedule, and you may have to wait. However, do not assume this will be the case. Ensure you arrive on time. Take along the examination announcement and a copy of your application to review. Do try to relax and compose yourself. Even the calmest, most self-assured person is usually somewhat nervous before his or her interview.

   2) <u>Dress appropriately.</u> This is a business interview, and your appearance should indicate that you regard it as such. The oral interview panel is forming impressions about you from your education and experience, your manners, your attitudes, the way you express yourself, and your appearance. Use perfumes/colognes and cosmetics sparingly, and be considerate that others may be allergic.

   3) <u>Know names of panel members.</u> As soon as you arrive at the interview area, ask the receptionist the name of each panel member. Make a note of how to pronounce those names if they seem difficult to pronounce.

c. **Beginning the Interview.**

   1) The chairperson will introduce you to the other panel member when you enter the interview room. After acknowledging introductions, sit down. The interview will now begin.

   2) Usually, the chairperson will start by briefly reviewing some of your background highlights as listed on your application. Do not interrupt unless there are important misinterpretations. You may be asked a general question to help you get started, such as, "What aspects of your background do you think have best prepared you for this job?" The interview is now underway. The members of the panel will proceed to ask you the kinds of questions they feel will give them an idea of your potential as a CHP officer.

d. **Making Interview Questions Work for You.**

   1) <u>Do your best.</u> Remember that the interview panel's job is to help you do your best. At times, you might feel that the panel individually and collectively is trying to seek out only your negative attributes. Actually, this is not true. They are obliged to make a fair and impartial appraisal of your qualifications for the classification of Cadet, CHP. They must consider both your strengths and your weaknesses, and want to see you in your best light. Remember, they must interview all candidates, and an uncooperative or complaining candidate may not do well in the interview in spite of their best efforts to bring out the candidate's strongest attributes. Your job is to let the panel see you at your best.

ANNEX A

2) <u>Be natural.</u> Keep your attitude enthusiastic and confident, but not cocky. If you are not confident that you can do the job, do not expect the interview panel to have confidence in you. Do not apologize for your weaknesses; rather try to bring out your strong points. The interview panel is interested in a positive, not a negative presentation. Cockiness and wordiness might make the panel wonder if you are covering up a weakness by a false show of strength. On the other hand, try to use more than a couple of words when you answer each of the panel's questions.

3) <u>Get comfortable, but do not lounge or sprawl.</u> Sit upright but not stiffly. A careless posture may lead the interview panel to conclude that you are not impressed by the importance of the occasion. This conclusion is natural, even if incorrect. Do not fuss with your clothing or with a pencil or paper. Your hands may occasionally be useful to emphasize a point, but do not let them become a point of distraction.

4) <u>Be pleasant, but do not wisecrack or initiate extensive small talk.</u> This is a business situation, and your attitude should show that you consider it as such. The interview panel's time is limited; the panel does not want to waste it, and neither should you. However, participate appropriately if a panel member chooses to make small talk at the beginning of the interview in order to make you feel more comfortable.

5) <u>Do not exaggerate your experience or abilities.</u> The interview panel may know more about you than you think. An experienced interview panel is rather adept at spotting such a situation. Do not take this chance.

6) <u>Knowledge of QAP member.</u> If you know a member of the interview panel, do not make an obvious point of it, but do not hide it. Remain as natural as possible. Go ahead and present your strong points to the panel, rather than waiting for the person you know to do so.

7) <u>Do not dominate the interview.</u> Let the interview panel direct the interview. The panel will give you the clues. Do not assume that you have to do all the talking. Realize that the panel has a number of questions to ask each candidate. Do not try to take up all the interview time by showing off your extensive knowledge. On the other hand, be sure you have prepared in advance to present the highlights of your strengths to the panel when they ask you for them (or at the end of the interview if they have not been mentioned earlier in the interview).

8) <u>Be attentive.</u> Usually, your interview lasts approximately 30 to 45 minutes. You should keep your attention at its sharpest throughout the interview. When a panel member is addressing a problem or a question to you, give that person your undivided attention. Address your reply principally to that person but continue eye contact with the other panel member.

ANNEX A

9) <u>Do not interrupt.</u> Panel members may be stating a problem for you to analyze. They will ask you a question when the time comes. Let the problem be stated and wait for the question.

10) <u>Make sure you understand the question.</u> Do not try to answer a question until you are sure what is being asked. If it is not clear, restate it in your own words or ask the panel member to clarify it for you. Do not argue about minor elements.

11) <u>Reply promptly but not hastily.</u> Respond as quickly as you can, but do not jump to a hasty, ill-considered answer. It is acceptable to pause before answering. Try not to stare at the window, wall, or ceiling while formulating your answer.

12) <u>Do not try to create the answer you think the panel member wants.</u> The panel is interested in how you analyze and solve problems. If you give an answer that you really do not think is correct, but believe it is an answer the panel wants, you may have difficulty defending your answer if the panel members ask you to clarify your answer.

13) <u>Do not switch sides in your reply merely to agree with a panel member.</u> Sometimes a panel member will appear to support the reverse of your answer merely to draw you out and to see if you are willing and able to defend your point of view. Do not start a heated debate; yet, do not surrender a good position. If a position is worth taking, it is worth defending.

14) <u>Do not be afraid to admit an error in judgment if you are shown to be wrong.</u> The panel knows that you are forced to reply without the opportunity for careful, prolonged consideration of the issue. Your answer may be demonstrably wrong. If so, admit it and get on with the interview.

15) <u>Do not bring in extraneous comments or tell lengthy anecdotes.</u> Keep your replies to the point. If you feel the need of an illustration from your personal experience, keep it brief and leave out minor details. If you think you might be giving the interview panel too much detail on a specific point, you may want to ask them whether they would like you to elaborate further.

16) <u>Do not use slang terms or use words improperly.</u> Many good replies have been weakened by the use of slang terms or other language faults. Frequently, the panel will not any errors in grammar or diction or other evidence of carelessness in your speech habits (i.e., use of phrases such as "yeah," "uh-huh," or "you know" and mumbling).

17) <u>Present your strengths in terms of how you could benefit the Department if hired.</u> Be ready to tell the panel how your education, prior work experience, military experience, volunteer work, hobbies/clubs/achievements, physical fitness, or other activities have helped prepare you for the position.

ANNEX A

e.  **Closing the Interview.**

   1) The chairperson usually concludes the interview by asking if you have anything to add. You should take advantage of this opportunity to make a closing statement. The closing statement should include your overall qualifications, personal achievements, methods of preparation, items that were not covered in the interview, and reasons why you should be given favorable consideration. The tone of your closing statement should be positive, upbeat, and brief (approximately 30 seconds).

   2) If it seems appropriate to shake hands with the interview panel members, it is fine to do so. If it would be awkward or uncomfortable for you, then you probably are better off not shaking their hands; however, should the panel members extend their hands first, you are recommended to shake hands. A smile and a statement from you such as, "Thanks again for your time," should end the interview on a positive note.

ANNEX A

# CHAPTER 5

## BACKGROUND INVESTIGATION, MEDICAL EVALUATION, PSYCHOLOGICAL EVALUATION, ACADEMY INVITATION

1. **BACKGROUND INVESTIGATION**

   An initial interview appointment will be made with the applicant by the CHP officers who conduct the background investigation.

   a. **Applicants are required to provide information in the following areas:**

      - References
      - Education
      - Residences (past seven years)
      - Other Peace Officer Applications (departments to which the applicant sent an application for employment
      - Employment History
      - Driving Record (all arrests, all citations)
      - Arrest/Legal History (all arrests, any civil litigation)
      - Financial History (all accounts, opened and closed)
      - Military Service

   b. **Applicants are required to show the following documents, and provide a photocopy of each, at the initial interview:**

      - Valid Driver's License
      - Birth Certificate
      - Verification of Education (high school diploma, college degree, GED certificate)
      - High School Transcripts
      - College or University Transcripts (sealed, official copies)
      - Marriage Certificate
      - Marriage Dissolution Documents
      - Vehicle Insurance Policies
      - Military Service Certificate (discharge documents [DD214], commendations, etc.)
      - Social Security Card
      - Proof of Legal U.S. Residency (birth certificate, naturalization papers)

   c. During the Background Investigation Phase, the applicant will be scheduled for a Computer Voice Stress Analysis (CVSA). The CVSA will verify the information the applicant provides to the background investigator.

   d. A final interview is conducted by the background investigator to review the findings of the investigation, and to notify the applicant whether he/she will be recommended to continue in the selection process. All information provided to the background investigator will be subject to truth verification.

2. **MEDICAL EVALUATION**

   a. The applicant will be notified when and how to arrange a medical appointment either during or after the background investigation.

   b. The medical evaluation is paid for by the state, and administered by doctors contracted by the state. A complete physical examination is conducted to ensure that the applicant is capable of performing the essential duties of a CHP officer.

   NOTE: Although the State Personnel Board allows 20 days to fill out the medical forms, it is recommended that the applicant complete the forms as soon as possible. Completion of the medical forms in a timely manner may expedite entry into the Academy.

3. **PSYCHOLOGICAL INTERVIEW**

   Applicants continuing in the selection process will be scheduled for an appointment with a departmentally selected psychologist. This interview is generally held after the background investigation and prior to the Academy invitation.

4. **ACADEMY INVITATION**

   There are generally four Academy cadet classes annually. Normally, 2 to 4 weeks prior to the start of the Academy class, either by mail or telephone, applicants receive formal notification of an invitation to the Academy. Refer to Chapter 1, Section 5 of this guide for a general overview about the Academy, Academy facilities and accommodations, and the type of training and courses provided.

# CHAPTER 6

# LIFE AT THE ACADEMY

1. **REPORTING TO THE ACADEMY**

   a. **Arrival.** Applicants will need to arrive at the Academy for the first day by 0730 hours for registration and orientation.

   b. **Attire.** Male and female cadets should report to the Academy in appropriate business attire.

   1) Males: Suit (sport coat), tie, dress shoes.

   2) Females: Business suit, dress shoes (skirt, dresses and high heel shoes not recommended).

   c. **Grooming Standards.** As with uniformed employees, cadets shall assume the responsibility of adopting high standards for personal grooming and cleanliness.

   1) Personal Grooming – Male: The following grooming standards are deemed reasonable and shall be the minimum standards for male uniformed employees while in uniform or appropriate civilian attire.

      a) Hair. Shall be neat, clean, trimmed (not shaved), and present a groomed appearance. Hair shall not interfere with the proper wearing of the uniform hat/cap or helmet. Hair shall not extend below the top of the uniform shirt collar while sitting or standing in an erect position. Hair color or style shall not be unusual or bizarre. Hair which is styled or combed forward shall not be lower than the relaxed eyebrow of an individual and shall not be visible on the forehead while the uniform hat/cap or helmet is worn.

      b) Sideburns and Mustaches. Skin shall be clean shaven; however, neatly trimmed sideburns and mustaches are permissible. Sideburns shall not extend below the bottom of the ear and shall end with a clean-shaven horizontal line. The maximum width at the bottom of the sideburns shall not exceed 1 – 1½ inches.

      Mustaches shall not extend more than ½-inch beyond the corners of the mouth nor below the vermillion border of the upper lip, or more than ¼-inch below the corner of the mouth. Waxed ends or points are prohibited.

   2) Personal Grooming – Female

      a) Hair. Same standards apply as with male hair grooming. In addition,

         (1) Decoration(s) shall not be worn in the hair. Hair clips and pins that match the color of the hair are permitted.

(2) Hair shall not be worn in a "ponytail" or similar style.

(3) Moderate "natural" or other hair styles are permitted in conforming with the hair standards described above; however, the maximum extension from the scalp shall not exceed two inches.

    b) **Cosmetics**. Cosmetics shall be subdued and blended to match the natural skin color of the individual.

        (1) False eyelashes are prohibited.

    c) **Fingernails**. Shall be clean and trimmed. Nails shall not extend beyond the tips of the fingers. Only clear nail polish is permitted.

    d) **Brassieres**. Brassieres shall provide adequate support.

d. **What to Bring**. It is imperative that each cadet possesses certain documents and information for the first day processing.

1) Driver license.
2) At least two blank checks, with $350 to $500 deposited in the account to cover the checks.
3) Social Security Numbers of beneficiaries.
4) Emergency contact information.
5) Vehicle Information: License plate number, color, make, and model.

e. **Other Items to Bring**. One clock radio, dusting supplies, shoe polishing items, plain white crewneck tee-shirts, a minimum amount of civilian attire, swimsuit, toiletries (prescription medications), boots/shoes (black, all leather), a pair of running shoes, and non-marking court shoes.

## 2. ACADEMY LIFESTYLE

a. **Live-in Training**. The Academy is a live-in training facility. Training day typically begins at 0800 hours and ends at approximately 1700 hours. Cadets are required to remain on the Academy grounds after training hours.

b. **Drill**. Cadets learn drill procedures necessary to participate in ceremonies and tactical formations.

c. **Inspections**. To ensure each cadet adheres to the high standards of the Department, personnel and dorm inspections are held at various intervals during cadet training.

d. **Liberty**. Cadets receive liberty on Wednesday nights and weekends, contingent on passing the tests each week and absent any disciplinary actions.

1) Wednesday – 1700 to 2359 hours
2) Weekends – 1700 hours Friday to 2359 Sunday

e. **Meals**. Meals are served between 0645 – 0730, 1145 – 1230, and 1700 – 1730 hours Monday through Saturday, and 0800, 1200, and 1700 hours on Sunday.

   1) The Academy cafeteria provides a variety of prepared foods. Cadets are responsible for choosing meals appropriately. Cadets not meeting the body composition requirements will be placed on the training table and must adhere to a strict diet.

f. **Salary/Pay**. Cadets receive full salary during the 27-week training period at the Academy. Pay warrants will be issued once a month, after the first of every month. Arrange with creditors and budget your finances accordingly.

g. **Medical Care**. Medical and dental benefits are provided after the cadet's first thirty days of training. **NOTE: Cadets are responsible for any medical costs incurred during the first thirty days of training**. Treatment for injuries that cadets suffer as a result of training will be covered by the Department.

h. **Mail/Mailing Address**.

   1) Incoming mail is delivered to the Academy on a daily basis, except Sundays and holidays. Correspondents address cadet mail as follows:

      Cadet (cadet's full name)
      C.T.C. (e.g., CTC II-06 [class/year])
      California Highway Patrol Academy
      3500 Reed Avenue
      West Sacramento, CA 95605-1699

i. **Housing**. Cadets are assigned to a dormitory quad. Eight cadets or more may be assigned to each quad, sharing common restroom and showers. Cadets will share a room with another cadet from the same class. Cadets are responsible for maintaining its appearance.

j. **Emergencies**. Cadets may receive emergency telephone calls once an emergency is verified. Cadets should tell their family/friends that they cannot receive any other phone calls during the 27 weeks of training.

k. **Personal Affairs**. Personal and family conflict (marriage problems, homesickness, etc.) is the main cause for early separation from cadet training. Cadets should have their personal affairs in order prior to reporting to the Academy. Cadets should be prepared to be separated from their families for several months.

3. **ACADEMY TRAINING**

Cadets will be required to meet the standards set forth by the Commission on Peace Officer Standards and Training (POST) for cadet training ranging from academics and physical training to enforcement tactics, weapons training and vehicle operations. The following descriptions will give a brief overview of the type of training and what you should expect in each phase.

a. **Academics**

   1) Cadets are responsible for 67 "learning domains" (LDs) mandated by POST, in addition to agency specific policies and procedures. Cadets will receive over 1,255 hours of training. Cadets are required to take a remedial exam in addition to serving a weekend restriction if an LD is failed. Failure of the remedial examination will result in termination from cadet training.

   2) Cadets are certified as an Emergency Medical Responder (EMR) during Academy training.

   3) Cadets are also required to complete and pass an Accident Investigation course, Spanish Language training, and Criminal Law courses.

b. **Physical Training**. Cadets are expected to pass a variety of Physical Fitness Tests and the Physical Performance Program Test. To prepare, cadets should be involved in some form of strength training program (a circuit weight training program is advisable). In addition, prior to reporting to the Academy, cadets should develop an endurance to:

   1) run at least three miles, three times a week, at a 9-minute-per-mile pace

   2) perform 50 to 75 sit-ups (unassisted)

   3) perform 50 push-ups, and

   4) perform four pull-ups

   This will ensure each cadet meets the minimum incoming acceptable level.

c. **Enforcement Tactics**. During this 108-hour course, cadets will learn the basics for and be tested on general knowledge of Use of Force, Patrol Techniques, Vehicle Pullovers, Unusual Occurrences, Simunitions Training and Crimes in Progress, as well as the ability to apply that knowledge during both day and night scenario testing.

d. **Weapons Training**. This program prepares the cadet to meet the challenge of "real world" encounters.

   1) Each cadet will be instructed in the safe handling and effective use of the Department's general duty weapons; Smith & Wesson Model 4006-TSW, semi-automatic pistol, and Remington Model 870 shotgun, both in daylight and night conditions.

   2) Each cadet will also complete a firing course to familiarize him/herself with tactical rifles.

   3) Each cadet will be trained in the proper use of Oleoresin Capsicum (OC), "pepper spray," operations in a chemical environment (CS gas), and basic recognition and handling of confiscated and clandestine weapons.

e. **Emergency Vehicle Operations Course (EVOC)**

   1) Cadets will be trained in enforcement driving at the Emergency Vehicle Operations Course. Cadets will receive a minimum of 24 hours lecture on vehicle dynamics, performance driving techniques, and departmental policy. Cadets will also receive a minimum of 22 hours of hands-on driver training. Training includes:

      a) Vehicle placement
      b) skid control techniques
      c) performance driving
      d) defensive driving
      e) Code-3 pursuit driving

   2) Each cadet will be required to meet minimum performance objectives during hands-on training as well as successfully completing a written examination.

f. **Customs and Courtesies**. Cadets are to become familiar with customs and courtesies such as how to address staff members or any persons on Academy grounds by using "Sir" or "Ma'am," "Yes, Sir," or "Yes, Ma'am," and assuming the position of attention and remaining in that position until told otherwise.

# CHAPTER 7

# CADET FIELD ASSIGNMENT PROTOCOL

1. **ASSIGNMENTS/GRADUATION**

    During the period between weeks 19 and 21 prior to graduation, cadets receive a "Dream Sheet"; a list of those CHP Area offices that have openings for new officers. Cadets list their choices of locations by order to personal preference. The lists are then returned to headquarters for processing. The following information shows how the cadet's first duty assignment is determined/prioritized:

    a. **The needs of the Department** (Bilingual, etc.)

    b. **Hardship** (Only person available to care for sick relative, etc. – very rare)

    c. **Home ownership with school age children.** The commute time must be one hour or less from the Area office assigned. Home must have been purchased prior to Academy appointment, grant deed in cadet's name. (Area commander may be contacted to verify distance to Area office if it is not apparent.)

    d. **Home ownership with children under school age** (children under five). Same criteria as above.

    e. **Home ownership with no children.** Same criteria as above.

    **Note: Home ownership also includes mobile homes 101 feet or longer.**

    f. **Rental unit with school age children.** Same distance requirements apply as in "c".

    g. **The last four digits of the cadet's Social Security Number** (e.g., the higher the number, the higher the priority). Most cadet assignments are determined in this manner.

2. **FIELD TRAINING AND PROBATION**

    a. **Field Training.** New officers in the field are required to successfully complete a 50-working day, Field Training and Evaluation period. New officers will usually work with three separate Field Training Officers (FTOs) for a period of 15 days each (Phase I, Phase II, and Phase III). Upon successfully completing the 45-working day, Field Training and Evaluation period, the new officer will then be re-assigned back to the first Field Training Officer for an additional five-day Field Training and Evaluation period (Shadow Phase). During field training, the FTOs evaluate their trainee's performance and application of skills learned at the Academy.

    b. **Shift Assignment.** Shift assignments typically encompass the following hours: "A" Watch: 5:45 A.M. – 2:15 P.M., "B" watch: 1:45 P:.M. – 10: 15 P.M.; and "C" Watch: 9:45 P.M. – 6:15 A.M., although there may be other shifts/shift hours assigned within the command. Assigned workdays include weekends and holidays.

c. **12-Month Probation.** New officers may be assigned anywhere in the state and are required to serve a 12-month probationary term at their first command assignment. Following the completion of probation, officers may submit a request to voluntarily transfer to any field command in the state. Transfers are made on a state-wide seniority basis.

# HOW TO TAKE A TEST

I. YOU MUST PASS AN EXAMINATION

### A. WHAT EVERY CANDIDATE SHOULD KNOW

Examination applicants often ask us for help in preparing for the written test. What can I study in advance? What kinds of questions will be asked? How will the test be given? How will the papers be graded?

As an applicant for a civil service examination, you may be wondering about some of these things. Our purpose here is to suggest effective methods of advance study and to describe civil service examinations.

Your chances for success on this examination can be increased if you know how to prepare. Those "pre-examination jitters" can be reduced if you know what to expect. You can even experience an adventure in good citizenship if you know why civil service exams are given.

### B. WHY ARE CIVIL SERVICE EXAMINATIONS GIVEN?

Civil service examinations are important to you in two ways. As a citizen, you want public jobs filled by employees who know how to do their work. As a job seeker, you want a fair chance to compete for that job on an equal footing with other candidates. The best-known means of accomplishing this two-fold goal is the competitive examination.

Exams are widely publicized throughout the nation. They may be administered for jobs in federal, state, city, municipal, town or village governments or agencies.

Any citizen may apply, with some limitations, such as the age or residence of applicants. Your experience and education may be reviewed to see whether you meet the requirements for the particular examination. When these requirements exist, they are reasonable and applied consistently to all applicants. Thus, a competitive examination may cause you some uneasiness now, but it is your privilege and safeguard.

### C. HOW ARE CIVIL SERVICE EXAMS DEVELOPED?

Examinations are carefully written by trained technicians who are specialists in the field known as "psychological measurement," in consultation with recognized authorities in the field of work that the test will cover. These experts recommend the subject matter areas or skills to be tested; only those knowledges or skills important to your success on the job are included. The most reliable books and source materials available are used as references. Together, the experts and technicians judge the difficulty level of the questions.

Test technicians know how to phrase questions so that the problem is clearly stated. Their ethics do not permit "trick" or "catch" questions. Questions may have been tried out on sample groups, or subjected to statistical analysis, to determine their usefulness.

Written tests are often used in combination with performance tests, ratings of training and experience, and oral interviews. All of these measures combine to form the best-known means of finding the right person for the right job.

## II. HOW TO PASS THE WRITTEN TEST

### A. NATURE OF THE EXAMINATION

To prepare intelligently for civil service examinations, you should know how they differ from school examinations you have taken. In school you were assigned certain definite pages to read or subjects to cover. The examination questions were quite detailed and usually emphasized memory. Civil service exams, on the other hand, try to discover your present ability to perform the duties of a position, plus your potentiality to learn these duties. In other words, a civil service exam attempts to predict how successful you will be. Questions cover such a broad area that they cannot be as minute and detailed as school exam questions.

In the public service similar kinds of work, or positions, are grouped together in one "class." This process is known as *position-classification*. All the positions in a class are paid according to the salary range for that class. One class title covers all of these positions, and they are all tested by the same examination.

### B. FOUR BASIC STEPS

#### 1) Study the announcement

How, then, can you know what subjects to study? Our best answer is: "Learn as much as possible about the class of positions for which you've applied." The exam will test the knowledge, skills and abilities needed to do the work.

Your most valuable source of information about the position you want is the official exam announcement. This announcement lists the training and experience qualifications. Check these standards and apply only if you come reasonably close to meeting them.

The brief description of the position in the examination announcement offers some clues to the subjects which will be tested. Think about the job itself. Review the duties in your mind. Can you perform them, or are there some in which you are rusty? Fill in the blank spots in your preparation.

Many jurisdictions preview the written test in the exam announcement by including a section called "Knowledge and Abilities Required," "Scope of the Examination," or some similar heading. Here you will find out specifically what fields will be tested.

#### 2) Review your own background

Once you learn in general what the position is all about, and what you need to know to do the work, ask yourself which subjects you already know fairly well and which need improvement. You may wonder whether to concentrate on improving your strong areas or on building some background in your fields of weakness. When the announcement has specified "some knowledge" or "considerable knowledge," or has used adjectives like "beginning principles of..." or "advanced ... methods," you can get a clue as to the number and difficulty of questions to be asked in any given field. More questions, and hence broader coverage, would be included for those subjects which are more important in the work. Now weigh your strengths and weaknesses against the job requirements and prepare accordingly.

#### 3) Determine the level of the position

Another way to tell how intensively you should prepare is to understand the level of the job for which you are applying. Is it the entering level? In other words, is this the position in which beginners in a field of work are hired? Or is it an intermediate or advanced level? Sometimes this is indicated by such words as "Junior" or "Senior" in the class title. Other jurisdictions use Roman numerals to designate the level – Clerk I, Clerk II, for example. The word "Supervisor" sometimes appears in the title. If the level is not indicated by the title, check the description of duties. Will you be working under very close supervision, or will you have responsibility for independent decisions in this work?

### 4) Choose appropriate study materials

Now that you know the subjects to be examined and the relative amount of each subject to be covered, you can choose suitable study materials. For beginning level jobs, or even advanced ones, if you have a pronounced weakness in some aspect of your training, read a modern, standard textbook in that field. Be sure it is up to date and has general coverage. Such books are normally available at your library, and the librarian will be glad to help you locate one. For entry-level positions, questions of appropriate difficulty are chosen – neither highly advanced questions, nor those too simple. Such questions require careful thought but not advanced training.

If the position for which you are applying is technical or advanced, you will read more advanced, specialized material. If you are already familiar with the basic principles of your field, elementary textbooks would waste your time. Concentrate on advanced textbooks and technical periodicals. Think through the concepts and review difficult problems in your field.

These are all general sources. You can get more ideas on your own initiative, following these leads. For example, training manuals and publications of the government agency which employs workers in your field can be useful, particularly for technical and professional positions. A letter or visit to the government department involved may result in more specific study suggestions, and certainly will provide you with a more definite idea of the exact nature of the position you are seeking.

## III. KINDS OF TESTS

Tests are used for purposes other than measuring knowledge and ability to perform specified duties. For some positions, it is equally important to test ability to make adjustments to new situations or to profit from training. In others, basic mental abilities not dependent on information are essential. Questions which test these things may not appear as pertinent to the duties of the position as those which test for knowledge and information. Yet they are often highly important parts of a fair examination. For very general questions, it is almost impossible to help you direct your study efforts. What we can do is to point out some of the more common of these general abilities needed in public service positions and describe some typical questions.

1) General information

Broad, general information has been found useful for predicting job success in some kinds of work. This is tested in a variety of ways, from vocabulary lists to questions about current events. Basic background in some field of work, such as sociology or economics, may be sampled in a group of questions. Often these are principles which have become familiar to most persons through exposure rather than through formal training. It is difficult to advise you how to study for these questions; being alert to the world around you is our best suggestion.

2) Verbal ability

An example of an ability needed in many positions is verbal or language ability. Verbal ability is, in brief, the ability to use and understand words. Vocabulary and grammar tests are typical measures of this ability. Reading comprehension or paragraph interpretation questions are common in many kinds of civil service tests. You are given a paragraph of written material and asked to find its central meaning.

3) Numerical ability

Number skills can be tested by the familiar arithmetic problem, by checking paired lists of numbers to see which are alike and which are different, or by interpreting charts and graphs. In the latter test, a graph may be printed in the test booklet which you are asked to use as the basis for answering questions.

4) Observation

A popular test for law-enforcement positions is the observation test. A picture is shown to you for several minutes, then taken away. Questions about the picture test your ability to observe both details and larger elements.

5) Following directions

In many positions in the public service, the employee must be able to carry out written instructions dependably and accurately. You may be given a chart with several columns, each column listing a variety of information. The questions require you to carry out directions involving the information given in the chart.

6) Skills and aptitudes

Performance tests effectively measure some manual skills and aptitudes. When the skill is one in which you are trained, such as typing or shorthand, you can practice. These tests are often very much like those given in business school or high school courses. For many of the other skills and aptitudes, however, no short-time preparation can be made. Skills and abilities natural to you or that you have developed throughout your lifetime are being tested.

Many of the general questions just described provide all the data needed to answer the questions and ask you to use your reasoning ability to find the answers. Your best preparation for these tests, as well as for tests of facts and ideas, is to be at your physical and mental best. You, no doubt, have your own methods of getting into an exam-taking mood and keeping "in shape." The next section lists some ideas on this subject.


IV. KINDS OF QUESTIONS

Only rarely is the "essay" question, which you answer in narrative form, used in civil service tests. Civil service tests are usually of the short-answer type. Full instructions for answering these questions will be given to you at the examination. But in case this is your first experience with short-answer questions and separate answer sheets, here is what you need to know:

**1) Multiple-choice Questions**

Most popular of the short-answer questions is the "multiple choice" or "best answer" question. It can be used, for example, to test for factual knowledge, ability to solve problems or judgment in meeting situations found at work.

A multiple-choice question is normally one of three types—
- It can begin with an incomplete statement followed by several possible endings. You are to find the one ending which *best* completes the statement, although some of the others may not be entirely wrong.
- It can also be a complete statement in the form of a question which is answered by choosing one of the statements listed.

- It can be in the form of a problem – again you select the best answer.

Here is an example of a multiple-choice question with a discussion which should give you some clues as to the method for choosing the right answer:

When an employee has a complaint about his assignment, the action which will *best* help him overcome his difficulty is to
   A. discuss his difficulty with his coworkers
   B. take the problem to the head of the organization
   C. take the problem to the person who gave him the assignment
   D. say nothing to anyone about his complaint

In answering this question, you should study each of the choices to find which is best. Consider choice "A" – Certainly an employee may discuss his complaint with fellow employees, but no change or improvement can result, and the complaint remains unresolved. Choice "B" is a poor choice since the head of the organization probably does not know what assignment you have been given, and taking your problem to him is known as "going over the head" of the supervisor. The supervisor, or person who made the assignment, is the person who can clarify it or correct any injustice. Choice "C" is, therefore, correct. To say nothing, as in choice "D," is unwise. Supervisors have and interest in knowing the problems employees are facing, and the employee is seeking a solution to his problem.

## 2) True/False Questions

The "true/false" or "right/wrong" form of question is sometimes used. Here a complete statement is given. Your job is to decide whether the statement is right or wrong.

SAMPLE: A roaming cell-phone call to a nearby city costs less than a non-roaming call to a distant city.

This statement is wrong, or false, since roaming calls are more expensive.

This is not a complete list of all possible question forms, although most of the others are variations of these common types. You will always get complete directions for answering questions. Be sure you understand *how* to mark your answers – ask questions until you do.

## V. RECORDING YOUR ANSWERS

Computer terminals are used more and more today for many different kinds of exams.

For an examination with very few applicants, you may be told to record your answers in the test booklet itself. Separate answer sheets are much more common. If this separate answer sheet is to be scored by machine – and this is often the case – it is highly important that you mark your answers correctly in order to get credit.

An electronic scoring machine is often used in civil service offices because of the speed with which papers can be scored. Machine-scored answer sheets must be marked with a pencil, which will be given to you. This pencil has a high graphite content which responds to the electronic scoring machine. As a matter of fact, stray dots may register as answers, so do not let your pencil rest on the answer sheet while you are pondering the correct answer. Also, if your pencil lead breaks or is otherwise defective, ask for another.

Since the answer sheet will be dropped in a slot in the scoring machine, be careful not to bend the corners or get the paper crumpled.

The answer sheet normally has five vertical columns of numbers, with 30 numbers to a column. These numbers correspond to the question numbers in your test booklet. After each number, going across the page are four or five pairs of dotted lines. These short dotted lines have small letters or numbers above them. The first two pairs may also have a "T" or "F" above the letters. This indicates that the first two pairs only are to be used if the questions are of the true-false type. If the questions are multiple choice, disregard the "T" and "F" and pay attention only to the small letters or numbers.

Answer your questions in the manner of the sample that follows:

32. The largest city in the United States is
    A. Washington, D.C.
    B. New York City
    C. Chicago
    D. Detroit
    E. San Francisco

1) Choose the answer you think is best. (New York City is the largest, so "B" is correct.)
2) Find the row of dotted lines numbered the same as the question you are answering. (Find row number 32)
3) Find the pair of dotted lines corresponding to the answer. (Find the pair of lines under the mark "B.")
4) Make a solid black mark between the dotted lines.


## VI. BEFORE THE TEST

Common sense will help you find procedures to follow to get ready for an examination. Too many of us, however, overlook these sensible measures. Indeed, nervousness and fatigue have been found to be the most serious reasons why applicants fail to do their best on civil service tests. Here is a list of reminders:

- Begin your preparation early – Don't wait until the last minute to go scurrying around for books and materials or to find out what the position is all about.
- Prepare continuously – An hour a night for a week is better than an all-night cram session. This has been definitely established. What is more, a night a week for a month will return better dividends than crowding your study into a shorter period of time.
- Locate the place of the exam – You have been sent a notice telling you when and where to report for the examination. If the location is in a different town or otherwise unfamiliar to you, it would be well to inquire the best route and learn something about the building.
- Relax the night before the test – Allow your mind to rest. Do not study at all that night. Plan some mild recreation or diversion; then go to bed early and get a good night's sleep.
- Get up early enough to make a leisurely trip to the place for the test – This way unforeseen events, traffic snarls, unfamiliar buildings, etc. will not upset you.
- Dress comfortably – A written test is not a fashion show. You will be known by number and not by name, so wear something comfortable.

- Leave excess paraphernalia at home – Shopping bags and odd bundles will get in your way. You need bring only the items mentioned in the official notice you received; usually everything you need is provided. Do not bring reference books to the exam. They will only confuse those last minutes and be taken away from you when in the test room.
- Arrive somewhat ahead of time – If because of transportation schedules you must get there very early, bring a newspaper or magazine to take your mind off yourself while waiting.
- Locate the examination room – When you have found the proper room, you will be directed to the seat or part of the room where you will sit. Sometimes you are given a sheet of instructions to read while you are waiting. Do not fill out any forms until you are told to do so; just read them and be prepared.
- Relax and prepare to listen to the instructions
- If you have any physical problem that may keep you from doing your best, be sure to tell the test administrator. If you are sick or in poor health, you really cannot do your best on the exam. You can come back and take the test some other time.

## VII. AT THE TEST

The day of the test is here and you have the test booklet in your hand. The temptation to get going is very strong. Caution! There is more to success than knowing the right answers. You must know how to identify your papers and understand variations in the type of short-answer question used in this particular examination. Follow these suggestions for maximum results from your efforts:

### 1) Cooperate with the monitor

The test administrator has a duty to create a situation in which you can be as much at ease as possible. He will give instructions, tell you when to begin, check to see that you are marking your answer sheet correctly, and so on. He is not there to guard you, although he will see that your competitors do not take unfair advantage. He wants to help you do your best.

### 2) Listen to all instructions

Don't jump the gun! Wait until you understand all directions. In most civil service tests you get more time than you need to answer the questions. So don't be in a hurry. Read each word of instructions until you clearly understand the meaning. Study the examples, listen to all announcements and follow directions. Ask questions if you do not understand what to do.

### 3) Identify your papers

Civil service exams are usually identified by number only. You will be assigned a number; you must not put your name on your test papers. Be sure to copy your number correctly. Since more than one exam may be given, copy your exact examination title.

### 4) Plan your time

Unless you are told that a test is a "speed" or "rate of work" test, speed itself is usually not important. Time enough to answer all the questions will be provided, but this does not mean that you have all day. An overall time limit has been set. Divide the total time (in minutes) by the number of questions to determine the approximate time you have for each question.

### 5) Do not linger over difficult questions

If you come across a difficult question, mark it with a paper clip (useful to have along) and come back to it when you have been through the booklet. One caution if you do this – be sure to skip a number on your answer sheet as well. Check often to be sure that you have not lost your place and that you are marking in the row numbered the same as the question you are answering.

### 6) Read the questions

Be sure you know what the question asks! Many capable people are unsuccessful because they failed to *read* the questions correctly.

### 7) Answer all questions

Unless you have been instructed that a penalty will be deducted for incorrect answers, it is better to guess than to omit a question.

### 8) Speed tests

It is often better NOT to guess on speed tests. It has been found that on timed tests people are tempted to spend the last few seconds before time is called in marking answers at random – without even reading them – in the hope of picking up a few extra points. To discourage this practice, the instructions may warn you that your score will be "corrected" for guessing. That is, a penalty will be applied. The incorrect answers will be deducted from the correct ones, or some other penalty formula will be used.

### 9) Review your answers

If you finish before time is called, go back to the questions you guessed or omitted to give them further thought. Review other answers if you have time.

### 10) Return your test materials

If you are ready to leave before others have finished or time is called, take ALL your materials to the monitor and leave quietly. Never take any test material with you. The monitor can discover whose papers are not complete, and taking a test booklet may be grounds for disqualification.

## VIII. EXAMINATION TECHNIQUES

1) Read the general instructions carefully. These are usually printed on the first page of the exam booklet. As a rule, these instructions refer to the timing of the examination; the fact that you should not start work until the signal and must stop work at a signal, etc. If there are any *special* instructions, such as a choice of questions to be answered, make sure that you note this instruction carefully.

2) When you are ready to start work on the examination, that is as soon as the signal has been given, read the instructions to each question booklet, underline any key words or phrases, such as *least, best, outline, describe* and the like. In this way you will tend to answer as requested rather than discover on reviewing your paper that you *listed without describing*, that you selected the *worst* choice rather than the *best* choice, etc.

3) If the examination is of the objective or multiple-choice type – that is, each question will also give a series of possible answers: A, B, C or D, and you are called upon to select the best answer and write the letter next to that answer on your answer paper – it is advisable to start answering each question in turn. There may be anywhere from 50 to 100 such questions in the three or four hours allotted and you can see how much time would be taken if you read through all the questions before beginning to answer any. Furthermore, if you come across a question or group of questions which you know would be difficult to answer, it would undoubtedly affect your handling of all the other questions.

4) If the examination is of the essay type and contains but a few questions, it is a moot point as to whether you should read all the questions before starting to answer any one. Of course, if you are given a choice – say five out of seven and the like – then it is essential to read all the questions so you can eliminate the two that are most difficult. If, however, you are asked to answer all the questions, there may be danger in trying to answer the easiest one first because you may find that you will spend too much time on it. The best technique is to answer the first question, then proceed to the second, etc.

5) Time your answers. Before the exam begins, write down the time it started, then add the time allowed for the examination and write down the time it must be completed, then divide the time available somewhat as follows:
    - If 3-1/2 hours are allowed, that would be 210 minutes. If you have 80 objective-type questions, that would be an average of 2-1/2 minutes per question. Allow yourself no more than 2 minutes per question, or a total of 160 minutes, which will permit about 50 minutes to review.
    - If for the time allotment of 210 minutes there are 7 essay questions to answer, that would average about 30 minutes a question. Give yourself only 25 minutes per question so that you have about 35 minutes to review.

6) The most important instruction is to *read each question* and make sure you know what is wanted. The second most important instruction is to *time yourself properly* so that you answer every question. The third most important instruction is to *answer every question*. Guess if you have to but include something for each question. Remember that you will receive no credit for a blank and will probably receive some credit if you write something in answer to an essay question. If you guess a letter – say "B" for a multiple-choice question – you may have guessed right. If you leave a blank as an answer to a multiple-choice question, the examiners may respect your feelings but it will not add a point to your score. Some exams may penalize you for wrong answers, so in such cases *only*, you may not want to guess unless you have some basis for your answer.

7) Suggestions
   a. Objective-type questions
      1. Examine the question booklet for proper sequence of pages and questions
      2. Read all instructions carefully
      3. Skip any question which seems too difficult; return to it after all other questions have been answered
      4. Apportion your time properly; do not spend too much time on any single question or group of questions

5. Note and underline key words – *all, most, fewest, least, best, worst, same, opposite,* etc.
6. Pay particular attention to negatives
7. Note unusual option, e.g., unduly long, short, complex, different or similar in content to the body of the question
8. Observe the use of "hedging" words – *probably, may, most likely,* etc.
9. Make sure that your answer is put next to the same number as the question
10. Do not second-guess unless you have good reason to believe the second answer is definitely more correct
11. Cross out original answer if you decide another answer is more accurate; do not erase until you are ready to hand your paper in
12. Answer all questions; guess unless instructed otherwise
13. Leave time for review

b. Essay questions
1. Read each question carefully
2. Determine exactly what is wanted. Underline key words or phrases.
3. Decide on outline or paragraph answer
4. Include many different points and elements unless asked to develop any one or two points or elements
5. Show impartiality by giving pros and cons unless directed to select one side only
6. Make and write down any assumptions you find necessary to answer the questions
7. Watch your English, grammar, punctuation and choice of words
8. Time your answers; don't crowd material

8) Answering the essay question

Most essay questions can be answered by framing the specific response around several key words or ideas. Here are a few such key words or ideas:

M's: manpower, materials, methods, money, management
P's: purpose, program, policy, plan, procedure, practice, problems, pitfalls, personnel, public relations

a. Six basic steps in handling problems:
1. Preliminary plan and background development
2. Collect information, data and facts
3. Analyze and interpret information, data and facts
4. Analyze and develop solutions as well as make recommendations
5. Prepare report and sell recommendations
6. Install recommendations and follow up effectiveness

b. Pitfalls to avoid
1. *Taking things for granted* – A statement of the situation does not necessarily imply that each of the elements is necessarily true; for example, a complaint may be invalid and biased so that all that can be taken for granted is that a complaint has been registered

2. *Considering only one side of a situation* – Wherever possible, indicate several alternatives and then point out the reasons you selected the best one
3. *Failing to indicate follow up* – Whenever your answer indicates action on your part, make certain that you will take proper follow-up action to see how successful your recommendations, procedures or actions turn out to be
4. *Taking too long in answering any single question* – Remember to time your answers properly

## IX. AFTER THE TEST

Scoring procedures differ in detail among civil service jurisdictions although the general principles are the same. Whether the papers are hand-scored or graded by machine we have described, they are nearly always graded by number. That is, the person who marks the paper knows only the number – never the name – of the applicant. Not until all the papers have been graded will they be matched with names. If other tests, such as training and experience or oral interview ratings have been given, scores will be combined. Different parts of the examination usually have different weights. For example, the written test might count 60 percent of the final grade, and a rating of training and experience 40 percent. In many jurisdictions, veterans will have a certain number of points added to their grades.

After the final grade has been determined, the names are placed in grade order and an eligible list is established. There are various methods for resolving ties between those who get the same final grade – probably the most common is to place first the name of the person whose application was received first. Job offers are made from the eligible list in the order the names appear on it. You will be notified of your grade and your rank as soon as all these computations have been made. This will be done as rapidly as possible.

People who are found to meet the requirements in the announcement are called "eligibles." Their names are put on a list of eligible candidates. An eligible's chances of getting a job depend on how high he stands on this list and how fast agencies are filling jobs from the list.

When a job is to be filled from a list of eligibles, the agency asks for the names of people on the list of eligibles for that job. When the civil service commission receives this request, it sends to the agency the names of the three people highest on this list. Or, if the job to be filled has specialized requirements, the office sends the agency the names of the top three persons who meet these requirements from the general list.

The appointing officer makes a choice from among the three people whose names were sent to him. If the selected person accepts the appointment, the names of the others are put back on the list to be considered for future openings.

That is the rule in hiring from all kinds of eligible lists, whether they are for typist, carpenter, chemist, or something else. For every vacancy, the appointing officer has his choice of any one of the top three eligibles on the list. This explains why the person whose name is on top of the list sometimes does not get an appointment when some of the persons lower on the list do. If the appointing officer chooses the second or third eligible, the No. 1 eligible does not get a job at once, but stays on the list until he is appointed or the list is terminated.

## X. HOW TO PASS THE INTERVIEW TEST

The examination for which you applied requires an oral interview test. You have already taken the written test and you are now being called for the interview test – the final part of the formal examination.

You may think that it is not possible to prepare for an interview test and that there are no procedures to follow during an interview. Our purpose is to point out some things you can do in advance that will help you and some good rules to follow and pitfalls to avoid while you are being interviewed.

*What is an interview supposed to test?*

The written examination is designed to test the technical knowledge and competence of the candidate; the oral is designed to evaluate intangible qualities, not readily measured otherwise, and to establish a list showing the relative fitness of each candidate – as measured against his competitors – for the position sought. Scoring is not on the basis of "right" and "wrong," but on a sliding scale of values ranging from "not passable" to "outstanding." As a matter of fact, it is possible to achieve a relatively low score without a single "incorrect" answer because of evident weakness in the qualities being measured.

Occasionally, an examination may consist entirely of an oral test – either an individual or a group oral. In such cases, information is sought concerning the technical knowledges and abilities of the candidate, since there has been no written examination for this purpose. More commonly, however, an oral test is used to supplement a written examination.

*Who conducts interviews?*

The composition of oral boards varies among different jurisdictions. In nearly all, a representative of the personnel department serves as chairman. One of the members of the board may be a representative of the department in which the candidate would work. In some cases, "outside experts" are used, and, frequently, a businessman or some other representative of the general public is asked to serve. Labor and management or other special groups may be represented. The aim is to secure the services of experts in the appropriate field.

However the board is composed, it is a good idea (and not at all improper or unethical) to ascertain in advance of the interview who the members are and what groups they represent. When you are introduced to them, you will have some idea of their backgrounds and interests, and at least you will not stutter and stammer over their names.

*What should be done before the interview?*

While knowledge about the board members is useful and takes some of the surprise element out of the interview, there is other preparation which is more substantive. It *is* possible to prepare for an oral interview – in several ways:

**1) Keep a copy of your application and review it carefully before the interview**

This may be the only document before the oral board, and the starting point of the interview. Know what education and experience you have listed there, and the sequence and dates of all of it. Sometimes the board will ask you to review the highlights of your experience for them; you should not have to hem and haw doing it.

**2) Study the class specification and the examination announcement**

Usually, the oral board has one or both of these to guide them. The qualities, characteristics or knowledges required by the position sought are stated in these documents. They offer valuable clues as to the nature of the oral interview. For example, if the job involves supervisory responsibilities, the announcement will usually indicate that knowledge of modern supervisory methods and the qualifications of the candidate as a supervisor will be tested. If so, you can expect such questions, frequently in the form of a hypothetical situation which you are expected to solve. NEVER go into an oral without knowledge of the duties and responsibilities of the job you seek.

### 3) Think through each qualification required

Try to visualize the kind of questions you would ask if you were a board member. How well could you answer them? Try especially to appraise your own knowledge and background in each area, *measured against the job sought*, and identify any areas in which you are weak. Be critical and realistic – do not flatter yourself.

### 4) Do some general reading in areas in which you feel you may be weak

For example, if the job involves supervision and your past experience has NOT, some general reading in supervisory methods and practices, particularly in the field of human relations, might be useful. Do NOT study agency procedures or detailed manuals. The oral board will be testing your understanding and capacity, not your memory.

### 5) Get a good night's sleep and watch your general health and mental attitude

You will want a clear head at the interview. Take care of a cold or any other minor ailment, and of course, no hangovers.

*What should be done on the day of the interview?*

Now comes the day of the interview itself. Give yourself plenty of time to get there. Plan to arrive somewhat ahead of the scheduled time, particularly if your appointment is in the fore part of the day. If a previous candidate fails to appear, the board might be ready for you a bit early. By early afternoon an oral board is almost invariably behind schedule if there are many candidates, and you may have to wait. Take along a book or magazine to read, or your application to review, but leave any extraneous material in the waiting room when you go in for your interview. In any event, relax and compose yourself.

The matter of dress is important. The board is forming impressions about you – from your experience, your manners, your attitude, and your appearance. Give your personal appearance careful attention. Dress your best, but not your flashiest. Choose conservative, appropriate clothing, and be sure it is immaculate. This is a business interview, and your appearance should indicate that you regard it as such. Besides, being well groomed and properly dressed will help boost your confidence.

Sooner or later, someone will call your name and escort you into the interview room. *This is it*. From here on you are on your own. It is too late for any more preparation. But remember, you asked for this opportunity to prove your fitness, and you are here because your request was granted.

*What happens when you go in?*

The usual sequence of events will be as follows: The clerk (who is often the board stenographer) will introduce you to the chairman of the oral board, who will introduce you to the other members of the board. Acknowledge the introductions before you sit down. Do not be surprised if you find a microphone facing you or a stenotypist sitting by. Oral interviews are usually recorded in the event of an appeal or other review.

Usually the chairman of the board will open the interview by reviewing the highlights of your education and work experience from your application – primarily for the benefit of the other members of the board, as well as to get the material into the record. Do not interrupt or comment unless there is an error or significant misinterpretation; if that is the case, do not hesitate. But do not quibble about insignificant matters. Also, he will usually ask you some question about your education, experience or your present job -- partly to get you to start talking and to establish the interviewing "rapport." He may start the actual questioning, or turn it over to one of the other members. Frequently, each member undertakes the questioning on a particular area, one in which he is perhaps most competent, so you can expect each member to participate in the examination. Because time is limited, you may also expect some rather abrupt switches in the direction the questioning takes, so do not be upset by it. Normally, a board member will not pursue a single line of questioning unless he discovers a particular strength or weakness.

After each member has participated, the chairman will usually ask whether any member has any further questions, then will ask you if you have anything you wish to add. Unless you are expecting this question, it may floor you. Worse, it may start you off on an extended, extemporaneous speech. The board is not usually seeking more information. The question is principally to offer you a last opportunity to present further qualifications or to indicate that you have nothing to add. So, if you feel that a significant qualification or characteristic has been overlooked, it is proper to point it out in a sentence or so. Do not compliment the board on the thoroughness of their examination – they have been sketchy, and you know it. If you wish, merely say, "No thank you, I have nothing further to add." This is a point where you can "talk yourself out" of a good impression or fail to present an important bit of information. Remember, *you close the interview yourself.*

The chairman will then say, "That is all, Mr. _____, thank you." Do not be startled; the interview is over, and quicker than you think. Thank him, gather your belongings and take your leave. Save your sigh of relief for the other side of the door.


*How to put your best foot forward*

Throughout this entire process, you may feel that the board individually and collectively is trying to pierce your defenses, seek out your hidden weaknesses and embarrass and confuse you. Actually, this is not true. They are obliged to make an appraisal of your qualifications for the job you are seeking, and they want to see you in your best light. Remember, they must interview all candidates and a non-cooperative candidate may become a failure in spite of their best efforts to bring out his qualifications. Here are 15 suggestions that will help you:

**1) Be natural – Keep your attitude confident, not cocky**

If you are not confident that you can do the job, do not expect the board to be. Do not apologize for your weaknesses, try to bring out your strong points. The board is interested in a positive, not negative, presentation. Cockiness will antagonize any board member and make him wonder if you are covering up a weakness by a false show of strength.

**2) Get comfortable, but don't lounge or sprawl**

Sit erectly but not stiffly. A careless posture may lead the board to conclude that you are careless in other things, or at least that you are not impressed by the importance of the occasion. Either conclusion is natural, even if incorrect. Do not fuss with your clothing, a pencil or an ashtray. Your hands may occasionally be useful to emphasize a point; do not let them become a point of distraction.

**3) Do not wisecrack or make small talk**

This is a serious situation, and your attitude should show that you consider it as such. Further, the time of the board is limited – they do not want to waste it, and neither should you.

**4) Do not exaggerate your experience or abilities**

In the first place, from information in the application or other interviews and sources, the board may know more about you than you think. Secondly, you probably will not get away with it. An experienced board is rather adept at spotting such a situation, so do not take the chance.

**5) If you know a board member, do not make a point of it, yet do not hide it**

Certainly you are not fooling him, and probably not the other members of the board. Do not try to take advantage of your acquaintanceship – it will probably do you little good.

**6) Do not dominate the interview**

Let the board do that. They will give you the clues – do not assume that you have to do all the talking. Realize that the board has a number of questions to ask you, and do not try to take up all the interview time by showing off your extensive knowledge of the answer to the first one.

**7) Be attentive**

You only have 20 minutes or so, and you should keep your attention at its sharpest throughout. When a member is addressing a problem or question to you, give him your undivided attention. Address your reply principally to him, but do not exclude the other board members.

**8) Do not interrupt**

A board member may be stating a problem for you to analyze. He will ask you a question when the time comes. Let him state the problem, and wait for the question.

**9) Make sure you understand the question**

Do not try to answer until you are sure what the question is. If it is not clear, restate it in your own words or ask the board member to clarify it for you. However, do not haggle about minor elements.

**10) Reply promptly but not hastily**

A common entry on oral board rating sheets is "candidate responded readily," or "candidate hesitated in replies." Respond as promptly and quickly as you can, but do not jump to a hasty, ill-considered answer.

**11) Do not be peremptory in your answers**

A brief answer is proper – but do not fire your answer back. That is a losing game from your point of view. The board member can probably ask questions much faster than you can answer them.

**12) Do not try to create the answer you think the board member wants**

He is interested in what kind of mind you have and how it works – not in playing games. Furthermore, he can usually spot this practice and will actually grade you down on it.

**13) Do not switch sides in your reply merely to agree with a board member**

Frequently, a member will take a contrary position merely to draw you out and to see if you are willing and able to defend your point of view. Do not start a debate, yet do not surrender a good position. If a position is worth taking, it is worth defending.

**14) Do not be afraid to admit an error in judgment if you are shown to be wrong**

The board knows that you are forced to reply without any opportunity for careful consideration. Your answer may be demonstrably wrong. If so, admit it and get on with the interview.

**15) Do not dwell at length on your present job**

The opening question may relate to your present assignment. Answer the question but do not go into an extended discussion. You are being examined for a *new* job, not your present one. As a matter of fact, try to phrase ALL your answers in terms of the job for which you are being examined.

*Basis of Rating*

Probably you will forget most of these "do's" and "don'ts" when you walk into the oral interview room. Even remembering them all will not ensure you a passing grade. Perhaps you did not have the qualifications in the first place. But remembering them will help you to put your best foot forward, without treading on the toes of the board members.

Rumor and popular opinion to the contrary notwithstanding, an oral board wants you to make the best appearance possible. They know you are under pressure – but they also want to see how you respond to it as a guide to what your reaction would be under the pressures of the job you seek. They will be influenced by the degree of poise you display, the personal traits you show and the manner in which you respond.


ABOUT THIS BOOK

This book contains tests divided into Examination Sections. Go through each test, answering every question in the margin. We have also attached a sample answer sheet at the back of the book that can be removed and used. At the end of each test look at the answer key and check your answers. On the ones you got wrong, look at the right answer choice and learn. Do not fill in the answers first. Do not memorize the questions and answers, but understand the answer and principles involved. On your test, the questions will likely be different from the samples. Questions are changed and new ones added. If you understand these past questions you should have success with any changes that arise. Tests may consist of several types of questions. We have additional books on each subject should more study be advisable or necessary for you. Finally, the more you study, the better prepared you will be. This book is intended to be the last thing you study before you walk into the examination room. Prior study of relevant texts is also recommended. NLC publishes some of these in our Fundamental Series. Knowledge and good sense are important factors in passing your exam. Good luck also helps. So now study this Passbook, absorb the material contained within and take that knowledge into the examination. Then do your best to pass that exam.

# EXAMINATION SECTION

# EXAMINATION SECTION
## TEST 1

DIRECTIONS: Each question or incomplete statement is followed by several suggested answers or completions. Select the one that BEST answers the question or completes the statement. *PRINT THE LETTER OF THE CORRECT ANSWER IN THE SPACE AT THE RIGHT.*

1. Which of the following events would typically cause the GREATEST amount of stress in a person's life?
   A. A major change in financial status
   B. Vacation
   C. Pregnancy
   D. Marital separation

   1.____

2. A local shopping center has experienced a recent rash of shoplifting. Officer Jones is patrolling the mall parking lot frequently.
   Which situation below should Officer Jones regard as MOST suspicious?
   A. A man running out a store entrance with a shopping bag from the store under his arm
   B. A car parked for a long time near the front entrance of the store
   C. A woman loading a pile of clothes, some with plastic security tags still attached, into the trunk of her car
   D. A young man walking around looking in through the windows of various parked cars

   2.____

3. An officer is faced with the responsibility of telling a woman her husband has been murdered. While the officers should phrase the news as gently as possible, he or she should also demonstrate empathy nonverbally.
   The BEST way to do this is to
   A. stand with arms crossed
   B. hold the woman closely
   C. maintain eye contact
   D. tell the woman you understand her pain

   3.____

4. Cognitive symptoms of anxiety include
   A. rapid heart rate              B. feelings of fear of helplessness
   C. poor social functioning       D. euphoria

   4.____

5. Which of the following is MOST likely to help a person to improve her attitude?
   A. Avoiding people who make her feel bad about herself
   B. Learning to become more goal-oriented
   C. Learning to look more clearly at her own faults
   D. Taking charge of an unruly situation

   5.____

1

6. A suspect has been handcuffed, but refuses to take a seat in the patrol car after several requests.
   The arresting officer should
   A. tap the suspect behind the knees with the baton, just hard enough so that the suspect's legs will fold and he can be inserted into the car
   B. tighten the handcuffs until the pain compel compliance
   C. try to frighten the suspect with threats
   D. inform the suspect of the consequences for resisting arrest

   6._____

7. Each of the following is likely to be a cause of stress on the job, EXCEPT
   A. work overload
   B. differences in organizational and personal values
   C. a narrowly-defined role
   D. time pressures

   7._____

8. In communicating with people, especially in stressful or high-conflict situations, nonverbal communication is
   A. more important than the verbal message
   B. less important than the verbal message
   C. universal across all cultures
   D. typically contradictory to the verbal message

   8._____

9. Problem-oriented police work does NOT
   A. help officers get to the roots of a crime problem
   B. offer a proactive model for policing
   C. focus on responding to calls for service
   D. have any impact on preventing or reducing crime

   9._____

10. The difference between assertiveness and aggressiveness is that
    A. assertiveness is not potentially harmful to others
    B. aggressiveness involves strangers
    C. aggressiveness has to do with achieving goals
    D. assertiveness is always negative

    10._____

11. As an officer and his partner arrive to investigate a reported domestic disturbance, the husband and wife are still arguing. In the presence of the officers, each spouse makes a verbal threat of physical harm against the other. In resolving this conflict, the FINAL step that should be taken by the officers is to
    A. indicate the consequences if this behavior continues
    B. empathize with each of the spouses
    C. present the spouses with problem-solving strategies
    D. describe the behaviors that appeared to cause the disturbance

    11._____

12. Elements of community policing include
    I. the police           II. the business community
    III. the media          IV. religious institutions
    The CORRECT ANSWER IS:
    A. I, II        B. I, II, III        C. I, III        D. I, II, III, IV

    12._____

13. In a grocery store parking lot, a pair of officers arrest both the buyer and seller in an alleged drug transaction in a grocery store parking lot. After the suspects have been handcuffed and placed in a patrol car, one of the officers notices a wad of bills on the ground where the transaction took place. The officer pockets the money and decides to keep it, telling herself that the money is "dirty" and that she has more of a right to it than either of the criminal suspects. Legally, the officer has committed a crime; ethically, she has committed a(n)
    A. rationalization   B. kickback   C. stereotyping   D. deviance

13.____

14. Probably the MOST effective way to deal with on-the-job stress is to
    A. find alternative employment
    B. take early retirement
    C. participate in a personal wellness program
    D. acquire assertiveness skills that will help confront the people responsible for the stress

14.____

Questions 15-16.

DIRECTIONS:   Questions 15 and 16 deal with the following situation.

A pharmacist has complained to the police department that several drug addicts in his neighborhood have been attempting to obtain drugs legally, usually by passing fake prescriptions.

15. Which of the following people should arouse the MOST suspicion when approaching the prescription counter?
    A. A middle-aged woman who appears homeless and is poorly groomed
    B. A young African-American male in a hooded sweatshirt on a hot day
    C. A man in his thirties who glances around furtively and brings a large amount of nonprescription items to the counter for purchase
    D. None of the above should be regarded as suspicious on the basis of their appearance alone

15.____

16. After refusing to fill several prescriptions, the pharmacist describes or gives each of the prescriptions to an investigating officer.
    Which of the following MOST warrants investigation?
    A. A written investigation that is covered with several coffee rings
    B. A prescription written on a Post-It note
    C. A written prescription for pain killers with a date indicating it was written more than a week ago
    D. A prescription that is phoned in by a doctor

16.____

17. An individual's personality, whether normal or deviant, will ALWAYS
    A. refer to the person's deep inner self, rather than just superficial aspects
    B. involve unique characteristics that are all different from another person's
    C. be a product of social and cultural environments, with no biological foundation
    D. be organized into patterns that are observable and measurable to some degree

17.____

18. Change in a person's life that is due to personal growth is almost always
    A. negative    B. dramatic    C. positive    D. minor

19. Residents in an urban neighborhood have complained of a recent increase in gang-related graffiti in their community.
    Which of the following should be regarded as MOST suspicious by an officer on patrol?
    A. One young man walking down the street and flashing gang signs at passing cars
    B. A pair of teenagers riding their bicycles in a tenement parking lot late at night
    C. A group of teenagers hanging out in a convenience store parking lot, leaning against a wall that is covered with graffiti
    D. A group of teenagers hanging out in a convenience store parking lot. One of the teenagers has a spray paint can.

20. Common symptoms of stress include each of the following EXCEPT
    A. digestive problem    B. sluggishness
    C. sleep problems    D. emotional instability

21. The general goal of community policing is
    A. a lower overall crime rate
    B. conviction of criminals who are caught in the community
    C. fewer violent crimes
    D. a higher quality of life in the community

22. In most settings, the simplest and most effective method of stopping sexual harassment is to
    A. threaten the person with legal or administrative consequences
    B. ignore it
    C. avoid the person as much as possible
    D. ask or tell the person to stop

23. Of the following types of crime, the one MOST likely to have a widespread impact on a victims community is
    A. hate or bias crime    B. workplace violence
    C. theft    D. sexual assault

24. Functional roles of the police include:
    I. Crime prevention    II. Order maintenance
    III. Public service    IV. Criminal prosecution
    The CORRECT answer is:
    A. I only    B. I, II    C. I, II, III    D. I, II, III, IV

25. A pre-existing thought or belief that people have about members of a given group—whether the belief is positive, negative, or neutral—is
    A. ethnocentrism    B. a stereotype
    C. self-centeredness    D. discrimination

## KEY (CORRECT ANSWERS)

| | | | |
|---|---|---|---|
| 1. | D | 11. | A |
| 2. | C | 12. | D |
| 3. | C | 13. | A |
| 4. | B | 14. | C |
| 5. | B | 15. | D |
| 6. | D | 16. | B |
| 7. | C | 17. | D |
| 8. | A | 18. | B |
| 9. | C | 19. | D |
| 10. | A | 20. | B |

21. D
22. D
23. A
24. C
25. B

# TEST 2

DIRECTIONS: Each question or incomplete statement is followed by several suggested answers or completions. Select the one that BEST answers the question or completes the statement. *PRINT THE LETTER OF THE CORRECT ANSWER IN THE SPACE AT THE RIGHT.*

1. Role expectations for police officers generally
   A. are consistent across the country, with a strong focus on peacekeeping
   B. change from community to community, depending on the local culture
   C. direct them to be more lenient with juvenile offenders
   D. direct them to be self-reliant in both preventing and investigating crime

   1.____

2. Officer Shinjo takes a complaint from a woman who says she is being stalked by a man who is a classmate in one of her night business courses. The man has sent her unwanted gifts and left numerous unanswered telephone messages, but she did not become concerned until last night, when she noticed the man following her home from class. She asks Officer Shinjo what to do about the situation.
   At least part of Officer Shinjo's advice to the woman should include the suggestion that she
   A. immediately apply for a restraining order
   B. create a logbook to document each of the stalking incidents in as much detail as possible
   C. answer one of the man's telephone calls and try to explain that the unwanted attention is making her uncomfortable
   D. call the man herself and threaten legal action if he doesn't stop bothering her

   2.____

3. Which of the following is an element of self-direction?
   A. Knowing when to seek help from others
   B. Being able to get from one geographic location to another without a map
   C. Establishing and reaching both short- and long-term goals
   D. Adopting healthier lifestyle habits

   3.____

4. Each of the following factors is typically associated with ethnicity, EXCEPT
   A. culture         B. language
   C. economic status    D. physical characteristics

   4.____

5. Among the communication skills necessary for effective communication with people, the foundation upon which all others are based is considered to be
   A. confrontation    B. authoritativeness
   C. attending behavior    D. observation

   5.____

6. Which of the following offers the BEST definition of the word "ethics"?
   A. An individual's means of obtaining what he wants from and for other people in a society
   B. Standards of conduct that express a society's concept of right and wrong

   6.____

C. A formal code of conduct that delineates a strict set of rules and framework for punishment
D. Morality and the consequences of behaviors

7. Which of the following is a measurement of a rate?
   A. The ratio of the number of new African-American arrestees for drug-related crimes in the 35-49 age bracket during a specific year, compared to the number of African-Americans in the same age group in the entire community
   B. The number of white females, aged 18-25, who are arrested each year on child endangerment charges
   C. The percentage change in the number of property crimes in a given year, compared to the previous year
   D. The ratio of the number of persons currently under prosecution for violent crimes to the number of people, aged 14-55, in the entire community

8. In recent weeks, several patrons at a local restaurant have had their cars broken into by having a window smashed in, and then having valuable items taken from the car. Officer Jackson is patrolling the restaurant parking lot.
   Which situation below should she regard as MOST suspicious?
   A. A young man in a hooded sweatshirt walking around the parking lot at lunchtime, carrying a long, heavy flashlight
   B. A car parked so as to partially block other cars from exiting the parking lot
   C. A man's voice raised in anger coming from the parking lot
   D. Several young men leaning against the outside of the parking lot fence in the early evening, bouncing a basketball and apparently waiting for the arrival of another person

9. Among the skills important to effective communication with people, the MOST complex and difficult to master are those that help to
   A. encourage    B. confront    C. influence    D. summarize

10. The FIRST step in dealing with an alcohol or drug addiction is to
    A. admit there is a problem
    B. talk to a counselor or close friend
    C. stop taking the drug or drinking alcohol
    D. join a support group or enter a rehabilitation center

11. Key elements of police professionalism include:
    I. an advanced education
    II. a clearly stated code of ethics
    III. accountability through peer review
    IV. demonstrated understanding of the field's core body of knowledge
    The CORRECT answer is:
    A. I, II          B. I, III, IV     C. II, III, IV     D. I, II, III, IV

12. A factor that makes a police officer susceptible to corruption is that the officer
    A. is typically different from most members of society
    B. can be sure that if a suspect is arrested, the suspect will be prosecuted and punished
    C. is usually better off financially than most of the people she interacts with in carrying out her duties
    D. has the professional discretion not to enforce the law

13. In resolving an ethical dilemma, a police officer's FIRST step should generally be to
    A. identify the ethical issues that are in conflict
    B. identify the people and organizations likely to be affected by the decision
    C. consult with colleagues and appropriate experts
    D. examine the reasons in favor of and opposed to each possible course of action

14. During a lengthy interview with a witness, an officer decides to use "reflection of meaning" strategies in order to clarify the information he's being given.
    This strategy would involve each of the following EXCEPT
    A. trying to paraphrase longer statements offered by the witness
    B. closing with a check on the witness's words, such as "So do I understand this correctly?"
    C. beginning sentences with phrases such as "You mean....." or "Sounds as if you saw....."
    D. offering an interpretation of the witness's words

15. Officer McGee is meeting with several community members to determine a course of action for reducing gang-related activities in the area.
    Each of the following is a guideline to be used by an officer in building a constructive relationship with community members, EXCEPT
    A. viewing community members as equals
    B. adopting a completely neutral tone of voice when speaking with people
    C. using a shared vocabulary of easily understood, nonoffensive words
    D. asking for the input of community members before making any suggestions

16. In solving a complex problem, the FIRST step is always to
    A. develop a plan          B. gather information
    C. define the problem      D. envision contingencies

17. Role conflict can occur when an officer encounters two sets of expectations that are inconsistent with each other. Role strain can occur when an officer's role is limited by what he or she is authorized to do.
    The MAIN difference between these two is that role
    A. conflict is relatively rare among police officers
    B. conflict can be resolved; role strain cannot
    C. strain creates stressful situations for officers
    D. strain has a greater influence on the officer's exercise of discretion

18. Generally, police community relations differs from public relations in that they
    A. consider the needs of the community first
    B. are much more successful in reducing social problems
    C. are without inherent spheres of interest
    D. encourage two-way communications

19. Factors that place a man at risk as a potential batterer include each of the following, EXCEPT
    A. poverty
    B. drug or alcohol use
    C. 30-45 years of age
    D. witnessing spousal abuse between parents

20. The four major categories of commonly abused substances include
    A. stimulants    B. alcohol    C. nicotine    D. caffeine

21. After receiving their monthly assistance payments from the local social services agency, some members of the homeless community immediately use the money to carry out drug transactions.
    In his patrol of the area around the agency, which situation below should Officer Garcia regard as MOST suspicious?
    A. A group of several homeless people who meet every day in a local park, where they sit together for about three hours and then move on
    B. A homeless woman who walks up and down the entire length of a busy city street all day long, endlessly smoking cigarettes
    C. An abandoned car that sits on a privately-owned lot and is used as a sleeping place by several homeless people throughout the day
    D. A single man remaining in the same area for several hours at a time, during which many homeless people approach him and greet him with handshakes

22. The MOST significant factor that requires police to perform functions other than law enforcement is
    A. greater public trust relative to other agencies or institutions
    B. a broader resource base
    C. round-the-clock availability
    D. the level of police interaction with community members

23. A "minority" group is a group that is discriminated against on the basis of
    A. physical or cultural characteristics
    B. the size of the group relative to the majority
    C. race
    D. the group's degree of conformity to the norms of the majority

24. An officer is talking with a resident of a high-crime urban neighborhood about a recent increase in drug-related activities. Because of the active police presence in the area, some residents are suspicious of the police.
    Each of the following nonverbal cues is a likely indicator of distrust on the part of a listener, EXCEPT

A. holding arms crossed over one's chest
B. steady eye contact
C. clenched jaw
D. shoulders angled away from speaker

25. Personality characteristics necessary for the successful performance of police duties include
    I. dependent style in problem-solving
    II. emotional expressiveness in interpersonal communication
    III. cohesiveness in group performance
    IV. emotional restraint
    The CORRECT answer is:
    A. I, III  B. I, II, IV  C. II, III, IV  D. I, II, III, IV

25.____

## KEY (CORRECT ANSWERS)

| | | | |
|---|---|---|---|
| 1. | B | 11. | D |
| 2. | B | 12. | D |
| 3. | C | 13. | A |
| 4. | C | 14. | D |
| 5. | C | 15. | B |
| 6. | B | 16. | C |
| 7. | B | 17. | B |
| 8. | A | 18. | D |
| 9. | C | 19. | C |
| 10. | A | 20. | A |

21. D
22. C
23. A
24. B
25. C

# EXAMINATION SECTION
## TEST 1

DIRECTIONS: Each question or incomplete statement is followed by several suggested answers or completions. Select the one that BEST answers the question or completes the statement. *PRINT THE LETTER OF THE CORRECT ANSWER IN THE SPACE AT THE RIGHT.*

1. Officer Hayes has arrived at the scene of an automobile accident to find the two drivers arguing heatedly in the middle of the intersection, where their two cars remain entangled by their front bumpers. Traffic has backed up on all four sides of the intersection. As Officer Hayes approaches, the two drivers each begin to tell their side of the story at the same time. As they grow more agitated and begin to call each other names, one of the drivers threatens the other with physical harm.
Officer Hayes' FIRST action should be to
     A. ask each driver to stand on an opposite corner of the intersection and wait for him to begin documenting the accident
     B. call a tow truck to clear the accident from the intersection
     C. arrest the driver who made the threat
     D. ask the drivers to pull their cars out of the intersection and off to the side of the road

2. Probably the MOST important thing a police officer can do to build and strengthen a trusting relationship with community members is to
     A. patrol the area often and conspicuously
     B. listen to them in a respectful and nonjudgmental way
     C. make sure people understand his background and qualifications
     D. establish clear, reachable goals for improving the community

3. Which of the following is NOT a factor that should influence an officer's exercise of discretion?
     A. Clear statutes and protocols
     B. Informal expectations of legislatures and the public
     C. Use of force
     D. Limited resources

4. The term for the policing style which emphasizes order maintenance is _____ style.
     A. service     B. coercive     C. watchman     D. legalistic

5. Officer Torres, a community service law enforcement officer, approaches the home of recent Vietnamese immigrants to speak to several community members gathered there. He notices several pairs of shoes on the front porch.

It is reasonable for Officer Torres too assume that
- A. the people in the home are superstitious
- B. the house must have some religious significance
- C. if he removes his own shoes before entering, it will be perceived as a sign of respect
- D. the homeowners are having their carpets cleaned

6. Ethical issues are
   - A. usually a problem only in individual behaviors
   - B. relevant to all aspects of police work
   - C. usually referred to a board or committee for decision-making
   - D. the same as legal issues

7. In using the "reflection of meaning" technique in a client interview, a social worker should do each of the following, EXCEPT
   - A. begin with a sentence stem such as "You mean…" or "Sounds like you believe…"
   - B. offer an interpretation of the client's words
   - C. add paraphrasing of longer client statements
   - D. close with a "check-out" such as, "Am I hearing you right?"

8. A police officer is speaking with a victim who is hearing-impaired. The police officer should try to do each of the following, EXCEPT
   - A. speak slowly and clearly
   - B. gradually increase the volume of his voice
   - C. face the victim squarely
   - D. reduce or eliminate any background or ambient noise

9. An officer is interviewing a witness who is a recent immigrant from China. In general, the officer should avoid
   - A. verbal tracking or requests for clarification
   - B. open-ended questions
   - C. sustained eye contact
   - D. attentive body language

10. Which of the following statements about rape is FALSE?
    - A. The use of alcohol and drugs can reduce sexual inhibitions.
    - B. Rape is a crime of violence.
    - C. Rape is a crime that can only be committed against women.
    - D. It is not a sustainable legal charge if the partner has already consented to sex in the past.

11. A person's individual code of ethics is typically determined by each of the following factors, EXCEPT
    - A. reason    B. religion    C. emotion    D. law

12. Officer Long, new to the urban precinct where he is assigned patrol, has received a pair of complaints from two customers about the owner of a local convenience store, who works the cash register on most days. According to one customer, the owner became angry and ordered her out of the store after she had asked the price of a certain item. The other customer claims that on another occasion, the owner pulled a handgun from behind the counter and trained it on him as he walked slowly out of the store with his hands up. Each of the customers has lived in the neighborhood for many years and has never before seen or heard of any strange behavior on the owner's part.
    In investigating these complaints, Officer Long should suspect that
    A. the owner should be considered armed and dangerous and any entry into the store should be made with weapons drawn
    B. the cause of the problem is most likely the onset of a serious psychological disturbance
    C. the customers may have reasons to be untruthful about the convenience store owner
    D. the store owner has probably experienced a recent trauma, such as a robber attempt or a personal loss

13. Typical signs and symptoms of stress include
    I. weakened immune system
    II. prolonged, vivid daydreams
    III. insomnia
    IV. depression
    The CORRECT answer is:
    A. I only   B. I, III, IV   C. III, IV   D. I, II, III, IV

14. Other than solid, ethical police work, an officer's BEST defense against a lawsuit or complaint is usually
    A. detailed case records
    B. a capable advocate
    C. a vigorous counterclaim against the plaintiff
    D. the testimony of professional character witnesses

15. Assertive people
    A. avoid stating feelings, opinions, or desires
    B. appear passive, but behave aggressively
    C. state their views and needs directly
    D. appear aggressive, but behave passively

16. In the non-verbal communication process, meaning is MOST commonly provided by
    A. body language
    B. touch
    C. tone of voice
    D. context

17. The MOST obvious practical benefit that deviance has on a society is the
    A. advancement of the status quo
    B. vindication of new laws
    C. inducement to reach cultural goals
    D. promotion of social unity

18. What is the term for policing that focuses on providing a wider and more thorough array of social services to defeat the social problems that cause crime?  18.____
    A. Reflecting policing
    B. Order maintenance
    C. Social engineering
    D. Holistic policing

19. The term "active listening" MOSTLY refers to a person's ability to  19.____
    A. both listen and accomplish other tasks at the same time
    B. take an active role in determining which information is provided by the speaker
    C. concentrate on what is being said
    D. indicate with numerous physical cues that he/she is listening

20. Police officers in any jurisdiction are MOST likely to receive calls about  20.____
    A. threats
    B. suspicious persons
    C. petty theft or property crime
    D. disturbances, such as family arguments

21. Which of the following is NOT a physiological explanation for rape?  21.____
    A. Uncontrollable sex drive
    B. Lack of available partners
    C. Reaction to repressed desires
    D. Consequence of the natural selection process

22. Which of the following is an element of self-discipline?  22.____
    A. Establishing and reaching short-term goals
    B. Establishing and reaching long-term goals
    C. Taking an honest look at one's lifestyle and making conscious changes toward improvement
    D. Taking an honest look at one's personality and revealing traits, both good and bad, to others

23. Most of the events in a person's life are the result of  23.____
    A. chance events
    B. a sense of intuition
    C. individual choices and decisions
    D. the decisions of one's parents or other authority figures

24. Which of the following is the MOST effective way for a department to limit the discretion exercised by police officers?  24.____
    A. Open and flexible departmental directives
    B. Close supervision by departmental management
    C. Broadening role definitions for officers
    D. Statutory protection from civil liability lawsuits

25. Police officers who demonstrate critical thinking skills are also more likely to demonstrate each of the following, EXCEPT   25._____
    A. the ability to empathize
    B. the tendency to criticize
    C. self-awareness
    D. reflective thinking

## KEY (CORRECT ANSWERS)

| | | | |
|---|---|---|---|
| 1. | A | 11. | D |
| 2. | B | 12. | D |
| 3. | A | 13. | B |
| 4. | C | 14. | A |
| 5. | C | 15. | C |
| 6. | B | 16. | A |
| 7. | B | 17. | D |
| 8. | B | 18. | D |
| 9. | C | 19. | C |
| 10. | D | 20. | D |

| | |
|---|---|
| 21. | C |
| 22. | C |
| 23. | C |
| 24. | B |
| 25. | B |

# TEST 2

DIRECTIONS: Each question or incomplete statement is followed by several suggested answers or completions. Select the one that BEST answers the question or completes the statement. *PRINT THE LETTER OF THE CORRECT ANSWER IN THE SPACE AT THE RIGHT.*

1. Officer Park responds to a domestic disturbance call to find a mother and her two young children huddled together in the living room, all of them crying. The mother explains that her husband is no longer there; he flew into a fit of rage and then stormed out to join his friends for a night of drinking.
   Officer Park's FIRST action would MOST likely be to
   A. determine the location of the husband
   B. contact the appropriate social services agency to arrange a consultation
   C. try to calm the family down and ask the mother to explain what happened
   D. refer the mother to a local battered-spouse shelter

   1.____

2. Most commonly, the reason for crimes involving stranger violence is
   A. anger     B. retaliation     C. hate     D. robbery

   2.____

3. For a police officer, "burst stress" is MOST likely to be caused by
   A. a shootout          B. financial troubles
   C. departmental politics     D. substance abuse

   3.____

4. The MOST significant factor in whether a person achieves success in his/her personal life, school, and career is
   A. intelligence            B. a positive attitude
   C. existing financial resources     D. innate ability

   4.____

5. Typically, a professional code of ethics
   A. embodies a broad picture of expected moral conduct
   B. is voluntary
   C. provides specific guidance for performance in situations
   D. are decided by objective ethicists outside of the profession

   5.____

6. Components recognized by contemporary society as elements of sexual harassment include
   I. abuse of power            II. immature behavior
   III. sexual desire            IV. hormonal imbalance
   The CORRECT answer is:
   A. I only     B. I, III     C. II, III     D. I, II, III, IV

   6.____

7. The phrase "substance abuse" is typically defined as
   A. an addiction to an illegal substance
   B. the continued use of a psychoactive substance even after it creates problems in a person's life
   C. the overuse of an illegal substance
   D. a situation in which a person craves a drug and organizes his or her life around obtaining it

   7.____

2 (#2)

8. The humanist perspective of behavior holds that people who commit crimes or otherwise act badly are
   A. willfully disregarding societal norms
   B. reacting to the deprivation of basic needs
   C. suffering from a psychological illness
   D. experiencing a moral lapse

8.____

9. Which of the following is NOT involved in the process of empathic listening?
   A. Actually hearing exactly what the other person is saying
   B. Searching for the "hidden meanings" behind statements
   C. Listening without judgment
   D. Communicating that you're hearing what the other person is saying, both verbally and nonverbally

9.____

10. Which of the following is NOT a component in developing a stress-resistant lifestyle?
    A. Finding leisure time
    B. Eating nutritious foods
    C. Getting enough sleep
    D. Seeking financial independence

10.____

11. Which of the following was NOT a factor that led to the expansion of a community policing model?
    A. Information obtained at a crime scene during a preliminary investigation was the most important factor determining the probability of an arrest.
    B. Police response times typically had little to do with the probability of making an arrest.
    C. Traditional "preventive patrols" generally failed to reduce crime.
    D. People who knew police officers personally often tried to take advantage of them.

11.____

12. Most of the correspondence in a pyramid scheme that has defrauded several elderly victims has been traced to a post office box in a rural area.
    Probably the simplest and most efficient way of arresting the suspect(s) in this case would be to
    A. use an elderly man as a "victim" to lure the suspects into an attempt to defraud him
    B. address a letter to the post office box asking the user to come in for questioning
    C. check Postal Service records to see who is leasing the post office box
    D. physically observe the post office box for a while, to see who is using it

12.____

13. The process of hiring a police officer typically involves each of the following, EXCEPT
    A. technical preparation
    B. medical examination
    C. background checks
    D. physical ability test

13.____

14. The MOST common form of rape is _____ rape.
    A. stranger
    B. acquaintance
    C. sadistic
    D. spousal

14.____

15. Officer Stevens and his partner respond to a domestic disturbance call involving a father and his teenage daughter. As the officers arrive at their home, the two are still arguing heatedly, but when the officers enter, the daughter retreats to the kitchen, where she continues crying. The father explains that his wife, the daughter's mother, died last year, and the daughter's behavior and school performance have suffered as a result. The father is afraid that the daughter is falling in with the wrong crowd, and may be getting involved with drugs. He is afraid for her and doesn't know what to do.
Within the scope of his police role, the MOST appropriate action for Officer Stevens to take in this case would be to
    A. warn both the father and the daughter of the potential consequences of conviction on a charge of disturbing the peace
    B. refer the father and the daughter to a social services or counseling agency
    C. inform the daughter of the drug statutes that may apply in her case as a way to influence her choices
    D. question the daughter about her feelings surrounding the death of her mother

16. During an interview, a suspect confesses to the rape of a co-worker that occurred in the office after the rest of the employees had left for the day. The suspect says he was tormented by the seductive behavior of the co-worker until he could no longer stand it. He was himself a victim, he says.
In this case, the suspect is making use of the psychological defense mechanism known as
    A. projection    B. regression    C. denial    D. sublimation

17. Which of the following is NOT a good stress-reduction strategy?
    A. Spend some time each day doing absolutely nothing
    B. Become more assertive
    C. Develop a hobby
    D. Have a sense of humor

18. The term for the policing style which emphasizes problem-solving is _____ style.
    A. watchman          B. order maintenance
    C. service           D. legalistic

19. According to current rules and statutes, any employer
    A. may inquire as to a job applicant's age or date of birth
    B. may keep on file information regarding an employee's race, color, religion, sex, or national origin
    C. may refuse employment to someone without a car
    D. must give a woman who has taken time off for maternity leave her same job and salary when she is read to return to work

4 (#2)

20. During a conversation with the mother of a teenage boy who has been arrested   20.____
twice for shoplifting, an officer attempts to be an active listener as the mother
explains why she thinks the boy is having so much trouble.
Being an active listener includes each of the following strategies, EXCEPT
    A. putting the speaker at ease
    B. interrupting with questions to clarify meaning
    C. summarizing the speaker's major ideas and feelings
    D. withholding criticism

21. Which of the following is NOT a characteristic of the typical poverty-class family?   21.____
    A. Female-headed, single-parent families
    B. Unwed parents
    C. Isolated from neighbors and relatives
    D. High divorce rates

22. When speaking with community members about improving the quality of life   22.____
in the neighborhood, an officer should look for signs of social desirability bias
among the people with whom he's talking.
Social desirability bias often causes people to
    A. judge other people based on their social role rather than inner character
    B. attribute their successes to skill, while blaming external factors for failures
    C. modify their interactions or behaviors based on what they think is
       acceptable to others
    D. contend for leadership positions

23. For a number of reasons, Officer Stone thinks a fellow officer might have a   23.____
drinking problem, and decides to talk to her about it. The officer says she
doesn't have a drinking problem; she doesn't even take a drink until after it gets
dark.
Her answer indicates that she
    A. doesn't have a drinking problem
    B. is probably a social drinker
    C. drinks more during the winter months
    D. is in denial

24. Factors which shape the police role include each of the following, EXCEPT   24.____
    A. individual goals           B. role expectations
    C. role acquisition           D. multiple-role phenomenon

25. "Deviance" is a social term denoting   25.____
    A. any violation of norms
    B. any serious violation of norms
    C. a type of nonconforming behavior recognizable in all cultures
    D. a specific set of crime statistics

## KEY (CORRECT ANSWERS)

| | | | |
|---|---|---|---|
| 1. | C | 11. | D |
| 2. | D | 12. | D |
| 3. | A | 13. | A |
| 4. | B | 14. | B |
| 5. | A | 15. | B |
| 6. | A | 16. | A |
| 7. | B | 17. | A |
| 8. | B | 18. | C |
| 9. | B | 19. | B |
| 10. | D | 20. | B |

21. C
22. C
23. D
24. A
25. A

# EXAMINATION SECTION
# TEST 1

DIRECTIONS: This section contains descriptions of problem situations. Each problem situation has four alternative actions that might be taken to deal with the problem. You are to make two judgments for each problem.

First, decide which alternative you would MOST LIKELY choose in response to the problem. It might not be exactly what you would do in that situation, but it should be the alternative that comes closest to what you would actually do. Record your answers on the answer sheet by writing the appropriate letter next to the prompt for MOST LIKELY.

Second, decide which alternative you would be LEAST LIKELY to choose in that situation. Write the letter of that alternative next to the prompt for LEAST LIKELY.

1. You realize that an error has been made in the documentation of evidence for a case. The amount of the cash reported seized at the scene is now significantly less than when it was originally recorded. You would
    A. go back and talk to everyone who was involved in the chain of custody
    B. immediately tell a supervisor about the problem
    C. consider it a clerical error and try to conceal the discrepancy while you try to figure out how it happened but tell a supervisor if you cannot figure out what happened
    D. consider that the mistake was made when the evidence was seized, and alter the log to reflect the existing amount

    Most likely:_____ Least likely:_____

2. You are assigned to lead a search for evidence that may have been deposited somewhere within a large tract of woods. The recovery of this evidence is critical to the prosecution of the suspect in the crime. For this task, you are MOST likely to lead by
    A. blazing a trail for others to follow
    B. helping people choose the best course of action
    C. punishing mistakes
    D. appealing to shared goals and values

    Most likely:_____ Least likely:_____

3. Your partner, who has become your oldest and dearest friend, recently admitted to you that he removed something from the evidence room that might suggest the innocence of a suspect whom he knew without a doubt to be guilty. Your supervisor has discovered that the evidence is missing, and your partner asks you to say that you forgot to log the evidence in. You know that this would easily resolve the situation. You would
    A. not go along with the idea to say the mistake was yours, and tell the supervisor what happened
    B. not go along with the idea, but would say nothing about your partner's admission

C. not go along with the idea, and encourage your partner to own up to what he did
D. go along with your partner; he broke the rules but his intentions were good

Most likely:_____ Least likely:_____

4. You are having a telephone conversation with a supervisor who is leaving a confidential message to another agent in your office about facts pertaining to an important case. You are on your cellphone, in a public area, surrounded by many unfamiliar people. In order to verify that you have correctly taken the message, you
   A. read the message back to the supervisor
   B. ask the supervisor to call you back later
   C. explain that you will call back when you can find a more private location
   D. ask the supervisor to repeat the message

   Most likely:_____ Least likely:_____

5. You're in a conversation with someone who has difficulty finding the proper words to say. You
   A. wait for the person to finish, and then offer a restatement of what you think she was trying to say
   B. gladly interrupt and supply the words for her
   C. wait for her to finish, and then ask a series of clarifying questions
   D. interrupt and ask that she take some time to think about it before speaking

   Most likely:_____ Least likely:_____

6. You are meeting with several other law enforcement officials and community members to determine a course of action for reducing drug trafficking in the area. In order to build a constructive relationship with officials and community members, you
   A. assure the group that you are an expert who has a long record of experience in these matters, and tell them how the problem can be solved
   B. advise them that the solution to the problem can be solved
   C. ask for input from representatives from each group before making suggestions
   D. adopt a completely neutral tone of voice when addressing group members

   Most likely:_____ Least likely:_____

7. When working in a group, someone raises a question that you've already given a lot of thought. You're not sure, however, about how the question should best be answered. You decide to
   A. speak up, briefly explaining the different alternatives that occurred to you
   B. wait for somebody to mention something that has already occurred to you, and then voice your agreement
   C. advise the group that this is a thorny problem that probably can't be solved
   D. keep quiet and listen to the group's discussion, offering feedback when you think it's appropriate

   Most likely:_____ Least likely:_____

8. Completely by accident, you notice a significant error in a colleague's report. The report is about to be released to key decision-makers, and you have absolutely no responsibility for the report. You would MOST likely
   A. spread the word about the error to the colleague's co-workers, in the hope that the information makes its way to the report's author
   B. take a mental note of the error and mention it if anyone asks
   C. keep quiet—it's not your responsibility and you don't want to create friction
   D. find the person who wrote the report and point out the mistake

   Most likely:_____ Least likely:_____

9. A detective who is often nasty to you and your colleagues has compiled an impressive record of success in her investigations; nearly all have led to arrests, and every one of those arrests has ended in conviction. In going over one of the detective's reports, you notice that she has neglected to properly document the chain of custody for a piece of evidence. You aren't that familiar with the case, and don't know how important it is to the case. You have a feeling that the detective will be angry if you point out her mistake. You
   A. do nothing and let her deal with the consequences
   B. pull her aside and tell her about the mistake
   C. tell her you noticed a mistake in her report, and ask her if she is interested in knowing what it is
   D. inform her supervisor and her partner about the mistake

   Most likely:_____ Least likely:_____

10. A crime was recently committed. You believe that, among the following, the MOST useful interview subject would probably be a(n)
    A. informant     B. victim     C. suspect     D. witness

    Most likely:_____ Least likely:_____

11. In order to complete a certain task, you need to ask a favor of a colleague whom you don't know very well. The BEST way to do this would be to
    A. ask the colleague briefly for assistance, stating your reasons for asking
    B. ask the colleague and offer to do something for him in return
    C. tell the colleague there will be many intangible rewards associated with his cooperation
    D. explain that one of the ways the colleague can gain favor with his superiors is to cooperate with you

    Most likely:_____ Least likely:_____

12. A team composed of you and your colleagues encounters a problem similar to one you have encountered when working within another team in the past. Together, you and your team come up with a solution that has the potential for success, even though it is significantly different from the one that worked for you in the past. Your reaction to this new solution is to

A. feel good about the team's originality and go along for the ride on this new plan
B. be concerned about the possibility of failure with the new solution, but accept that there may be more than one way to solve the problem
C. tell them there is a proven way to succeed in solving this problem, and insist that they adopt your solution
D. tell colleagues you're uneasy with the unknowns and variables involved in this new solution, and then urge them to go with your proven success

Most likely:_____ Least likely:_____

13. You have become so proficient at the documentation/paperwork part of your job that you actually now have some time to spare during work hours. With this extra time, you decide to
    A. take initiative and propose a new project to the supervisor
    B. see your supervisor and tell him or her you are ready for more work
    C. take care of some personal errands that you have been unable to do because of work
    D. take some of the pressure off existing work and take more time to complete existing tasks

    Most likely:_____ Least likely:_____

14. Your investigative team is having a disagreement about strategy that has become a heated debate, with members divided nearly equally between two strategic choices. You think both choices have some merit, and don't feel strongly one way or the other about which is selected. You
    A. take the side of the group that contains more of your friends and associates
    B. calmly wait for them to work out their differences
    C. try to figure out which side is more likely to win the argument before taking sides
    D. calmly point out the benefits of both plans and suggest a compromise

    Most likely:_____ Least likely:_____

15. You turn the corner at the office one day and spot an agent altering the evidence log, which has been left unattended. Later, you look and see that the entry was for an amount of an illicit substance, and the new entry appears to match the amount that exists in the evidence room. You are not sure how much of the substance was initially collected. You would
    A. ask the agent to return the missing evidence and tell him/her that if you see it happen again you will tell your supervisor
    B. tell the agent you saw him making the change, and ask him why it was necessary
    C. let the matter drop; you don't know that anything untoward occurred, and bringing it up will only result in bad feelings
    D. tell other colleagues and try to confront the agent as a group to try to deal with the problem on your own

    Most likely:_____ Least likely:_____

16. In developing a plan for investigating a crime spree that has taken place on both sides of the state line, a team encounters problems in how to coordinate the input of federal and state resources. The FIRST step in solving this problem would be to
    A. gather information
    B. define the problem as completely as possible
    C. envision contingencies
    D. develop a plan for solving the problem

    Most likely:_____ Least likely:_____

17. Because your work unit has recently become severely understaffed, you are asked to perform a task that you believe is far beneath the skills and capabilities associated with your position. You respond to this request by
    A. performing the task slowly or inadequately before resuming your more important work, in order to insure that you won't be asked again
    B. doing what is asked, but asking a supervisor to make sure these tasks are evenly distributed among co-workers until the unit can be fully staffed
    C. refusing it on the grounds of professional integrity
    D. complying cheerfully and accepting the task as part of a new expanded job description

    Most likely:_____ Least likely:_____

18. Your supervisor has decided to transfer you to an unfamiliar department as part of an agency restructuring of your organization. The department is in the same building and there will be no changes in compensation or benefits. Your reaction is to be
    A. thrilled at the opportunity to push yourself and learn new skills
    B. not to mind the transfer, because it is likely to teach you something new
    C. entirely neutral, since you won't have to relocate or take a pay cut
    D. disappointed that you will have to change your regular routine

    Most likely:_____ Least likely:_____

19. Your investigative team has developed a plan for investigating a series of violent crimes that have occurred in the tri-state area. In developing the plan, your team must balance the need to conduct the investigation "by the book" meticulously gathering and documenting a body of evidence and testimony, with the need to catch the criminal before another person becomes a victim. The plan, in attempting to balance these concerns, includes a few procedures that involve certain risks. The team should attempt to minimize the consequences of risk-taking by
    A. keeping the focus on capturing the suspect as soon as possible, and dealing with the consequences as they come
    B. reworking the plan to avoid risk whenever possible
    C. setting aside emotional concerns about victims and assembling an airtight case
    D. planning ahead and preparing for each outcome

    Most likely:_____ Least likely:_____

20. An informant has come forward to offer information about a crime. You believe it is important to understand the informant's motivation for coming forward, so you ask him about this
    A. when he least expects it
    B. after he has given an account, but before you have asked any questions
    C. at the conclusion of the interview
    D. at the beginning of the interview

    Most likely:_____ Least likely:_____

21. You are faced with a problem that, try as you might, you're unable to solve. You
    A. ask your most trusted associate
    B. ask for input from several people who you know will have different viewpoints
    C. drop it, hope that it won't become a significant concern, and move on to another task
    D. shift your focus to another problem for a while before giving this problem a fresh look

    Most likely:_____ Least likely:_____

22. You are interviewing several witnesses to a particularly violent crime that was committed recently. One of the witnesses, an older woman, is so upset that she can barely speak coherently. Her testimony does not seem to make much sense, especially when compared to that of others. In continuing to interview her, you make a mental note to document her emotional state when you write up the interview, because strong emotional responses are likely to affect a person's
    A. prior knowledge              B. intelligence
    C. perceptions of current reality    D. reflexes

    Most likely:_____ Least likely:_____

23. An informant in an ongoing investigation tells you that he resents having to work with you because you have adopted a superior attitude with him and made work unpleasant. The informant is working on the investigation as a condition of a prior court plea. Your BEST response would be to
    A. tell the informant that you are not interested in his opinion of you; he is required to cooperate on the case
    B. try to find out why the offender cannot work with you and tell him that his work is important to the case
    C. consider the informant as rebellious, and inform the court that the terms of his sentencing have been violated
    D. apologize to the offender and tell him you have been under a lot of strain

    Most likely:_____ Least likely:_____

24. Within a few days, you will meet with supervisors for a scheduled work evaluation. For the review, you will
    A. take the evaluation as it comes and improvise your responses
    B. prepare a list of your accomplishments, skills, and ideas for how to contribute more to the organization

C. assume that your performance will be criticized, and prepare for the attack
D. undertake a little reflection on your failures and successes, but nothing elaborate

Most likely:_____ Least likely:_____

25. You and your partner are in the middle of a very heated argument about the conduct of an investigation. You normally like your partner and get along very well with her, but you are so furious that you are about to say something very nasty that you know will hurt her feelings. Your MOST likely reaction would be to
    A. walk away immediately without saying a word
    B. say what is on your mind and sort it out later
    C. say that you are too angry to talk right now and give yourself time to calm down
    D. leave the room while mumbling the comment in a low voice

    Most likely:_____ Least likely:_____

26. In casual conversation, a person asks you for information about your work as an FBI agent. You should
    A. explain that you are not supposed to talk about your responsibilities to outsiders
    B. refer the person to the public relations department
    C. speak vaguely and give out as few facts as possible
    D. be frank and tell the person as much factual information as you can about your general responsibilities

    Most likely:_____ Least likely:_____

27. In the field, you are in an isolated and rural area and find yourself in a situation with circumstances you have never encountered before. You would be MOST likely to use your own judgment
    A. when existing policy and rules appear to be unfair in their application
    B. when immediate action is necessary and the rules do not cover the situation
    C. only if a superior is present
    D. whenever a situation is not covered by established rules

    Most likely:_____ Least likely:_____

28. One of your colleagues has gone on vacation and his mother, an elderly woman who lives in another state, has filed a complaint with your office; she thinks she may have been defrauded via an e-mail scam. The case has been assigned to Agent Broom, who works in your office. Your colleague phones you from his vacation and asks if you can find out more about her case. Your reaction is to
    A. simply refuse to answer your colleague's questions
    B. find the case file and tell the colleague what he wants to know
    C. speak to your supervisor, explain the situation and ask for the information that your colleague wants
    D. ask the mother if she gives permission for you to find out more from Agent Broom

    Most likely:_____ Least likely:_____

29. When working with team members, you offer what you think is a well-reasoned solution to a problem. Your team members reject it out of hand, saying that it could never work. In a later meeting with mid-level administrators, your supervisor makes the same suggestion. You
    A. say nothing to the supervisor, but later make sure your team members understand that they should be more deferential to your judgment
    B. make sure the supervisor knows you suggested the same solution, but were ignored
    C. feel vindicated by the supervisor's concurrence, but don't feel the need to say anything
    D. demand an apology from your team members for being so closed-minded

    Most likely:_____ Least likely:_____

30. After your partner conducts an interview with an informant, the informant emerges from the interrogation room with some swelling around his right eye. You are pretty sure the swelling was not present when the informant entered the room. You
    A. do nothing; you can't be certain your partner did anything wrong
    B. immediately report the partner's abuse to a supervisor
    C. ask other agents in the office if anything like this has ever happened before
    D. confront your partner and ask what happened

    Most likely:_____ Least likely:_____

31. You and another agent in your unit do not get along, to put it mildly. The problem is, you and she have been assigned to direct an investigation together, and in order to have a good outcome, the two of you need to get along. You
    A. realize the destructive potential for run-ins with her, and quietly get yourself assigned to another case
    B. make an effort to be civil, but if she isn't returning the favor, try to keep a low profile and get the work done
    C. take this as a personal challenge and make it your mission to win her over
    D. try to get your supervisors to understand the seriousness of the friction between you, and ask that they reassign her to another case

    Most likely:_____ Least likely:_____

32. At the end of a busy day at work, you accidentally send an e-mail containing an attachment with some confidential case file information to the wrong person. Which of the following would be the BEST thing to do?
    A. Forget what happened and send the e-mail to the correct person
    B. Leave the office for the day and deal with it tomorrow
    C. Explain to your supervisor what has happened and let her handle the issue
    D. Immediately send another e-mail to the 'wrong' person explaining your mistake

    Most likely:_____ Least likely:_____

9 (#1)

33. A crime has just been committed at a bank, and you arrive at the scene first, before any local law enforcement personnel. Before the police arrive, a handful of bank officials arrive and ask to enter the crime scene. You would
    A. request their cooperation in remaining outside the scene until the area can be properly secured
    B. keep them out by any means necessary
    C. tell them to take it up with the police when they arrive
    D. defer to their wishes

    Most likely:_____ Least likely:_____

34. You are interviewing the victim of a crime that was committed only about an hour ago. During the course of the interview you try to
    A. maintain a calm and steady demeanor
    B. make sure at least one other agent is present before beginning
    C. get the facts by any means necessary
    D. keep the victim away from others who are familiar to him/her

    Most likely:_____ Least likely:_____

35. You inherit a large sum of money, and your financial advisor suggests two types of investments. In the first, you invest a moderate, set amount each year, and receive a modest guaranteed payoff at the end of the investment period. The second choice includes a much larger investment (most of your inheritance), but also has a larger potential payoff, with the possibility of losing all your money in an economic downturn. Which type of investment would you choose?
    A. A combination of the two
    B. The first type of investment
    C. The second type of investment
    D. Neither. You wouldn't risk your savings on investments.

    Most likely:_____ Least likely:_____

36. You and your partner are working on a complex project that demands a great deal of effort from both of you. Your partner is frequently absent as a result of burnout and stress from his personal problems. You do not know much about the circumstances, nor have you known him for long. Your partner contributes very little to the project, and, as a result, you are putting in an excessive amount of overtime in order to keep the project moving ahead. You feel that your health may begin to suffer if you continue to work this many hours. You handle this situation by
    A. raising the issue with your supervisor and request additional help to ensure that the project is completed on schedule
    B. offering to help your partner deal with his personal problems
    C. continuing to put in overtime to keep the project moving ahead
    D. meeting with your partner to request that he does his share of the work

    Most likely:_____ Least likely:_____

37. For the first time, you are assigned the lead on a case. You oversee a team of about five people. Your supervisor has assigned you a fairly clear-cut case, and in the end, despite a few logistical and technical problems, you and your team wrap things up fairly quickly. After a speedy conviction, you meet with a group of three supervisors, who congratulate you on your success. They then launch a critique of your leadership of the case that, while pointing out your strengths as a leader, can only be interpreted as somewhat unfavorable, given the team's logistical and technical problems. Most likely, your reaction is to feel that
    A. it probably would not be a good idea for you to assume leadership of a more difficult case in the future
    B. you should keep this critique in mind the next time you take charge of a team
    C. the bottom line is that the case resulted in a conviction, and this is the only measure that really matters
    D. the members of your team really let you down with their mistakes

    Most likely:_____ Least likely:_____

38. You and another agent are conducting an investigation together. You have noticed that the other agent is taking some shortcuts as he collects evidence and obtains statements from the victims and witnesses. These shortcuts are reducing the quality of the investigation. You would MOST likely
    A. point out to the trooper the impact his shortcuts will have on the traffic investigation
    B. notify your supervisor of the shortcuts being taken by the other agent
    C. go back and redo those aspects of the investigation on which the agent has taken shortcuts
    D. ignore the agent's work performance, since it is not your responsibility to monitor his performance

    Most likely:_____ Least likely:_____

39. During a meeting, you and a group of supervisors are discussing your performance on a recently completed project. Using a list of objective criteria, the supervisors explain where you performed most successfully. They then shift their focus to areas in which your performance fell short of the standards. Your reaction is to
    A. launch a vigorous defense of your performance and explain why you think the standards are not appropriate in your case
    B. listen carefully, ask for clarification when necessary, and then discuss with them why these shortcomings occurred
    C. tell them you are very sorry and promise to do better in the future
    D. explain that you did your best and are skeptical that any of them could have done better, given the circumstances

    Most likely:_____ Least likely:_____

40. While you are conducting an investigation at a crime scene, a citizen walks past you and makes a demeaning and derogatory comment about your law enforcement responsibilities. You would MOST likely

A. ask the person to come back and explain why he made such a comment
B. ask the person to show you some identification, so that you can take his name down in case of further trouble
C. ignore the comment and continue with your work
D. confront the individual and demand an apology for the comment

Most likely:_____ Least likely:_____

41. You are working on a case under the direct supervision of a regional supervisor. In your opinion, she has her mind set on a plan that is mediocre, uninspired, and likely to meet only a minimal set of objectives. She is happy with having finally made a decision, wants to finalize, and makes a point of telling you not to try to talk her out of her plan. You think the plan is a waste of resources and perhaps even a mistake, even though most of your colleagues have already told you to let it go. How would you deal with the situation?
    A. Quietly work to get transferred to another project
    B. Tell the supervisor that she is making a mistake, and try to convince her to change her mind
    C. Resist the temptation to try changing her mind
    D. Ask if she is certain she doesn't want to think it over one last time

Most likely:_____ Least likely:_____

42. When interviewing a potential witness, you notice that she has a tendency to wander off the subject and talk about herself and her family for expended intervals. When you ask her where she was at about noon the day before yesterday, she launches into a long description of her normal daily routine. You respond by
    A. telling her sternly that your time is limited and you would like her to stick to answering your questions
    B. waiting for a pauses in her speech during which you can politely steer the conversation back toward her whereabouts yesterday at noon
    C. cutting her off and repeating the question, as if she hadn't been speaking at all
    D. letting her "talk herself out" and then repeating the question, this time in a more closed-ended format

Most likely:_____ Least likely:_____

43. You are the leader of an investigative team, and wonder about the role of praise in the team's success. As the leader, your philosophy about praise is that it
    A. can improve performance if it is given when it is most appropriate
    B. should almost always be withheld in order to make team members understand there is always room for improvement
    C. should be given sparely, and reserved for truly exceptional achievements
    D. should be given to team members even, and perhaps especially, when they perform poorly, in order to boost their self-esteem

Most likely:_____ Least likely:_____

44. You are assigned to an investigation with Agent Stark, who is known to be somewhat inattentive to detail. His mistakes or omissions have resulted in at least one case dismissal that you know of. Throughout the course of the investigation, you
    A. make it a point to be involved in every aspect of the investigation, accompanying Agent Stark on every interview, and insisting on collaboration in written work
    B. leave Agent Stark mostly alone, and then go back and make corrections to his work and documentation when they are necessary
    C. work to block Agent Stark's access to important witnesses, evidence, and case files, thereby minimizing the harm he is likely to do
    D. document every one of Agent Stark's missteps and report them to your superiors as they occur, in order to avoid jeopardizing the case

    Most likely:_____ Least likely:_____

45. An interview has strayed far beyond what you had intended. To redirect the subject's response, you say
    A. "I'm interested in what you were saying a few minutes ago. Can you tell me more about it?"
    B. "Why are we talking about this?"
    C. "Let me ask the rest of the questions I need answered, then we can talk."
    D. "This is interesting, but it isn't related to the business of this interview."

    Most likely:_____ Least likely:_____

46. You have been asked to recruit a new detective to come work for your regional office. She is an up-and-coming star with a lot of potential, and you and your supervisor both feel she would be a good fit for your office. Unfortunately, despite your best efforts, she ends up seeking and receiving an assignment elsewhere. You later find out through your supervisor that you came off as seeming a little too aggressive and desperate. Your supervisor offers you some suggestions for how to handle this situation if it ever comes up again. Your reaction is to think that
    A. putting you in charge of the detective's recruitment was a terrible idea to begin with
    B. the detective's choice was her own loss; you made it clear that your office had the most to offer
    C. you wish there was some way you could make it up to your supervisor
    D. maybe you did come on too strong and should re-examine your methods

    Most likely:_____ Least likely:_____

47. You have become aware that a colleague, who is nearing retirement and now working only part-time for the bureau, has been using office phone and tax facilities to run his own private investigation business. You think that he may have been warned about this once before and that he promised to stop. You have just found a fax for his business placed in your mailbox by mistake. You would MOST likely
    A. Put the fax in your colleague's mailbox without saying anything to anyone
    B. Politely inform your colleague that you will tell your supervisor the next time you catch him using agency resources for his own private business.

C. Put the fax in your supervisor's mailbox without saying anything to anyone
D. Give the fax to your co-worker and remind her that office equipment is not supposed to be used for personal use.

48. You are working on a case with a detective in another regional office who has, once again, rescheduled your meeting appointment at the last minute. Apparently, he left a last-minute message for you this time, but you didn't get it because you were already on your way. This is not the first time you have canceled prior engagements to accommodate his schedule. Each time you have been inconvenienced and very irritated, but this is a very important case and he is a good detective when he is at work. How do you react to this person?
    A. Tell the detective it is disrespectful and inconvenient when he makes last-minute changes to your schedule
    B. Don't let on that you are irritated, but ask the detective to give you longer notice the next time he has to cancel.
    C. Maintain a cold professionalism when rescheduling the appointment
    D. Don't let on that you are irritated, but make a point to subject the detective to a few last-minute cancellations of his own, so he'll know how it feels

    Most likely:_____ Least likely:_____

49. A pharmacist has complained to the police department that several drug addicts in his neighborhood have been attempting to obtain drugs illegally, often by passing fake prescriptions. Based only on this information during a stakeout of the prescription counter, you would be MOST likely to find suspicious
    A. a young African-American male in a hooded sweatshirt on a hot day
    B. a woman in her thirties who glances around furtively and brings a large amount of nonprescription items to the counter for purchase
    C. a middle-aged man who appears homeless and is poorly groomed
    D. none of the above should be regarded as suspicious on the basis of their appearance alone

    Most likely:_____ Least likely:_____

50. At a work meeting, your supervisor mentions an interesting new assignment that has not been assigned yet. It sounds like something you could handle, though it would be demanding. You
    A. grow increasingly nervous about the possibility that you would be assigned the job
    B. immediately volunteer to handle the project yourself
    C. tell the supervisor that you would be willing to take it on, but ask if it might be possible to delegate some of your current workload
    D. tell the supervisor that you would be willing to take it on, but only if you receive a raise in pay

    Most likely:_____ Least likely:_____

# SITUATIONAL JUDGMENT
# KEY TO EXERCISES

NOTE: While a few situations in the examination have one choice that is clearly better or worse than the others, some have two or even three choices that would be equally as good or bad as the rest. The key that follows should be taken as a rough guideline and not a definitive formula for success on the test. The answers below reflect the fact that the situational judgment test is designed to measure your:
- Ability to Organize, Plan, and Prioritize
- Ability to Relate Effectively with Others
- Ability to Maintain a Positive Image
- Ability to Evaluate Information and Make Judgment Decisions
- Ability to Adapt to Changing Situations Integrity

1. Most Likely: B; Least Likely: D
2. Most Likely: D, Least Likely: C
3. Most Likely: A or C; Least Likely: D
4. Most Likely: D; Least Likely: A
5. Most Likely: A or C; Least Likely: D

6. Most Likely: C; Least Likely; A or B
7. Most Likely: A; Least Likely: C
8. Most Likely: D; Least Likely: C
9. Most Likely: B; Least Likely: A
10. Most Likely: D; Least Likely: C

11. Most Likely: A; Least Likely: D
12. Most Likely: B; Least Likely: C
13. Most Likely: B; Least Likely: C or D
14. Most Likely: D; Least Likely: A, B, or C
15. Most Likely: B; Least Likely: A

16. Most Likely: B; Least Likely: A, C, or D
17. Most Likely: B; Least Likely: C
18. Most Likely: B; Least Likely: D
19. Most Likely: D; Least Likely: A, B, or C
20. Most Likely: C; Least Likely: A, B, or D

21. Most Likely: B; Least Likely: C
22. Most Likely: C; Least Likely: A, B, or D
23. Most Likely: B; Least Likely: C
24. Most Likely: B; Least Likely: C
25. Most Likely: C; Least Likely: B

15 (#1)

26. Most Likely: D; Least Likely: A
27. Most Likely: B; Least Likely: D
28. Most Likely: C; Least Likely: A
29. Most Likely: C; Least Likely: D
30. Most Likely: D; Least Likely: A

31. Most Likely: C; Least Likely: A or D
32. Most Likely: C; Least Likely: A
33. Most Likely: A; Least Likely: B, C, or D
34. Most Likely: A; Least Likely: C or D
35. Most Likely: A; Least Likely: D

36. Most Likely: A; Least Likely: C
37. Most Likely: B; Least Likely: A, C, or D
38. Most Likely: A; Least Likely: D
39. Most Likely: B; Least Likely: C or D
40. Most Likely: C; Least Likely: A, B, or D

41. Most Likely: D; Least Likely: A
42. Most Likely: B; Least Likely: A
43. Most Likely: A; Least Likely: B or D
44. Most Likely: A; Least Likely: C
45. Most Likely: A; Least Likely: B

46. Most Likely: D; Least Likely: A or B
47. Most Likely: D; Least Likely: A
48. Most Likely: B; Least Likely: D
49. Most Likely: D; Least Likely: A, B, or C
50. Most Likely: C; Least Likely: A or D

# EXAMINATION SECTION
# TEST 1

DIRECTIONS: This inventory contains 50 questions about yourself. You are to read each question and select the answer that best describes you from the choices provided. *PRINT THE LETTER OF YOUR ANSWER IN THE SPACE AT THE RIGHT.*

1. What has given you the most difficulty in any job that you have had?

    A. A supervisor who watched over my work too closely
    B. A supervisor who gave inconsistent direction
    C. Disagreements or gossip among co-workers
    D. Having to deal with too many insignificant details

2. I _____ put off doing a chore that I could have taken care of right away.

    A. often    B. sometimes    C. seldom    D. never

3. During high school, the number of clubs or organizations I belonged/ belong to is:

    A. 0    B. 1 or 2    C. 2 to 3    D. more than 3

4. In the past, when I have given a speech or presentation, I was likely to have prepared ahead of time:

    A. much less than others did
    B. less than others
    C. more than others
    D. about the same as others

5. When working as a member of a team, I prefer to:

    A. take on challenging tasks but not take the lead
    B. do less complex tasks
    C. take the lead
    D. keep a low profile

6. Generally, in my work assignments, I would prefer to work:

    A. on one thing at a time.
    B. on a couple of things at a time.
    C. on many things at the same time.
    D. on something I have never done before.

7. In the course of a week, the thing that gives me the greatest satisfaction is

    A. coming up with a new or unique way to handle a situation.
    B. helping other people to solve problems.
    C. having free time to devote to personal interests.
    D. being told I have done a good job.

8. My health or fitness has _____ limited my ability to perform certain tasks.   8._____

   A. often   B. sometimes   C. seldom   D. never

9. In the past, when faced with an ethical dilemma, my first step has usually been to   9._____

   A. identify the issues that are in conflict
   B. reflect on the punishment or rewards likely to result from either course of action
   C. try to find someone else who is more appropriate for making such a decision
   D. identify the people and organizations likely to be affected by the decision

10. My leadership style could be best described as   10._____

    A. autocratic              B. democratic/participative
    C. permissive/laissez faire   D. motivational

11. In the past, when I have been part of a team, I most often felt   11._____

    A. as if I were a cut above, and ready to lead
    B. a sense of equality and belonging
    C. uncertain about the next step
    D. isolated and marginalized

12. I usually enjoy thinking about the plusses and minuses of alternative approaches to solving a problem:   12._____

    A. very true for me-describes me perfectly
    B. somewhat true of me
    C. somewhat false for me
    D. absolutely false for me-doesn't describe me at all

13. When I have participated in team activities in the past and found that other group members performed better than I have, I most often   13._____

    A. examined the skills and strategies that made them so successful
    B. made a last-gasp attempt to measure up
    C. tried to reconfigure the team members so that I wouldn't end up looking bad
    D. resented the easier set of circumstances that made such success possible

14. In the past, when I failed to adequately learn a skill, concept or body of knowledge, the failure was most often the result of   14._____

    A. other peoples' interference with my approach to learning or solving the problem
    B. poor instruction
    C. having too little time to adequately study and practice
    D. a study plan that aimed too high, without learning the basics first

15. My energy is usually highest when   15._____

    A. I work as part of a collaborative team
    B. I work completely on my own
    C. I work mostly on my own, with input from others when I ask for it
    D. I work with ongoing evaluations from superiors

16. My own work standards are  16.____

    A. usually completely different from those of others
    B. usually in tune with those of others
    C. always frustratingly more demanding than those of others
    D. sometimes different from others, but easily adapted to fit the group

17. In the past, when I have worked with a group on a task for which I had little experience, I have most often  17.____

    A. asked questions and contributed as much as I was able
    B. tried to alter the parameters of the task in order to suit my own abilities
    C. asked for direction and hoped for clear guidance
    D. I don't recall being in this situation.

18. How much do you agree with the following statement: "Unless I am assigned to a team that is made up of people just like myself, the team is not likely to succeed."  18.____

    A. Strongly agree          B. Agree somewhat
    C. Disagree somewhat       D. Strongly disagree

19. I am _____ giving other people feedback on their work because _____ .  19.____

    A. very comfortable; I usually know more about what it takes to succeed than they do
    B. comfortable; it is a normal and useful part of teamwork
    C. uncomfortable; I don't usually have anything to add
    D. very uncomfortable; I'm afraid I will be resented or rejected

20. In my career, I have changed jobs  20.____

    A. only through promotion          B. once or twice
    C. on the average, every few years D. never

21. In the past, whenever I've been unable to achieve all that I set out to do in a given time period, I have  21.____

    A. tried to figure out where I came up short, and devised new strategies
    B. looked for ways to redefine "success"
    C. felt angry or hopeless
    D. I have never failed to achieve what I've set out to do.

22. Other people have _____ referred to me as an over-achiever.  22.____

    A. always     B. often     C. occasionally     D. never

23. When it comes to competitiveness, I am  23.____

    A. much more competitive than others
    B. slightly more competitive than others
    C. about as competitive as others
    D. generally less competitive than others

24. In the past, when I have achieved an important goal, I have

    A. not made a big deal of it, as it is only one small step toward an ultimate goal
    B. often gone back and tried to imagine how it could have been achieved mere successfully
    C. enjoyed the feeling of satisfaction for a while, before moving on to another goal
    D. tried to make the feeling of accomplishment last for as long as I could

25. My first impressions of people

    A. are almost always dead-on
    B. usually give an incomplete perception that evolves over time
    C. are often wrong, to my delight
    D. are often wrong, to my disappointment

26. When assigned a task, I believe

    A. success is imperative, and I'll do anything to achieve it
    B. success is important, and I focus on doing my best
    C. my investment in the success of the task correlates to my opinion of the task's importance
    D. my investment in the success of the task correlates to my opinion of the task's achievability

27. When trying to evaluate whether I have succeeded on a certain task, I rely mostly on

    A. my own gut feeling
    B. the opinions of peers
    C. a list of objective criteria
    D. people who fill leadership positions and are in a position to judge

28. If I fail to do something well,

    A. it usually isn't my fault
    B. it's probably time to give someone else a chance
    C. I'll look for feedback, reflect on it, and approach it differently another time
    D. I'll redouble my efforts, and won't give up until I succeed

29. At work or in school, when somebody has stood up to me or disagreed with me, I have tended to

    A. make a mental note that the person is an enemy who can't be trusted
    B. react angrily and heatedly, and then tried to make amends afterward
    C. listen carefully and assume that the person's opinion deserves respect
    D. apologize and try to soothe the person

30. In the past, when an assigned task has been altered during the course of my work, my reaction has usually been to

    A. adapt my strategy to fit the new circumstances
    B. wish that the people who first assigned it could make up their minds
    C. wonder what I've been doing wrong
    D. This has never happened to me

31. When times get tough, I usually 31._____

    A. become emotionally fragile or volatile
    B. feel more stressed, but make the effort to meet demands
    C. become depressed and find it more difficult to work
    D. tend to engage in unhealthy behaviors such as overeating or getting less sleep

32. I second-guess my decisions 32._____

    A. almost never
    B. when there is evidence to suggest that another way might be better
    C. when I feel poorly about myself or my performance
    D. constantly, always mindful of the different available courses of action

33. When I engage in an activity that requires moderate physical exertion, I usually 33._____

    A. push myself to ratchet up the physical demands of the activity
    B. feel challenged and energized
    C. come up with ways to make it less strenuous
    D. feel winded and depleted

34. If it were up to me, my success on a certain task would be defined by 34._____

    A. myself alone
    B. a set of fair and objective criteria
    C. my friends
    D. the strictest standards available

35. When I have been assigned to work in a group in the past, I have usually 35._____

    A. insisted on a leadership position
    B. been asked to assume a leadership position
    C. participated as an equal, and deferred to others when their opinions merited it
    D. been frozen out of decision-making by the more aggressive group members

36. When my regular work schedule changes, I most often 36._____

    A. try to stick with my proven formula for success
    B. feel angry and resentful at the whimsy of outside forces
    C. laugh it off as the result of a bureaucracy that often works against logic
    D. try to go with the flow and produce results

37. If somebody tries to talk me out of a decision, I am most likely to 37._____

    A. tell them they are wasting their time
    B. say I agree with them to minimize conflict, and then stick to my original plan
    C. try to figure out where they are coming from
    D. ask what I can do to make them happy

38. When I find a task to be unpleasant, but necessary,

    A. it is usually difficult to motivate myself to work on the task
    B. I try to pass it on to someone who will enjoy it more
    C. I am able to motivate myself to complete the task satisfactorily
    D. I place the task low on my priorities list

39. It seems as if it is _____ case that some people find what I say to be rude or offensive.

    A. always
    B. often
    C. sometimes
    D. never

40. When I have finished a particular task, I usually find that the time it took to complete was

    A. about what I had expected and planned for
    B. more than I had expected and planned for
    C. less than I had expected and planned for
    D. other more or less than I had planned for, with no consistent means of predicting either

41. When I undertake a task with several different parts, I usually

    A. tackle the easiest work first
    B. start organizing the different parts into categories that I can prioritize
    C. start working on them in no particular order it all has to get done anyway
    D. have a difficult time deciding which part to do first

42. When I am assigned a new project, I'm usually

    A. a little apprehensive about adding to my workload
    B. hopeful that it will be more interesting than the drudgery that takes up most of my time
    C. excited to take on something new and different
    D. nervous about whether I'm up to the task

43. On the occasions when I have been in a position to lead others, I have most often tried to lead by

    A. isolating and marginalizing the weak links
    B. offering appropriate rewards and punishments
    C. trying to inspire confidence and innovation
    D. allowing decisions to be made by other group members

44. My own academic career has been one characterized by

    A. achievement beyond even my own expectations
    B. hard work
    C. success without having to try very hard
    D. bitter disappointment in those charged with the task of educating me

45. I believe that when a group composed of talented people fails to achieve an assigned task, it is usually the case that

    A. A the group failed to appoint a leader who could have directed their talents toward a result
    B. the group probably didn't do as good a job at communicating as they could have
    C. some group members were working harder than others
    D. the people who assigned the task had unrealistic expectations

46. I feel that whatever success I have achieved in life has been attributable largely to

    A. myself alone
    B. hard work and the support of others
    C. the fact that tasks were clearly defined and not too difficult
    D. D. pure luck

47. In my academic career, I have tended to focus the most energy on course work that

    A. allowed me to express my creativity
    B. I knew would later help to advance my career
    C. challenged me to think in new and different ways
    D. involved memorization and repetition

48. I usually get a physical workout _____ a week.

    A. 0-1    B. 2-3    C. 3-5    D. 5-7

49. Of the following, my favorite academic subjects could be most accurately described as

    A. the empirical subjects, such as math and science
    B. expressive and creative subjects such as art
    C. subjects that involved a lot of reading, such as history and English literature
    D. entirely dependent on how the subjects were taught, and in what kind of environment

50. Of the following, the information sources I tend to trust the most are

    A. network television news programs
    B. Internet blogs
    C. professional and scholarly journals, such as *Scientific American*
    D. other print media such as newspapers and magazines

## Biodata Inventory
## Key to Exercises

*Note: In a biographical inventory, which asks for factual data, there are no right or wrong answers. It may also be true that for a particular question, more than one answer reflects a trait or viewpoint that might qualify one as a special agent: there is no single type of person or personality type that is acceptable. At the same time, there are some qualities or experiences that would probably suggest that a person is less than an ideal candidate. Generally, you are likely to be considered "qualified" if your answers tend to reveal the skills and abilities that the Biodata Inventory is designed to look for:*

- Ability to Organize, Plan, and Prioritize
- Ability to Maintain a Positive Image
- Ability to Evaluate Information and Make Judgment Decisions
- Initiative and Motivation
- Ability to Adapt to Changing Situations
- Physical Requirements

*The following responses are the ones most indicative of these skills and abilities:*

1. No choice here is better than the others; all describe a problem.
2. D
3. D
4. C
5. A or C

6. No answer is inherently better than the others; candidate suitability will probably depend on the task at hand.
7. A or B
8. D
9. A
10. B or D

11. B
12. A or B
13. A
14. D
15. A

16. D
17. A
18. C or D
19. B
20. None is "right," but choice C is the least desirable, labeling you as one who can't stick with a job.

21. A
22. None is "right," but choice D is the least desirable—it's better to have over-achieved at least once or twice.
23. None is "right," but choice D is the least desirable.
24. C
25. B

**Biodata Inventory**
**Key to Exercises (continued)**

26. B
27. C
28. C
29. C
30. A

31. B
32. B
33. B
34. B
35. B or C

36. D
37. C
38. C
39. D
40. A

41. B
42. C
43. C
44. B
45. B

46. B
47. C
48. D
49. None is the "right" answer, but A or C are the best choices.
50. C

# PERSONALITY/AUTOBIOGRAPHICAL INVENTORY
## EXAMINATION SECTION
## TEST 1

DIRECTIONS: Each question or incomplete statement is followed by several suggested answers or completions. Select the one that BEST answers the question or completes the statement. *PRINT THE LETTER OF THE CORRECT ANSWER IN THE SPACE AT THE RIGHT.*

1. While a senior in high school, I was absent  1.____
   A. never
   B. seldom
   C. frequently
   D. more than 10 days
   E. only when I felt bored

2. While in high school, I failed classes  2.____
   A. never
   B. once
   C. twice
   D. more than twice
   E. at least four times

3. During class discussions in my high school classes, I usually  3.____
   A. listened without participating
   B. participated as much as possible
   C. listened until I had something to add to the discussion
   D. disagreed with others simply for the sake of argument
   E. laughed at stupid ideas

4. My high school grade point average (on a 4.0 scale) was  4.____
   A. 2.0 or lower
   B. 2.1 to 2.5
   C. 2.6 to 3.0
   D. 3.1 to 3.5
   E. 3.6 to 4.0

5. As a high school student, I completed my assignments  5.____
   A. as close to the due date as I could manage
   B. whenever the teacher gave me an extension
   C. frequently
   D. on time
   E. when they were interesting

6. While in high school, I participated in  6.____
   A. athletic and nonathletic extracurricular activities
   B. athletic extracurricular activities
   C. nonathletic extracurricular activities
   D. no extracurricular activities
   E. mandatory after-school programs

7. In high school, I made the honor roll 7.____
   A. several times
   B. once
   C. more than once
   D. twice
   E. I can't remember if I made the honor role

8. Upon graduation from high school, I received 8.____
   A. academic and nonacademic honors
   B. academic honors
   C. nonacademic honors
   D. no honors
   E. I can't remember if I received honors

9. While attending high school, I worked at a paid job or as a volunteer 9.____
   A. never
   B. every so often
   C. 5 to 10 hours a month
   D. more than 10 hours a month
   E. more than 15 hours a month

10. During my senior year of high school, I skipped school 10.____
    A. whenever I could
    B. once a week
    C. several times a week
    D. not at all
    E. when I got bored

11. I was suspended from high school 11.____
    A. not at all
    B. once or twice
    C. once or twice, for fighting
    D. several times
    E. more times than I can remember

12. During high school, my fellow students and teachers considered me 12.____
    A. above average
    B. below average
    C. average
    D. underachieving
    E. underachieving and prone to fighting

13. The ability to _____ is most important to a Police Officer 13.____
    A. draw his/her gun quickly
    B. see over great distances and difficult terrain
    C. verbally and physically intimidate criminals
    D. communicate effectively in circumstances which can be dangerous
    E. hear over great distances

14. I began planning for college                                                                       14.____
    A. when my parents told me to
    B. when I entered high school
    C. during my junior year
    D. during my senior hear
    E. when I signed up for my SAT (or other standardized exam)

15. An effective leader is someone who                                                                  15.____
    A. inspires confidence in his/her followers
    B. inspires fear in his/her followers
    C. tells subordinates exactly what they should do
    D. creates an environment in which subordinates feel insecure about their
       job security and performance
    E. makes as few decisions as possible

16. I prepared myself for college by                                                                    16.____
    A. learning how to get extensions on major assignments
    B. working as many hours as possible at my after-school job
    C. spending as much time with my friends as possible
    D. getting good grades and participating in extracurricular activities
    E. watching television shows about college kids

17. I paid for college by                                                                               17.____
    A. supplementing my parents contributions with my own earnings
    B. relying on scholarships, loans, and my own earnings
    C. relying on my parents and student loans
    D. relying on my parents to pay my tuition, room and board
    E. relying on sources not listed here

18. While a college student, I spent my summers and holiday breaks                                      18.____
    A. in summer or remedial classes      B. traveling
    C. working                            D. relaxing
    E. spending time with my friends

19. My final college grade point average (on a 4.0 scale) was                                           19.____
    A. 3.8 to 4.0         B. 3.5 to 3.8         C. 3.0 to 3.5
    D. 2.5 to 3.0         E. 2.0 to 2.5

20. As a college student, I cut classes                                                                 20.____
    A. frequently                         B. when I didn't like them
    C. sometimes                          D. rarely
    E. when I needed the sleep

21. In college, I received academic honors                                                              21.____
    A. not at all
    B. once
    C. twice
    D. several times
    E. I can't remember if I received academic honors

22. While in college, I declared a major
   A. during my first year
   B. during my sophomore year
   C. during my junior year
   D. during my senior year
   E. several times

23. While on patrol as a Police Officer, you spot someone attempting to flee the scene of a crime. Your first reaction is to
   A. draw your weapon
   B. observe the person until he or she completes the fleeing
   C. identify yourself as a Police Officer
   D. fire your weapon over the person's head in order to scare him or her
   E. call immediately for backup

24. As a college student, I failed _____ classes.
   A. no
   B. two
   C. three
   D. four
   E. more than four

25. Friends describe me as
   A. introverted
   B. hot-tempered
   C. unpredictable
   D. quiet
   E. easygoing

# KEY (CORRECT ANSWERS)

PLEASE NOTE: The answers listed are the best answers. However, you are to answer the exam honestly. Your personal answer may differ from the *best* answers.

| | | | | |
|---|---|---|---|---|
| 1. | A | | 11. | A |
| 2. | A | | 12. | A |
| 3. | C | | 13. | D |
| 4. | E | | 14. | B |
| 5. | D | | 15. | A |
| 6. | A | | 16. | D |
| 7. | A | | 17. | B |
| 8. | A | | 18. | C |
| 9. | E | | 19. | A |
| 10. | D | | 20. | D |

21. D
22. A
23. C
24. A
25. E

# TEST 2

DIRECTIONS: Each question or incomplete statement is followed by several suggested answers or completions. Select the one that BEST answers the question or completes the statement. *PRINT THE LETTER OF THE CORRECT ANSWER IN THE SPACE AT THE RIGHT.*

1. As a Police Officer, you apprehend three men whom you believe are in the country illegally. However, none of the men speaks English, and you don't speak their language.
   Your reaction should be to
   A. draw your weapon so that they understand the seriousness of the situation
   B. take them into custody, where they will have access to a translator
   C. attempt to communicate through hand gestures and shouting
   D. call for a translator to come and meet you at your location
   E. pretend you understand their language and apprehend them

   1.____

2. During my college classes, I preferred to
   A. remain silent during class discussions
   B. do other homework during class discussions
   C. participate frequently in class discussions
   D. argue with others as much as possible
   E. laugh at the stupid opinions of others

   2.____

3. As a Police Officer, you are chasing a small group of people who are running away from the scene of a crime. During your pursuit, one member of the group is left behind. You see that she is injured and in need of medical attention.
   Your reaction is to
   A. fire your weapon at the group members to get them to stop
   B. cease pursuit of the group members and take the woman into custody
   C. continue pursuit of the group members, leaving the woman behind since acting ill is a common trick
   D. radio for backup to stay with the woman while medical help arrives while you continue pursuit of the group members
   E. radio for backup to continue pursuit of the group members while you stay with the woman and wait for medical help to arrive

   3.____

4. As a college student, I was placed on academic probation
   A. not at all            B. once
   C. twice                 D. three times
   E. more than three times

   4.____

5. At work, being a team player means to
   A. compromise your ideals and beliefs
   B. compensate for the incompetence of others
   C. count on others to compensate for my inexperience
   D. cooperate with others to get a project finished
   E. rely on others to get the job done

   5.____

6. As a Police Officer, you confront someone you believe has just committed a crime. After identifying yourself, you notice the suspect holding something that looks like a knife.
   Your FIRST reaction should be to
   A. draw your weapon and fire
   B. call immediately for backup
   C. keep your weapon drawn until you get the suspect into a position that is controllable
   D. ask the suspect if he is armed
   E. talk to the suspect without drawing your weapon

7. My friends from college remember me primarily as a(n)
   A. person who loved to party   B. ambitious student
   C. athlete                     D. joker
   E. fighter

8. My college experience is memorable primarily because of
   A. the friends I made
   B. the sorority/fraternity I was able to join
   C. the social activities I participated in
   D. my academic achievements
   E. the money I spent

9. A friend who is applying for a job asks you to help him pass the mandatory drug test by substituting a sample of your urine for his.
   You should
   A. help him by supplying the sample
   B. help him by supplying the sample and insisting he seek drug counseling
   C. supply the sample, but tell him that this is the only time you'll help in this way
   D. call the police
   E. refuse

10. As a college student, I handed in my assignments
    A. when they were due          B. whenever I could get an extension
    C. when they were interesting  D. when my friends reminded me to
    E. when I was able

11. At work you are accused of a minor infraction which you didn't commit.
    Your FIRST reaction is to
    A. call a lawyer
    B. speak to your supervisor about the mistake
    C. call the police
    D. yell at the person who did commit the infraction
    E. accept the consequences regardless of your guilt or innocence

12. While on patrol, you are surprised by a large group of disorderly teenage gang members. You are greatly outnumbered.
    As a Police Officer, your FIRST reaction is to
    A. draw your weapon and identify yourself
    B. get back into your vehicle and wait for help to arrive
    C. call for backup
    D. pretend you are part of a large group of police in the area
    E. identify yourself and get the group members into a controllable position

13. As a college student, I began to prepare for final exams
    A. the night before taking them
    B. when the professor handed out the review sheets
    C. several weeks before taking them
    D. when my friends began to prepare for their exams
    E. the morning of the exam

14. As a Police Officer in the field, you confront a small group of people you believe to be wanted criminals.
    Your MOST important consideration during this exchange should be
    A. apprehension of criminals
    B. safety of county citizens in nearby towns
    C. safety of the criminals
    D. number of criminals you must apprehend in order to receive a commendation'
    E. the amount of respect the criminals show to you and your position

15. At work, I am known as
    A. popular         B. quiet          C. intense
    D. easygoing       E. dedicated

16. The MOST important quality in a coworker is
    A. friendliness                B. cleanliness
    C. a good sense of humor       D. dependability
    E. good listening skills

17. In the past year, I have stayed home from work
    A. frequently                  B. only when I felt depressed
    C. rarely                      D. only when I felt overwhelmed
    E. only to run important errands

18. As a Police Officer, the BEST way to collect information from a suspect during an interview is to
    A. physically intimidate the suspect
    B. verbally intimidate the suspect
    C. threaten the suspect's family and/or friend with criminal prosecution
    D. encourage a conversation with the suspect
    E. sit in silence until the suspect begins speaking

19. For me, the BEST thing about college was the
    A. chance to strengthen my friendships and develop new ones
    B. chance to test my abilities and develop new ones
    C. number of extracurricular activities and clubs
    D. chance to socialize
    E. chance to try several different majors

19.____

20. As an employee, my WEAKEST skill is
    A. controlling my temper
    B. my organizational ability
    C. my ability to effectively understand directions
    D. my ability to effectively manage others
    E. my ability to communicate my thoughts in writing

20.____

21. As a Police Officer, my GREATEST strength would be
    A. my sense of loyalty          B. my organizational ability
    C. punctuality                  D. dedication
    E. my ability to intimidate others

21.____

22. As a Police Officer, you find a group of suspicious youths gathered around a truck which is on fire.
    Your FIRST reaction is to
    A. call the fire department
    B. arrest them all for destruction of property
    C. draw your weapon and begin questioning them
    D. return to your vehicle and wait for the fire department
    E. instruct the group to remain while you return to your vehicle and request backup

22.____

23. If asked by my company to learn a new job-related skill, my reaction would be to
    A. ask for a raise
    B. ask for overtime pay
    C. question the necessity of the skill
    D. cooperate with some reluctance
    E. cooperate with enthusiasm

23.____

24. When I disagree with others, I tend to
    A. listen quietly despite my disagreement
    B. laugh openly at the person I disagree with
    C. ask the person to explain their views before I respond
    D. leave the conversation before my anger gets the best of me
    E. point out exactly why the person is wrong

24.____

25. When I find myself in a situation which is confusing or unclear, my reaction is to
    A. pretend I am not confused
    B. remain calm and, if necessary, ask someone else for clarification
    C. grow frustrated and angry
    D. walk away from the situation
    E. immediately insist that someone explain things to me

25.____

# KEY (CORRECT ANSWERS)

PLEASE NOTE: The answers listed are the best answers. However, you are to answer the exam honestly. Your personal answer may differ from the *best* answers.

| | | | | |
|---|---|---|---|---|
| 1. | B | | 11. | B |
| 2. | C | | 12. | E |
| 3. | E | | 13. | C |
| 4. | A | | 14. | A |
| 5. | D | | 15. | E |
| | | | | |
| 6. | C | | 16. | D |
| 7. | B | | 17. | C |
| 8. | D | | 18. | D |
| 9. | E | | 19. | B |
| 10. | A | | 20. | E |

21. D
22. A
23. E
24. C
25. B

# TEST 3

DIRECTIONS: Each question or incomplete statement is followed by several suggested answers or completions. Select the one that BEST answers the question or completes the statement. *PRINT THE LETTER OF THE CORRECT ANSWER IN THE SPACE AT THE RIGHT.*

1. While on patrol as a Police Officer, you find a dead body lying in the open. Hiding a few feet away, behind some rocks, you find a suspicious person who is holding items which seem to have been taken from the dead body, including a pair of shoes and some jewelry.
   You should
   A. apprehend the suspect and bring him to the station for further questioning
   B. arrest the suspect for murder and robbery
   C. arrest the suspect for murder
   D. subdue the suspect with force and check the area for his accomplices
   E. subdue the suspect with force and call for backup to check the area for his accomplices

1.____

2. If you were placed in a supervisory position, which of the following abilities would you consider to be MOST important to your job performance?
   A. Stubborness
   B. The ability to hear all sides of a story before making a decision
   C. Kindness
   D. The ability to make and stick to a decision
   E. Patience

2.____

3. What is your HIGHEST level of education?
   A. Less than a high school diploma
   B. A high school diploma or equivalency
   C. A graduate of community college
   D. A graduate of a four-year accredited college
   E. A degree from graduate school

3.____

4. When asked to supervise other workers, your approach should be to
   A. ask for management wages since you're doing management work
   B. give the workers direction and supervise every aspect of the process
   C. give the workers direction and then allow them to do the job
   D. and the workers their job specifications
   E. do the work yourself, since you're uncomfortable supervising others

4.____

5. Which of the following BEST describes you?
   A. Need little or no supervision
   B. Resent too much supervision
   C. Require as much supervision as my peers
   D. Require slightly more supervision than my peers
   E. Require close supervision

5.____

6. You accept a job which requires an ability to perform several tasks at once. What is the BEST way to handle such a position?
   A. With strong organizational skills and a close attention to detail
   B. By delegating the work to someone with strong organizational skills
   C. Staying focused on one task at a time, no matter what happens
   D. Working on one task at a time until each task is successfully completed
   E  Asking my supervisor to help me

7. As a Police Officer, you take a suspected perpetrator into custody. After returning to the field, you notice that your gun is missing.
   You should
   A. retrace your steps to see if you dropped it somewhere
   B. report the loss immediately
   C. ask your partner to borrow his or her gun
   D. pretend that nothing's happened
   E. rely on your hands for defense and protection

8. Which of the following BEST describes your behavior when you disagree with someone?
   You
   A. state your own point of view as quickly and loudly as you can
   B. listen quietly and keep your opinions to yourself
   C. listen to the other person's perspective and then carefully point out all the flaws in their logic
   D. list all of the ignorant people who agree with the opposing point of view
   E. listen to the other person's perspective and then explain your own perspective

9. As a new Police Officer, you make several mistakes during your first week of work.
   You react by
   A. learning from your mistakes and moving on
   B. resigning
   C. blaming it on your supervisor
   D. refusing to talk about it
   E. blaming yourself

10. My ability to communicate effectively with others is _____ average.
    A. below          B. about          C. above
    D. far above      E. far below

11. In which of the following areas are you MOST highly skilled?
    A. Written communication
    B. Oral communication
    C. Ability to think quickly in difficult situations
    D. Ability to work with a broad diversity of people and personalities
    E. Organizational skills

12. As a Police Officer, you are assigned to work with a partner whom you dislike.  12.____
You should
    A. immediately report the problem to your supervisor
    B. ask your partner not to speak to you during working hours
    C. tell your colleagues about your differences
    D. tell your partner why you dislike him/her
    E. work with your partner regardless of your personal feelings

13. During high school, what was your MOST common after-school activity?  13.____
    A. Remaining after school to participate in various clubs and organizations (such as band, sports, etc.)
    B. Remaining after school to make up for missed classes
    C. Remaining after school as punishment (detention, etc.)
    D. Going straight to an after-school job
    E. Spending the afternoon at home or with friends

14. During high school, in which of the following subjects did you receive the HIGHEST grades?  14.____
    A. English, History, Social Studies
    B. Math, Science
    C. Vocational classes
    D. My grades were consistent in all subjects
    E. Classes I liked

15. When faced with an overwhelming number of duties at work, your reaction is to  15.____
    A. do all of the work yourself, no matter what the cost
    B. delegate some responsibilities to capable colleagues
    C. immediately ask your supervisor for help
    D. put off as much work as possible until you can get to it
    E. take some time off to relax and clear your mind

16. As a Police Officer, your supervisor informs you that a prisoner whom you arrested has accused you of beating him. You know you are innocent.  16.____
You react by
    A. quitting your job
    B. hiring a lawyer
    C. challenging your supervisor to prove the charges against you
    D. calmly tell your supervisor what really happened and presenting evidence to support your position
    E. insisting that you be allowed to speak alone to the prisoner

17. Which of the following BEST describes your desk at your current or most recent job?  17.____
    A. Messy and disorganized        B. Neat and organized
    C. Messy but organized           D. Neat but disorganized
    E. Messy

18. The _____ BEST describes your reasons for wanting to become a Police Officer.   18._____
    A. ability to carry and use a weapon
    B. excitement and challenges of the career
    C. excellent salary and benefits package
    D. chance to tell other people what to do
    E. chance to help people find a better life

19. As a Police Officer in the field, you are approached by a man who is frantic   19._____
    but unable to speak English. After several minutes of trying to communicate,
    you realize that the man is asking you to come with him in order to help
    someone who has been hurt.
    You should
    A. ignore him, since it might be a trap
    B. call for backup
    C. immediately offer to help the man
    D. return to your vehicle and wait for the man to leave
    E. radio your position and situation to another officer, then go with the man
       to offer help

20. When asked to take on extra responsibility at work, in order to help out a   20._____
    coworker who is overwhelmed, your response is to
    A. ask for overtime pay
    B. complain to your supervisor that you are being taken advantage of
    C. help the coworker to the best of your ability
    D. ask the coworker to come back some other time
    E. give the coworker some advice on how to get his/her job done

21. At my last job, I was promoted   21._____
    A. not at all            B. once
    C. twice                 D. three times
    E. more than three times

22. As a Police Officer, you discover the body of a person whom you suspect   22._____
    to be a gang member. You also suspect that there are several other gang
    members hiding in the nearby vicinity.
    Your FIRST reaction should be to
    A. begin a search of the nearby area for the other gang members
    B. return to your vehicle and call for backup
    C. return to your vehicle with the body of the person you found
    D. check whether the person you found is dead or alive
    E. draw your weapon and identify yourself

23. You are faced with an overwhelming deadline at work.
Your reaction is to
    A. procrastinate until the last minute
    B. procrastinate until someone notices you need some help
    C. notify your supervisor that you can't complete the work on your own
    D. work in silence without asking any questions
    E. arrange your schedule so that you can get the work done before the deadline

24. When you feel yourself under deadline pressures at work, your response is to
    A. make sure you keep to a schedule which allows you to complete the work on time
    B. wait until just before the deadline to complete the work
    C. ask someone else to do the work
    D. grow so obsessive about the work that your coworkers feel compelled to help you
    E. ask your supervisor immediately for help

25. Which of the following BEST describes your appearance at your current or most recent position?
    A. Well-groomed, neat, and clean
    B. Unkempt, but dressed neatly
    C. Messy and dirty clothing
    D. Unshaven and untidy
    E. Clean-shaven, but sloppily dressed

6 (#3)

# KEY (CORRECT ANSWERS)

PLEASE NOTE: The answers listed are our preferred answers. However, you are to answer the exam honestly. Your personal answer may differ from our answers.

1. A
2. D
3. E
4. C
5. A

6. A
7. B
8. E
9. A
10. C

11. C
12. E
13. A
14. D
15. B

16. D
17. B
18. B
19. E
20. C

21. C
22. D
23. E
24. A
25. A

# TEST 4

DIRECTIONS: Each question or incomplete statement is followed by several suggested answers or completions. Select the one that BEST answers the question or completes the statement. *PRINT THE LETTER OF THE CORRECT ANSWER IN THE SPACE AT THE RIGHT.*

1. Which of the following BEST describes the way you react to making a difficult decision?
    A. Consult with the people you're closest to before making the decision
    B. Make the decision entirely on your own
    C. Consult only with those people whom your decision will affect
    D. Consult with everyone you known, in an effort to make a decision that will please everyone
    E. Forget about the decision until you have to make it

1.____

2. If placed in a supervisory role, which of the following characteristics would you rely on most heavily when dealing with the employees you supervise?
    A. Kindness   B. Cheeriness   C. Honesty
    D. Hostility  E. Aloofness

2.____

3. As a Police Officer, you are pursuing a suspect when he turns and pulls something out of his pocket that looks like a gun.
   You should
    A. run away and call for backup
    B. assure the man that you mean him no harm
    C. draw your gun and order the man to stop and drop his weapon
    D. draw your gun and fire a warning shot
    E. draw your gun and fire immediately

3.____

4. In addition to English, in which of the following languages are you also fluent?
    A. Spanish    B. French    C. Italian
    D. German     E. Other

4.____

5. When confronted with gossip at work, your typical reaction is to
    A. participate
    B. listen without participating
    C. notify your supervisor
    D. excuse yourself from the discussion
    E. confront your coworkers about their problem

5.____

6. In the past two years, how many jobs have you held?
    A. None       B. One       C. Two
    D. Three      E. More than three

6.____

2 (#4)

7. In your current or most recent job, you favorite part of the job is the part which involves
   A. telling other people what they're doing wrong
   B. supervising others
   C. working without supervision to finish a project
   D. written communication
   E. oral communication

   7.____

8. Your supervisor asks you about a colleague who is applying for a position which you also want.
   You react by
   A. commenting honestly on the person's work performance
   B. enhancing the person's negative traits
   C. informing your supervisor about your colleague's personal problems
   D. telling your supervisor that would be better in the position
   E. refusing to comment

   8.____

9. As a Police Officer, you confiscate some contraband which was being imported by an illegal alien who is now in your custody. Your partner asks you not to turn the contraband in to your supervisor.
   Your response is to
   A. inform your supervisor of your partner's request immediately
   B. tell your partner you feel uncomfortable with his request
   C. pretend you didn't hear you partner's request
   D. tell your supervisor and all your colleagues about your partner's request
   E. give the contraband to your partner and let him handle it

   9.____

10. Which of the following BEST describes your responsibilities in your last job?
    A. Entirely supervisory
    B. Much supervisory responsibility
    C. Equal amounts of supervisory and nonsupervisory responsibility
    D. Some supervisory responsibilities
    E. No supervisory responsibilities

    10.____

11. How much written communication did your previous or most recent job require of you?
    A. A great deal of written communication
    B. Some written communication
    C. I don't remember
    D. A small amount of written communication
    E. No written communication

    11.____

12. In the past two years, how many times have you been fired from a job?
    A. None              B. Once
    C. Twice             D. Three times
    E. More than three times

    12.____

63

13. How much time have you spent working for volunteer organizations in the past year?    13.____
    A. 10 to 20 hours per week
    B. 5 to 10 hours per week
    C. 3 to 5 hours per week
    D. 1 to 3 hours per week
    E. I have spent no time volunteering in the past year

14. Your efforts at volunteer work usually revolve around which of the following types of organizations?    14.____
    A. Religious
    B. Community-based organizations working to improve the community
    C. Charity organizations working on behalf of the poor
    D. Charity organizations working on behalf of the infirm or handicapped
    E. Other

15. Which of the following BEST describes your professional history?    15.____
    Promoted at _____ coworkers
    A. a much faster rate than        B. a slightly faster rate than
    C. the same rate as               D. a slightly slower rate than
    E. a much slower rate than

16. Which of the following qualities do you MOST appreciate in a coworker?    16.____
    A. Friendliness      B. Dependability      C. Good looks
    D. Silence           E. Forgiveness

17. When you disagree with a supervisor's instructions or opinion about how to complete a project, your reaction is to    17.____
    A. inform your supervisor that you refuse to complete the project according to his or her instructions
    B. inform your colleague of you supervisor's incompetence
    C. accept your supervisor's instructions in silence
    D. voice your concerns and then complete the project according to your own instincts
    E. voice your concerns and then complete the project according to your supervisor's instructions

18. Which of the following BEST describes your reaction to close supervision and specific direction from your supervisor?    18.____
    You
    A. listen carefully to the directions, and then figure out a way to do the job more effectively
    B. complete the job according to the given specifications
    C. show some initiative by doing the job your way
    D. ask someone else to do the job for you
    E. listen carefully to the directions, and then figure out a better way to do the job which will save more money

19. How should a Police Officer handle a situation in which he or she is offered a bribe not to issue a traffic ticket?
    A. Pretend the bribe was never offered
    B. Accept the money as evidence and release the person
    C. Draw your weapon and call for backup
    D. Refuse the bribe and then arrest the person
    E. Accept the bribe and then arrest the person

19._____

20. At work you are faced with a difficult decision.
    You react by
    A. seeking advice from your colleagues
    B. following your own path regardless of the consequences
    C. asking your supervisor what you should do
    D. keeping the difficulties to yourself
    E. working for a solution which will please everyone

20._____

21. If asked to work with a person whom you dislike, your response would be
    A. to ask your supervisor to allow you to work with someone else
    B. to ask your coworker to transfer to another department or project
    C. talk to your coworker about the proper way to behave at work
    D. pretend the coworker is your best friend for the sake of your job
    E. to set aside your personal differences in order to complete the job

21._____

22. As a supervisory, which of the following incentives would you use to motivate your employees?
    A. Fear of losing their jobs
    B. Fear of their supervisors
    C. Allowing employees to provide their input on a number of policies
    D. Encouraging employees to file secret reports regarding colleagues' transgressions
    E. All of the above

22._____

23. A fellow Police Officer, with whom you enjoy a close friendship, has a substance-abuse problem which has gone undetected. You suspect the problem may be affecting his job.
    You would
    A. ask the Police Officer if the problem is affecting his job performance
    B. warn the Police Officer that he must seek counseling or you will report him
    C. wait a few weeks to see whether the officer's problem really is affecting his job
    D. discuss it with your supervisor
    E. wait for the supervisor to discover the problem

23._____

24. In the past two months, you have missed work
    A. zero times           B. once
    C. twice                D. three times
    E. more than three times

24._____

25. As a Police Officer, you are pursuing a group of robbers when you discover two small children who have been abandoned near a railroad crossing.
You should
   A. tell the children to stay put while you continue your pursuit
   B. lock the children in your vehicle and continue your pursuit
   C. stay with the children and radio for help in the pursuit of the robbers
   D. use the children to set a trap for the robbers
   E. ignore the children and continue your pursuit

## KEY (CORRECT ANSWERS)

PLEASE NOTE: The answers listed are our preferred answers. However, you are to answer the exam honestly. Your personal answer may differ from our answers.

1. A
2. C
3. C
4. A
5. D

6. B
7. C
8. A
9. A
10. D

11. B
12. A
13. C
14. B
15. A

16. B
17. E
18. B
19. D
20. A

21. E
22. C
23. D
24. A
25. C

# SAMPLE QUESTIONS
# BIOGRAPHICAL INVENTORY

The questions included in the Biographical Inventory ask for information about you and your background. These kinds of questions are often asked during an oral interview. For years, employers have been using interviews to relate personal history, preferences, and attitudes to job success. This Biographical Inventory attempts to do the same and includes questions which have been shown to be related to job success. It has been found that successful employees tend to select some answers more often than other answers, while less successful employees tend to select different answers. The questions in the Biographical Inventory do not have a single correct answer. Every choice is given some credit. More credit is given for answers selected more often by successful employees.

These Biographical Inventory questions are presented for illustrative purposes only. The answers have not been linked to the answers of successful employees; therefore, we cannot designate any "correct" answer(s).

DIRECTIONS: You may only mark ONE response to each question. It is possible that none of the answers applies well to you. However, one of the answers will surely be true (or less inaccurate) for you than others. In such a case, mark that answer. <u>Answer each question honestly.</u> The credit that is assigned to each response on the actual test is based upon how successful employees described themselves when honestly responding to the questions. *PRINT THE LETTER OF THE CORRECT ANSWER IN THE SPACE AT THE RIGHT.*

1. Generally, in your work assignments, would you prefer
    A. to work on one thing at a time
    B. to work on a couple of things at a time
    C. to work on many things at the same time

2. In the course of a week, which of the following gives you the GREATEST satisfaction?
    A. Being told you have done a good job.
    B. Helping other people to solve their problems.
    C. Coming up with a new or unique way to handle a situation.
    D. Having free time to devote to personal interests.

# READING COMPREHENSION
## UNDERSTANDING AND INTERPRETING WRITTEN MATERIAL

# EXAMINATION SECTION
## TEST 1

DIRECTIONS: Each question or incomplete statement is followed by several suggested answers or completions. Select the one that BEST answers the question or completes the statement. *PRINT THE LETTER OF THE CORRECT ANSWER IN THE SPACE AT THE RIGHT.*

Questions 1-5.

DIRECTIONS: Questions 1 through 5 are to be answered on the basis of the following passage.

The laws with which criminal courts are concerned contain threats of punishment for infraction of specified rules. Consequently, the courts are organized primarily for implementation of the punitive societal reaction of crime. While the informal organization of most courts allows the judge to use discretion as to which guilty persons actually are to be punished, the threat of punishment for all guilty persons always is present. Also, in recent years a number of formal provisions for the use of non-punitive and treatment methods by the criminal courts have been made, but the threat of punishment remains, even for the recipients of the treatment and non-punitive measures. For example, it has become possible for courts to grant probation, which can be non-punitive, to some offenders, but the probationer is constantly under the threat of punishment, for, if he does not maintain the conditions of his probation, he may be imprisoned. As the treatment reaction to crime becomes more popular, the criminal courts may have as their sole function the determination of the guilt or innocence of the accused persons, leaving the problem of correcting criminals entirely to outsiders. Under such conditions, the organization of the court system, the duties and activities of court personnel, and the nature of the trial all would be decidedly different.

1. Which one of the following is the BEST description of the subject matter of the above passage?
The

   A. value of non-punitive measures for criminals
   B. effect of punishment on guilty individuals
   C. punitive functions of the criminal courts
   D. success of probation as a deterrent of crime

2. It may be INFERRED from the above passage that the present traditional organization of the criminal court system is a result of

   A. the nature of the laws with which these courts are concerned
   B. a shift from non-punitive to punitive measures for correctional purposes
   C. an informal arrangement between court personnel and the government
   D. a formal decision made by court personnel to increase efficiency

3. All persons guilty of breaking certain specified rules, according to the above passage, are subject to the threat of

   A. treatment
   B. punishment
   C. probation
   D. retrial

4. According to the above passage, the decision whether or not to punish a guilty person is a function USUALLY performed by

   A. the jury
   B. the criminal code
   C. the judge
   D. corrections personnel

5. According to the above passage, which one of the following is a possible effect of an increase in the *treatment reactions to crime?*

   A. A decrease in the number of court personnel
   B. An increase in the number of criminal trials
   C. Less reliance on probation as a non-punitive treatment measure
   D. A decrease in the functions of the court following determination of guilt

Questions 6-8.

DIRECTIONS: Questions 6 through 8 are to be answered on the basis of the following passage.

A glaring exception to the usual practice of the judicial trial as a means of conflict resolution is the utilization of administrative hearings. The growing tendency to create administrative bodies with rule-making and quasi-judicial powers has shattered many standard concepts. A comprehensive examination of the legal process cannot neglect these newer patterns.

In the administrative process, the legislative, executive, and judicial functions are mixed together, and many functions, such as investigating, advocating, negotiating, testifying, rule making, and adjudicating, are carried out by the same agency. The reason for the breakdown of the separation-of-powers formula is not hard to find. It was felt by Congress, and state and municipal legislatures, that certain regulatory tasks could not be performed efficiently, rapidly, expertly, and with due concern for the public interest by the traditional branches of government. Accordingly, regulatory agencies were delegated powers to consider disputes from the earliest stage of investigation to the final stages of adjudication entirely within each agency itself, subject only to limited review in the regular courts.

6. The above passage states that the usual means for conflict resolution is through the use of

   A. judicial trial
   B. administrative hearing
   C. legislation
   D. regulatory agencies

7. The above passage IMPLIES that the use of administrative hearing in resolving conflict is a(n) _____ approach.

   A. traditional
   B. new
   C. dangerous
   D. experimental

8. The above passage states that the reason for the breakdown of the separation-of-powers formula in the administrative process is that

A. Congress believed that certain regulatory tasks could be better performed by separate agencies
B. legislative and executive functions are incompatible in the same agency
C. investigative and regulatory functions are not normally reviewed by the courts
D. state and municipal legislatures are more concerned with efficiency than with legality

Questions 9-10.

DIRECTIONS: Questions 9 and 10 are to be answered SOLELY on the basis of the information given in the following paragraph.

An assumption commonly made in regard to the reliability of testimony is that when a number of persons report upon the same matter, those details upon which there is an agreement may, in general, be considered as substantiated. Experiments have shown, however, that there is a tendency for the same errors to appear in the testimony of different individuals, and that, quite apart from any collusion, agreement of testimony is no proof of dependability.

9. According to the above paragraph, it is commonly assumed that details of an event are substantiated when

   A. a number of persons report upon them
   B. a reliable person testifies to them
   C. no errors are apparent in the testimony of different individuals
   D. several witnesses are in agreement about them

9.____

10. According to the above paragraph, agreement in the testimony of different witnesses to the same event is

    A. evaluated more reliably when considered apart from collusion
    B. not the result of chance
    C. not a guarantee of the accuracy of the facts
    D. the result of a mass reaction of the witnesses

10.____

Questions 11-12.

DIRECTIONS: Questions 11 and 12 are to be answered SOLELY on the basis of the information given in the following paragraph.

The accuracy of the information about past occurrence obtainable in an interview is so low that one must take the stand that the best use to be made of the interview in this connection is a means of finding clues and avenues of access to more reliable sources of information. On the other hand, feelings and attitudes have been found to be clearly and correctly revealed in a properly conducted personal interview.

11. According to the above paragraph, information obtained in a personal interview

    A. can be corroborated by other clues and more reliable sources of information revealed at the interview
    B. can be used to develop leads to other sources of information about past events
    C. is not reliable
    D. is reliable if it relates to recent occurrences

11.____

12. According to the above paragraph, the personal interview is suitable for obtaining  12.____

   A. emotional reactions to a given situation
   B. fresh information on factors which may be forgotten
   C. revived recollection of previous events for later use as testimony
   D. specific information on material already reduced to writing

Questions 13-15.

DIRECTIONS: Questions 13 through 15 are to be answered on the basis of the following paragraph.

Admissibility of handwriting standards (samples of handwriting for the purpose of comparison) as a basis for expert testimony is frequently necessary when the authenticity of disputed documents may be at issue. Under the older rules of common law, only that writing relating to the issues in the case could be used as a basis for handwriting testimony by an expert. Today, most jurisdictions admit irrelevant writings as standards for comparison. However, their genuineness, in all instances, must be established to the satisfaction of the court. There are a number of types of documents, however, not ordinarily relevant to the issues which are seldom acceptable to the court as handwriting standards, such as bail bonds, signatures on affidavits, depositions, etc. These are usually already before the court as part of the record in a case. Exhibits written in the presence of a witness or prepared voluntarily for a law enforcement officer are readily admissible in most jurisdictions. Testimony of a witness who is considered familiar with the writing is admissible in some jurisdictions. In criminal cases, it is possible that the signature on the fingerprint card obtained in connection with the arrest of the defendant for the crime currently charged may be admitted as a handwriting standard. In order to give the defendant the fairest possible treatment, most jurisdictions do not admit the signatures on fingerprint cards pertaining to prior arrests. However, they are admitted sometimes. In such instances, the court usually requires that the signature be photographed or removed from the card and no reference be made to the origin of the signature.

13. Of the following, the types of handwriting standards MOST likely to be admitted in evidence by most jurisdictions are those  13.____

   A. appearing on depositions and bail bonds
   B. which were written in the presence of a witness or voluntarily given to a law enforcement officer
   C. identified by witnesses who claim to be familiar with the handwriting
   D. which are in conformity with the rules of common law only

14. The PRINCIPAL factor which generally determines the acceptance of handwriting standards by the courts is  14.____

   A. the relevance of the submitted documents to the issues of the case
   B. the number of witnesses who have knowledge of the submitted documents
   C. testimony that the writing has been examined by a handwriting expert
   D. acknowledgment by the court of the authenticity of the submitted documents

15. The MOST logical reason for requiring the removal of the signature of a defendant from fingerprint cards pertaining to prior arrests, before admitting the signature in court as a handwriting standard, is that  15.____

A. it simplifies the process of identification of the signature as a standard for comparison
B. the need for identifying the fingerprints is eliminated
C. mention of prior arrests may be prejudicial to the defendant
D. a handwriting expert does not need information pertaining to prior arrests in order to make his identification

Questions 16-20.

DIRECTIONS: Questions 16 through 20 are to be answered SOLELY on the basis of the information contained in the following paragraph.

A statement which is offered in an attempt to prove the truth of the matters therein stated, but which is not made by the author as a witness before the court at the particular trial in which it is so offered, is hearsay. This is so whether the statement consists of words (oral or written), of symbols used as a substitute for words, or of signs or other conduct offered as the equivalent of a statement. Subject to some well-established exceptions, hearsay is not generally acceptable as evidence, and it does not become competent evidence just because it is received by the court without objection. One basis for this rule is simply that a fact cannot be proved by showing that somebody stated it was a fact. Another basis for the rule is the fundamental principle that in a criminal prosecution the testimony of the witness shall be taken before the court, so that at the time he gives the testimony offered in evidence he will be sworn and subject to cross-examination, the scrutiny of the court, and confrontation by the accused.

16. Which of the following is hearsay? 16.____
A(n)

    A. written statement by a person not present at the court hearing where the statement is submitted as proof of an occurrence
    B. oral statement in court by a witness of what he saw
    C. written statement of what he saw by a witness present in court
    D. re-enactment by a witness in court of what he saw

17. In a criminal case, a statement by a person not present in court is 17.____

    A. *acceptable* evidence if not objected to by the prosecutor
    B. *acceptable* evidence if not objected to by the defense lawyer
    C. *not acceptable* evidence except in certain well-settled circumstances
    D. *not acceptable* evidence under any circumstances

18. The rule on hearsay is founded on the belief that 18.____

    A. proving someone said an act occurred is not proof that the act did occur
    B. a person who has knowledge about a case should be willing to appear in court
    C. persons not present in court are likely to be unreliable witnesses
    D. permitting persons to testify without appearing in court will lead to a disrespect for law

19. One reason for the general rule that a witness in a criminal case must give his testimony in court is that

    A. a witness may be influenced by threats to make untrue statements
    B. the opposite side is then permitted to question him
    C. the court provides protection for a witness against unfair questioning
    D. the adversary system is designed to prevent a miscarriage of justice

20. Of the following, the MOST appropriate title for the above passage would be

    A. WHAT IS HEARSAY?
    B. RIGHTS OF DEFENDANTS
    C. TRIAL PROCEDURES
    D. TESTIMONY OF WITNESSES

21. A person's statements are independent of who he is or what he is. Statements made by a person are not proved true or false by questioning his character or his position. A statement should stand or fall on its merits, regardless of who makes the statement. Truth is determined by evidence only. A person's character or personality should not be the determining factor in logic. Discussions should not become incidents of name calling.
    According to the above, whether or not a statement is true depends on the

    A. recipient's conception of validity
    B. maker's reliability
    C. extent of support by facts
    D. degree of merit the discussion has

Question 22-25.

DIRECTIONS: Questions 22 through 25 are to be answered on the basis of the following passage.

The question, whether an act, repugnant to the Constitution, can become the law of the land, is a question deeply interesting to the United States; but, happily, not of an intricacy proportioned to its interest. It seems only necessary to recognize certain principles, supposed to have been long and well-established, to decide it. That the people have an original right to establish, for their future government, such principles as, in their opinion, shall most conduce to their own happiness, is the basis on which the whole American fabric has been erected. The exercise of this original right is a very great exertion; nor can it, nor ought it, to be frequently repeated. The principles, therefore, so established are deemed fundamental; and as the authority from which they proceed is supreme, and can seldom act, they are designed to be permanent.

22. The BEST title for the above passage would be

    A. PRINCIPLES OF THE CONSTITUTION
    B. THE ROOT OF CONSTITUTIONAL CHANGE
    C. ONLY PEOPLE CAN CHANGE THE CONSTITUTION
    D. METHODS OF CONSTITUTIONAL CHANGE

23. According to the above passage, original right is

    A. fundamental to the principle that the people may choose their own form of government
    B. established by the Constitution

C. the result of a very great exertion and should not often be repeated
D. supreme, can seldom act, and is designed to be permanent

24. Whether an act not in keeping with Constitutional principles can become law is, according to the above passage,

   A. an intricate problem requiring great thought and concentration
   B. determined by the proportionate interests of legislators
   C. determined by certain long established principles, fundamental to Constitutional Law
   D. an intricate problem, but less intricate than it would seem from the interest shown in it

25. According to the above passage, the phrase *and can seldom act* refers to the

   A. principle enacted early into law by Americans when they chose their future form of government
   B. original rights of the people as vested in the Constitution
   C. original framers of the Constitution
   D. established, fundamental principles of government

---

# KEY (CORRECT ANSWERS)

| | | | |
|---|---|---|---|
| 1. | C | 11. | B |
| 2. | A | 12. | A |
| 3. | B | 13. | B |
| 4. | C | 14. | D |
| 5. | D | 15. | C |
| 6. | A | 16. | A |
| 7. | B | 17. | C |
| 8. | A | 18. | A |
| 9. | D | 19. | B |
| 10. | C | 20. | A |

21. C
22. B
23. A
24. D
25. A

# TEST 2

DIRECTIONS: Each question or incomplete statement is followed by several suggested answers or completions. Select the one that BEST answers the question or completes the statement. *PRINT THE LETTER OF THE CORRECT ANSWER IN THE SPACE AT THE RIGHT.*

Questions 1-3.

DIRECTIONS: Questions 1 through 3 are to be answered SOLELY on the basis of the following paragraph.

    The police laboratory performs a valuable service in crime investigation by assisting in the reconstruction of criminal action and by aiding in the identification of persons and things. When studied by a technician, physical things found at crime scenes often reveal facts useful in identifying the criminal and in determining what has occurred. The nature of substances to be examined and the character of the examination to be made vary so widely that the services of a large variety of skilled scientific persons are needed in crime investigations. To employ such a complete staff and to provide them with equipment and standards needed for all possible analysis and comparisons is beyond the means and the needs of any but the largest police departments. The search of crime scenes for physical evidence also calls for the services of specialists supplied with essential equipment and assigned to each tour of duty so as to provide service at any hour.

1. If a police department employs a large staff of technicians of various types in its laboratory, it will affect crime investigations to the extent that

   A. most crimes will be speedily solved
   B. identification of criminals will be aided
   C. search of crime scenes for physical evidence will become of less importance
   D. investigation by police officers will not usually be required

2. According to the above paragraph, the MOST complete study of objects found at the scenes of crimes is

   A. always done in all large police departments
   B. based on assigning one technician to each tour of duty
   C. probably done only in large police departments
   D. probably done in police departments of communities with low crime rates

3. According to the above paragraph, a large variety of skilled technicians is useful in criminal investigations because

   A. crimes cannot be solved without their assistance as part of the police team
   B. large police departments need large staffs
   C. many different kinds of tests on various substances can be made
   D. the police cannot predict what methods may be tried by wily criminals

Questions 4-6.

DIRECTIONS: Questions 4 through 6 are to be answered SOLELY on the basis of the following passage.

Probably the most important single mechanism for bringing the resources of science and technology to bear on the problems of crime would be the establishment of a major prestigious science and technology research program within a research institute. The program would create interdisciplinary teams of mathematicians, computer scientists, electronics engineers, physicists, biologists, and other natural scientists, psychologists, sociologists, economists, and lawyers. The institute and the program must be significant enough to attract the best scientists available, and, to this end, the director of this institute must himself have a background in science and technology and have the respect of scientists. Because it would be difficult to attract such a staff into the Federal government, the institute should be established by a university, a group of universities, or an independent nonprofit organization, and should be within a major metropolitan area. The institute would have to establish close ties with neighboring criminal justice agencies that would receive the benefit of serving as experimental laboratories for such an institute. In fact, the proposal for the institute might be jointly submitted with the criminal justice agencies. The research program would require, in order to bring together the necessary *critical mass* of competent staff, an annual budget which might reach 5 million dollars, funded with at least three years of lead time to assure continuity. Such a major scientific and technological research institute should be supported by the Federal government.

4. Of the following, the MOST appropriate title for the foregoing passage is

   A. RESEARCH - AN INTERDISCIPLINARY APPROACH TO FIGHTING CRIME
   B. A CURRICULUM FOR FIGHTING CRIME
   C. THE ROLE OF THE UNIVERSITY IN THE FIGHT AGAINST CRIME
   D. GOVERNMENTAL SUPPORT OF CRIMINAL RESEARCH PROGRAMS

5. According to the above passage, in order to attract the best scientists available, the research institute should

   A. provide psychologists and sociologists to counsel individual members of interdisciplinary teams
   B. encourage close ties with neighboring criminal justice agencies
   C. be led by a person who is respected in the scientific community
   D. be directly operated and funded by the Federal government

6. The term *critical mass,* as used in the above passage, refers MAINLY to

   A. a staff which would remain for three years of continuous service to the institute
   B. staff members necessary to carry out the research program of the institute successfully
   C. the staff necessary to establish relations with criminal justice agencies which will serve as experimental laboratories for the institute
   D. a staff which would be able to assist the institute in raising adequate funds

Questions 7-9.

DIRECTIONS: Questions 7 through 9 are to be answered SOLELY on the basis of the following paragraph.

The use of modern scientific methods in the examination of physical evidence often provides information to the investigator which he could not otherwise obtain. This applies particularly to small objects and materials present in minute quantities or trace evidence because the quantities here are such that they may be overlooked without methodical searching, and often special means of detection are needed. Whenever two objects come in contact with one another, there is a transfer of material, however slight. Usually, the softer object will transfer to the harder, but the transfer may be mutual. The quantity of material transferred differs with the type of material involved and the more violent the contact the greater the degree of transference. Through scientific methods of determining physical properties and chemical composition, we can add to the facts observable by the investigator's unaided senses, and thereby increase the chances of identification.

7. According to the above paragraph, the amount of material transferred whenever two objects come in contact with one another

   A. varies directly with the softness of the objects involved
   B. varies directly with the violence of the contact of the objects
   C. is greater when two soft, rather than hard, objects come into violent contact with each other
   D. is greater when coarse-grained, rather than smooth-grained, materials are involved

8. According to the above paragraph, the PRINCIPAL reason for employing scientific methods in obtaining trace evidence is that

   A. other methods do not involve a methodical search of the crime scene
   B. scientific methods of examination frequently reveal physical evidence which did not previously exist
   C. the amount of trace evidence may be so sparse that other methods are useless
   D. trace evidence cannot be properly identified unless special means of detection are employed

9. According to the above paragraph, the one of the following statements which BEST describes the manner in which scientific methods of analyzing physical evidence assists the investigator is that such methods

   A. add additional valuable information to the investigator's own knowledge of complex and rarely occurring materials found as evidence
   B. compensate for the lack of important evidential material through the use of physical and chemical analyses
   C. make possible an analysis of evidence which goes beyond the ordinary capacity of the investigator's senses
   D. identify precisely those physical characteristics of the individual which the untrained senses of the investigator are unable to discern

Questions 10-13.

DIRECTIONS: Questions 10 through 13 are to be answered SOLELY on the basis of the information contained in the following paragraph.

Under the provisions of the Bank Protection Act of 1968, enacted July 8, 1968, each Federal banking supervisory agency, as of January 7, 1969, had to issue rules establishing minimum standards with which financial institutions under their control must comply with respect to the installation, maintenance, and operation of security devices and procedures, reasonable in cost, to discourage robberies, burglaries, and larcenies, and to assist in the identification and apprehension of persons who commit such acts. The rules set the time limits within which the affected banks and savings and loan associations must comply with the standards, and the rules require the submission of periodic reports on the steps taken. A violator of a rule under this Act is subject to a civil penalty not to exceed $100 for each day of the violation. The enforcement of these regulations rests with the responsible banking supervisory agencies.

10. The Bank Protection Act of 1968 was designed to

    A. provide Federal police protection for banks covered by the Act
    B. have organizations covered by the Act take precautions against criminals
    C. set up a system for reporting all bank robberies to the FBI
    D. insure institutions covered by the Act from financial loss due to robberies, burglaries, and larcenies

11. Under the provisions of the Bank Protection Act of 1968, each Federal banking supervisory agency was required to set up rules for financial institutions covered by the Act governing the

    A. hiring of personnel
    B. punishment of burglars
    C. taking of protective measures
    D. penalties for violations

12. Financial institutions covered by the Bank Protection Act of 1968 were required to

    A. file reports at regular intervals on what they had done to prevent theft
    B. identify and apprehend persons who commit robberies, burglaries, and larcenies
    C. draw up a code of ethics for their employees
    D. have fingerprints of their employees filed with the FBI

13. Under the provisions of the Bank Protection Act of 1968, a bank which is subject to the rules established under the Act and which violates a rule is liable to a penalty of NOT _____ than $100 for each _____.

    A. more; violation
    B. less; day of violation
    C. less; violation
    D. more; day of violation

Questions 14-17.

DIRECTIONS: Questions 14 through 17 are to be answered SOLELY on the basis of the following passage.

Specific measures for prevention of pilferage will be based on careful analysis of the conditions at each agency. The most practical and effective method to control casual pilferage is the establishment of psychological deterrents.

One of the most common means of discouraging casual pilferage is to search individuals leaving the agency at unannounced times and places. These spot searches may occasionally detect attempts at theft, but greater value is realized by bringing to the attention of individuals the fact that they may be apprehended if they do attempt the illegal removal of property.

An aggressive security education program is an effective means of convincing employees that they have much more to lose than they do to gain by engaging in acts of theft. It is important for all employees to realize that pilferage is morally wrong no matter how insignificant the value of the item which is taken. In establishing any deterrent to casual pilferage, security officers must not lose sight of the fact that most employees are honest and disapprove of thievery. Mutual respect between security personnel and other employees of the agency must be maintained if the facility is to be protected from other more dangerous forms of human hazards. Any security measure which infringes on the human rights or dignity of others will jeopardize, rather than enhance, the overall protection of the agency.

14. The $100,000 yearly inventory of an agency revealed that $50 worth of goods had been stolen; the only individuals with access to the stolen materials were the employees. Of the following measures, which would the author of the above passage MOST likely recommend to a security officer?

   A. Conduct an intensive investigation of all employees to find the culprit.
   B. Make a record of the theft, but take no investigative or disciplinary action against any employee.
   C. Place a tight security check on all future movements of personnel.
   D. Remove the remainder of the material to an area with much greater security.

15. What does the passage imply is the percentage of employees whom a security officer should expect to be honest?

   A. No employee can be expected to be honest all of the time
   B. Just 50%
   C. Less than 50%
   D. More than 50%

16. According to the above passage, the security officer would use which of the following methods to minimize theft in buildings with many exits when his staff is very small?

   A. Conduct an inventory of all material and place a guard near that which is most likely to be pilfered
   B. Inform employees of the consequences of legal prosecution for pilfering
   C. Close off the unimportant exits and have all his men concentrate on a few exits
   D. Place a guard at each exit and conduct a casual search of individuals leaving the premises

17. Of the following, the title BEST suited for this passage is

   A. CONTROL MEASURES FOR CASUAL PILFERING
   B. DETECTING THE POTENTIAL PILFERER
   C. FINANCIAL LOSSES RESULTING FROM PILFERING
   D. THE USE OF MORAL PERSUASION IN PHYSICAL SECURITY

Questions 18-24.

DIRECTIONS: Questions 18 through 24 are to be answered SOLELY on the basis of the following passage.

Burglar alarms are designed to detect intrusion automatically. Robbery alarms enable a victim of a robbery or an attack to signal for help. Such devices can be located in elevators, hallways, homes and apartments, businesses and factories, and subways, as well as on the street in high-crime areas. Alarms could deter some potential criminals from attacking targets so protected. If alarms were prevalent and not visible, then they might serve to suppress crime generally. In addition, of course, the alarms can summon the police when they are needed.

All alarms must perform three functions: sensing or initiation of the signal, transmission of the signal and annunciation of the alarm. A burglar alarm needs a sensor to detect human presence or activity in an unoccupied enclosed area like a building or a room. A robbery victim would initiate the alarm by closing a foot or wall switch, or by triggering a portable transmitter which would send the alarm signal to a remote receiver. The signal can sound locally as a loud noise to frighten away a criminal, or it can be sent silently by wire to a central agency. A centralized annunciator requires either private lines from each alarmed point, or the transmission of some information on the location of the signal.

18. A conclusion which follows LOGICALLY from the above passage is that

    A. burglar alarms employ sensor devices; robbery alarms make use of initiation devices
    B. robbery alarms signal intrusion without the help of the victim; burglar alarms require the victim to trigger a switch
    C. robbery alarms sound locally; burglar alarms are transmitted to a central agency
    D. the mechanisms for a burglar alarm and a robbery alarm are alike

19. According to the above passage, alarms can be located

    A. in a wide variety of settings
    B. only in enclosed areas
    C. at low cost in high-crime areas
    D. only in places where potential criminals will be deterred

20. According to the above passage, which of the following is ESSENTIAL if a signal is to be received in a central office?

    A. A foot or wall switch
    B. A noise-producing mechanism
    C. A portable reception device
    D. Information regarding the location of the source

21. According to the above passage, an alarm system can function WITHOUT a

    A. centralized annunciating device
    B. device to stop the alarm
    C. sensing or initiating device
    D. transmission device

22. According to the above passage, the purpose of robbery alarms is to

    A. find out automatically whether a robbery has taken place
    B. lower the crime rate in high-crime areas
    C. make a loud noise to frighten away the criminal
    D. provide a victim with the means to signal for help

23. According to the above passage, alarms might aid in lessening crime if they were    23._____

    A. answered promptly by police
    B. completely automatic
    C. easily accessible to victims
    D. hidden and widespread

24. Of the following, the BEST title for the above passage is    24._____

    A. DETECTION OF CRIME BY ALARMS
    B. LOWERING THE CRIME RATE
    C. SUPPRESSION OF CRIME
    D. THE PREVENTION OF ROBBERY

25. Although the rural crime reporting area is much less developed than that for cities and    25._____
    towns, current data are collected in sufficient volume to justify the generalization that
    rural crime rates are lower than those or urban communities.
    According to this statement,

    A. better reporting of crime occurs in rural areas than in cities
    B. there appears to be a lower proportion of crime in rural areas than in cities
    C. cities have more crime than towns
    D. crime depends on the amount of reporting

## KEY (CORRECT ANSWERS)

| | |
|---|---|
| 1. B | 11. C |
| 2. C | 12. A |
| 3. C | 13. D |
| 4. A | 14. B |
| 5. C | 15. D |
| 6. B | 16. B |
| 7. B | 17. A |
| 8. C | 18. A |
| 9. C | 19. A |
| 10. B | 20. D |

21. A
22. D
23. D
24. A
25. B

# READING COMPREHENSION
# UNDERSTANDING AND INTERPRETING WRITTEN MATERIAL
## EXAMINATION SECTION
## TEST 1

DIRECTIONS: Each question or incomplete statement is followed by several suggested answers or completions. Select the one that BEST answers the question or completes the statement. *PRINT THE LETTER OF THE CORRECT ANSWER IN THE SPACE AT THE RIGHT.*

Questions 1-3.

DIRECTIONS: Questions 1 through 3 are to be answered SOLELY on the basis of the following paragraph.

The final step in an accident investigation is the making out of the police report. In the case of a traffic accident, the officer should go right from the scene to his office to write up the report. However, if a person was injured in the accident and taken to a hospital, the officer should visit him there before going to his office to prepare his report. This personal visit to the injured person does not mean that the office must make a physical examination; but he should make an effort to obtain a statement from the injured person or persons. If this is not possible, information should be obtained from the attending physician as to the extent of the injury. In any event, without fail, the name of the physician should be secured and the report should state the name of the physician and the fact that he told the officer that, at a certain stated time on a certain stated date, the injuries were of such and such a nature. If the injured person dies before the officer arrives at the hospital, it may be necessary to take the responsible person into custody at once.

1. When a person has been injured in a traffic accident, the one of the following actions which it is necessary for a police officer to take in connection with the accident report is to
   A. prepare the police report immediately after the accident, and then go to the hospital to speak to the victim
   B. do his utmost to verify the victim's story prior to preparing the official police report of the incident
   C. be sure to include the victim's statement in the police report in every case
   D. try to get the victim's version of the accident prior to preparing the police report

2. When one of the persons injured in a motor vehicle accident dies, the above paragraph provides that the police officer
   A. must immediately take the responsible person into custody, if the injured person is already dead when the officer appears at the scene of the accident
   B. must either arrest the responsible person or get a statement from him, if the injured person dies after arrival at the hospital

C. may have to immediately arrest the responsible person, if the injured person dies in the hospital prior to the officer's arrival there
D. may refrain from arresting the responsible person, but only if the responsible person is also seriously injured

3. When someone has been injured in a collision between two automobiles and is given medical treatment shortly thereafter by a physician, the one of the following actions which the police officer MUST take with regard to the physician is to 3.____
   A. obtain his name and his diagnosis of the injuries, regardless of the place where treatment was given
   B. obtain his approval of the portion of the police report relating to the injured person and the treatment given him prior to and after his arrival at the hospital
   C. obtain his name, his opinion of the extent of the person's injuries, and his signed statement of the treatment he gave the injured person
   D. set a certain stated time on a certain stated date for interviewing him, unless he is an attending physician in a hospital

Questions 4-7.

DIRECTIONS: Questions 4 through 7 are to be answered SOLELY on the basis of the following paragraph.

Because of the importance of preserving physical evidence, the patrolman should not enter a scene of a crime if it can be examined visually from one position and if no other pressing duty requires his presence there. However, there are some responsibilities that take precedence over preservation of evidence. Some examples are: rescue work, disarming dangerous persons, quelling a disturbance. However, the patrolman should learn how to accomplish these more vital tasks, while at the same time preserving as much evidence as possible. If he finds it necessary to enter upon the scene, he should quickly study the place of entry to learn if any evidence will suffer by his contact; then he should determine the routes to be used in walking to the spot where his presence is required. Every place where a foot will fall or where a hand or other part of his body will touch, should be examined with the eye. Objects should not be touched or moved unless there is a definite and compelling reason. For identification of most items of physical evidence at the initial investigation, it is seldom necessary to touch or move them.

4. The one of the following titles which is the MOST appropriate for the above paragraph is: 4.____
   A. Determining the Priority of Tasks at the Scene of a Crime
   B. The Principal Reasons for Preserving Evidence at the Scene of a Crime
   C. Precautions to Take at the Scene of a Crime
   D. Evidence to be Examined at the Scene of a Crime

5. When a patrolman feels that it is essential for him to enter the immediate area where a crime has been committed, he should
    A. quickly but carefully glance around to determine whether his entering the area will damage any evidence present
    B. remove all objects of evidence from his predetermined route in order to avoid stepping on them
    C. carefully replace any object immediately if it is moved or touched by his hands or any other part of his body
    D. use only the usual place of entry to the scene in order to avoid disturbing any possible clues left on rear doors and windows by the criminal

5._____

6. The one of the following which is the LEAST urgent duty of a police officer who has just reported to the scene of a crime is to
    A. disarm the hysterical victim of the crime who is wildly waving a loaded gun in all directions
    B. give first aid to a possible suspect who has been injured while attempting to leave the scene of the crime
    C. prevent observers from attacking and injuring the persons suspected of having committed the crime
    D. preserve from damage or destruction any evidence necessary for the proper prosecution of the case against the criminals

6._____

7. A police officer has just reported to the scene of a crime in response to a phone call.
The BEST of the following actions for him to take with respect to objects of physical evidence present at the scene is to
    A. make no attempt to enter the crime scene if his entry will disturb any vital physical evidence
    B. map out the shortest straight path to follow in walking to the spot where the physical evidence may be found
    C. move such objects of physical evidence as are necessary to enable him to assist the wounded victim of the crime
    D. quickly examine all objects of physical evidence in order to determine which objects may be touched and which may not

7._____

Questions 8-11.

DIRECTIONS: Questions 8 through 11 are to be answered SOLELY on the basis of the following paragraph.

After examining a document and comparing the characters with specimens of other specimens of other handwritings, the laboratory technician may conclude that a certain individual did write the questioned document. This opinion could be based on a large number of similar, as well as a small number of dissimilar but explainable characteristics. On the other hand, if the laboratory technician concludes that the person in question did not write the questioned document, such an opinion could be based on the large number of characteristics which are dissimilar, or even on a small number which are dissimilar provided that these are of overriding significance, and despite the presence of explainable similarities. The laboratory expert is not always able to give a positive opinion. He may state that a certain individual probably did or did not write the questioned document. Such an opinion is usually the result of insufficient material, either in the questioned document or in the specimens submitted for comparison. Finally, the expert may be unable to come to any conclusion at all because of insufficient material submitted for comparison or because of improper specimens.

8. The one of the following which is the MOST appropriate title for the above paragraph is:
   A. Similar and Dissimilar Characteristics in Handwriting
   B. The Limitations of Handwriting Analysis in Identifying the Writer
   C. The Positive Identification of Suspects Through Their Handwriting
   D. The Inability to Identify an Individual Through His Handwriting

9. When a handwriting expert compares the handwriting on two separate documents and decides that they were written by the same person, his conclusions are generally based on the fact that
   A. a large number of characteristics in both documents are dissimilar but the few similar characteristics are more important
   B. all the characteristics are alike in both documents
   C. similar characteristics need to be examined as to the cause for their similarity
   D. most of the characteristics in both documents are alike and their few differences are readily explainable

10. If a fingerprint technician carefully examines a handwritten threatening letter and compares it with specimens of handwriting made by a suspect, he would be MOST likely to decide that the suspect did NOT write the threatening letter when the handwriting specimens and the letter have
    A. a small number of dissimilarities
    B. a small number of dissimilar but explainable characteristics
    C. important dissimilarities despite the fact that these may be few
    D. some similar characteristics that are easily imitated or disguised

11. There are instances when even a trained handwriting expert cannot decide definitely whether or not a certain document and a set of handwriting specimens were written by the same person.
    This inability to make a positive decision generally arises in situations where
    A. only one document of considerable length is available for comparison with a sufficient supply of handwriting specimens
    B. the limited nature of the handwriting specimens submitted restricts their comparability with the questioned document
    C. the dissimilarities are not explainable
    D. the document submitted for comparison does not include all the characteristics included in the handwriting specimens

Questions 12-14.

DIRECTIONS: Questions 12 through 14 are to be answered SOLELY on the basis of the following paragraph.

In cases of drunken driving, or of disorderly conduct while intoxicated, too many times some person who had been completely under the influence of alcoholic liquor at the time of his arrest has walked out of court without any conviction just because an officer failed to make the proper observation. Many of the larger cities and counties make use of various scientific methods to determine the degree of intoxication of a person, such as breath, urine, and blood tests. Many of the smaller cities, however, do not have the facilities to make these various tests, and must, therefore, rely on the observation tests given at the scene. These consist, among other things, of noticing how the subject walked, talked, and acted. One test that is usually given at night is the eye reaction to light, which the officer gives by shining his flashlight into the eyes of the subject. The manner in which the pupils of the eyes react to the light helps to determine the sobriety of a person. If he is intoxicated, the pupils of his eyes are dilated more at night than the eyes of a sober person. Also, when a light is flashed into the eyes of a sober person, his pupils contract instantly, but in the case of a person under the influence of liquor, the pupils contract very slowly.

12. Many persons who have been arrested on a charge of driving while completely intoxicated have been acquitted by a judge because the arresting officer had neglected to
    A. bring the driver to court while he was still under the influence of alcohol
    B. make the required scientific tests to fully substantiate his careful personal observations of the driver's intoxicated condition
    C. submit to the court any test results showing the driver's condition or degree of drunkenness
    D. watch the driver closely for some pertinent facts which would support the officer's suspicions of the driver's intoxicated condition

13. When a person is arrested for acting in a disorderly and apparently intoxicated manner in public, the kind of test which would fit in BEST with the thought of the above statement is:
    A. In many smaller cities, a close watch on his behavior and of his reactions to various blood and body tests
    B. In many smaller cities, having him walk a straight line
    C. In most larger counties, close watch of the speed of his reactions to the flashlight test
    D. In most cities of all sizes, the application of the latest scientific techniques in the analysis of his breath

14. When a person suspected of driving a motor vehicle while intoxicated is being examined to determine whether or not he actually is intoxicated, one of the methods used is to shine the light of a flashlight into his eyes.

When this method is used, the NORMAL result is that the pupils of the suspect's eyes will
- A. expand instantly if he is fully intoxicated, and remain unchanged if he is completely sober
- B. expand very slowly if he has had only a small amount of alcohol, and very rapidly if he has had a considerable amount of alcohol
- C. grow smaller at once if he is sober, and grow smaller more slowly if he is intoxicated
- D. grow smaller very slowly if he is fully sober, and grow smaller instantaneously if he is fully intoxicated

Questions 15-17.

DIRECTIONS: Questions 15 through 17 are to be answered SOLELY on the basis of the following paragraph.

Where an officer has personal knowledge of facts, sufficient to constitute reasonable grounds to believe that a person has committed or is committing a felony, he may arrest him, and, after having lawfully placed him under arrest, may search and take into his possession any incriminating evidence. The right of an officer to make an arrest and search is not limited to cases where the officer has personal knowledge of the commission of a felony, because he may act upon information conveyed to him by third persons which he believes to be reliable. Where an officer, charged with the duty of enforcing the law, receives information from apparently reliable sources, which would induce in the mind of the prudent person a belief that a felony was being or had been committed, he may make an arrest and search the person of a defendant, but he is not justified in acting on anonymous information alone.

15. When a felony has been committed, an officer would be acting MOST properly if he arrested a man
    - A. when he, the officer, has a police report that the man is suspected of having been involved in several minor offenses
    - B. when he, the officer, has received information from a usually reliable source that the man was involved in the crime
    - C. only when he, the officer, has personal knowledge that the man has committed the felony
    - D. when he, the officer, knows for a fact that the man has associated in the past with several persons who had been seen near the scene of the felony

16. An officer would be acting MOST properly if he searched a suspect for incriminating evidence
    - A. when he has received detailed information concerning the fact that the suspect is going to commit a felony
    - B. only after having lawfully arrested the suspect and charged him with having committed a felony
    - C. when he has just received an anonymous tip that the suspect had just committed a felony and is in illegal possession of stolen goods

D. in order to find in his possession legally admissible evidence on the basis of which the officer could then proceed to arrest the suspect for having committed a felony

17. A police officer has received information from an informant that a crime has been committed. The informant has also named two persons who he says committed the crime.
The officer's decision to both arrest and search the two suspects would be
   A. *correct*, if it would not be unreasonable to assume that the crime committed is a felony, and if the informant has been trustworthy in the past
   B. *incorrect*, if the informant has no proof but his own word to offer that a felony has been committed, although he has always been trustworthy in the past
   C. *correct*, if it would be logical and prudent to assume that the information is accurate regardless of whether the offense committed is a felony or a less serious crime
   D. *incorrect*, even if the informant produces objective and seemingly convincing proof that a felony has been committed, but has a reputation of occasional past unreliability

17.____

Questions 18-20.

DIRECTIONS: Questions 18 through 20 are to be answered SOLELY on the basis of the following paragraph.

If there are many persons at the scene of a hit-and-run accident, it would be a waste of time to question all of them; the witness needed is the one who can best describe the missing auto. Usually the person most qualified to do this is a youth of fifteen or sixteen years of age. He is more likely to be able to tell the make and year of a car than most other persons. A woman may be a good witness as to how the accident occurred, but usually will be unable to tell the make of the car. As soon as any information with regard to the missing car or its description is obtained, the police officer should call or radio headquarters and have the information put on the air. This should be done without waiting for further details, for time is an important factor. If a good description of the wanted car is obtained, then the next task is to get a description of the driver. In this hunt, it is found that a woman is often a more accurate witness than a man. Usually she will be able to state the color of clothes worn by the driver. If the wanted driver is a woman, another woman will often be able to tell the color and sometimes even the material of the clothing worn.

18. A hit-and-run accident has occurred and a police officer is attempting to obtain information from persons who had witnessed the incident.
It would generally be BEST for him to question a
   A. boy in his late teens, when the officer is seeking an accurate description of the age, coloring, and physical build of the driver of the car
   B. man, when the officer is seeking an accurate description of the driver of the car and the color and material of his coat, suit, and hat

18.____

C. woman, when the officer is seeking an accurate description of the driver of the car
D. young teenage girl, when the officer is seeking an accurate description of the style and color of the clothes worn by the driver of the car

19. Time is an important factor when an attempt is being made to apprehend the guilty driver in a hit-and-run accident.
However, the EARLIEST moment when the police should broadcast a radio announcement of the crime is when a(n)
    A. description of the missing car or any facts concerning it have been obtained
    B. tentative identification of the driver of the missing car has been made
    C. detailed description of the missing car and its occupant has been obtained
    D. eyewitness account has been obtained of the accident, including the identity of the victim, the extent of injuries, and the make and license number of the car

19._____

20. The time when it would be MOST desirable to get a description of the driver of the hit-and-run car is
    A. after getting a description of the car itself
    B. before transmitting information concerning the car to headquarters for broadcasting
    C. as soon as the officer arrives at the scene of the accident
    D. as soon as the victim of the accident has been given needed medical assistance

20._____

## KEY (CORRECT ANSWERS)

| | | | |
|---|---|---|---|
| 1. | D | 11. | B |
| 2. | C | 12. | D |
| 3. | A | 13. | B |
| 4. | C | 14. | C |
| 5. | A | 15. | B |
| 6. | D | 16. | B |
| 7. | C | 17. | A |
| 8. | B | 18. | C |
| 9. | D | 19. | A |
| 10. | C | 20. | A |

# TEST 2

DIRECTIONS: Each question or incomplete statement is followed by several suggested answers or completions. Select the one that BEST answers the question or completes the statement. *PRINT THE LETTER OF THE CORRECT ANSWER IN THE SPACE AT THE RIGHT.*

Questions 1-4.

DIRECTIONS: Questions 1 through 4 are to be answered SOLELY on the basis of the following paragraph.

Automobile tire tracks found at the scene of a crime constitute an important link in the chain of physical evidence. In many cases, these are the only clues available. In some areas, unpaved ground adjoins the highway or paved streets. A suspect will often park his car off the paved portion of the street when committing a crime, sometimes leaving excellent tire tracks. Comparison of the tire track impressions with the tires is possible only when the vehicle has been found. However, the initial problem facing the police is the task of determining what kind of car probably made the impressions found at the scene of the crime. If the make, model, and year of the car which made the impressions can be determined, it is obvious that the task of elimination is greatly lessened.

1. The one of the following which is the MOST appropriate title for the above paragraph is:
   A. The Use of Automobiles in the Commission of Crimes
   B. The Use of Tire Tracks in Police Work
   C. The Capture of Criminals by Scientific Police Work
   D. The Positive Identification of Criminals Through Their Cars

2. When searching for clear signs left by the car used in the commission of a crime, the MOST likely place for the police to look would be on the
   A. highway adjoining unpaved streets
   B. highway adjacent to paved street
   C. paved street adjacent to the highway
   D. unpaved ground adjacent to a highway

3. Automobile tire tracks found at the scene of a crime are of value as evidence in that they are
   A. generally sufficient to trap and convict a suspect
   B. the most important link in the chain of physical evidence
   C. often the only evidence at hand
   D. circumstantial rather than direct

4. The PRIMARY reason for the police to try to find out which make, model, and year of car was involved in the commission of a crime is to
   A. compare the tire tracks left at the scene of the crime with the type of tires used on cars of that make
   B. determine if the mud on the tires of the suspected car matches the mud in the unpaved road near the scene of the crime

C. reduce to a large extent the amount of work involved in determining the particular car used in the commission of a crime
D. alert the police patrol forces to question the occupants of all automobiles of this type

Questions 5-8.

DIRECTIONS: Questions 5 through 8 are to be answered SOLELY on the basis of the following paragraph.

When stopping vehicles on highways to check for suspects or fugitives, the police use an automobile roadblock whenever possible. This consists of three cars placed in prearranged positions. Car number one is parked across the left lane of the roadway with the front diagonally facing toward the center line. Car number two is parked across the right lane, with the front of the vehicle also toward the center line, in a position perpendicular to car number one and approximately twenty feet to the rear. Continuing another twenty feet to the rear along the highway, car number three is parked in an identical manner to car number one. The width of the highway determines the angle or position in which the autos should be placed. In addition to the regular roadblock signs and the uses of flares at night only, there is an officer located at both the entrance and exit to direct and control traffic from both directions. This type of roadblock forces all approaching autos to reduce speed and zigzag around the police cars. Officers standing behind the parked cars can most safely and carefully view all passing motorists. Once a suspect is inside the block, it becomes extremely difficult to crash out.

5. Of the following, the MOST appropriate title for this paragraph is:
   A. The Construction of an Escape-Proof Roadblock
   B. Regulation of Automobile Traffic Through a Police Roadblock
   C. Safety Precautions Necessary in Making an Automobile Roadblock
   D. Structure of a Roadblock to Detain Suspects or Fugitives

5.____

6. When setting up a three-car roadblock, the *relative* positions of the cars should be such that
   A. the front of car number one is placed diagonally to the center line and faces car number three
   B. car number three is placed parallel to the center line and its front faces the right side of the road
   C. car number two is placed about 20 feet from car number one and its front faces the left side of the road
   D. car number three is parallel to and about 20 feet away from car number one

6.____

7. Officers can observe occupants of all cars passing through the roadblock with GREATEST safety when
   A warning flares are lighted to illuminate the area sufficiently at night
   B. warning signs are put up at each end of the roadblock
   C. they are stationed at both the exit and the entrance of the roadblock
   D. they take up positions behind cars in the roadblock

7.____

8. The type of automobile roadblock described in the above paragraph is of value in police work because
    A. a suspect is unable to escape its confines by using force
    B. it is frequently used to capture suspects with no danger to the police
    C. it requires only two officers to set up and operate
    D. vehicular traffic within its confines is controlled as to speed and direction

Questions 9-11.

DIRECTIONS: Questions 9 through 11 are to be answered SOLELY on the basis of the following paragraph.

A problem facing the police department in one area of the city was to try to reduce the number of bicycle thefts which had been increasing at an alarming rate in the past three or four years. A new program was adopted to get at the root of the problem. Tags were printed, reminding youngsters that bicycles left unlocked can be easily stolen. The police concentrated on such places as theaters, a municipal swimming pool, an athletic field, and the local high school, and tied tags on all bicycles which were not locked. The majority of bicycle thefts took place at the swimming pool. In 2019, during the first two weeks the pool was open, an average of 10 bicycle was stolen there daily. During the same two-week period, 30 bicycles a week were stolen at the athletic field, 15 at the high school, and 11 at all theaters combined. In 2020, after tagging the unlocked bicycles, it was found that 20 bicycles a week were stolen at the pool and 5 at the high school. It was felt that the police tags had helped the most, although the school officials had helped to a great extent in this program by distributing "locking" notices to parents and children, and the use of the loudspeaker at the pool urging children to lock their bicycles had also been very helpful.

9. The one of the following which had the GREATEST effect in the campaign to reduce bicycle stealing was the
    A. distribution of "locking" notices by the school officials
    B. locking of all bicycles left in public places
    C. police tagging of bicycles left unlocked by youngsters
    D. use of the loudspeaker at the swimming pool

10. The tagging program was instituted by the police department CHIEFLY to
    A. determine the areas where most bicycle thieves operated
    B. instill in youngsters the importance of punishing bicycle thieves
    C. lessen the rising rate of bicycle thefts
    D. recover as many as possible of the stolen bicycles

11. The figures showing the number of bicycle thefts in the various areas surveyed indicate that in 2019
    A. almost as many thefts occurred at the swimming pool as at all theaters combined
    B. fewer thefts occurred at the athletic field than at both the high school and all theaters combined
    C. more than half the thefts occurred at the swimming pool
    D. twice as many thefts occurred at the high school as at the athletic field

Questions 12-13.

DIRECTIONS: Questions 12 and 13 are to be answered SOLELY on the basis of the following paragraph.

A survey has shown that crime prevention work is most successful if the officers are assigned on rotating shifts to provide for around-the-clock coverage. An officer may work days for a time and then be switched to nights. The prime object of the night work is to enable the officer to spot conditions inviting burglars. Complete lack of, or faulty locations of, night lights and other conditions that may invite burglars, which might go unnoticed during daylight hours, can be located and corrected more readily through night work. Night work also enables the officer to check local hangouts of juvenile, such as bus and railway depots, certain cafes or pool halls, the local roller rink, and the building where a juvenile dance is held every Friday night. Detectives also join patrolmen cruising in radio patrol cars to check on juveniles loitering late at night and to spot-check local bars for juveniles.

12. The MOST important purpose of assigning officers to night shifts is to make it possible for them to
    A. correct conditions which may not be readily noticed during the day
    B. discover the locations of, and replace, missing and faulty night lights
    C. locate criminal hangouts
    D. notice things at night which cannot be noticed during the daytime

13. The type of shifting of officers which BEST prevents crime is to have
    A. day-shift officers rotated to night work
    B. rotating shifts provide sufficient officers for coverage 24 hours daily
    C. an officer work around the clock on a 24-hour basis as police needs arise
    D. rotating shifts to give the officers varied experience

Questions 14-15.

DIRECTIONS: Questions 14 and 15 are to be answered SOLELY on the basis of the following paragraph.

Proper firearms training is one phase of law enforcement which cannot be ignored. No part of the training of a police officer is more important or more valuable. The officer's life and often the lives of his fellow officers depend directly upon his skill with the weapon he is carrying. Proficiency with the revolver is not attained exclusively by the volume of ammunition used and the number of hours spent on the firing line. Supervised practice and the use of training aids and techniques help make the shooter. It is essential to have a good firing range where new officers are trained and older personnel practice in scheduled firearms sessions. The fundamental points to be stressed are grip, stance, breathing, sight alignment and trigger squeeze. Coordination of thought, vision, and motion must be achieved before the officer gains confidence in his shooting ability. Attaining this ability will make the student a better officer and enhance his value to the force.

14. A police officer will gain confidence in his shooting ability only after he has
    A. spent the required number of hours on the firing line
    B. been given sufficient supervised practice
    C. learned the five fundamental points
    D. learned to coordinate revolver movement with his sight and thought

15. Proper training in the use of firearms is one aspect of law enforcement which must be given serious consideration CHIEFLY because it is the
    A. most useful and essential single factor in the training of a police officer
    B. one phase of police officer training which stresses mental and physical coordination
    C. costliest aspect of police officer training involving considerable expense for the ammunition used in target practice
    D. most difficult part of police officer training, involving the expenditure of many hour on the firing line

Questions 16-20.

DIRECTIONS: Questions 16 through 20 are to be answered SOLELY on the basis of the following paragraph.

Lifting consists of transferring a print that has been dusted with powder to a transfer medium in order to preserve the print. Chemically developed prints cannot be lifted. Proper lifting of fingerprints is difficult and should be undertaken only when other means of recording the print are neither available nor suitable. Lifting should not be attempted from a porous surface. There are two types of commercial lifting tape which are good transfer mediums: rubber adhesive lift, one side of which is gummed and covered with thin, transparent celluloid; and transparent lifting tape, made of cellophane, one side of which is gummed. A package of acetate covers, frosted on one side and used to cover and protect the lifted print, accompanies each roll. If commercial tape is not available, transparent scotch tape may be used. The investigator should remove the celluloid or acetate cover from the lifting tape; smooth the tape, gummy side down, firmly and evenly over the entire print; gently peel the tape off the surface; replace the cover; and attach pertinent identifying data to the tape. All parts of the print should come in contact with the tape; air pockets should be avoided. The print will adhere to the lifting tape. The cover permits the print to be viewed and protects it from damage. Transparent lifting tape does not reverse the print. If a rubber adhesive lift is utilized, the print is reversed. Before a direct comparison can be made, the lifted print must be photographed, the negative reversed and a positive made.

16. An investigator wishing to preserve a record of fingerprints on a highly porous surface should
    A. develop them chemically before attempting to lift them
    B. lift them with scotch tape only when no other means of recording the prints are available
    C. employ some method other than lifting
    D. dust them with powder before attempting to lift them with rubber adhesive lift

17. Disregarding all other considerations, the SIMPLEST process to use in lifting a fingerprint from a window pane is that involving the use of
    A. rubber adhesive lift, because it gives a positive print in one step
    B. dusting powder and a camera, because the photograph is less likely to break than the window pane
    C. a chemical process, because it both develops and preserves the print at the same time
    D. transparent lifting tape, because it does not reverse the print

18. When a piece of commercial lifting tape is being used by an investigator wishing to lift a clear fingerprint from a smoothly-finished metal safe-door, he should
    A. prevent the ends of the tape from getting stuck to the metal surface because of the danger of forming air-pockets and thus damaging the print
    B. make certain that the tape covers all parts of the print and no air-pocket are formed
    C. carefully roll the tape over the most significant parts of the print only to avoid forming air-pockets
    D. be especially cautious not to destroy the air-pockets since this would tend to blur the print

19. When fingerprints lifted from an object found at the scene of a crime are to be compared with the fingerprints of a suspect, the lifted print
    A. can be compared directly only if a rubber adhesive lift was used
    B. cannot be compared directly if transparent scotch tape was used
    C. can be compared directly if transparent scotch tape was used
    D. must be photographed first and a positive made if any commercial lifting tape was used

20. When a rubber adhesive lift is to be used to lift a fingerprint, the one of the following which must be gently peeled off FIRST is the
    A. acetate cover                B. celluloid strip
    C. dusted surface               D. tape off the print surface

## KEY (CORRECT ANSWERS)

| | | | |
|---|---|---|---|
| 1. | B | 11. | C |
| 2. | D | 12. | A |
| 3. | C | 13. | B |
| 4. | C | 14. | D |
| 5. | D | 15. | A |
| 6. | C | 16. | C |
| 7. | D | 17. | D |
| 8. | D | 18. | B |
| 9. | C | 19. | C |
| 10. | C | 20. | B |

# READING COMPREHENSION
## UNDERSTANDING AND INTERPRETING WRITTEN MATERIAL
# EXAMINATION SECTION
# TEST 1

DIRECTIONS: Each question or incomplete statement is followed by several suggested answers or completions. Select the one that BEST answers the question or completes the statement. *PRINT THE LETTER OF THE CORRECT ANSWER IN THE SPACE AT THE RIGHT.*

Questions 1-4.

DIRECTIONS: Questions 1 through 4 are to be answered SOLELY on the basis of the information given in the paragraph below.

Abandoned cars – with tires gone, chrome stripped away, and windows smashed – have become a common sight on the city's streets. In 2000, more than 72,000 were deposited at curbs by owners who never came back, an increase of 15,000 from the year before and more than 30 times the number abandoned a decade ago. In January 2001, the city Environmental Protection Administrator asked the State Legislature to pass a law requiring a buyer of a new automobile to deposit $100 and an owner of an automobile at the time the law takes effect to deposit $50 with the State Department of Motor Vehicles. In return, they would be given a certificate of deposit which would be passed on to each succeeding owner. The final owner would get the deposit money back if he could present proof that he has disposed of his car *in an environmentally acceptable manner.* The Legislature has given no indication that it plans to rush ahead on the matter.

1. The number of cars abandoned in the city streets in 1990 was MOST NEARLY

    A. 2,500  B. 12,000  C. 27,500  D. 57,000

2. The proposed law would require a person who owned a car bought before the law was passed to deposit

    A. $100 with the State Department of Motor Vehicles
    B. $50 with the Environmental Protection Administration
    C. $100 with the State Legislature
    D. $50 with the State Department of Motor Vehicles

3. The proposed law would require the State to return the deposit money ONLY when the

    A. original owner of the car shows proof that he sold it
    B. last owner of the car shows proof that he got rid of the car in a satisfactory way
    C. owner of a car shows proof that he has transferred the certificate of deposit to the next owner
    D. last owner of a car returns the certificate of deposit

2 (#1)

4. The MAIN idea or theme of the above article is that 4.____

   A. a proposed new law would make it necessary for car owners in the State to pay additional taxes
   B. the State Legislature is against a proposed law to require deposits from automobile owners to prevent them from abandoning their cars
   C. the city is trying to find a solution for the increasing number of cars abandoned on its streets
   D. to pay for the removal of abandoned cars the city's Environmental Protection Administrator has asked the State to fine automobile owners who abandon their vehicles

Questions 5-7.

DIRECTIONS: Questions 5 through 7 are to be answered SOLELY on the basis of the information given in the paragraph below.

The regulations applying to parking meters provide that the driver is required to deposit the appropriate coin immediately upon parking and it is illegal for him to return at a later period to extend the parking time. If there is unused time on a parking meter, another car may be parked for a period not to exceed the unused time without the deposit of a coin. Operators of commercial vehicles are not required to deposit coins while loading or unloading expeditiously. By definition, a vehicle is considered parked even though there is a driver at the wheel and the meter must be used by the driver of such car.

5. According to the above paragraph, the regulations applying to parking meters do NOT 5.____

   A. allow the driver of a parked vehicle to stay in his car
   B. consider any loading or unloading of a vehicle as parking
   C. make any distinction between an unoccupied car and one with the driver at the wheel
   D. permit a driver who has parked a car at a meter with unused parking time to put a coin in the meter

6. According to the above paragraph, it is a violation of the parking meter regulations to 6.____

   A. load and unload slowly
   B. park commercial vehicles except for loading and unloading
   C. put a second coin in the meter in order to park longer
   D. use a parking space at any time without depositing a coin

7. The above paragraph CLEARLY indicates 7.____

   A. the number of minutes a vehicle may be parked
   B. the value of the coin that is to be put in the meter
   C. what is meant by a commercial vehicle
   D. when a car may be parked free

Questions 8-13.

DIRECTIONS: Questions 8 through 13 are to be answered on the basis of the information given in the paragraph below.

There are many types of reports. One of these is the field report, which requests information specified and grouped under columns or headings. A detailed, printed form is often used in submitting field reports. However, these printed, standardized forms provide a limited amount of space. The field man is required to make the decision as to how much of the information he has should go directly into the report and how much should be left for clarification if and when he is called in to explain a reported finding. In many instances, the addition of a short explanation of the finding might relieve the reader of the report of the necessity to seek an explanation. Therefore, the basic factual information asked for by the printed report form should often be clarified by some simple explanatory statement. If this is done, the reported finding becomes meaningful to the reader of the report who is far from the scene of the subject matter dealt with in the report. The significance of that which is reported finds its expression in the adoption of certain policies, improvements, or additions essential to furthering the effectiveness of the program.

8. According to the above paragraph, the field report asks for

   A. a detailed statement of the facts
   B. field information which comes under the heading of technical data
   C. replies to well-planned questions
   D. specific information in different columns

9. According to the above paragraph, the usual printed field report form

   A. does not have much room for writing
   B. is carefully laid out
   C. is necessary for the collection of facts
   D. usually has from three to four columns

10. According to the above paragraph, the man in the field MUST decide if

    A. a report is needed at all
    B. he should be called in to explain a reported finding
    C. he should put all the information he has into the report
    D. the reader of the report is justified in seeking an explanation

11. According to the above paragraph, the man in the field may be required to

    A. be acquainted with the person or persons who will read his report
    B. explain the information he reports
    C. give advice on specific problems
    D. keep records of the amount of work he completes

12. According to the above paragraph, the value of an explanatory statement added to the factual information reported in the printed forms is that it

    A. allows the person making the report to express himself briefly
    B. forces the person making the report to think logically
    C. helps the report reader understand the facts reported
    D. makes it possible to turn in the report later

13. According to the above paragraph, the importance of the information given by the field man in his report is shown by the

    A. adoption of policies and improvements
    B. effectiveness of the field staff
    C. fact that such a report is required
    D. necessary cost studies to back up the facts

13.\_\_\_\_

Questions 14-15.

DIRECTIONS: Questions 14 and 15 are to be answered on the basis of the information contained in the following paragraph.

    The driver of the collection crew shall at all times remain in or on a department vehicle in which there is revenue. In the event such driver must leave the vehicle, he shall designate one of the other members of the crew to remain in or on the vehicle. The member of the crew so designated by the driver shall remain in or on the vehicle until relieved by the driver or another member of the crew. The vehicle may be left unattended only when there is no revenue contained therein provided, however, that in that event the vehicle shall be locked. The loss of any vehicle or any of its contents, including revenue, resulting from any deviation from this rule, shall be the responsibility of the member or members of crew who shall be guilty of such deviation.

14. The vehicle of a collection crew may be left with no one in it only if

    A. it is locked
    B. there is a crew member nearby
    C. there is no money in it
    D. there is only one member in the crew

14.\_\_\_\_

15. If money is stolen from an unattended vehicle of a collection crew, the employee held responsible is the

    A. driver
    B. one who left the vehicle unattended
    C. one who left the vehicle unlocked
    D. one who relieved the driver

15.\_\_\_\_

Questions 16-18.

DIRECTIONS: Questions 16 through 18 are to be answered SOLELY on the basis of the information given in the paragraph below.

    Safety belts provide protection for the passengers of a vehicle by preventing them from crashing around inside if the vehicle is involved in a collision. They operate on the principle similar to that used in the packaging of fragile items. You become a part of the vehicle package, and you are kept from being tossed about inside if the vehicle is suddenly decelerated. Many injury-causing collisions at low speeds, for example at city intersections, could have been injury-free if the occupants had fastened their safety belts. There is a double advantage to the driver in that it not only protects him from harm, but prevents him from being yanked away from the wheel, thereby permitting him to maintain control of the car.

16. The principle on which seat belts work is that  16._____

    A. a car and its driver and passengers are fragile
    B. a person fastened to the car will not be thrown around when the car slows down suddenly
    C. the driver and passengers of a car that is suddenly decelerated will be thrown forward
    D. the driver and passengers of an automobile should be packaged the way fragile items are packaged

17. We can assume from the above passage that safety belts should be worn at all times because you can never tell when  17._____

    A. a car will be forced to turn off onto another road
    B. it will be necessary to shift into low gear to go up a hill
    C. you will have to speed up to pass another car
    D. a car may have to come to a sudden stop

18. Besides preventing injury, an ADDITIONAL benefit from the use of safety belts is that  18._____

    A. collisions are fewer
    B. damage to the car is kept down
    C. the car can be kept under control
    D. the number of accidents at city intersections is reduced

Questions 19-24.

DIRECTIONS: Questions 19 through 24 are to be answered on the basis of the following reading passage covering Procedures For Patrol.

### PROCEDURES FOR PATROL

The primary function of all Parking Enforcement Agents assigned to patrol duty shall be to patrol assigned areas and issue summonses to violators of various sections of the City Traffic Regulations, which sections govern the parking or operation of vehicles. Parking Enforcement Agents occasionally may be called upon to distribute educational pamphlets and perform other work, at the discretion of the Bureau Chief.

Each Agent on patrol duty will be assigned a certain area (or areas) to be patrolled. These areas will be assigned during the daily roll call. Walking Cards will describe the street locations of the patrol and the manner in which the patrol is to be walked.

A Traffic Department vehicle will be provided for daily patrol assignments when necessary.

Each Agent shall accomplish an assigned field patrol in the following manner:

a. Start each patrol at the location specified on the daily patrol sheet, and proceed as per walking instructions.
b. Approach each metered space being utilized (each metered space in which a vehicle is parked). If the meter shows the expired flag, the member of the force shall prepare and affix a summons to the vehicle parked at meter.

c. Any vehicle in violation of any regulation governing the parking, standing, stopping, or movement of vehicles will be issued a summons.
d. No summons will be issued to a vehicle displaying an authorized vehicle identification plate of the Police Department unless the vehicle is parked in violation of the No Standing, No Stopping, Hydrant, Bus Stop, or Double Parking Regulations. Identification plates for Police Department automobiles are made of plastic and are of rectangular shape, 10 3/4" long, 3 3/4" high, black letters and numerals on a white background. The words *POLICE DEPT.* are printed on the face with the identification number. Identification plates for private automobiles are the same size and shape as those used on Police Department automobiles.

An Agent on patrol, when observing a person *feeding* a street meter (placing an additional coin in a meter so as to leave the vehicle parked for an additional period) shall prepare and affix a summons to the vehicle.

An Agent on patrol shall note on a computer card each missing or defective, out of order, or otherwise damaged meter.

19. Of the following, the work which the Parking Enforcement Agent performs MOST often is

    A. issuing summonses for parking violations
    B. distributing educational pamphlets
    C. assisting the Bureau Chief
    D. driving a city vehicle

20. The area to be covered by a Parking Enforcement Agent on patrol is

    A. determined by the Police Department
    B. regulated by the city Traffic Regulations
    C. marked off with red flags
    D. described on Walking Cards

21. A Parking Enforcement Agent reports a broken meter by

    A. issuing a summons
    B. making a mark on a computer card
    C. raising the flag on the broken meter
    D. attending a daily roll call

22. With respect to the use of an automobile for patrol duty,

    A. Parking Enforcement Agents must supply their own cars for patrol
    B. automobiles for patrol will be supplied by the Police Department
    C. Parking Enforcement Agents are permitted to park in a bus stop
    D. department vehicles will be provided when required for patrol

23. Parking Enforcement Agents sometimes issue summonses to drivers for *feeding* a street meter in violation of parking regulations.
    Which one of the following situations describes such a violation?
    A driver

    A. has moved from one metered space to another
    B. has parked next to a Police Department No Standing sign
    C. is parked by a meter which shows 30 minutes time still remaining
    D. has used a coin to reset the meter after his first time period expired

24. Vehicles displaying an authorized vehicle identification plate of the Police Department are allowed to park at expired meters.
Which one of the following statements describes the proper size of identification plates for private automobiles used for police work?
They

   A. are 10 3/4" long and 3 3/4" high
   B. have white letters and numerals on a black background
   C. are 3 3/4" long and 10 3/4" high
   D. have black letters and numerals on a white background

24.____

Questions 25-30.

DIRECTIONS: Questions 25 through 30 are to be answered on the basis of the following reading passage covering the Operation of Department Motor Vehicles.

## OPERATION OF DEPARTMENT MOTOR VEHICLES

When operating a Traffic Department motor vehicle, a member of the force must show every courtesy to other drivers, obey all traffic signs and traffic regulations, obey all other lawful authority, and handle the vehicle in a manner which will foster safety practices in others and create a favorable impression of the Bureau, the Department, and the City. The operator and passengers MUST use the safety belts.

### Driving Rules

   a. DO NOT operate a mechanically defective vehicle.
   DO NOT race engine on starting.
   DO NOT tamper with mechanical equipment.
   DO NOT run engine if there is an indication of low engine oil pressure, overheating, or no transmission oil.

   b. When parking on highway, all safety precautions must be observed.

   c. When parking in a garage or parking field, observe a maximum speed of 5 miles per hour. Place shift lever in park or neutral position, effectively apply hand brake, then shut off all ignition and light switches to prevent excess battery drain, and close all windows.

### Reporting Defects

   a. Report all observed defects on Drivers' Vehicle Defect Card and on Monthly Vehicle Report Form 49 in sufficient detail so a mechanic can easily locate the source of trouble.
   b. Enter vehicle road service calls and actual time of occurrence on Monthly Vehicle Report.

### Reporting Accidents

Promptly report all facts of each accident as follows: For serious accidents, including those involving personal injury, call your supervisor as soon as possible. Give all the appropriate information about the accident to your supervisor. Record vehicle registration information, including the name of the registered owner, the state, year, and serial number, and the classification marking on the license plates. Also record the operator's license number and other identifying information, and, if it applies, the injured person's age and sex. Give a full description of how the accident happened, and what happened following the accident, including the vehicles in collision, witnesses, police badge number, hospital, condition of road surface, time of day, weather conditions, location (near, far, center of intersection), and damage.

### Repairs to Automobiles

When a Department motor vehicle requires repairs that cannot be made by the operator, or requires replacement of parts or accessories (including tires and tubes), or requires towing, the operator shall notify the District Commander.

When a Departmental motor vehicle is placed out of service for repairs, the Regional Commander shall assign another vehicle, if available.

### Daily Operator's Report

The operator of a Department automobile shall keep a daily maintenance record of the vehicle, and note any unusual occurrences, on the Daily Operator's Report.

25. Parking Enforcement Agents who are assigned to operate Department motor vehicles on patrol are expected to

    A. disregard the posted speed limits to save time
    B. remove their seat belts on short trips
    C. show courtesy to other drivers on the road
    D. take the right of way at all intersections

26. The driver of a Department motor vehicle should

    A. leave the windows open when parking the vehicle in a garage
    B. drive the vehicle at approximately 10 miles per hour in a parking field
    C. be alert for indication of low engine oil pressure and overheated engine
    D. start a cold vehicle by racing the engine for 5 minutes

27. The reason that all defects on a Department vehicle that have been observed by its driver should be noted on a Monthly Vehicle Report Form 49 is:

    A. This action will foster better safety practices among other Agents
    B. The source of the defect may be located easily by a trained mechanic
    C. All the facts of an accident will be reported promptly
    D. The District Commander will not have to make road calls

28. If the driver of a Department vehicle is involved in an accident, an Accident Report should be made out. This Report should include a full description of how the accident happened.
    Which of the following statements would PROPERLY belong in an Accident Report?

    A. The accident occurred at the intersection of Broadway and 42nd Street.
    B. The operator of the Department motor vehicle replaced the windshield wiper.
    C. The vehicle was checked for gas and water before the patrol began.
    D. A bus passed two parked vehicles.

29. When a Department vehicle is disabled, whom should the operator notify?
    The

    A. Traffic Department garage
    B. Assistant Bureau Chief
    C. Police Department
    D. District Commander

30. The PROPER way for an operator of a Department vehicle to report unusual occurrences with respect to the operation of the vehicle is to

    A. follow the same procedures as for reporting a defect
    B. request the Regional Commander to assign another vehicle
    C. phone the Bureau Chief as soon as possible
    D. make a note of the circumstances on the Daily Operator's Report

## KEY (CORRECT ANSWERS)

| | | | |
|---|---|---|---|
| 1. | A | 16. | B |
| 2. | D | 17. | D |
| 3. | B | 18. | C |
| 4. | C | 19. | A |
| 5. | C | 20. | D |
| 6. | C | 21. | B |
| 7. | D | 22. | D |
| 8. | D | 23. | D |
| 9. | A | 24. | A |
| 10. | C | 25. | C |
| 11. | B | 26. | C |
| 12. | C | 27. | B |
| 13. | A | 28. | A |
| 14. | C | 29. | D |
| 15. | B | 30. | D |

# TEST 2

DIRECTIONS: Each question or incomplete statement is followed by several suggested answers or completions. Select the one that BEST answers the question or completes the statement. *PRINT THE LETTER OF THE CORRECT ANSWER IN THE SPACE AT THE RIGHT.*

Questions 1-4.

DIRECTIONS: Questions 1 through 4 are to be answered SOLELY on the basis of the information contained in the following passage.

Of those arrested in the city in 2003 for felonies or misdemeanors, only 32% were found guilty of any charge. Fifty-six percent of such arrestees were acquitted or had their cases dismissed. 11% failed to appear for trial, and 1% received other dispositions. Of those found guilty, only 7.4% received any sentences of over one year in jail. Only 50% of those found guilty were sentenced to any further time in jail. When considered with the low probability of arrests for most crimes, these figures make it clear that the crime control system in the city poses little threat to the average criminal. Delay compounds the problem. The average case took four appearances for disposition after arraignment. Twenty percent of all cases took eight or more appearances to reach a disposition. Forty-four percent of all cases took more than one year to disposition.

1. According to the above passage, crime statistics for 2003 indicate that   1._____

    A. there is a low probability of arrests for all crimes in the city
    B. the average criminal has much to fear from the law in the city
    C. over 10% of arrestees in the city charged with felonies or misdemeanors did not show up for trial
    D. criminals in the city are less likely to be caught than criminals in the rest of the country

2. The percentage of those arrested in 2003 who received sentences of over one year in jail amounted to MOST NEARLY   2._____

    A. .237    B. 2.4    C. 23.7    D. 24.0

3. According to the above passage, the percentage of arrestees in 2003 who were found guilty was   3._____

    A. 20% of those arrested for misdemeanors
    B. 11% of those arrested for felonies
    C. 50% of those sentenced to further time in jail
    D. 32% of those arrested for felonies or misdemeanors

4. According to the above paragraph, the number of appearances after arraignment and before disposition amounted to   4._____

    A. an average of four
    B. eight or more in 44% of the cases
    C. over four for cases which took more than a year
    D. between four and eight for most cases

Questions 5-6.

DIRECTIONS: Questions 5 and 6 are to be answered on the basis of the following paragraph.

A person who, with the intent to deprive or defraud another of the use and benefit of property or to appropriate the same to the use of the taker, or of any other person other than the true owner, wrongfully takes, obtains or withholds, by any means whatever, from the possession of the true owner or of any other person any money, personal property, thing in action, evidence of debt or contract, or article of value of any kind, steals such property and is guilty of larceny.

5. This definition from the Penal Law has NO application to the act of      5._____

    A. fraudulent conversion by a vendor of city sales tax money collected from purchasers
    B. refusing to give proper change after a purchaser has paid for an article in cash
    C. receiving property stolen from the rightful owner
    D. embezzling money from the rightful owner

6. According to the above paragraph, an auto mechanic who claimed to have a lien on an automobile for completed repairs and refused to surrender possession until the bill was paid      6._____

    A. *cannot* be charged with larceny because his repairs increased the value of the car
    B. *can* be charged with larceny because such actual possession can be construed to include intent to deprive the owner of use of the car
    C. *cannot* be charged with larceny because the withholding is temporary and such possession is not an evidence of debt
    D. *cannot* be charged with larceny because intent to defraud is lacking

Questions 7-12.

DIRECTIONS: Questions 7 through 12 are to be answered on the basis of the information given in the passage below. Assume that all questions refer to the same state described in the passage.

The courts and the police consider an *offense* as any conduct that is punishable by a fine or imprisonment. Such offenses include many kinds of acts—from behavior that is merely annoying, like throwing a noisy party that keeps everyone awake, all the way up to violent acts like murder. The law classifies offenses according to the penalties that are provided for them. In one state, minor offenses are called *violations*. A violation is punishable by a fine of not more than $250 or imprisonment of not more than 15 days, or both. The annoying behavior mentioned above is an example of a violation. More serious offenses are classified as *crimes*. Crimes are classified by the kind of penalty that is provided. A *misdemeanor* is a crime that is punishable by a fine of not more than $1,000 or by imprisonment of not more than 1 year, or both. Examples of misdemeanors include stealing something with a value of $100 or less, turning in a false alarm, or illegally possessing less than 1/8 of an ounce of a dangerous drug. A *felony* is a criminal offense punishable by imprisonment of more than 1 year. Murder is clearly a felony.

7. According to the above passage, any act that is punishable by imprisonment or by a fine is called a(n)  7._____

   A. offense  B. violation  C. crime  D. felony

8. According to the above passage, which of the following is classified as a crime?  8._____

   A. Offense punishable by 15 days imprisonment
   B. Minor offense
   C. Violation
   D. Misdemeanor

9. According to the above passage, if a person guilty of burglary can receive a prison sentence of 7 years or more, burglary would be classified as a  9._____

   A. violation  B. misdemeanor
   C. felony  D. violent act

10. According to the above passage, two offenses that would BOTH be classified as misdemeanors are  10._____

    A. making unreasonable noise, and stealing a $90 bicycle
    B. stealing a $75 radio, and possessing 1/16 of an ounce of heroin
    C. holding up a bank, and possessing 1/4 of a pound of marijuana
    D. falsely reporting a fire, and illegally double-parking

11. The above passage says that offenses are classified according to the penalties provided for them.  11._____
    On the basis of clues in the passage, who probably decides what the maximum penalties should be for the different kinds of offenses?

    A. The State lawmakers  B. The City police
    C. The Mayor  D. Officials in Washington, D.C.

12. Of the following, which BEST describes the subject matter of the passage?  12._____

    A. How society deals with criminals
    B. How offenses are classified
    C. Three types of criminal behavior
    D. The police approach to offenders

Questions 13-20.

DIRECTIONS: Questions 13 through 20 are to be answered SOLELY on the basis of the following passage.

Auto theft is prevalent and costly. In 2005, 486,000 autos valued at over $500 million were stolen. About 28 percent of the inhabitants of Federal prisons are there as a result of conviction of interstate auto theft under the Dyer Act. In California alone, auto thefts cost the criminal justice system approximately $60 million yearly.

The great majority of auto theft is for temporary use rather than resale, as evidenced by the fact that 88 percent of autos stolen in 2005 were recovered. In Los Angeles, 64 percent of stolen autos that were recovered were found within two days, and about 80 percent within a week. Chicago reports that 71 percent of the recovered autos were found within four miles of the point of theft. The FBI estimates that 8 percent of stolen cars are taken for the purpose of stripping them for parts, 12 percent for resale, and 5 percent for use in another crime. Auto thefts are primarily juvenile acts. Although only 21 percent of all arrests for nontraffic offenses in 2005 were of individuals under 18 years of age, 63 percent of auto theft arrests were of persons under 18. Auto theft represents the start of many criminal careers; in an FBI sample of juvenile auto theft offenders, 41 percent had no prior arrest record.

13. In the above passage, the discussion of the reasons for auto theft does NOT include the percent of

    A. autos stolen by prior offenders
    B. recovered stolen autos found close to the point of theft
    C. stolen autos recovered within a week
    D. stolen autos which were recovered

14. Assuming the figures in the above passage remain constant, you may logically estimate the cost of auto thefts to the California criminal justice system over a five-year period beginning in 2005 to have been about _____ million.

    A. $200   B. $300   C. $440   D. $500

15. According to the above passage, the percent of stolen autos in Los Angeles which were not recovered within a week was _____ percent.

    A. 12   B. 20   C. 29   D. 36

16. According to the above passage, MOST auto thefts are committed by

    A. former inmates of Federal prisons   B. juveniles
    C. persons with a prior arrest record   D. residents of large cities

17. According to the above passage, MOST autos are stolen for

    A. resale                B. stripping of parts
    C. temporary use         D. use in another crime

18. According to the above passage, the percent of persons arrested for auto theft who were under 18

    A. equals nearly the same percent of stolen autos which were recovered
    B. equals nearly two-thirds of the total number of persons arrested for nontraffic offenses
    C. is the same as the percent of persons arrested for nontraffic offenses who were under 18
    D. is three times the percent of persons arrested for nontraffic offenses who were under 18

19. An APPROPRIATE title for the above passage is

    A. HOW CRIMINAL CAREERS BEGIN
    B. RECOVERY OF STOLEN CARS
    C. SOME STATISTICS ON AUTO THEFT
    D. THE COSTS OF AUTO THEFT

20. Based on the above passage, the number of cars taken for use in another crime in 2005 was

 A. 24,300   B. 38,880   C. 48,600   D. 58,320

Questions 21-22.

DIRECTIONS: Questions 21 and 22 are to be answered SOLELY on the basis of the following paragraph.

If the second or third felony is such that, upon a first conviction, the offender would be punishable by imprisonment for any term less than his natural life, then such person must be sentenced to imprisonment for an indeterminate term, the minimum of which shall be not less than one-half of the longest term prescribed upon a first conviction, and the maximum of which shall be not longer than twice such longest term, provided, however, that the minimum sentence imposed hereunder upon such second or third felony offender shall in no case be less than five years; except that where the maximum punishment for a second or third felony offender hereunder is five years or less, the minimum sentence must be not less than two years.

21. According to the above paragraph, a person who has a second felony conviction shall receive as a sentence for that second felony an indeterminate term

 A. not less than twice the minimum term prescribed upon a first conviction as a maximum
 B. not less than one-half the maximum term of his first conviction as a minimum
 C. not more than twice the minimum term prescribed upon a first conviction as a minimum
 D. with a maximum of not more than twice the longest term prescribed for a first conviction for this crime

22. According to the above paragraph, if the term for this crime for a first offender is up to three years, the possible indeterminate term for this crime as a second or third felony shall have a _____ of not _____ than _____ years.

 A. minimum; less; five
 B. maximum; more; five
 C. minimum; less; one and one-half
 D. maximum; less; six

23. A statute states: *A person who steals an article worth $1,000 or less where no aggravating circumstances accompany the act is guilty of petit larceny. If the article is worth more than $1,000, it may be grand larceny.*
 If all you know is that Edward Smith stole an article worth $1,000, it may reasonably be said that

 A. Smith is guilty of petit larceny
 B. Smith is guilty of grand larceny
 C. Smith is guilty of neither petit larceny nor grand larceny
 D. precisely what charge will be placed against Smith is uncertain

Questions 24-25.

DIRECTIONS: Questions 24 and 25 are to be answered on the basis of the following section of a law.

A person who, after having been three times convicted within this state of felonies or attempts to commit felonies, or under the law of any other state, government, or country, of crimes which if committed within this state would be felonious, commits a felony, other than murder, first or second degree, or treason, within this state, shall be sentenced upon conviction of such fourth, or subsequent, offense to imprisonment in a state prison for an indeterminate term the minimum of which shall be not less than the maximum term provided for first offenders for the crime for which the individual has been convicted, but, in any event, the minimum term upon conviction for a felony as the fourth or subsequent, offense shall be not less than fifteen years, and the maximum thereof shall be his natural life.

24. Under the terms of the above law, a person must receive the increased punishment therein provided if

   A. he is convicted of a felony and has been three times previously convicted of felonies
   B. he has been three times previously convicted of felonies, regardless of the nature of his present conviction
   C. his fourth conviction is for murder, first or second degree, or treason
   D. he has previously been convicted three times of murder, first or second degree, or treason

25. Under the terms of the above law, a person convicted of a felony for which the penalty is imprisonment for a term not to exceed ten years, and who has been three times previously convicted of felonies in this state, shall be sentenced to a term, the MINIMUM of which shall be

   A. 10 years           B. 15 years
   C. indeterminate      D. his natural life

7 (#2)

# KEY (CORRECT ANSWERS)

1. C
2. B
3. D
4. A
5. C

6. D
7. A
8. D
9. C
10. B

11. A
12. B
13. A
14. B
15. B

16. B
17. C
18. D
19. C
20. A

21. D
22. C
23. D
24. A
25. B

---

# READING COMPREHENSION
## UNDERSTANDING AND INTERPRETING WRITTEN MATERIAL

## EXAMINATION SECTION
## TEST 1

DIRECTIONS: Each question or incomplete statement is followed bpy several suggested answers or completions. Select the one that BEST answers the question or completes the statement. *PRINT THE LETTER OF THE CORRECT ANSWER IN THE SPACE AT THE RIGHT.*

Questions 1-4.

DIRECTIONS: Questions 1 through 4 are to be answered on the basis of the following passage.

It should be emphasized that one goal of law enforcement is the reduction of stress between one population group and another. When no stress exists between populations, law enforcement can deal with other tensions or simply perform traditional police functions. However, when stress between populations does exist, law enforcement, in its efforts to prevent disruptive behavior, becomes committed to reducing that stress (if for no other reason than its responsibility to maintain an orderly environment). The type of stress to be reduced, unlike the tension stemming from social change, is stress generated through intergroup and interracial friction. Of course, all sources of tension are inextricably interrelated, but friction between different populations in the community is of immediate concern to law enforcement.

1. The above passage emphasizes that, during times of stress between groups in the community, it is necessary for the police to attempt to

    A. continue their traditional duties
    B. eliminate tension resulting from social change
    C. reduce intergroup stress
    D. punish disruptive behavior

1.____

2. Based on the above passage, police concern with tension among groups in a community is MOST likely to stem primarily from their desire to

    A. establish racial justice
    B. prevent violence
    C. protect property
    D. unite the diverse groups

2.____

3. According to the above passage, enforcers of the law are responsible for

    A. analyzing consequences of population-group hostility
    B. assisting social work activities
    C. creating order in the environment
    D. explaining group behavior

3.____

4. The factor which produces the tension accompanying social change is 4._____

   A. a disorderly environment
   B. disruptive behavior
   C. inter-community hostility
   D. not discussed in the above passage

Questions 5-7.

DIRECTIONS: Questions 5 through 7 are to be answered SOLELY on the basis of the following paragraphs.

Perhaps the most difficult administrative problem of the police records unit is the maintenance of cooperative relationships with the operating units in the department. Unless these relationships are completely accepted by the operating units, some records activities will result in friction. The records system is a tool of the chief administrative officer and the various supervising officers in managing personnel, police operations, and procedures. However, the records unit must constantly check on the records activities of all members of the department if the records system is to serve as a really effective tool for these supervisory officers.

The first step in avoiding conflict between the records and the operating units is to develop definite policies and regulations governing the records system. These regulations should be prepared jointly by the head of the records unit and the heads of the operating units under the leadership of the chief administrative officer of the department. Once the records policies and regulations have been agreed upon, the task is to secure conformity. Theoretically, if a patrolman fails to prepare a report of an investigation, his commanding officer should be notified by the records unit and he, in turn, should take appropriate measures to secure the report. Practically, this line of command must be cut across in the case of such routine matters, or the commanding officer will spend time in keeping the records system going that should be devoted to the other police duties which comprise the major work of the department. However, if the patrolman is persistently negligent, or if a new policy or procedure is being initiated, the records unit must deal through the commanding officer.

5. According to the above passage, the one of the following situations in which the records unit would MOST likely contact a commanding officer of an operating unit is when 5._____

   A. a patrolman has expressed disagreement with a records unit policy and suggests a modification of the policy
   B. an important report, which involves more than one operating unit, has been carelessly prepared by a patrolman
   C. the commanding officer of the operating unit devotes little time to police duties which comprise the major work of the department
   D. the records unit has received orders from the chief administrative officer to institute several changes in previous records procedures

6. According to the above paragraph, obtaining agreement as to definite policies, and regulations governing the records system 6._____

   A. guarantees the avoidance of conflict between the records and operating divisions
   B. is of lesser importance than the maintenance of cooperative relationships thereafter

C. should precede any active records division efforts to gain compliance with such policies and regulations
D. should be preceded by an evaluation of the extent to which supervisory officers consider the system an effective management tool

7. According to the above passage, conflict between the records division and the operating divisions is MOST likely to result when the

   A. chief administrative officer denies to the records division the authority to check on the records activities of all members of the department
   B. operating divisions are not convinced that their work contacts with the records division are useful and desirable
   C. records division voluntarily attempts to establish productive relationships with operating divisions
   D. operating divisions understand the specific nature i of records division duties

7.____

Questions 8-10.

DIRECTIONS: Questions 8 through 10 are to be answered SOLELY on the basis of the following paragraph.

Early in the development of police service, legislators granted powers and authority to policemen beyond their inherent rights as citizens in order that they would be able to act effectively in the discharge of their duties. The law makers also recognized the fact that unless policemen were excused from complete obedience to certain laws and regulations, they would be seriously encumbered in the effective discharge of their duties. The exemptions were specifically provided for by legislative action because of the danger of abuse of power involved in granting blanket privileges and powers. The public, however, has not been so discriminating and has gone well beyond the law in excusing policemen from full obedience to regulatory measures. The liberal interpretation that the public has placed upon the right of police officers to disobey the law has been motivated in part by public confidence in law enforcement and in part by a sincere desire of the public to assist the police in every way in the performance of their duties. Further, the average citizen is not interested in the technicalities of law enforcement nor is he aware of the legal limitations that are placed upon the authority of policemen. It is a regrettable fact that many policemen assume so-called rights of law that either do not exist or that are subject to well-defined legal limitations, because the public generally is unaware of the limitations placed by law upon policemen.

8. According to the above paragraph, the one of the following statements which BEST explains the reason for granting special legal powers to policemen is that such powers are granted

   A. because the exercise of their inherent rights by citizens frequently conflicted with efficient law enforcement
   B. because the public has not been sufficiently vigilant in objecting to blanket grants of power
   C. in order to excuse policemen from full obedience to laws and regulations which they are unable to enforce
   D. in order to remove certain handicaps experienced by policemen in law enforcement operations

8.____

9. According to the above paragraph, specific legislative exemptions for policemen from complete obedience to certain laws and regulations

    A. are based largely on so-called rights of law that either do not exist or are misinterpreted by the public
    B. have not been abused by the police even though most individual policemen ignore proper legal limitations
    C. have not provided a fully effective limitation on the exercise of unwarranted police authority
    D. have been misunderstood by the police and the public partly because they are based on unduly technical laws

10. According to the above paragraph, the one of the following statements which BEST explains the liberal attitude of the public toward the special powers of policemen is that the public

    A. believes that the police are justified in disregarding the technicalities of law enforcement and also wants to assist the police in the performance of their duties
    B. feels that the laws restricting police authority are overly strict and also believes that the police are performing their duties in a proper manner
    C. is not aware of the legal restrictions on police authority and also believes that the police are performing their duties in a proper manner
    D. wants to assist the police in the performance of their duties and also feels that the laws on police authority are sufficiently restrictive

Questions 11-12.

DIRECTIONS: Questions 11 and 12 are to be answered SOLELY on the basis of the following paragraph.

The personal conduct of each member of the department is the primary factor in promoting desirable police-community relations. Tact, patience, and courtesy shall be strictly observed under all circumstances. A favorable public attitude toward the police must be earned; it is influenced by the personal conduct and attitude of each member of the force; by his personal integrity and courteous manner; by his respect for due process of law; by his devotion to the principles of justice, fairness, and impartiality.

11. According to the above paragraph, what is the BEST action an officer can take in dealing with people in a neighborhood?

    A. Assist neighborhood residents by doing favors for them
    B. Give special attention to the community leaders in order to be able to control them effectively
    C. Behave in an appropriate manner and give all community members the same just treatment
    D. Prepare a plan detailing what he, the officer, wants to do for the community and submit it for approval

12. As used in the above paragraph, the word impartiality means MOST NEARLY

    A. observant        B. unbiased
    C. righteousness    D. honesty

Questions 13-16.

DIRECTIONS: Questions 13 through 16 are to be answered on the basis of the information given in the following passage.

The public often believes that the main job of a uniformed officer is to enforce laws by simply arresting people. In reality, however, many of the situations that an officer deals with do not call for the use of his arrest power. In the first place, an officer spends much of his time preventing crimes from happening, by spotting potential violations or suspicious behavior and taking action to prevent illegal acts. In the second place, many of the situations in which officers are called on for assistance involve elements like personal arguments, husband-wife quarrels, noisy juveniles, or mentally disturbed persons. The majority of these problems do not result in arrests and convictions, and often they do not even involve illegal behavior. In the third place, even in situations where there seems to be good reason to make an arrest, an officer may have to exercise very good judgment. There are times when making an arrest too soon could touch off a riot, or could result in the detention of a minor offender while major offenders escaped, or could cut short the gathering of necessary on-the-scene evidence.

13. The above passage IMPLIES that most citizens

    A. will start to riot if they see an arrest being made
    B. appreciate the work that law enforcement officers do
    C. do not realize that making arrests is only a small part of law enforcement
    D. never call for assistance unless they are involved in a personal argument or a husband-wife quarrel

14. According to the above passage, one way in which law enforcement officers can prevent crimes for happening is by

    A. arresting suspicious characters
    B. letting minor offenders go free
    C. taking action on potential violations
    D. refusing to get involved in husband-wife fights

15. According to the above passage, which of the following statements is NOT true of situations involving mentally disturbed persons?

    A. It is a waste of time to call on law enforcement officers for assistance in such situations.
    B. Such situations may not involve illegal behavior.
    C. Such situations often do not result in arrests.
    D. Citizens often turn to law enforcement officers for help in such situations.

16. The last sentence in the passage mentions *detention of minor offenders.*
    Of the following, which BEST explains the meaning of the word *detention* as used here?

    A. Sentencing someone
    B. Indicting someone
    C. Calling someone before a grand jury
    D. Arresting someone

Questions 17-18.

DIRECTIONS: Questions 17 and 18 are to be answered SOLELY on the basis of the following paragraph.

In order that the police officer can function in a role that is outside the area of his personal prejudices, it is necessary to develop in him a real sense of professionalism. Policing is increasingly recognized as requiring a high degree of technical knowledge and skill. This, however, is only one mark of a profession. Another is the increasing emphasis upon public duty and service to the community. The time has long passed in enlightened police circles when a man became an officer of the law by merely donning a uniform and flashing a star. Training, dedication, and understanding are the cornerstones of modern police science. The police officer must become increasingly aware of the role he plays as a symbol of society's authority - aware that only by examining the relation of his personal sentiments and feelings to his public duties can he achieve true impartiality and neutrality. This is an educational problem in its own right, and it is equal in importance to the acquisition of new information as to the technicalities of crime detection.

17. According to the above paragraph, 17.____

   A. the achievement of true neutrality in law enforcement is the most important problem facing the police officer
   B. the emphasis on community service is one of the characteristics of a profession that is being increasingly stressed as a part of police work
   C. the emphasis on the technicalities of crime detection is improper if it detracts from the need of the police to be a symbol of society's authority
   D. technical training is an area of police work which has always received recognition as an important aspect of police science

18. According to the above paragraph, 18.____

   A. a consideration of the distinguishing characteristics of other professions leads to the conclusion that police work is not a profession
   B. concern for impartiality in law enforcement has always characterized police administration
   C. the absence of personal prejudice in a police officer determines his effectiveness
   D. the police officer should aim to achieve impartiality by examining his personal sentiments and prejudices, since he serves as a symbol of society's authority

Questions 19-22.

DIRECTIONS: Questions 19 through 22 are to be answered on the basis of the following paragraph.

During actual pursuit of a traffic offender and particularly in speed cases when the operator of the police vehicle is maneuvering for clocking, there is a need for haste so that the clocking may be applied when the motorist is traveling in violation of the speed laws. However, necessary haste cannot include rashness. The pursuit, for whatever purpose, must not be at the expense of the safety of other users of the road. When changing lanes to get ahead, the police operator must do it safely or not at all. Giving proper and clear signals as to his intentions is a must but should not be construed as a guarantee of completing the maneuver safely. He must use good judgment in determining whether his *S* pass can be made safely. If there is a possibility that the motorist to be passed would be forced to apply his brakes to avoid a collision, the passing should be delayed. Instead, he should be notified by hand signal of the police vehicle operator's intention to pass and directed to reduce speed so that the police vehicle can be driven past safely. In other than emergencies, sudden stops should be avoided. In a situation where law enforcement needs require a sudden reduction in speed, consideration must be given to the vehicles behind to preclude rear-end collisions. A gradual reduction in speed, coupled with a sufficient warning to convey the intention to stop or turn is the preferential course of action. Similarly, if at all possible, the police operator should avoid turning at locations that are clearly unfavorable for turning, such as through safety zones or between stanchions placed to prohibit passage, since such maneuvers increase the probability of an accident.

19. The one of the following which MOST adequately describes the central theme of the paragraph is the _____ motorized traffic offenders.

    A. essentiality of maintaining maximum speed during the pursuit of
    B. danger of passing intervening vehicles while pursuing
    C. precautions to take in the pursuit of
    D. methods of attaining greater speed while pursuing

20. According to the above paragraph, when the operator of a police vehicle is pursuing an offender in the same lane, and approaches another vehicle which is between him and the offender's vehicle, it would be MOST correct to state that the operator of the police vehicle

    A. may attempt to by-pass the vehicle between him and the offender with complete safety so long as he has given proper and clear automatic and hand signals to its operator
    B. may attempt to by-pass the vehicle between him and the offender even if it would be necessary for him to make an *S* pass to do so
    C. must not attempt to by-pass the vehicle between him and the offender until he has directed its operator to reduce speed
    D. must not attempt to by-pass the vehicle between him and the offender unless he can do so safely without leaving the lane

21. According to the above paragraph, when the operator of a police vehicle notices a motorist driving along and suspects that the motorist may have just violated some traffic law, he MAY

    A. not exceed the posted speed limit except when he is attempting to get into position to clock the offender's speed
    B. travel at whatever speed he deems necessary in order to catch up with and clock the speeding suspect but only as long as both remain in the same lane and the lane remains clear
    C. not exceed the posted speed limit unless he feels certain that the offender has exceeded or can be reasonably expected to exceed the posted speed limit
    D. exceed the posted speed limit in order to apprehend the violator but must never do so if there is any possibility of danger to anyone else using the road

22. A police vehicle is in pursuit of a motorized traffic offender who is attempting to evade capture by alternating between weaving in and out of slower-moving traffic, making sudden stops, and going through safety zones or stanchions placed to prohibit passage.
According to the above paragraph, the operator in pursuit should GENERALLY

    A. follow right behind the offender through all these maneuvers but keep alert for sudden changes in tactics
    B. avoid engaging in such of these maneuvers as he can without increasing the distance between him and the offender
    C. refrain from engaging in driving maneuvers similar to the offender's without duly considering the inherent dangers
    D. anticipate the offender's actions and take the steps necessary to cut him off when he emerges from safety zones

23. Citizens understand in a vague and general way that their civil liberties must be respected by the police, but they do not appreciate that this protection necessarily extends both to those who consider themselves to be law observers and to those who are law violators.
The MOST important deduction to be made from this by a police officer is that

    A. public opinion is uninformed and hence may be disregarded
    B. the basis is laid for serious misunderstanding between the police and the public
    C. the public attitude toward severe arrest procedures depends on the personal character of the arrestee and not the crime charged
    D. the public favors a policy of selective law enforcement

Questions 24-25.

DIRECTIONS: Questions 24 and 25 are to be answered on the basis of the following paragraph.

The most significant improvements in personnel selection procedures can be expected from a program designed to obtain more precise statements of the requirements for a particular position and from the development of procedures that will make it possible to select not just those applicants who are generally best, but those whose abilities and personal characteristics provide the closest fit to the specific job requirement.

24. According to the above paragraph, better personnel selection procedures will result from

    A. simplification of job description
    B. better recruiting procedures
    C. obtaining more detailed experience data from applicants
    D. detailed statements of training and skills required for positions

25. According to the above paragraph, the MOST desirable applicant for a position is

    A. the one who has all the necessary training, even though he lacks the necessary personal characteristics
    B. the one whose abilities and personal characteristics are of the highest order
    C. generally not the same as the best qualified person
    D. the one whose qualifications are most nearly the same as the job requirement

# KEY (CORRECT ANSWERS)

1. C
2. B
3. C
4. D
5. D

6. C
7. B
8. D
9. C
10. C

11. C
12. B
13. C
14. C
15. A

16. D
17. B
18. D
19. C
20. B

21. D
22. C
23. B
24. D
25. D

# TEST 2

DIRECTIONS: Each question or incomplete statement is followed by several suggested answers or completions. Select the one that BEST answers the question or completes the statement. *PRINT THE LETTER OF THE CORRECT ANSWER IN THE SPACE AT THE RIGHT.*

Questions 1-3.

DIRECTIONS: Questions 1 through 3 are to be answered SOLELY on the basis of the following paragraph.

Every organization needs a systematic method of checking its operation as a means to increase efficiency and promote economy. Many successful private firms have instituted a system of audits or internal inspections to accomplish these ends. Law enforcement organizations, which have an extremely important service to *sell*, should be no less zealous in developing efficiency and economy in their operations. Periodic, organized, and systematic inspections are one means of promoting the achievement of these objectives. The necessity of an organized inspection system is perhaps greatest in those law enforcement groups which have grown to such a size that the principal officer can no longer personally supervise or be cognizant of every action taken. Smooth and effective operation demands that the head of the organization have at hand some tool with which he can study and enforce general policies and procedures and also direct compliance with day-to-day orders, most of which are put into execution outside his sight and hearing. A good inspection system can serve as that tool.

1. The central thought of the above paragraph is that a system of inspections within a police department

    A. is unnecessary for a department in which the principal officer can personally supervise all official actions taken
    B. should be instituted at the first indication that there is any deterioration in job performance by the force
    C. should be decentralized and administered by first-line supervisory officers
    D. is an important aid to the police administrator in the accomplishment of law enforcement objectives

1.____

2. The MOST accurate of the following statements concerning the need for an organized inspection system in a law enforcement organization is:
It is

    A. never needed in an organization of small size where the principal officer can give personal supervision
    B. most needed where the size of the organization prevents direct supervision by the principal officer
    C. more needed in law enforcement organizations than in private firms
    D. especially needed in an organization about to embark upon a needed expansion of services

2.____

3. According to the above paragraph, the head of the police organization utilizes the internal inspection system

   A. as a tool which must be constantly re-examined in the light of changing demands for police service
   B. as an administrative technique to increase efficiency and promote economy
   C. by personally visiting those areas of police operation which are outside his sight and hearing
   D. to augment the control of local commanders over detailed field operations

Questions 4-6.

DIRECTIONS: Questions 4 through 6 are to be answered SOLELY on the basis of the following paragraph.

Every officer in a department, from the chief of police to the new recruit, should participate if a human relations program is to be effective. The policies, programs, and examples which the chief initiates become the guide for action by all other officers. Through the command group, lieutenants and above in rank, the chief disseminates throughout the department his policies and ideas for application. It is that group which in essence holds control over a department. Implementation of a human relations program must always be through them, with their full support and understanding obtained. They are the link between the sergeants and the chief; they train and assist the sergeants in all operations and give up some of their authority so the sergeants may have freedom to act. The police sergeant is probably the key to success of any police human relations program, since it is his responsibility to develop a wholesome and loyal attitude in the policemen toward their job, themselves, and toward other officers in the department. Instilling of job satisfaction in the patrolmen becomes his responsibility. If changes are to be made in departmental practices or procedures, it is the sergeant's job to change the policemen's attitudes and to condition them for the change.

4. According to this paragraph, one of the responsibilities of a sergeant is to

   A. inform the command group of any changes in attitude on the part of the policemen
   B. inform the command group of needed changes in practices and procedures and inform the policemen of accomplishments and problems of the command group
   C. insist upon a demonstration of job satisfaction by the policemen
   D. prepare the policemen to accept any impending changes in departmental procedure

5. According to this paragraph, the MOST accurate of the following statements concerning a police human relations program is:

   A. Application of policies and ideas is less the responsibility of the sergeant than of the command group
   B. Newly appointed patrolmen should not participate in a human relations program until the sergeant has had an opportunity to change their attitudes
   C. The key to a successful human relations program is the patrolmen's acceptance of basic departmental procedures
   D. The human relations program can never be successful without being actively supported by the lieutenants

6. According to this paragraph, the command group 6.____
   A. assists the sergeant in the accomplishment of police objectives in the area of human relations
   B. delegates responsibility to the sergeant in this critical area of administration so that he has freedom to develop a more wholesome program
   C. initiates the programs and policies which reflect the general views of the chief
   D. should direct but not participate in a human relations program

Questions 7-9.

DIRECTIONS: Questions 7 through 9 are to be answered SOLELY on the basis of the following paragraph.

The sentiment of the community is not always favorable to procedures designed to accomplish the police purpose. Unfavorable public attitudes may make the immediate adoption of a superior procedure impractical. A necessary part of the task of achieving police objectives is the development of public attitudes favorable to their attainment. The police, therefore, must be organized to inform the public regarding the significance and consequences of failures in law enforcement and compliance, and also regarding police requirements and the results of failure to meet them. The police cannot progress ahead of public sentiment since there must be general acceptance by the people of controls that are applied by the police in order to completely accomplish the basic police objectives. The development of favorable public sentiment is a relatively long-range project, whereas organization requirements are immediate. The organizational structure, therefore, must be designed to conform somewhat to public attitudes. As public sentiment changes, modification of the structure may be desirable.

7. According to the above paragraph, modifications of the police organizational structure should 7.____
   A. be considered in instances where public sentiment has also changed
   B. be designed to anticipate major changes in public attitudes
   C. be regarded as a relatively long-range project
   D. follow closely any changes in public sentiment

8. According to the above paragraph, the development of favorable public attitudes towards the police is important because 8.____
   A. failures in law enforcement activity are thereby more likely to be quickly corrected
   B. the accomplishment of primary police purposes is largely dependent on such favorable attitudes
   C. the improvement of the conditions of work of the police are ultimately determined by the public
   D. no one will comply with police regulations without a favorable public attitude

9. According to the above paragraph, it would be MOST advisable that a decision to adopt a new police procedure 9.____
   A. be determined mainly by its crime deterring effect on the community
   B. not be made if any community objection has been expressed towards the procedure

C. be made only after favorable public attitudes have been developed in all community groups
D. be partly based on a consideration of its community acceptance

Questions 10-12.

DIRECTIONS: Questions 10 through 12 are to be answered SOLELY on the basis of the following paragraph.

All members of the police force must recognize that the people, through their representatives, hire and pay the police and that, as in any other employment, there must exist a proper employer-employee relationship. The police officer must understand that the essence of a correct police attitude is a willingness to serve, but at the same time he should distinguish between service and servility, and between courtesy and softness. He must be firm but also courteous, avoiding even an appearance of rudeness. He should develop a position that is friendly and unbiased, pleasant and sympathetic, in his relations with the general public, but firm and impersonal on occasions calling for regulation and control. A police officer should understand that his primary purpose is to prevent violations, not to arrest people. He should recognize the line of demarcation between a police function and passing judgment which is a court function. On the other side, a public that cooperates with the police, that supports them in their efforts and that observes laws and regulations may be said to have a desirable attitude.

10. In accordance with this paragraph, the PROPER attitude for a police officer to take is to

    A. be pleasant and sympathetic at all times
    B. be friendly, firm, and impartial
    C. be stern and severe in meting out justice to all
    D. avoid being rude, except in those cases where the public is uncooperative

11. Assume that an officer is assigned by his superior officer to a busy traffic intersection and is warned to be on the lookout for motorists who skip the light or who are speeding. According to this paragraph, it would be PROPER for the officer in this assignment to

    A. give a summons to every motorist whose car was crossing when the light changed
    B. hide behind a truck and wait for drivers who violate traffic laws
    C. select at random motorists who seem to be impatient and lecture them sternly on traffic safety
    D. stand on post in order to deter violations and give offenders a summons or a warning as required

12. According to this paragraph, a police officer must realize that the PRIMARY purpose of police work is to

    A. provide proper police service in a courteous manner
    B. decide whether those who violate the law should be punished
    C. arrest those who violate laws
    D. establish a proper employer-employee relationship

Questions 13-15.

DIRECTIONS: Questions 13 through 15 are to be answered SOLELY on the basis of the following paragraphs.

In cases of accident, it is most important for an officer to obtain the name, age, residence, occupation, and a full description of the person injured, names and addresses of witnesses. He shall also obtain a statement of the attendant circumstances. He shall carefully note contributory conditions, if any, such as broken pavement, excavation, lights not burning, snow and ice on the roadway, etc. He shall enter all the facts in his memorandum book and on Form 17 or Form 18, and promptly transmit the original of the form to his superior officer and the duplicate to headquarters.

An officer shall render reasonable assistance to sick or injured persons. If the circumstances appear to require the services of a physician, he shall summon a physician by telephoning the superior officer on duty and notifying him of the apparent nature of the illness or accident and the location where the physician will be required. He may summon other officers to assist if circumstances warrant.

In case of an accident or where a person is sick on city property, an officer shall obtain the information necessary to fill out card Form 18 and record this in his memorandum book and promptly telephone the facts to his superior officer. He shall deliver the original card at the expiration of his tour to his superior officer and transmit the duplicate to headquarters.

13. According to this passage, the MOST important consideration in any report on a case of accident or injury is to

    A. obtain all the facts
    B. telephone his superior officer at once
    C. obtain a statement of the attendant circumstances
    D. determine ownership of the property on which the accident occurred

14. According to this passage, in the case of an accident on city property, the officer should ALWAYS

    A. summon a physician before filling out any forms or making any entries in his memorandum book
    B. give his superior officer on duty a prompt report by telephone
    C. immediately bring the original of Form 18 to his superior officer on duty
    D. call at least one other officer to the scene to witness conditions

15. If the procedures stated in this passage were followed for all accidents in the city, an impartial survey of accidents occurring during any period of time in this city may be MOST easily made by

    A. asking a typical officer to show you his memorandum book
    B. having a superior officer investigate whether contributory conditions mentioned by witnesses actually exist
    C. checking all the records of all superior officers
    D. checking the duplicate card files at headquarters

Questions 16-18.

DIRECTIONS: Questions 16 through 18 are to be answered SOLELY on the basis of the following paragraph.

When the frequency of special situations that create extraordinary needs for police service is nearly continuous, as is often the case in a large city, a separate unit for each is desirable even though in some communities these needs are met by the force assigned to deal with the average need. Variations in the manpower needed to deal with special situations further complicate the problem. Special squads created to meet unusual needs are not likely to be adequate to deal with all situations. One unit must be used to supplement the other in some situations. Likewise, the force normally used to meet the average need must be used in some other situations to supplement the efforts of both. For example, the entire force is likely to be pressed into overtime duty when disaster strikes. The existence of special units, however, diminishes the frequency and extent of necessary requisitions of unspecialized manpower from their regular assignments. The special squads should also be used as a manpower reserve to fill vacancies in or absences from regular assignments when the regular services must be maintained exactly as before.

16. The one of the following situations which would MOST justify the creation of a separate unit, according to the above passage, is when

    A. the force assigned to deal with the average need, in small or large cities, is assigned continuously to handle all extraordinary needs for police service
    B. the frequency of the situations that create above average needs is somewhat in proportion to the size of the city
    C. the force assigned to deal with the average need has to give nearly continuous attention to above-average needs
    D. in a large city the separate unit can be used to supplement the force assigned to deal with the average need

17. When a special squad is unable to meet adequately one of the needs for police service which it was assigned to provide, it would be MOST correct, according to the above passage, to state that

    A. the force normally used to meet the average need should not be used unless some other special squad has first been assigned
    B. the force normally used to meet the average need as well as any other special squad should not both be used at the same time
    C. some other special unit should be used to supplement the special squad while attempting to avoid assigning the force normally used to meet the average need
    D. some other special unit should not be used unless it is likely that its own efforts can be supplemented by the special squad at some future time

18. The decision as to whether officers assigned to a special unit should be used to replace absent officers in a regular unit depends MAINLY on the

    A. extent to which unspecialized manpower must be requisitioned
    B. effect of the absences on the regular services which should not be even temporarily diminished

C. extent to which the services provided by the force normally assigned to the regular unit have been diminished by the absences
D. relative importance of maintaining the services of the special squad exactly as before

Questions 19-20.

DIRECTIONS: Questions 19 through 20 are to be answered SOLELY on the basis of the following paragraph.

The traditional characteristics of a police organization, which do not foster group-centered leadership, are being changed daily by progressive police administrators. These characteristics are authoritarian and result in a leader-centered style with all deter- mination of policy and procedure made by the leader. In the group-centered style, policies and procedures are a matter for group discussion and decision. The supposedly modern view is that the group-centered style is the most conducive to improving organizational effectiveness. By contrast, the traditional view regards the group-centered style as an idealistic notion of psychologists. It is questionable, however, that the situation determines the appropriate leadership style. In some circumstances, it will be leader-centered; in others, group-centered. Nevertheless, police supervisors will see more situations calling for a leadership style that, while flexible, is primarily group-centered. Thus, the supervisor in a police department must have a capacity not just to issue orders, but to engage in behavior involving organizational leadership which primarily emphasizes goals and work facilitation.

19. According to the above passage, there is reason to believe that with regard to the effectiveness of different types of leadership, the

    A. leader-centered type is better than the individual-centered type or the group-centered type
    B. leader-centered type is best in some situations and the group-centered type best in other situations
    C. group-centered type is better than the leader-centered type in all situations
    D. authoritarian type is least effective in democratic countries

20. According to the above passage, police administrators today are

    A. more likely than in the past to favor making decisions on the basis of discussions with subordinates
    B. likely in general to favor traditional patterns of leadership in their organizations
    C. more likely to be progressive than conservative
    D. practical and individualistic rather than idealistic in their approach to police problems

## KEY (CORRECT ANSWERS)

| | | | |
|---|---|---|---|
| 1. | D | 11. | D |
| 2. | B | 12. | A |
| 3. | B | 13. | A |
| 4. | D | 14. | B |
| 5. | D | 15. | D |
| 6. | A | 16. | C |
| 7. | A | 17. | C |
| 8. | B | 18. | B |
| 9. | D | 19. | B |
| 10. | B | 20. | A |

# ENGLISH EXPRESSION
# CHOICE OF EXPRESSION
# COMMENTARY

One special form of the English Expression multiple-choice question in current use requires the candidate to select from among five (5) versions of a particular part of a sentence (or of an entire sentence), the one version that expresses the idea of the sentence most clearly, effectively, and accurately. Thus, the candidate is required not only to recognize errors, but also to choose the best way of phrasing a particular part of the sentence.

This is a test of choice of expression, which assays the candidate's ability to express himself correctly and effectively, including his sensitivity to the subtleties and nuances of the language.

## SAMPLE QUESTIONS

DIRECTIONS: In each of the following sentences, some part of the sentence or the entire sentence is underlined. The underlined part presents a problem in the appropriate use of language. Beneath each sentence you will find five ways of writing the underlined part. The first of these indicates no change (that is, it repeats the original), but the other four are all different. If you think the original sentence is better than any of the suggested changes, you should choose answer A; otherwise you should mark one of the other choices. Select the BEST answer and print the letter in the space at the right.

This is a test of correctness and effectiveness of expression. In choosing answers, follow the requirements of standard written English; that is, pay attention to acceptable usage in grammar, diction (choice of words), sentence construction, and punctuation. Choose the answer that produces the most effective sentence—clear and exact, without awkwardness or ambiguity. Do not make a choice that changes the meaning of the original sentence.

### SAMPLE QUESTION 1

Although these states now trade actively with the West, and although they are willing to exchange technological information, their arts and thoughts and social structure <u>remains substantially similar to what it has always been</u>.
  A. remains substantially similar to what it has always been
  B. remain substantially unchanged
  C. remains substantially unchanged
  D. remain substantially similar to what they have always been
  E. remain substantially without being changed

The purpose of questions of this type is to determine the candidate's ability to select the clearest and most effective means of expressing what the statement attempts to say. In this example, the phrasing in the statement, which is repeated in A, presents a problem of agreement between a subject and its verb (<u>their arts and thought and social structure</u> and <u>remains</u>), a problem of agreement between a pronoun and its antecedent (<u>their arts and thought and social structure</u> and <u>it</u>), an a problem of precise and concise phrasing (<u>remains</u>

substantially similar to what it has always been for remains substantially unchanged). Each of the four remaining choices in some way corrects one or more of the faults in the sentence, but only one deals with all three problems satisfactorily. Although C presents a more careful and concise wording of the phrasing of the statement and, in the process, eliminates the problem of agreement between pronoun and antecedent, it fails to correct the problem of agreement between the subject and its verb. In D, the subject agrees with its verb and the pronoun agrees with its antecedent, but the phrasing is not so accurate as it should be. The same difficulty persists in E. Only in B are all the problems presented corrected satisfactory. The question is not difficult.

## SAMPLE QUESTION 2

Her latest novel is the largest in scope, the most accomplished in technique, and <u>it is more significant in theme than anything</u> she has written.
- A. it is more significant in theme than anything
- B. It is most significant in theme of anything
- C. more significant in theme than anything
- D. the most significant in theme than anything
- E. the most significant in theme of anything

This question is of greater difficulty than the preceding one. The problem posed in the sentence and repeated in A is essentially one of parallelism; Does the underlined portion of the sentence follow the pattern established by the first two elements of the series (<u>the largest</u>...<u>the most accomplished</u>)? It does not, for it introduces a pronoun and verb (<u>it is</u>) that the second term of the series indicates should be omitted and a degree of comparison (<u>more significant</u>) that is not in keeping with the superlatives used earlier in the sentence. B uses the superlative degree of <u>significant</u> but retains the unnecessary <u>it is</u>; C removes the <u>it is</u>, but retains the faulty comparative form of the adjective. D corrects both errors in parallelism, but introduces an error in idiom (<u>the most</u>...<u>than</u>). Only E corrects all the problems without introducing another fault.

## SAMPLE QUESTION 3

Desiring to insure the continuity of their knowledge, <u>magical lore is transmitted by the chiefs</u> to their descendants.
- A. magical lore is transmitted by the chiefs
- B. transmission of magical lore is made by the chiefs
- C. the chiefs' magical lore is transmitted
- D. the chiefs transmit magical lore
- E. the chiefs make transmission of magical lore

The CORRECT answer is D.

## SAMPLE QUESTION 4

<u>As Malcolm walks quickly and confident</u> into the purser's office, the rest of the crew wondered whether he would be charged with the theft.
- A. As Malcolm walks quickly and confident
- B. As Malcolm was walking quick and confident
- C. As Malcom walked quickly and confident

D. As Malcolm walked quickly and confidently
E. As Malcolm walks quickly and confidently
The CORRECT answer is D.

## SAMPLE QUESTION 5

The chairman, <u>granted the power to assign any duties to whoever he</u> wished, was still unable to prevent bickering.
A. granted the power to assign any duties to whoever he wished
B. granting the power to assign any duties to whoever he wished
C. being granted the power to assign any duties to whoever he wished
D. having been granted the power to assign any duties to whosoever he wished
E. granted the power to assign any duties to whomever he wished
The CORRECT answer is E.

## SAMPLE QUESTION 6

Certainly, well-seasoned products are more expensive, <u>but those kinds prove chaper</u> in the end.
A. but those kinds prove cheaper
B. but these kinds prove cheaper
C. but that kind proves cheaper
D. but those kind prove cheaper
E. but this kind proves cheaper
The CORRECT answer is A.

## SAMPLE QUESTION 7

"We shall not," he shouted, "whatever the <u>difficulties." "lose faith in the success of our plan!!</u>"
A. difficulties," "lose faith in the success of our plan!"
B. difficulties, "lose faith in the success of our plan"!
C. "difficulties, lose faith in the success of our plan!"
D. difficulties, lose faith in the success of our plan"!
E. difficulties, lose faith in the success of our plan!"

## SAMPLE QUESTION 8

<u>Climb up the tree</u>, the lush foliage obscured the chattering monkeys.
A. Climbing up the tree
B. Having climbed up the tree
C. Clambering up the tree
D. After we had climbed up the tree
E. As we climbed up the tree
The CORRECT answer is E.

# EXAMINATION SECTION
## TEST 1

DIRECTIONS: See DIRECTIONS for Sample Questions on Page 1. *PRINT THE LETTER OF THE CORRECT ANSWER IN THE SPACE AT THE RIGHT.*

1. At the opening of the story, Charles Gilbert <u>has just come</u> to make his home with his two unmarried aunts.　　　　　　　　　　　　　　　　　　1.____
   A. No change
   B. hadn't hardly come
   C. has just came
   D. had just come
   E. has hardly came

2. The sisters, who are no longer young, <u>are use to living</u> quiet lives.　　2.____
   A. No change
   B. are used to live
   C. are use'd to living
   D. are used to living
   E. are use to live

3. They <u>willingly except</u> the child.　　　　　　　　　　　　　　　　　3.____
   A. No change
   B. willingly eccepted
   C. willingly accepted
   D. willingly acepted
   E. willingly accept

4. As the months pass, Charles' presence <u>affects many changes</u> in their household.　　　　　　　　　　　　　　　　　　　　　　　　　　　　4.____
   A. No change
   B. affect many changes
   C. effects many changes
   D. effect many changes
   E. affected many changes

5. These changes <u>is not all together</u> to their liking.　　　　　　　　　　5.____
   A. No change
   B. is not altogether
   C. are not all together
   D. are not altogether
   E. is not alltogether

6. In fact, they have some difficulty in adapting <u>theirselves</u> to these changes　　6.____
   A. No change
   B. in adopting theirselves
   C. in adopting themselves
   D. in adapting theirselves
   E. in adapting themselves

7. That is the man <u>whom I believe</u> was the driver of the car.　　　　　　7.____
   A. No change
   B. who I believed
   C. whom I believed
   D. who to believe
   E. who I believe

8. John's climb to fame was more rapid <u>than his brother's</u>.　　　　　　8.____
   A. No change
   B. than his brother
   C. than that of his brother's
   D. than for his brother
   E. than the brother

9. We knew that he had formerly swam on an Olympic team.
   A. No change
   B. has formerly swum
   C. did formerly swum
   D. had formerly swum
   E. has formerly swam

10. Not one of us loyal supporters ever get a pass to a game.
    A. No change
    B. ever did got a pass
    C. ever has get a pass
    D. ever had get a pass
    E. ever gets a pass

11. He was complemented on having done a fine job.
    A. No change
    B. was compliminted
    C. was compleminted
    D. was complimented
    E. did get complimented

12. This play is different from the one we had seen last night.
    A. No change
    B. have seen
    C. had saw
    D. have saw
    E. saw

13. A row of trees was planted in front of the house.
    A. No change
    B. was to be planted
    C. were planted
    D. were to be planted
    E. are planted

14. The house looked its age in spite of our attempts to beautify it.
    A. No change
    B. looks its age
    C. looked its' age
    D. looked it's age
    E. looked it age

15. I do not know what to council in this case.
    A. No change
    B. where to council
    C. when to councel
    D. what to counsel
    E. what to counsil

16. She is more capable than any other girl in the office.
    A. No change
    B. than any girl
    C. than any other girls
    D. than other girl
    E. than other girls

17. At the picnic the young children behaved very good.
    A. No change
    B. behave very good
    C. behaved better
    D. behave very well
    E. behaved very well

18. I resolved to go irregardless of the consequences.
    A. No change
    B. to depart irregardless of
    C. to go regarding of
    D. to go regardingly of
    E. to go regardless of

19. The new movie has a number of actors which have been famous on Broadway.
    A. No change
    B. which had been famous
    C. who had been famous
    D. that are famous
    E. who have been famous

20. I am certain that these books are not our's.
    A. No change
    B. have not been ours'
    C. have not been our's
    D. are not ours
    E. are not ours'

21. Each of your papers is filed for future reference.
    A. No change
    B. Each of your papers are filed
    C. Each of your papers have been filed
    D. Each of your papers are to be filed
    E. Each of your paper is filed

22. I wish that he would take his work more serious.
    A. No change
    B. he took his work more serious
    C. he will take his work more serious
    D. he shall take his work more seriously
    E. he would take his work more seriously

23. After the treasurer report had been read, the chairman called for the reports of the committees.
    A. No change
    B. After the treasure's report had been read
    C. After the treasurers' report had been read
    D. After the treasurerer's report had been read
    E. After the treasurer's report had been read

24. Last night the stranger lead us down the mountain.
    A. No change
    B. leaded us down the mountain
    C. let us down the mountain
    D. led us down the mountain
    E. had led us down the mountain

25. It would not be safe for either you or I to travel in Viet Nam.
    A. No change
    B. for either you or me
    C. for either I or you
    D. for either of you or I
    E. for either of I or you

## KEY (CORRECT ANSWERS)

| | | | | |
|---|---|---|---|---|
| 1. | A | | 11. | D |
| 2. | D | | 12. | E |
| 3. | E | | 13. | A |
| 4. | C | | 14. | A |
| 5. | D | | 15. | D |
| 6. | E | | 16. | A |
| 7. | E | | 17. | E |
| 8. | A | | 18. | E |
| 9. | D | | 19. | E |
| 10. | E | | 20. | D |

| | |
|---|---|
| 21. | A |
| 22. | E |
| 23. | E |
| 24. | D |
| 25. | B |

# TEST 2

DIRECTIONS: See DIRECTIONS for Sample Questions on Page 1. *PRINT THE LETTER OF THE CORRECT ANSWER IN THE SPACE AT THE RIGHT.*

1. Both the body and the mind <u>needs exercise</u>.
   A. No change
   B. have needs of exercise
   C. is needful of exercise
   D. needed exercise
   E. need exercise

   1._____

2. <u>It's paw injured</u>, the animal limped down the road.
   A. No change
   B. It's paw injured
   C. Its paw injured
   D. Its' paw injured
   E. Its paw injure

   2._____

3. The butter <u>tastes rancidly</u>.
   A. No change
   B. tastes rancid
   C. tasted rancidly
   D. taste rancidly
   E. taste rancid

   3._____

4. <u>Who do you think</u> has sent me a letter?
   A. No change
   B. Whom do you think
   C. Whome do you think
   D. Who did you think
   E. Whom can you think

   4._____

5. If more nations <u>would have fought</u> against tyranny, the course of history would have been different.
   A. No change
   B. would fight
   C. could have fought
   D. fought
   E. had fought

   5._____

6. Radio and television programs, along with other media of communication, <u>helps us to appreciate the arts and to keep informed</u>.
   A. No change
   B. helps us to appreciate the arts and to be informed
   C. helps us to be appreciative of the arts and to keep informed
   D. helps us to be appreciative of the arts and to be informed
   E. help us to appreciate the arts and to keep informed

   6._____

7. Music, <u>for example most always</u> has listening and viewing audiences numbering in the hundreds of thousands.
   A. No change
   B. for example, most always
   C. for example, almost always
   D. for example nearly always
   E. for example, near always

   7._____

8. When operas are performed on radio or television, <u>they effect the listener</u>.
   A. No change
   B. they inflict the listener
   C. these effect the listeners
   D. they affects the listeners
   E. they affect the listener

   8._____

141

9. After hearing then the listener wants to buy recordings of the music.
   A. No change
   B. After hearing them, the listener wants
   C. After hearing them, the listener want
   D. By hearing them the listener wants
   E. By hearing them, the listener wants

10. To we Americans the daily news program has become important.
    A. No change
    B. To we the Americans
    C. To us Americans
    D. To us the Americans
    E. To we and us Americans

11. This has resulted from it's coverage of a days' events.
    A. No change
    B. from its coverage of a days' events
    C. from it's coverage of a day's events
    D. from its' coverage of a day's events
    E. from its coverage of a day's events

12. In schools, teachers advice their students to listen to or to view certain programs.
    A. No change
    B. teachers advise there students
    C. teachers advise their students
    D. the teacher advises their students
    E. teachers advise his students

13. In these ways we are preceding toward the goal of an educated and an informed public.
    A. No change
    B. we are preeceding toward the goal
    C. we are proceeding toward the goal
    D. we are preceding toward the goal
    E. we are proceeding toward the goal

14. The cost of living is raising again.
    A. No change
    B. are raising again
    C. is rising again
    D. are rising again
    E. is risen again

15. We did not realize that the boys' father had forbidden them to keep there puppy.
    A. No change
    B. had forbade them to keep there puppy
    C. had forbade them to keep their puppy
    D. has forbidden them to keep their puppy
    E. had forbidden them to keep their puppy

16. Her willingness to help others' was her outstanding characteristic.
    A. No change
    B. Her willingness to help other's,
    C. Her willingness to help others's
    D. Her willingness to help others
    E. Her willingness to help each other

17. Because he did not have an invitation, the girls objected to him going.
    A. No change
    B. the girls object to him going
    C. the girls objected to him's going
    D. the girls objected to his going
    E. the girls object to his going

18. Weekly dances have become a popular accepted feature of the summer schedule.
    A. No change
    B. have become a popular accepted feature
    C. have become a popular excepted feature
    D. have become a popularly excepted feature
    E. have become a popularly accepted feature

19. I couldn't hardly believe that he would desert our party.
    A. No change
    B. would hardly believe
    C. didn't hardly believe
    D. should hardly believe
    E. could hardly believe

20. I found the place in the book more readily than she.
    A. No change
    B. more readily than her
    C. more ready than she
    D. more quickly than her
    E. more ready than her

21. A good example of American outdoor activities are sports.
    A. No change
    B. is sports
    C. are sport
    D. are sports events
    E. are to be found in sports

22. My point of view is much different from your's.
    A. No change
    B. much different from your's
    C. much different than yours
    D. much different from yours
    E. much different than yours'

23. The cook was suppose to use two spoonfuls of dressing for each serving.
    A. No change
    B. was supposed to use two spoonsful
    C. was suppose to use two spoonful
    D. was supposed to use two spoonsfuls
    E. was supposed to use two spoonfuls

24. If anyone has any doubt about the values of the tour, <u>refer him to me</u>.   24.____
    A. No change
    B. refer him to I
    C. refer me to he
    D. refer them to me
    E. refer he to I

25. We expect that the affects of <u>the trip will be neneficial</u>.   25.____
    A. No change
    B. the effects of the trip will be beneficial
    C. the effects of the trip should be beneficial
    D. the affects of the trip would be beneficial
    E. the effects of the trip will be benificial

## KEY (CORRECT ANSWERS)

| | | | | |
|---|---|---|---|---|
| 1. | E | | 11. | E |
| 2. | C | | 12. | C |
| 3. | B | | 13. | E |
| 4. | A | | 14. | C |
| 5. | E | | 15. | E |
| 6. | E | | 16. | D |
| 7. | C | | 17. | D |
| 8. | E | | 18. | E |
| 9. | B | | 19. | E |
| 10. | C | | 20. | A |

| | |
|---|---|
| 21. | B |
| 22. | D |
| 23. | E |
| 24. | A |
| 25. | B |

# TEST 3

DIRECTIONS: See DIRECTIONS for Sample Questions on Page 1. *PRINT THE LETTER OF THE CORRECT ANSWER IN THE SPACE AT THE RIGHT.*

1. That, my friend is not the proper attitude.
   - A. No change
   - B. That my friend
   - C. That my fried,
   - D. That—my friend
   - E. That, my friend,

   1.____

2. The girl refused to admit that the note was her's.
   - A. No change
   - B. that the note were her's
   - C. that the note was hers'
   - D. that the note was hers
   - E. that the note might be hers

   2.____

3. There were fewer candidates that we had been lead to expect
   - A. No change
   - B. was fewer candidates than we had been lead
   - C. were fewer candidates than we had been lead
   - D. was fewer candidates than we had been led
   - E. were fewer candidates than we had been led

   3.____

4. When I first saw the car, its steering wheel was broke.
   - A. No change
   - B. its' steering wheel was broken
   - C. it's steering wheel had been broken
   - D. its steering wheel were broken
   - E. its steering wheel was broken

   4.____

5. I find that the essential spirit for we beginners is missing.
   - A. No change
   - B. we who begin are missing
   - C. us beginners are missing
   - D. us beginners is missing
   - E. we beginners are missing

   5.____

6. I believe that you had ought to study harder.
   - A. No change
   - B. you should have ought
   - C. you had better
   - D. you ought to have
   - E. you ought

   6.____

7. This is Tom, whom I am sure, will be glad to help you.
   - A. No change
   - B. Tom whom, I am sure,
   - C. Tom, whom I am sure
   - D. Tom who I am sure,
   - E. Tom, who, I am sure,

   7.____

8. His father or his mother has read to him every night since he was very small.
   - A. No change
   - B. did read to him
   - C. have been reading to him
   - D. had read to him
   - E. have read to him

   8.____

9. He <u>become an authority</u>
   A. No change
   B. becomed an authority
   C. become the authority
   D. became an authority
   E. becamed an authority

10. I know of no other reason in the club <u>who is more kind-hearted than her</u>.
    A. No change
    B. who are more kind-hearted than they
    C. who are more kind-hearted than them
    D. whom are more kind-hearted than she
    E. who is more kind-hearted than she

11. After Bill <u>had ran the mile</u>, he was breathless.
    A. No change
    B. had runned the mile
    C. has ran the mile
    D. had ranned the mile
    E. had run the mile

12. Wilson <u>has scarcely no equal</u> as a pitcher.
    A. No change
    B. has scarcely an equal
    C. has hardly no equal
    D. had scarcely no equal
    E. has scarcely any equals

13. It <u>was the worse storm</u> that the inhabitants of the island could remember.
    A. No change
    B. were the worse storm
    C. was the worst storm
    D. was the worsest storm
    E. was the most worse storm

14. If only <u>we had began</u> before it was too late.
    A. No change
    B. we had began
    C. we would have begun
    D. we had begun
    E. we had beginned

15. <u>Lets evaluate</u> our year's work.
    A. No change
    B. Let us' evaluate
    C. Lets' evaluate
    D. Lets' us evaluate
    E. Let's evaluate

16. This is an organization <u>with which I wouldn't want to be associated with</u>.
    A. No change
    B. with whom I wouldn't want to be associated with
    C. that I wouldn't want to be associated
    D. with which I would want not to be associated with
    E. with which I wouldn't want to be associated

17. The enemy fled in many directions, <u>leaving there weapons</u> on the field.
    A. No change
    B. leaving its weapons
    C. letting their weapons
    D. leaving alone there weapons
    E. leaving their weapons

18. I hoped that John could effect a compromise between the approved forces.    18._____
    A. No change
    B. could accept a compromise between
    C. could except a compromise between
    D. would have effected a compromise among
    E. could effect a compromise among

19. I was surprised to learn that he has not always spoke English fluently.    19._____
    A. No change
    B. that he had not always spoke English
    C. that he did not always speak English
    D. that he has not always spoken English
    E. that he could not always speak English

20. The lawyer promised to notify my father and I of his plans for a new trial.    20._____
    A. No change
    B. to notify I and my father
    C. to notify me and our father
    D. to notify my father and me
    E. to notify mine father and me

21. The most important feature of the series of tennis lessons were the large amount of strokes taught.    21._____
    A. No change
    B. were the large number
    C. was the large amount
    D. was the largeness of the amount
    E. was the large number

22. That the prize proved to be beyond her reach did not surprise him.    22._____
    A. No change
    B. has not surprised him
    C. had not ought to have surprised him
    D. should not surprise him
    E. would not have surprised him

23. I am not all together in agreement with the author's point of view.    23._____
    A. No change
    B. all together of agreement
    C. all together for agreement
    D. altogether with agreement
    E. altogether in agreement

24. Windstorms have recently established a record which meteorologists hope will not be equal for many years to come.    24._____
    A. No change
    B. will be equal
    C. will not be equalized
    D. will be equaled
    E. will not be equaled

25. A large number of Shakespeare's soliloquies must be considered <u>as representing thought</u>, not speech.   25.____
     A. No change
     B. as representative of speech, not thought
     C. as represented by thought, not speech
     D. as indicating thought, not speech
     E. as representative of thought, more than speech

## KEY (CORRECT ANSWERS)

| | | | | |
|---|---|---|---|---|
| 1. | E | | 11. | E |
| 2. | D | | 12. | B |
| 3. | E | | 13. | C |
| 4. | E | | 14. | D |
| 5. | D | | 15. | E |
| 6. | E | | 16. | E |
| 7. | E | | 17. | E |
| 8. | A | | 18. | A |
| 9. | D | | 19. | D |
| 10. | E | | 20. | D |

21. E
22. A
23. E
24. E
25. A

# TEST 4

DIRECTIONS: See DIRECTIONS for Sample Questions on Page 1. *PRINT THE LETTER OF THE CORRECT ANSWER IN THE SPACE AT THE RIGHT.*

1. A sight to inspire fear <u>are wild animals on the lose</u>.
   A. No change
   B. are wild animals on the loose
   C. is wild animals on the loose
   D. is wild animals on the lose
   E. are wild animals loose

   1._____

2. For many years, the settlers <u>had been seeking to workship as they please</u>.
   A. No change
   B. had seeked to workship as they pleased
   C. sought to workship as they please
   D. sought to have worshiped as they pleased
   E. had been seeking to worship as they pleased

   2._____

3. The girls stated that the dresses were <u>their's</u>.
   A. No change
   B. there's
   C. theirs
   D. theirs'
   E. there own

   3._____

4. <u>Please fellows</u> don't drop the ball.
   A. No change
   B. Please, fellows
   C. Please fellows;
   D. Please, fellows,
   E. Please! fellows

   4._____

5. Your sweater <u>has laid</u> on the floor for a week.
   A. No change
   B. has been laying
   C. has been lying
   D. laid
   E. has been lain

   5._____

6. I wonder whether <u>you're sure that scheme of yours'</u> will work.
   A. No change
   B. your sure that scheme of your's
   C. you're sure that scheme of yours
   D. your sure that scheme of yours
   E. you're sure that your scheme's

   6._____

7. Please let <u>her and me</u> do it.
   A. No change
   B. she and I
   C. she and me
   D. her and I
   E. her and him

   7._____

8. I expected him to be angry <u>and to scold</u> her.
   A. No change
   B. and that he would scold
   C. and that he might scold
   D. and that he should scold
   E. , scolding

   8._____

149

9. Knowing little about algebra, <u>it was difficult to solve the equation</u>.
   A. No change
   B. the equation was difficult to solve
   C. the solution to the equation was difficult to find
   D. I found it difficult to solve the equation
   E. it being difficult to solve the equation

10. He <u>worked more diligent</u> now that he had become vice president of the company.
    A. No change
    B. works more diligent
    C. works more diligently
    D. began to work more diligent
    E. worked more diligently

11. <u>Flinging himself at the barricade he</u> pounded on it furiously.
    A. No change
    B. Flinging himself at the barricade: he
    C. Flinging himself at the barricade—he
    D. Flinging himself at the barricade; he
    E. Flinging himself at the barricade, he

12. When he <u>begun to give us advise</u>, we stopped listening.
    A. No change
    B. began to give us advise
    C. begun to give us advice
    D. began to give us advice
    E. begin to give us advice

13. John was only one of the boys <u>whom as you know was</u> not eligible.
    A. No change
    B. who as you know were
    C. whom as you know were
    D. who as you know was
    E. who as you know is

14. <u>Why was Jane and he</u> permitted to go?
    A. No change
    B. was Jane and him
    C. were Jane and he
    D. were Jane and him
    E. weren't Jane and he

15. <u>Take courage Tom:  we</u> all make mistakes.
    A. No change
    B. Take courage Tom—we
    C. Take courage, Tom; we
    D. Take courage, Tom we
    E. Take courage! Tom: we

16. Henderson, the president of the class and <u>who is also captain of the team</u>, will lead the rally.
    A. No change
    B. since he is captain of the team
    C. captain of the team
    D. also being captain of the team
    E. who be also captain of the team

17. Our car has always <u>run good</u> on that kind of gasoline.
    A. No change
    B. run well
    C. ran good
    D. ran well
    E. done good

18. There was a serious difference of opinion among her and I.
    A. No change
    B. among she and I
    C. between her and I
    D. between her and me
    E. among her and me

19. "This is most unusual," said Helen, "the mailman has never been this late before."
    A. No change
    B. Helen, "The
    C. Helen—"The
    D. Helen; "The
    E. Helen." The

20. The three main characters in the story are Johnny Hobart a teenager, his mother a widow, and the local druggist.
    A. No change
    B. teenager; his mother, a widow; and
    C. teenager; his mother a widow; and
    D. teenager, his mother, a widow and
    E. teenager, his mother, a widow; and

21. How much has food costs raised during the past year?
    A. No change
    B. have food costs rose
    C. have food costs risen
    D. has food costs risen
    E. have food costs been raised

22. "Will you come too" she pleaded?
    A. No change
    B. too,?"she pleaded
    C. too?" she pleaded
    D. too," she pleaded?
    E. too, she pleaded?"

23. If he would have drank more milk, his health would have been better.
    A. No change
    B. would drink
    C. had drank
    D. had he drunk
    E. had drunk

24. Jack had no sooner laid down and fallen asleep when the alarm sounded.
    A. No change
    B. no sooner lain down and fallen asleep than
    C. no sooner lay down and fell asleep when
    D. no sooner laid down and fell asleep than
    E. no sooner lain down than he fell asleep when

25. Jackson is one of the few Sophomores, who has ever made the varsity team.
    A. No change
    B. one of the few Sophomores, who have
    C. one of the few sophomores, who has
    D. one of the few sophomores who have
    E. one of the few sophomores who has

## KEY (CORRECT ANSWERS)

| | | | | |
|---|---|---|---|---|
| 1. | C | | 11. | E |
| 2. | E | | 12. | D |
| 3. | C | | 13. | B |
| 4. | D | | 14. | C |
| 5. | C | | 15. | C |
| 6. | C | | 16. | C |
| 7. | A | | 17. | B |
| 8. | A | | 18. | D |
| 9. | D | | 19. | E |
| 10. | E | | 20. | B |

| | |
|---|---|
| 21. | C |
| 22. | C |
| 23. | E |
| 24. | B |
| 25. | D |

# TEST 5

DIRECTIONS: See DIRECTIONS for Sample Questions on Page 1. *PRINT THE LETTER OF THE CORRECT ANSWER IN THE SPACE AT THE RIGHT.*

1. The lieutenant had ridden almost a kilometer when the scattering shells <u>begin landing</u> uncomfortably close.
   A. No change
   B. beginning to land
   C. began to land
   D. having begun to land
   E. begin to land

   1.____

2. <u>Having studied eight weeks</u>, he now feels sufficiently prepared for the examination.
   A. No change
   B. For eight weeks he studies so
   C. Due to eight weeks of study
   D. After eight weeks of studying
   E. Since he's been spending the last eight weeks in study

   2.____

3. <u>Coming from the Greek, and the word "democracy" means government by the people</u>.
   A. No change
   B. "Democracy," the word which comes from the Greek, means government by the people.
   C. Meaning government by the people, the word "democracy" comes from the Greek.
   D. Its meaning being government by the people in Greek, the word is "democracy."
   E. The word "democracy" comes from the Greek and means government by the people.

   3.____

4. Moslem universities were one of the chief agencies <u>in the development</u> and spreading Arabic civilization.
   A. No change
   B. in the development of
   C. to develop
   D. in developing
   E. for the developing of

   4.____

5. The water of Bering Strait <u>were closing</u> to navigation by ice early in the fall.
   A. No change
   B. has closed
   C. have closed
   D. had been closed
   E. closed

   5.____

6. The man, <u>since he grew up</u> on the block, felt sentimental when returning to it.
   A. No change
   B. having grown up
   C. growing up
   D. since he had grown up
   E. whose growth had been

   6.____

153

7. Jack and Jill watched the canoe to take their parents out of sight round the bend of the creek.
   A. No change
   B. The canoe, taking their parents out of sight, rounds the bend as Jack and Jill watch.
   C. Jack and Jill watched the canoe round the bend of the creek, taking their parents out of sight,
   D. The canoe rounded the bend of the creek as it took their parents out of sight, Jack and Jill watching.
   E. Jack and Jill watching, the canoe is rounding the bend of the creek to take their parents out of sight.

7._____

8. Chaucer's best-known work is THE CANTERBURY TALES, a collection of stories which he tells with a group of pilgrims as they travel to the town of Canterbury.
   A. No change
   B. which he tells through
   C. who tell
   D. told by
   E. told through

8._____

9. The Estates-General, the old feudal assembly of France, had not met for one hundred and seventy-five years when it convened in 1789.
   A. No change
   B. has not met
   C. has not been meeting
   D. had no meeting
   E. has no meeting

9._____

10. Just forty years ago, there had been fewer than one hundred symphony orchestras in the United States.
    A. No change
    B. there had
    C. there were
    D. there was
    E. there existed

10._____

11. Mrs. Smith complained that her son's temper tantrums aggravated her and caused her to have a headache.
    A. No change
    B. gave her aggravation
    C. were aggravating to her
    D. aggravated her condition
    E. instigated

11._____

12. A girl like I would never be seen in a place like that.
    A. No change    B. as I    C. as me
    D. like I am    E. like me

12._____

13. Between you and me, my opinion is that this room is certainly nicer than the first one we saw.
    A. No change
    B. between you and I
    C. among you and me
    D. betwixt you and I
    E. between we

13._____

14. It is important to know for <u>what kind of a person you are working</u>.
    A. No change
    B. what kind of a person for whom you are working
    C. what kind of person you are working
    D. what kind of person you are working for
    E. what kind of a person you are working for

15. I had <u>all ready</u> finished the book before you came in.
    A. No change      B. already          C. previously
    D. allready       E. all

16. <u>Ask not for who the bell tolls, it tolls for thee</u>.
    A. No change
    B. Ask not for whom the bell tolls, it tolls for thee.
    C. Ask not whom the bell tolls for; it tolls for thee.
    D. Ask not for whom the bell tolls; it tolls for thee.
    E. As not who the bell tolls for: It tolls for thee.

17. It is a far better thing I do, than <u>ever I did</u> before.
    A. No change              B. never I did
    C. I have ever did        D. I have ever been done
    E. ever have I done

18. <u>Ending a sentence with a preposition is something up with which I will not put</u>.
    A. No change
    B. Ending a sentence with a preposition is something with which I will not put up.
    C. To end a sentence with a preposition is that which I will not put up with.
    D. Ending a sentence with a preposition is something of which I will not put up.
    E. Something I will not put up with is ending a sentence with a preposition.

19. Everyone <u>took off their hats and stand up</u> to sing the national anthem.
    A. No change
    B. took off their hats and stood up
    C. take off their hats and stand up
    D. took off his hat and stood up
    E. have taken off their hats and standing up

20. <u>She promised me that if she had the opportunity she would have came irregardless of the weather</u>.
    A. No change
    B. She promised me that if she had the opportunity she would have come regardless of the weather.
    C. She assured me that had she had the opportunity he would have come regardless of the weather.
    D. She assured me that if she would have had the opportunity she would have come regardless of the weather.

E. She promised me that if she had had the opportunity she would have came irregardless of the weather.

21. The man decided it would be advisable to marry a girl <u>somewhat younger than him</u>.
    A. No change
    B. somehow younger than him
    C. some younger than him
    D. somewhat younger from him
    E. somewhat younger than he

22. Sitting near the campfire, the old man told <u>John and I about many exciting adventures he had had</u>.
    A. No change
    B. John and me about many exciting adventures he had,
    C. John and I about much exciting adventure which he'd had
    D. John and me about many exciting adventures he had had
    E. John and me about many exciting adventures he has had.

23. <u>If you had stood at home and done your homework</u>, you would not have failed the course.
    A. No change
    B. If you had stood at home and done you're homework,
    C. If you had staid at home and done your homework,
    D. Had you stayed at home and done your homework,
    E. Had you stood at home and done your homework,

24. The children didn't, as a rule, <u>do anything beyond</u> what they were told to do.
    A. No change
    B. do hardly anything beyond
    C. do anything except
    D. do hardly anything except for
    E. do nothing beyond

25. <u>Either the girls or him is</u> right.
    A. No change
    B. Either the girls or he is
    C. Either the girls or him are
    D. Either the girls or he are
    E. Either the girls nor he is

## KEY (CORRECT ANSWERS)

| | | | |
|---|---|---|---|
| 1. | C | 11. | D |
| 2. | A | 12. | E |
| 3. | E | 13. | A |
| 4. | D | 14. | C |
| 5. | D | 15. | B |
| 6. | B | 16. | D |
| 7. | C | 17. | E |
| 8. | D | 18. | E |
| 9. | A | 19. | D |
| 10. | C | 20. | C |

| | |
|---|---|
| 21. | E |
| 22. | D |
| 23. | D |
| 24. | A |
| 25. | B |

# EXAMINATION SECTION
## TEST 1

DIRECTIONS: In each of the following questions, only one of the four sentences conforms to standards of correct usage. The other three contain errors in grammar, diction, or punctuation. Select the choice in each question which BEST conforms to standards of correct usage. Consider a choice correct if it contains none of the errors mentioned above, even though there may be other ways of expressing the same thought. *PRINT THE LETTER OF THE CORRECT ANSWER IN THE SPACE AT THE RIGHT.*

1.  A. Because he was ill was no excuse for his behavior
    B. I insist that he see a lawyer before he goes to trial.
    C. He said "that he had not intended to go."
    D. He wasn't out of the office only three days.

2.  A. He came to the station and pays a porter to carry his bags into the train.
    B. I should have liked to live in medieval times.
    C. My father was born in Linville. A little country town where everybody knows everyone else.
    D. The car, which is parked across the street, is disabled.

3.  A. He asked the desk clerk for a clean, quiet, room.
    B. I expected James to be lonesome and that he would want to go home.
    C. I have stopped worrying because I have heard nothing further on the subject.
    D. If the board of directors controls the company, they may take actions which are disapproved by the stockholders.

4.  A. Each of the players knew their place.
    B. He whom you saw on the stage is the son of an actor.
    C. Susan is the smartest of the twin sisters.
    D. Who ever thought of him winning both prizes?

5.  A. An outstanding trait of early man was their reliance on omens.
    B. Because I had never been there before.
    C. Neither Mr. Jones nor Mr. Smith has completed his work.
    D. While eating my dinner, a dog came to the window.

6.  A. A copy of the lease, in addition to the Rules and Regulations, are to be given to each tenant.
    B. The Rules and Regulations and a copy of the lease is being given to each tenant.
    C. A copy of the lease, in addition to the Rules and Regulations, is to be given to each tenant.
    D. A copy of the lease, in addition to the Rules and Regulations, are being given to each tenant.

7. A. Although we understood that for him music was a passion, we were disturbed  7.____
      by the fact that he was addicted to sing along with the soloists.
   B. Do you believe that Steven is liable to win a scholarship?
   C. Give the picture to whomever is a connoisseur of art.
   D. Whom do you believe to be the most efficient worker in the office?

8. A. Each adult who is sure they know all the answers will some day realize  8.____
      their mistake.
   B. Even the most hardhearted villain would have to feel bad about so horrible
      a tragedy.
   C. Neither being licensed teachers, both aspirants had to pass rigorous tests
      before being appointed.
   D. The principal reason why he wanted to be designated was because he had
      never before been to a convention.

9. A. Being that the weather was so inclement, the party has been postponed for  9.____
      at least a month.
   B. He is in New York City only three weeks and he has already seen all the
      thrilling sights in Manhattan and in the other four boroughs.
   C. If you will look it up in the official directory, which can be consulted in the
      library during specified hours, you will discover that the chairman and
      director are Mr. T. Henry Long.
   D. Working hard at college during the day and at the post office during the
      night, he appeared to his family to be indefatigable.

10. A. I would have been happy to oblige you if you only asked me to do it.  10.____
    B. The cold weather, as well as the unceasing wind and rain, have made us
       decide to spend the winter in Florida.
    C. The politician would have been more successful in winning office if he
       would have been less dogmatic.
    D. These trousers are expensive; however, they will wear well.

11. A. All except him wore formal attire at the reception for the ambassador.  11.____
    B. If that chair were to be blown off of the balcony, it might injure someone
       below.
    C. Not a passenger, who was in the crash, survived the impact.
    D. To borrow money off friends is the best way to lose them.

12. A. Approaching Manhattan on the ferry boat from Staten Island, an  12.____
       unforgettable sight of the skyscrapers is seen.
    B. Did you see the exhibit of modernistic paintings as yet?
    C. Gesticulating wildly and ranting in stentorian tones, the speaker was the
       sinecure of all eyes.
    D. The airplane with crew and passengers was lost somewhere in the Pacific
       Ocean.

3 (#1)

13.  A. If one has consistently had that kind of training, it is certainly too late to change your entire method of swimming long distances.
    B. The captain would have been more impressed if you would have been more conscientious in evacuation drills.
    C. The passengers on the stricken ship were all ready to abandon it at the signal.
    D. The villainous shark lashed at the lifeboat with it's tail, trying to upset the rocking boat in order to partake of it's contents.

13.____

14.  A. As one whose been certified as a professional engineer, I believe that the decision to build a bridge over that harbor is unsound.
    B. Between you and me, this project ought to be completed long before winter arrives.
    C. He fervently hoped that the men would be back at camp and to find them busy at their usual chores.
    D. Much to his surprise, he discovered that the climate of Korea was like his home town.

14.____

15.  A. An industrious executive is aided, not impeded, by having a hobby which gives him a fresh point of view on life and its problems.
    B. Frequent absence during the calendar year will surely mitigate against the chances of promotion.
    C. He was unable to go to the committee meeting because he was very ill.
    D. Mr. Brown expressed his disapproval so emphatically that his associates were embarassed

15.____

16.  A. At our next session, the office manager will have told you something about his duties and responsibilities.
    B. In general, the book is absorbing and original and have no hesitation about recommending it.
    C. The procedures followed by private industry in dealing with lateness and absence are different from ours.
    D  We shall treat confidentially any information about Mr. Doe, to whom we understand you have sent reports to for many years.

16.____

17.  A. I talked to one official, whom I knew was fully impartial.
    B. Everyone signed the petition but him.
    C. He proved not only to be a good student but also a good athlete.
    D. All are incorrect.

17.____

18.  A. Every year a large amount of tenants are admitted to housing projects.
    B. Henry Ford owned around a billion dollars in industrial equipment.
    C. He was aggravated by the child's poor behavior.
    D. All are incorrect.

18.____

19. A. Before he was committed to the asylum he suffered from the illusion that he was Napoleon.
    B. Besides stocks, there were also bonds in the safe.
    C. We bet the other team easily.
    D. All are incorrect.

19.____

20. A. Bring this report to your supervisory.
    B. He set the chair down near the table.
    C. The capitol of New York is Albany.
    D. All are incorrect.

20.____

21. A. He was chosen to arbitrate the dispute because everyone knew he would be disinterested.
    B. It is advisable to obtain the best council before making an important decision.
    C. Less college students are interested in teaching than ever before.
    D. All are incorrect.

21.____

22. A. She, hearing a signal, the source lamp flashed.
    B. While hearing a signal, the source lamp flashed.
    C. In hearing a signal, the source lamp flashed.
    D. As she heard a signal, the source lamp flashed.

22.____

23. A. Every one of the time records have been initialed in the designated spaces.
    B. All of the time records has been initialed in the designated spaces.
    C. Each one of the time records was initialed in the designated spaces.
    D. The time records all been initialed in the designated spaces.

23.____

24. A. If there is no one else to answer the phone, you will have to answer it.
    B. You will have to answer it yourself if no one else answers the phone.
    C. If no one else is not around to pick up the phone, you will have to do it.
    D. You will have to answer the phone when nobodys here to do it.

24.____

25. A. Dr. Barnes not in his office. What could I do for you?
    B. Dr. Barnes is not in his office. Is there something I can do for you?
    C. Since Dr. Barnes is not in his office, might there be something I may do for you?
    D. Is there any ways I can assist you since Dr. Barnes is not in his office?

25.____

26. A. She do not understand how the new console works.
    B. The way the new console works, she doesn't understand.
    C. She doesn't understand how the new console works.
    D. The new console works, so that she doesn't understand.

26.____

27. A. Certain changes in my family income must be reported as they occur.
    B. When certain changes in family income occur, it must be reported.
    C. Certain family income change must be reported as they occur.
    D. Certain changes in family income must be reported as they have been occurring.

27.____

28. A. Each tenant has to complete the application themselves.
    B. Each of the tenants have to complete the application by himself.
    C. Each of the tenants has to complete the application himself.
    D. Each of the tenants has to complete the application by themselves.

28.____

29. A. Yours is the only building that the construction will effect.
    B. Your's is the only building affected by the construction.
    C. The construction will only effect your building.
    D. Yours is the only building that will be affected by the construction.

29.____

30. A. There is four tests left.
    B. The number of tests left are four.
    C. There are four tests left.
    D. Four of the tests remains.

30.____

31. A. Each of the applicants takes a test.
    B. Each of the applicant take a test.
    C. Each of the applicants take tests.
    D. Each of the applicants have taken tests.

31.____

32. A. The applicant, not the examiners, are ready.
    B. The applicants, not the examiners, is ready.
    C. The applicants, not the examiner, are ready.
    D. The applicant, not the examiner, are ready

32.____

33. A. You will not progress except you practice.
    B. You will not progress without you practicing.
    C. You will not progress unless you practice.
    D. You will not progress provided you do not practice.

33.____

34. A. Neither the director or the employees will be at the office tomorrow.
    B. Neither the director nor the employees will be at the office tomorrow.
    C. Neither the director, or the secretary nor the other employees will be at the office tomorrow.
    D. Neither the director, the secretary or the other employees will be at the office tomorrow.

34.____

35. A. In my absence, he and her will have to finish the assignment.
    B. In my absence he and she will have to finish the assignment.
    C. In my absence she and him, they will have to finish the assignment.
    D. In my absence he and her both will have to finish the assignment.

35.____

## KEY (CORRECT ANSWERS)

| | | | |
|---|---|---|---|
| 1. B | 11. A | 21. A | 31. A |
| 2. B | 12. D | 22. D | 32. C |
| 3. C | 13. C | 23. C | 33. C |
| 4. B | 14. B | 24. A | 34. B |
| 5. C | 15. A | 25. B | 35. B |
| 6. C | 16. C | 26. C | |
| 7. D | 17. B | 27. A | |
| 8. B | 18. D | 28. C | |
| 9. D | 19. B | 29. D | |
| 10. D | 20. B | 30. C | |

# TEST 2

DIRECTIONS: Each question or incomplete statement is followed by several suggested answers or completions. Select the one that BEST answers the question or completes the statement. *PRINT THE LETTER OF THE CORRECT ANSWER IN THE SPACE AT THE RIGHT.*

Questions 1-4.

DIRECTIONS: Questions 1 through 4 consist of three sentences each. For each question, select the sentence which contains NO error in grammar or usage.

1. A. Be sure that everybody brings his notes to the conference.  1.____
   B. He looked like he meant to hit the boy.
   C. Mr. Jones is one of the clients who was chosen to represent the district.
   D. All are incorrect.

2. A. He is taller than I.  2.____
   B. I'll have nothing to do with these kind of people.
   C. The reason why he will not buy the house is because it is too expensive.
   D. All are incorrect.

3. A. Aren't I eligible for this apartment.  3.____
   B. Have you seen him anywheres?
   C. He should of come earlier.
   D. All are incorrect.

4. A. He graduated college in 2022.  4.____
   B. He hadn't but one more line to write.
   C. Who do you think is the author of this report?
   D. All are incorrect.

Questions 5-35.

DIRECTIONS: In each of the following questions, only one of the four sentences conforms to standards of correct usage. The other three contain errors in grammar, diction, or punctuation. Select the choice in each question which BEST conforms to standards of correct usage. Consider a choice correct if it contains none of the errors mentioned above, even though there may be other ways of expressing the same thought.

5. A. It is obvious that no one wants to be a kill-joy if they can help it.  5.____
   B. It is not always possible, and perhaps it never ispossible, to judge a person's character by just looking at him.
   C. When Yogi Berra of the New York Yankees hit an immortal grandslam home run, everybody in the huge stadium including Pittsburgh fans, rose to his feet.
   D. Every one of us students must pay tuition today.

6. A. The physician told the young mother that if the baby is not able to digest its milk, it should be boiled.
   B. There is no doubt whatsoever that he felt deeply hurt because John Smith had betrayed the trust.
   C. Having partaken of a most delicious repast prepared by Tessie Breen, the hostess, the horses were driven home immediately thereafter.
   D. The attorney asked my wife and myself several questions.

6.____

7. A. Despite all denials, there is no doubt in my mind that
   B. At this time everyone must deprecate the demogogic attack made by one of our Senators on one of our most revered statesmen.
   C. In the first game of a crucial two-game series, Ted Williams, got two singles, both of them driving in a run.
   D. Our visitor brought good news to John and I.

7.____

8. A. If he would have told me, I should have been glad to help him in his dire financial emergency.
   B. Newspaper men have often asserted that diplomats or so-called official spokesmen sometimes employ equivocation in attempts to deceive.
   C. I think someones coming to collect money for the Red Cross.
   D. In a masterly summation, the young attorney expressed his belief that the facts clearly militate against this opinion.

8.____

9. A. We have seen most all the exhibits.
   B. Without in the least underestimating your advice, in my opinion the situation has grown immeasurably worse in the past few days.
   C. I wrote to the box office treasurer of the hit show that a pair of orchestra seats would be preferable.
   D. As the grim story of Pearl Harbor was broadcast on that fateful December 7, it was the general opinion that war was inevitable.

9.____

10. A. Without a moment's hesitation, Casey Stengel said that Larry Berra works harder than any player on the team.
    B. There is ample evidence to indicate that many animals can run faster than any human being.
    C. No one saw the accident but I.
    D. Example of courage is the heroic defense put up by the paratroopers against overwhelming odds.

10.____

11. A. If you prefer these kind, Mrs. Grey, we shall be more than willing to let you have them reasonably.
    B. If you like these here, Mrs. Grey, we shall be more than willing to let you have them reasonably.
    C. If you like these, Mrs. Grey, we shall be more than willing to let you have them.
    D. Who shall we appoint?

11.____

12. A. The number of errors are greater in speech than in writing.
    B. The doctor rather than the nurse was to blame for his being neglected.
    C. Because the demand for these books have been so great, we reduced the price.
    D. John Galsworthy, the English novelist, could not have survived a serious illness; had it not been for loving care.

    12.____

13. A. Our activities this year have seldom ever been as interesting as they have been this month.
    B. Our activities this month have been more interesting, or at least as interesting as those of any month this year.
    C. Our activities this month has been more interesting than those of any other month this year.
    D. Neither Jean nor her sister was at home.

    13.____

14. A. George B. Shaw's view of common morality, as well as his wit sparkling with a dash of perverse humor here and there, have led critics to term him "The Incurable Rebel."
    B. The President's program was not always received with the wholehearted endorsement of his own party, which is why the party faces difficulty in drawing up a platform for the coming election.
    C. The reason why they wanted to travel was because they had never been away from home.
    D. Facing a barrage of cameras, the visiting celebrity found it extremely difficult to express his opinions clearly.

    14.____

15. A. When we calmed down, we all agreed that our anger had been kind of unnecessary and had not helped the situation.
    B. Without him going into all the details, he made us realize the horror of the accident.
    C. Like one girl, for example, who applied for two positions.
    D. Do not think that you have to be so talented as he is in order to play in the school orchestra.

    15.____

16. A. He looked very peculiarly to me.
    B. He certainly looked at me peculiar.
    C. Due to the train's being late, we had to wait an hour.
    D. The reason for the poor attendance is that it is raining.

    16.____

17. A. About one out of four own an automobile.
    B. The collapse of the old Mitchell Bridge was caused by defective construction in the central pier.
    C. Brooks Atkinson was well acquainted with the best literature, thus helping him to become an able critic.
    D. He has to stand still until the relief man comes up, thus giving him no chance to move about and keep warm.

    17.____

18. A. He is sensitive to confusion and withdraws from people whom he feels are too noisy.
    B. Do you know whether the data is statistically correct?
    C. Neither the mayor or the aldermen are to blame.
    D. Of those who were graduated from high school, a goodly percentage went to college.

18.____

19. A. Acting on orders, the offices were searched by a designated committee.
    B. The answer probably is nothing.
    C. I thought it to be all right to excuse them from class.
    D. I think that he is as successful a singer, if not more successful, than Mary.

19.____

20. A. $360,000 is really very little to pay for such a wellbuilt house.
    B. The creatures looked like they had come from outer space.
    C. It was her, he knew!
    D. Nobody but me knows what to do.

20.____

21. A. Mrs. Smith looked good in her new suit.
    B. New York may be compared with Chicago.
    C. I will not go to the meeting except you go with me.
    D. I agree with this editorial.

21.____

22. A. My opinions are different from his.
    B. There will be less students in class now.
    C. Helen was real glad to find her watch.
    D. It had been pushed off of her dresser.

22.____

23. A. Almost everyone, who has been to California, returns with glowing reports.
    B. George Washington, John Adams, and Thomas Jefferson, were our first presidents.
    C. Mr. Walters, whom we met at the bank yesterday, is the man, who gave me my first job.
    D. One should study his lessons as carefully as he can.

23.____

24. A. We had such a good time yesterday.
    B. When the bell rang, the boys and girls went in the schoolhouse.
    C. John had the worst headache when he got up this morning.
    D. Today's assignment is somewhat longer than yesterday's.

24.____

25. A. Neither the mayor nor the city clerk are willing to talk.
    B. Neither the mayor nor the city clerk is willing to talk.
    C. Neither the mayor or the city clerk are willing to talk.
    D  Neither the mayor or the city clerk is willing to talk.

25.____

26. A. Being that he is that kind of boy, cooperation cannot be expected.
    B. He interviewed people who he thought had something to say.
    C. Stop whomever enters the building regardless of rank or office held.
    D. Passing through the countryside, the scenery pleased us.

26.____

27. A. The childrens' shoes were in their closet.  27.____
    B. The children's shoes were in their closet.
    C. The childs' shoes were in their closet.
    D. The childs' shoes were in his closet.

28. A. An agreement was reached between the defendant, the plaintiff, the  28.____
       plaintiff's attorney and the insurance company as to the amount of the
       settlement.
    B. Everybody was asked to give their versions of the accident.
    C. The consensus of opinion was that the evidence was inconclusive.
    D. The witness stated that if he was rich, he wouldn't have had to loan the
       money.

29. A. Before beginning the investigation, all the materials related to the case were  29.____
       carefully assembled.
    B. The reason for his inability to keep the appointment is because of his injury
       in the accident.
    C. This here evidence tends to support the claim of the defendant.
    D. We interviewed all the witnesses who, according to the driver, were still in
       town.

30. A. Each claimant was allowed the full amount of their medical expenses.  30.____
    B. Either of the three witnesses is available.
    C. Every one of the witnesses was asked to tell his story.
    D. Neither of the witnesses are right.

31. A. The commissioner, as well as his deputy and various bureau heads, were  31.____
       present.
    B. A new organization of employers and employees have been formed.
    C. One or the other of these men have been selected.
    D. The number of pages in the book is enough to discourage a reader.

32. A. Between you and me, I think he is the better man.  32.____
    B. He was believed to be me.
    C. Is it us that you wish to see?
    D. The winners are him and her.

33. A. Beside the statement to the police, the witness spoke to no one.  33.____
    B. He made no statement other than to the police and I.
    C. He made no statement to any one else, aside from the police.
    D. The witness spoke to no one but me.

34. A. The claimant has no one to blame but himself.  34.____
    B. The boss sent us, he and I, to deliver the packages.
    C. The lights come from mine and not his car.
    D. There was room on the stairs for him and myself.

35. A. Admission to this clinic is limited to patients' inability to pay for medical care.
    B. Patients who can pay little or nothing for medical care are treated in this clinic.
    C. The patient's ability to pay for medical care is the determining factor in his admission to this clinic.
    D. This clinic is for the patient's that cannot afford to pay or that can pay a little for medical care.

35.____

## KEY (CORRECT ANSWERS)

| | | | | | | | |
|---|---|---|---|---|---|---|---|
| 1. | A | 11. | C | 21. | A | 31. | D |
| 2. | A | 12. | B | 22. | A | 32. | A |
| 3. | D | 13. | D | 23. | D | 33. | D |
| 4. | C | 14. | D | 24. | D | 34. | A |
| 5. | D | 15. | D | 25. | B | 35. | B |
| 6. | D | 16. | D | 26. | B | | |
| 7. | B | 17. | B | 27. | B | | |
| 8. | B | 18. | D | 28. | C | | |
| 9. | D | 19. | B | 29. | D | | |
| 10. | B | 20. | D | 30. | C | | |

# EXAMINATION SECTION

# TEST 1

DIRECTIONS: Each question or incomplete statement is followed by several suggested answers or completions. Select the one that BEST answers the question or completes the statement. *PRINT THE LETTER OF THE CORRECT ANSWER IN THE SPACE AT THE RIGHT.*

Questions 1-25. A student has written an article for the high school newspaper, using the skills learned in a stenography and typewriting class in its preparation. In the article which follows, certain words or groups of words are underlined and numbered. The underlined word or group of words may be incorrect because they present an error in grammar, usage, sentence structure, capitalization, diction, or punctuation. For each numbered word or group of words, there is an identically numbered question consisting of four choices based only on the underlined portion. Indicate the BEST choice. <u>Unnecessary changes will be considered incorrect.</u>

### TIGERS VIE FOR CITY CHAMPIONSHIP

In their second year of varsity football, the North Shore Tigers have gained a shot at the city championship. Last Saturday in the play-offs, the Tigers defeated the Western High School Cowboys, <u>thus eliminated that team</u> from contention. Most of the credit for the
(1)
team's improvement must go to Joe Harris, the coach. <u>To play as well as they do</u> now,
(2)
the coach must have given the team superior instruction. There is no doubt that,

<u>if a coach is effective, his influence is over</u> many young minds.
(3)
With this major victory behind them, the Tigers can now look forward <u>to meet the</u>
(4)
defending champions, the Revere Minutemen, in the finals.

The win over the Cowboys was <u>due</u> to North Side's supremacy in the air. The Tigers'
(5)
players have the advantages of strength and of <u>being speedy</u>. Our sterling quarterback, Butch
(6)
Carter, a master of the long pass, used <u>these kind of passes</u> to bedevil the boys from Western.
(7)
As a matter of fact, if the Tigers <u>would have used</u> the passing offense earlier in the game, the
(8)
score would have been more one-sided. Butch, by the way, our all-around senior student, has already been tapped for bigger things. Having the highest marks in his class, <u>Barton College</u>

has offered him a scholarship.
         (9)

The team's defense is another story.  During the last few weeks, neither the linebackers nor the safety man have shown sufficient ability to contain their opponents' running game.  In
                                                    (10)
the city final, the defensive unit's failing to complete it's assignments may lead to disaster.
                    (11)
However, the coach said that this unit not only has been cooperative but also the coach raise
                                                    (12)
their eagerness to learn.  He also said that this team has not and never will give up.  This kind
                                                                   (13)
of spirit is contagious, therefore I predict that the Tigers will win because I have affection and full
                        (14)                                                                (15)
confidence in the team.

One of the happy surprises this season is Peter Yisko, our punter.  Peter is in the United
                                                                            (16)
States for only two years.  When he was in grammar school in the old country, it was not necessary for him to have studied hard.  Now, he depends on the football team to help him with
                  (17)
his English.  Everybody but the team mascot and I have been pressed into service.  Peter was
                        (18
ineligible last year when he learned that he would only obtain half of the credits he had
                            (19)
completed in Europe.  Nevertheless, he attended occasional practice sessions, but he soon found out that, if one wants to be a successful player, you must realize that regular practice is
                                                        (20)
required.  In fact, if a team is to be successful, it is necessary that everyone be present for all
                                                                              (21)
practice sessions.  "The life of a football player," says Peter, "is better than a scholar."
                                                                       (22)
Facing the Minutemen, the Tigers will meet their most formidable opposition yet.  This team is not only gaining a bad reputation but also indulging in illegal practices on the field.
        (23)
They can't hardly object to us being technical about penalties under these circumstances.
     (24)
As far as the Minutemen are concerned, a victory will taste sweet like a victory should.
                                            (25)

1.   A.   that eliminated that team     B.   and they were eliminated       1.____
     C.   and eliminated them           D.   Correct as is

3 (#1)

2.  A. To make them play as well as they do
    B. Having played so well
    C. After they played so well
    D. Correct as is

    2.____

3.  A. if coaches are effective; they have influence over
    B. to be effective, a coach influences over
    C. if a coach is effective, he influences
    D. Correct as is

    3.____

4.  A. to meet with           B. to meeting
    C. to a meeting of        D. Correct as is

    4.____

5.  A. because of             B. on account of
    C. motivated by           D. Correct as is

    5.____

6.  A. operating swiftly      B. speed
    C. running speedily       D. Correct as is

    6.____

7.  A. these kinds of pass    B. this kind of passes
    C. this kind of pass      D. Correct as is

    7.____

8.  A. would of used          B. had used
    C. were using             D. Correct as is

    8.____

9.  A. he was offered a scholarship by Barton College.
    B. Barton College offered a scholarship to him.
    C. a scholarship was offered him by Barton College
    D. Correct as is

    9.____

10. A. had shown              B. were showing
    C. has shown              D. Correct as is

    10.____

11. A. the defensive unit failing to complete its assignment
    B. the defensive unit's failing to complete its assignment
    C. the defensive unit failing to complete it's assignment
    D. Correct as is

    11.____

12. A. has been not only cooperative, but also eager to learn
    B. has not only been cooperative, but also shows eagerness to learn
    C. has been not only cooperative, but also they were eager to learn
    D. Correct as is

    12.____

13. A. has not given up and never will
    B. has not and never would give up
    C. has not given up and never will give up
    D. Correct as is

    13.____

4 (#1)

14. A. .Therefore  B. : therefore  14.____
    C. —therefore  D. Correct as is

15. A. full confidence and affection for  15.____
    B. affection for and full confidence in
    C. affection and full confidence concerning
    D. Correct as is

16. A. is living  B. was living  16.____
    C. has been  D. Correct as is

17. A. to study  B. to be studying  17.____
    C. to have been studying  D. Correct as is

18. A. but the team mascot and me has  18.____
    B. but the team mascot and myself has
    C. but the team mascot and me have
    D. Correct as is

19. A. only learned that he would obtain half  19.____
    B. learned that he would obtain only half
    C. learned that he only would obtain half
    D. Correct as is

20. A. a person  B. one  20.____
    C. one  D. every

21. A. is  B. will be  21.____
    C. shall be  D. Correct as is

22. A. to be a scholar  B. being a scholar  22.____
    C. that of a scholar  D. Correct as is

23. A. not only is gaining a bad reputation  23.____
    B. is gaining not only a bad reputation
    C. is not gaining only a bad reputation
    D. Correct as is

24. A. can hardly object to us being  B. can hardly object to our being  24.____
    C. can't hardly object to our being  D. Correct as is

25. A victory will taste sweet like it should  25.____
    B. victory will taste sweetly as it should taste
    C. victory will taste sweet as a victory should
    D. Correct as is

Questions 26-30.

DIRECTIONS: Questions 26 through 30 are to be answered on the basis of the instructions and paragraph which follow.

The paragraph which follows is part of report prepared by a buyer for submission to his superior. The paragraph contains 5 underlined groups of words, each one bearing a number which identifies the question relating to it. Each of these groups of words MAY or MAY NOT represent standard written English, suitable for use in a formal report. For each question, decide whether the group of words used in the paragraph which is always choice A is standard written English and should be retained, or whether choice B, C, or D.

On October 23, 2009 the vendor delivered two microscopes to the using agency. <u>When they inspected</u>, one microscope was found to have a defective part. The vendor was
(26)
notified, and offered to replace the defective part; the using agency, however, requested <u>that the microscope be replaced</u>. The vendor claimed that complete replacement was
(27)
unnecessary and refused to comply with the agency's demand, <u>having the result that the
(28)
agency declared</u> that it will pay only for the acceptable microscope. At that point
<u>I got involved by the agency's contacting me</u>. The agency requested that I speak to the vendor
(29)
<u>since I handled the original purchase and have dealed with this vendor before.</u>
(30)

26. A. When they inspected  26.____
    B. Upon inspection
    C. The inspection report said that
    D. Having inspected,

27. A. that the microscope be replaced  27.____
    B. a whole new microscope in replacement
    C. to have a replacement for the microscope
    D. that they get the microscope replaced

28. A. , having the result that the agency declared  28.____
    B. ; the agency consequently declared
    C. , which refusal caused the agency to consequently declare
    D. , with the result of the agency's declaring

29. A. I got involved by the agency's contacting me  29.____
    B. I became involved, being contacted by the agency
    C. the agency contacting me, I got involved
    D. the agency contacted me and I became involved

30. A. have dealed with this vendor before.
    B. done business before with this vendor.
    C. know this vendor by prior dealings
    D. have dealt with this vendor before.

30._____

## KEY (CORRECT ANSWERS)

| | | | | | | | |
|---|---|---|---|---|---|---|---|
| 1. | C | 11. | B | 21. | D | | |
| 2. | A | 12. | A | 22. | C | | |
| 3. | C | 13. | B | 23. | D | | |
| 4. | B | 14. | A | 24. | A | | |
| 5. | A | 15. | B | 25. | C | | |
| 6. | B | 16. | C | 26. | B | | |
| 7. | C | 17. | A | 27. | A | | |
| 8. | B | 18. | A | 28. | B | | |
| 9. | D | 19. | B | 29. | D | | |
| 10. | C | 20. | C | 30. | D | | |

# EXAMINATION SECTION
## TEST 1

DIRECTIONS: Each question or incomplete statement is followed by several suggested answers or completions. Select the one that BEST answers the question or completes the statement. *PRINT THE LETTER OF THE CORRECT ANSWER IN THE SPACE AT THE RIGHT.*

1. Which of the following sentences is punctuated INCORRECTLY?
    A. Johnson said, "One tiny virus, Blanche, can multiply so fast that it will become 200 viruses in 25 minutes."
    B. With economic pressures hitting them from all sides, American farmers have become the weak link in the food chain.
    C. The degree to which this is true, of course, depends on the personalities of the people involved, the subject matter, and the atmosphere in general.
    D. "What loneliness, asked George Eliot, is more lonely than distrust?"

2. Which of the following sentences is punctuated INCORRECTLY?
    A. Based on past experiences, do you expect the plumber to show up late, not have the right parts, and overcharge you.
    B. When polled, however, the participants were most concerned that it be convenient.
    C. No one mentioned the flavor of the coffee, and no one seemed to care that china was used instead of plastic.
    D. As we said before, sometimes people view others as things; they don't see them as living, breathing beings like themselves.

3. Convention members travelled here from Kingston New York Pittsfield Massachusetts Bennington Vermont and Hartford Connecticut.
   How many commas should there be in the above sentence?
    A. 3     B. 4     C. 5     D. 6

4. Of the two speakers the one who spoke about human rights is more famous and more humble.
   How many commas should there be in the above sentence?
    A. 1     B. 2     C. 3     D. 4

5. Which sentence is punctuated INCORRECTLY?
    A. Five people voted no; two voted yes; one person abstained.
    B. Well, consider what has been said here today, but we won't make any promises.
    C. Anthropologists divide history into three major periods: the Stone Age, the Bronze Age, and the Iron Age.
    D. Therefore, we may create a stereotype about people who are unsuccessful; we may see them as lazy, unintelligent, or afraid of success.

6. Which sentence is punctuated INCORRECTLY?
   A. Studies have found that the unpredictability of customer behavior can lead to a great deal of stress, particularly if the behavior is unpleasant or if the employee has little control over it.
   B. If this degree of emotion and variation can occur in spectator sports, imagine the role that perceptions can play when there are real stakes involved.
   C. At other times, however hidden expectations may sabotage or severely damage an encounter without anyone knowing what happened.
   D. There are usually four issues to look for in a conflict: differences in values, goals, methods, and facts.

Questions 7-10.

DIRECTIONS: Questions 7 through 10 test your ability to distinguish between words that sound alike but are spelled differently and have different meanings. In the following groups of sentences, one of the underlined words is used incorrectly.

7. A. By accepting responsibility for their actions, managers promote trust.
   B. Dropping hints or making illusions to things that you would like changed sometimes leads to resentment.
   C. The entire unit loses respect for the manager and resents the reprimand.
   D. Many people are averse to confronting problems directly; they would rather avoid them.

8. A. What does this say about the effect our expectations have on those we supervise?
   B. In an effort to save time between 9 A.M. and 1 P.M., the staff members devised their own interpretation of what was to be done on these forms.
   C. The taskmaster's principal concern is for getting the work done; he or she is not concerned about the need or interests of employees.
   D. The advisor's main objective was increasing Angela's ability to invest her capitol wisely.

9. A. A typical problem is that people have to cope with the internal censer of their feelings.
   B. Sometimes, in their attempt to sound more learned, people speak in ways that are barely comprehensible.
   C. The council will meet next Friday to decide whether Abrams should continue as representative.
   D. His descent from grace was assured by that final word.

10. A. The doctor said that John's leg had to remain stationary or it would not heal properly.
    B. There is a city ordinance against parking too close to fire hydrants.
    C. Meyer's problem is that he is never discrete when talking about office politics.
    D. Mrs. Thatcher probably worked harder than any other British Prime Minister had ever worked.

Questions 11-20.

DIRECTIONS: For each of the following groups of sentences in Questions 11 through 20, select the sentence which is the BEST example of English usage and grammar.

11. A. She is a woman who, at age sixty, is distinctly attractive and cares about how they look.
    B. It was a seemingly impossible search, and no one knew the problems better than she.
    C. On the surface, they are all sweetness and light, but his morbid character is under it.
    D. The minicopier, designed to appeal to those who do business on the run like architects in the field or business travelers, weigh about four pounds.

11._____

12. A. Neither the administrators nor the union representative regret the decision to settle the disagreement.
    B. The plans which are made earlier this year were no longer being considered.
    C. I would have rode with him if I had known he was leaving at five.
    D. I don't know who she said had it.

12._____

13. A. Writing at a desk, the memo was handed to her for immediate attention.
    B. Carla didn't water Carl's plants this week, which she never does.
    C. Not only are they good workers, with excellent writing and speaking skills, and they get to the crux of any problem we hand them.
    D. We've noticed that this enthusiasm for undertaking new projects sometimes interferes with his attention to detail.

13._____

14. A. It's obvious that Nick offends people by being unruly, inattentive, and having no patience.
    B. Marcia told Genie that she would have to leave soon.
    C. Here are the papers you need to complete your investigation.
    D. Julio was startled by you're comment.

14._____

15. A. The new manager has done good since receiving her promotion, but her secretary has helped her a great deal.
    B. One of the personnel managers approached John and tells him that the client arrived unexpectedly.
    C. If somebody can supply us with the correct figures, they should do so immediately.
    D. Like zealots, advocates seek power because they want to influence the policies and actions of an organization.

15._____

16. A. Between you and me, Chris probably won't finish this assignment in time.  16.___
    B. Rounding the corner, the snack bar appeared before us.
    C. Parker's radical reputation made to the Supreme Court his appointment impossible.
    D. By the time we arrived, Marion finishes briefing James and returns to Hank's office.

17. A. As we pointed out earlier, the critical determinant of the success of middle managers is their ability to communicate well with others.  17.___
    B. The lecturer stated there wasn't no reason for bad supervision.
    C. We are well aware whose at fault in this instance.
    D. When planning important changes, it's often wise to seek the participation of others because employees often have much valuable ideas to offer.

18. A. Joan had ought to throw out those old things that were damaged when the roof leaked.  18.___
    B. I spose he'll let us know what he's decided when he finally comes to a decision.
    C. Carmen was walking to work when she suddenly realized that she had left her lunch on the table as she passed the market.
    D. Are these enough plants for your new office?

19. A. First move the lever forward, and then they should lift the ribbon casing before trying to take it out.  19.___
    B. Michael finished quickest than any other person in the office.
    C. There is a special meeting for we committee members today at 4 p.m.
    D. My husband is worried about our having to work overtime next week.

20. A. Another source of conflicts are individuals who possess very poor interpersonal skills.  20.___
    B. It is difficult for us to work with him on projects because these kinds of people are not interested in team building.
    C. Each of the departments was represented at the meeting.
    D. Poor boy, he never should of past that truck on the right.

Questions 21-28.

DIRECTIONS: In Questions 21 through 28, there may be a problem with English grammar or usage. If a problem does exist, select the letter that indicates the most effective change. If no problem exists, select Choice A.

21. He rushed her to the hospital and stayed with her, even though this took quite a bit of his time, he didn't charge her anything.  21.___
    A. No changes are necessary.
    B. Change even though to although
    C. Change the first comma to a period and capitalize even
    D. Change rushed to had rushed

22. Waiting that appears unfairly feels longer than waiting that seems justified.  22.____
    A. No changes are necessary.
    B. Change unfairly to unfair
    C. Change appears to seems
    D. Change longer to longest

23. May be you and the person who argued with you will be able to reach an agreement.  23.____
    A. No changes are necessary
    B. Change will be to were
    C. Change argued with to had an argument with
    D. Change May be to Maybe

24. Any one of them could of taken the file while you were having coffee.  24.____
    A. No changes are necessary
    B. Change any one to anyone
    C. Change of to have
    D. Change were having to were out having

25. While people get jobs or move from poverty level to better paying employment, they stop receiving benefits and start paying taxes.  25.____
    A. No changes are necessary
    B. Change While to As
    C. Change stop to will stop
    D. Change get to obtain

26. Maribeth's phone rang while talking to George about the possibility of their meeting Tom at three this afternoon.  26.____
    A. No changes are necessary
    B. Change their to her
    C. Move to George so that it follows Tom
    D. Change talking to she was talking

27. According to their father, Lisa is smarter than Chris, but Emily is the smartest of the three sisters.  27.____
    A. No changes are necessary
    B. Change their to her
    C. Change is to was
    D. Make two sentences, changing the second comma to a period and omitting but

28. Yesterday, Mark and he claim that Carl took Carol's ideas and used them inappropriately.  28.____
    A. No changes are necessary
    B. Change claim to claimed
    C. Change inappropriately to inappropriate
    D. Change Carol's to Carols'

Questions 29-34.

DIRECTIONS: For each group of sentences in Questions 29 through 34, select the choice that represents the BEST editing of the problem sentence.

29. The managers expected employees to be at their desks at all times, but they would always be late or leave unannounced.
    A. The managers wanted employees to always be at their desks, but they would always be late or leave unannounced.
    B. Although the managers expected employees to be at their desks no matter what came up, they would always be late and leave without telling anyone.
    C. Although the managers expected employees to be at their desks at all times, the managers would always be late or leave without telling anyone.
    D. The managers expected the employee to never leave their desks, but they would always be late or leave without telling anyone.

29.____

30. The one who is department manager he will call you to discuss the problem tomorrow morning at 10 A.M.
    A. The one who is department manager will call you tomorrow morning at ten to discuss the problem.
    B. The department manager will call you to discuss the problem tomorrow at 10 A.M.
    C. Tomorrow morning at 10 A.M., the department manager will call you to discuss the problem.
    D. Tomorrow morning the department manager will call you to discuss the problem.

30.____

31. A conference on child care in the workplace the $200 cost of which to attend may be prohibitive to childcare workers who earn less than that weekly.
    A. A conference on child care in the workplace that costs $200 may be too expensive for childcare workers who earn less than that each week.
    B. A conference on child care in the workplace, the cost of which to attend is $200, may be prohibitive to childcare workers who earn less than that weekly.
    C. A conference on child care in the workplace who costs $200 may be too expensive for childcare workers who earn less than that a week.
    D. A conference on child care in the workplace which costs $200 may be too expensive to childcare workers who earn less than that on a weekly basis.

31.____

32. In accordance with estimates recently made, there are 40,000 to 50,000 nuclear weapons in our world today.
    A. Because of estimates recently, there are 40,000 to 50,000 nuclear weapons in the world today.
    B. In accordance with estimates made recently, there are 40,000 to 50,000 nuclear weapons in the world today.

32.____

C. According to estimates made recently, there are 40,000 to 50,000 weapons in the world today.
D. According to recent estimates, there are 40,000 to 50,000 nuclear weapons in the world today.

33. Motivation is important in problem solving, but they say that excessive motivation can inhibit the creative process. 33.____
    A. Motivation is important in problem solving, but, as they say, too much of it can inhibit the creative process.
    B. Motivation is important in problem solving and excessive motivation will inhibit the creative process.
    C. Motivation is important in problem solving, but excessive motivation can inhibit the creative process.
    D. Motivation is important in problem solving because excessive motivation can inhibit the creative process.

34. In selecting the best option calls for consulting with all the people that are involved in it. 34.____
    A. In selecting the best option consulting with all people concerned with it.
    B. Calling for the best option, we consulted all the affected people.
    C. We called all the people involved to select the best option.
    D. To be sure of selecting the best option, one should consult all the people involved.

35. There are a number of problems with the following letter. From the options below, select the version that is MOST in accordance with standard business style, tone, and form. 35.____

    Dear Sir:

    We are so sorry that we have had to backorder your order for 15,000 widgets and 2,300 whatzits for such a long time. We have been having incredibly bad luck lately. When your order first came in no one could get to it because my secretary was out with the flu and her replacement didn't know what she was doing, then there was the dock strike in Cucamonga which held things up for awhile, and then it just somehow got lost. We think it may have fallen behind the radiator.
    We are happy to say that all these problems have been taken care of, we are caught up on supplies, and we should have the stuff to you soon, in the near future—about two weeks. You may not believe us after everything you've been through with us, but it's true.
    We'll let you know as soon as we have a secure date for delivery. Thank you so much for continuing to do business with us after all the problems this probably has caused you.

    Yours very sincerely,
    Rob Barker

## 8 (#1)

A. Dear Sir:

   We are so sorry that we have had to backorder your order for 15,000 widgets and 2,300 whatzits. We have been having problems with staff lately and the dock strike hasn't helped anything.
   We are happy to say that all these problems have been taken care of. I've told my secretary to get right on it, and we should have the stuff to you soon. Thank you so much for continuing to do business with us after all the problems this must have caused you.
   We'll let you know as soon as we have a secure date for delivery.

   Sincerely,
   Rob Barker

B. Dear Sir:

   We regret that we haven't been able to fill your order for 15,000 widgets and 2,300 whatzits in a timely fashion.
   We'll let you know as soon as we have a secure date for delivery.

   Sincerely,
   Rob Barker

C. Dear Sir:

   We are so very sorry that we haven't been able to fill your order for 15,000 widgets and 2,300 whatzits. We have been having incredibly bad luck lately, but things are much better now.
   Thank you so much for bearing with us through all of this. We'll let you know as soon as we have a secure date for delivery.

   Sincerely,
   Rob Barker

D. Dear Sir:

   We are very sorry that we haven't been able to fill your order for 15,000 widgets and 2,300 whatzits. Due to unforeseen difficulties, we have had to back-order your request. At this time, supplies have caught up to demand, and we foresee a delivery date within the next two weeks.
   We'll let you know as soon as we have a secure date for delivery. Thank you for your patience.

   Sincerely,
   Rob Barker

## KEY (CORRECT ANSWERS)

| | | | | | | | |
|---|---|---|---|---|---|---|---|
| 1. | D | 11. | B | 21. | C | 31. | A |
| 2. | A | 12. | D | 22. | B | 32. | D |
| 3. | B | 13. | D | 23. | D | 33. | C |
| 4. | A | 14. | C | 24. | C | 34. | D |
| 5. | B | 15. | D | 25. | B | 35. | D |
| 6. | C | 16. | A | 26. | D | | |
| 7. | B | 17. | A | 27. | A | | |
| 8. | D | 18. | D | 28. | B | | |
| 9. | A | 19. | D | 29. | C | | |
| 10. | C | 20. | C | 30. | B | | |

# PREPARING WRITTEN MATERIAL
## EXAMINATION SECTION
## TEST 1

DIRECTIONS: Each question or incomplete statement is followed by several suggested answers or completions. Select the one that BEST answers the question or completes the statement. *PRINT THE LETTER OF THE CORRECT ANSWER IN THE SPACE AT THE RIGHT.*

1. The one of the following sentences which is LEAST acceptable from the viewpoint of correct usage is:
   A. The police thought the fugitive to be him.
   B. The criminals set a trap for whoever would fall into it.
   C. It is ten years ago since the fugitive fled from the city.
   D. The lecturer argued that criminals are usually cowards.
   E. The police removed four bucketfuls of earth from the scene of the crime.

1.____

2. The one of the following sentences which is LEAST acceptable from the viewpoint of correct usage is:
   A. The patrolman scrutinized the report with great care.
   B. Approaching the victim of the assault, two bruises were noticed by the patrolman.
   C. As soon as I had broken down the door, I stepped into the room.
   D. I observed the accused loitering near the building, which was closed at the time.
   E. The storekeeper complained that his neighbor was guilty of violating a local ordinance.

2.____

3. The one of the following sentences which is LEAST acceptable from the viewpoint of correct usage is:
   A. I realized immediately that he intended to assault the woman, so I disarmed him.
   B. It was apparent that Mr. Smith's explanation contained many inconsistencies.
   C. Despite the slippery condition of the street, he managed to stop the vehicle before injuring the child.
   D. Not a single one of them wish, despite the damage to property, to make a formal complaint.
   E. The body was found lying on the floor.

3.____

4. The one of the following sentences which contains NO error in usage is:
   A. After the robbers left, the proprietor stood tied in his chair for about two hours before help arrived.
   B. In the cellar I found the watchman's hat and coat.
   C. The persons living in adjacent apartments stated that they had heard no unusual noises.

4.____

187

D. Neither a knife or any firearms were found in the room.
E. Walking down the street, the shouting of the crowd indicated that something was wrong.

5. The one of the following sentences which contains NO error in usage is:
    A. The policeman lay a firm hand on the suspect's shoulder.
    B. It is true that neither strength nor agility are the most important requirement for a good patrolman.
    C. Good citizens constantly strive to do more than merely comply the restraints imposed by society.
    D. No decision was made as to whom the prize should be awarded.
    E. Twenty years is considered a severe sentence for a felony.

6. Which of the following sentences is NOT expressed in standard English usage?
    A. The victim reached a pay-phone booth and manages to call police headquarters.
    B. By the time the call was received, the assailant had left the scene.
    C. The victim has been a respected member of the community for the past eleven years.
    D. Although the lighting was bad and the shadows were deep, the storekeeper caught sight of the attacker.
    E. Additional street lights have since been installed, and the patrols have been strengthened.

7. Which of the following sentences is NOT expressed in standard English usage?
    A. The judge upheld the attorney's right to question the witness about the missing glove.
    B. To be absolutely fair to all parties is the jury's chief responsibility.
    C. Having finished the report, a loud noise in the next room startled the sergeant.
    D. The witness obviously enjoyed having played a part in the proceedings.
    E. The sergeant planned to assign the case to whoever arrived first.

8. In which of the following sentences is a word misused?
    A. As a matter of principle, the captain insisted that the suspect's partner be brought for questioning.
    B. The principle suspect had been detained at the station house for most of the day.
    C. The principal in the crime had no previous criminal record, but his closest associate had been convicted of felonies on two occasions.
    D. The interest payments had been made promptly, but the firm had been drawing upon the principal for these payments.
    E. The accused insisted that his high school principal would furnish him a character reference.

3 (#1)

9. Which of the following statements is ambiguous?      9.____
   A. Mr. Sullivan explained why Mr. Johnson had been dismissed from his job.
   B. The storekeeper told the patrolman he had made a mistake.
   C. After waiting three hours, the patients in the doctor's office were sent home.
   D. The janitor's duties were to maintain the building in good shape and to answer tenants' complaints.
   E. The speed limit should, in my opinion, be raised to sixty miles an hour on that stretch of road.

10. In which of the following is the punctuation or capitalization faulty?      10.____
    A. The accident occurred at an intersection in the Kew Gardens section of Queens, near the bus stop.
    B. The sedan, not the convertible, was struck in the side.
    C. Before any of the patrolmen had left the police car received an important message from headquarters.
    D. The dog that had been stolen was returned to his master, John Dempsey, who lived in East Village.
    E. The letter had been sent to 12 Hillside Terrace, Rutland, Vermont 05702.

Questions 11-25.

DIRECTIONS:  Questions 11 through 25 are to be answered in accordance with correct English usage; that is, standard English rather than nonstandard or substandard. Nonstandard and substandard English includes words or expressions usually classified as slang, dialect, illiterate, etc., which are not generally accepted as correct in current written communication. Standard English also requires clarity, proper punctuation and capitalization and appropriate use of words. Write the letter of the sentence NOT expressed in standard English usage in the space at the right.

11. A. There were three witnesses to the accident.      11.____
    B. At least three witnesses were found to testify for the plaintiff.
    C. Three of the witnesses who took the stand was uncertain about the defendant's competence to drive.
    D. Only three witnesses came forward to testify for the plaintiff.
    E. The three witnesses to the accident were pedestrians.

12. A. The driver had obviously drunk too many martinis before leaving for home.      12.____
    B. The boy who drowned had swum in these same waters many times before.
    C. The petty thief had stolen a bicycle from a private driveway before he was apprehended.
    D. The detectives had brung in the heroin shipment they intercepted.
    E. The passengers had never ridden in a converted bus before.

13. A. Between you and me, the new platoon plan sounds like a good idea.
    B. Money from an aunt's estate was left to his wife and he.
    C. He and I were assigned to the same patrol for the first time in two months.
    D. Either you or he should check the front door of that store.
    E. The captain himself was not sure of the witness's reliability.

14. A. The alarm had scarcely begun to ring when the explosion occurred.
    B. Before the firemen arrived at the scene, the second story had been destroyed.
    C. Because of the dense smoke and heat, the firemen could hardly approach the now-blazing structure.
    D. According to the patrolman's report, there wasn't nobody in the store when the explosion occurred.
    E. The sergeant's suggestion was not at all unsound, but no one agreed with him.

15. A. The driver and the passenger they were both found to be intoxicated.
    B. The driver and the passenger talked slowly and not too clearly.
    C. Neither the driver nor his passengers were able to give a coherent account of the accident.
    D. In a corner of the room sat the passenger, quietly dozing.
    E. the driver finally told a strange and unbelievable story, which the passenger contradicted.

16. A. Under the circumstances I decided not to continue my examination of the premises.
    B. There are many difficulties now not comparable with those existing in 1960.
    C. Friends of the accused were heard to announce that the witness had better been away on the day of the trial.
    D. The two criminals escaped in the confusion that followed the explosion.
    E. The aged man was struck by the considerateness of the patrolman's offer.

17. A. An assemblage of miscellaneous weapons lay on the table.
    B. Ample opportunities were given to the defendant to obtain counsel.
    C. The speaker often alluded to his past experience with youthful offenders in the armed forces.
    D. The sudden appearance of the truck aroused my suspicions.
    E. Her studying had a good affect on her grades in high school.

18. A. He sat down in the theater and began to watch the movie.
    B. The girl had ridden horses since she was four years old.
    C. Application was made on behalf of the prosecutor to cite the witness for contempt.
    D. The bank robber, with his two accomplices, were caught in the act.
    E. His story is simply not credible.

19.  A. The angry boy said that he did not like those kind of friends.
     B. The merchant's financial condition was so precarious that he felt he must avail himself of any offer of assistance.
     C. He is apt to promise more than he can perform.
     D. Looking at the messy kitchen, the housewife felt like crying.
     E. A clerk was left in charge of the stolen property.

20.  A. His wounds were aggravated by prolonged exposure to sub-freezing temperatures.
     B. The prosecutor remarked that the witness was not averse to changing his story each time he was interviewed.
     C. The crime pattern indicated that the burglars were adapt in the handling of explosives.
     D. His rigid adherence to a fixed plan brought him into renewed conflict with his subordinates.
     E. He had anticipated that the sentence would be delivered by noon.

21.  A. The whole arraignment procedure is badly in need of revision.
     B. After his glasses were broken in the fight, he would of gone to the optometrist if he could.
     C. Neither Tom nor Jack brought his lunch to work.
     D. He stood aside until the quarrel was over.
     E. A statement in the psychiatrist's report disclosed that the probationer vowed to have his revenge.

22.  A. His fiery and intemperate speech to the striking employees fatally affected any chance of a future reconciliation.
     B. The wording of the statute has been variously construed.
     C. The defendant's attorney, speaking in the courtroom, called the official a demagogue who contempuously disregarded the judge's orders.
     D. The baseball game is likely to be the most exciting one this year.
     E. The mother divided the cookies among her two children.

23.  A. There was only a bed and a dresser in the dingy room.
     B. John was one of the few students that have protested the new rule.
     C. It cannot be argued that the child's testimony is negligible; it is, on the contrary, of the greatest importance.
     D. The basic criterion for clearance was so general that officials resolved any doubts in favor of dismissal.
     E. Having just returned from a long vacation, the officer found the city unbearably hot.

24.  A. The librarian ought to give more help to small children.
     B. The small boy was criticized by the teacher because he often wrote careless.
     C. It was generally doubted whether the women would permit the use of her apartment for intelligence operations.
     D. The probationer acts differently every time the officer visits him.
     E. Each of the newly appointed officers has 12 years of service.

25. A. The North is the most industrialized region in the country.
    B. L. Patrick Gray 3d, the bureau's acting director, stated that, while "rehabilitation is fine" for some convicted criminals, "it is a useless gesture for those who resist every such effort."
    C. Careless driving, faulty mechanism, narrow or badly kept roads all play their part in causing accidents.
    D. The childrens' books were left in the bus.
    E. It was a matter of internal security; consequently, he felt no inclination to rescind his previous order.

25._____

## KEY (CORRECT ANSWERS)

| | | | |
|---|---|---|---|
| 1. | C | 11. | C |
| 2. | B | 12. | D |
| 3. | D | 13. | B |
| 4. | C | 14. | D |
| 5. | E | 15. | A |
| 6. | A | 16. | C |
| 7. | C | 17. | E |
| 8. | B | 18. | D |
| 9. | B | 19. | A |
| 10. | C | 20. | C |

21. B
22. E
23. B
24. B
25. D

# TEST 2

DIRECTIONS: Each question or incomplete statement is followed by several suggested answers or completions. Select the one that BEST answers the question or completes the statement. *PRINT THE LETTER OF THE CORRECT ANSWER IN THE SPACE AT THE RIGHT.*

Questions 1-6.

DIRECTIONS: Each of Questions 1 through 6 consists of a statement which contains a word (one of those underlined) that is either incorrectly used because it is not in keeping with the meaning the quotation is evidently intended to convey, or is misspelled. There is only one INCORRECT word in each quotation. Of the four underlined words, determine if the first one should be replaced by the word lettered A, the second replaced by the word lettered B, the third replaced by the word lettered C, or the fourth replaced by the word lettered D.

1. Whether one depends on fluorescent or artificial light or both, adequate standards should be maintained by means of systematic tests.  
   A. natural    B. safeguards    C. established    D. routine

1.____

2. A police officer has to be prepared to assume his knowledge as a social scientist in the community.  
   A. forced    B. role    C. philosopher    D. street

2.____

3. It is practically impossible to indicate whether a sentence is too long simply by measuring its length.  
   A. almost    B. tell    C. very    D. guessing

3.____

4. Strong leaders are required to organize a community for delinquency prevention and for dissemination of organized crime and drug addiction.  
   A. tactics    B. important    C. control    D. meetings

4.____

5. The demonstrators who were taken to the Criminal Courts building in Manhattan (because it was large enough to accommodate them), contended that the arrests were unwarranted.  
   A. demonstraters    B. Manhatten  
   C. accomodate    D. unwarranted

5.____

6. They were guaranteed a calm atmosphere, free from harassment, which would be conducive to quiet consideration of the indictments.  
   A. guarenteed    B. atmspher  
   C. harassment    D. inditements

6.____

Questions 7-11.

DIRECTIONS: Each of Questions 7 through 11 consists of a statement containing four words in capital letters. One of these words in capital letters is not in keeping with the meaning which the statement is evidently intended to carry. The four words in capital letters in each statement are reprinted after the statement. Print the capital letter preceding the one of the four words which does MOST to spoil the true meaning of the statement in the space at the right.

7. Retirement and pension systems are essential not only to provide employees with with a means of support in the future, but also to prevent longevity and CHARITABLE considerations from UPSETTING the PROMOTIONAL opportunities RETIRED members of the career service.
   A. charitable    B. upsetting    C. promotional    D. retired

7._____

8. Within each major DIVISION in a properly set up public or private organization, provision is made so that each NECESSARY activity is CARED for and lines of authority and responsibility are clear-cut and INFINITE.
   A. division    B. necessary    C. cared    D. infinite

8._____

9. In public service, the scale of salaries paid must be INCIDENTAL to the services rendered, with due CONSIDERATION for the attraction of the desired MANPOWER and for the maintenance of a standard of living COMMENSURATE with the work to be performed.
   A. incidental            B. consideration
   C. manpower              D. commensurate

9._____

10. An understanding of the AIMS of an organization by the staff will AID greatly in increasing the DEMAND of the correspondence work of the office, and will to a large extent DETERMINE the nature of the correspondence.
    A. aims    B. aid    C. demand    D. determine

10._____

11. BECAUSE the Civil Service Commission strongly feels that the MERIT system is a key factor in the MAINTENANCE of democratic government, it has adopted as one of its major DEFENSES the progressive democratization of its own procedures in dealing with candidates for positions in the public service.
    A. Because    B. merit    C. maintenance    D. defenses

11._____

Questions 12-14.

DIRECTIONS: Questions 12 through 14 consist of one sentence each. Each sentence contains an incorrectly used word. First, decide which is the incorrectly used word. Then, from among the options given, decide which word, when substituted for the incorrectly used word, makes the meaning of the sentence clear.
EXAMPLE:
The U.S. national income exhibits a pattern of long term deflection.
   A. reflection    B. subjection    C. rejoicing    D. growth

The word *deflection* in the sentence does not convey the meaning the sentence evidently intended to convey. The word *growth* (Answer D), when substituted for the word *deflection*, makes the meaning of the sentence clear. Accordingly, the answer to the question is D.

12. The study commissioned by the joint committee fell compassionately short of the mark and would have to be redone.
    A. successfully
    B. insignificantly
    C. experimentally
    D. woefully

13. He will not idly exploit any violation of the provisions of the order.
    A. tolerate
    B. refuse
    C. construe
    D. guard

14. The defendant refused to be virile and bitterly protested service.
    A. irked
    B. feasible
    C. docile
    D. credible

Questions 15-25.

DIRECTIONS: Questions 15 through 25 consist of short paragraphs. Each paragraph contains one word which is INCORRECTLY used because it is NOT in keeping with the meaning of the paragraph. Find the word in each paragraph which is INCORRECTLY used and then select as the answer the suggested word which should be substituted for the incorrectly used word.

SAMPLE QUESTION:
In determining who is to do the work in your unit, you will have to decide just who does what from day to day. One of your lowest responsibilities is to assign work so that everybody gets a fair share and that everyone can do his part well.
A. new   B. old   C. important   D. performance

EXPLANATION:
The word which is NOT in keeping with the meaning of the paragraph is *lowest*. This is the INCORRECTLY used word. The suggested word *important* would be in keeping with the meaning of the paragraph and should be substituted for *lowest*. Therefore, the CORRECT answer is choice C.

15. If really good practice in the elimination of preventable injuries is to be achieved and held in any establishment, top management must refuse full and definite responsibility and must apply a good share of its attention to the task.
    A. accept
    B. avoidable
    C. duties
    D. problem

16. Recording the human face for identification is by no means the only service performed by the camera in the field of investigation. When the trial of any issue takes place, a word picture is sought to be distorted to the court of incidents, occurrences, or events which are in dispute.
    A. appeals
    B. description
    C. portrayed
    D. deranged

17. In the collection of physical evidence, it cannot be emphasized too strongly that a haphazard systematic search at the scene of the crime is vital. Nothing must be overlooked. Often the only leads in a case will come from the results of this search.
    A. important  B. investigation  C. proof  D. thorough

17.____

18. If an investigator has reason to suspect that the witness is mentally stable, or a habitual drunkard, he should leave no stone unturned in his investigation to determine if the witness was under the influence of liquor or drugs, or was mentally unbalanced either at the time of the occurrence to which he testified or at the time of the trial.
    A. accused  B. clue  C. deranged  D. question

18.____

19. The use of records is a valuable step in crime investigation and is the main reason every department should maintain accurate reports. Crimes are not committed through the use of departmental records alone but from the use of all records, of almost every type, wherever they may be found and whenever they give any incidental information regarding the criminal.
    A. accidental  B. necessary  C. reported  D. solved

19.____

20. In the years since passage of the Harrison Narcotic Act of 1914, making the possession of opium amphetamines illegal in most circumstances, drug use has become a subject of considerable scientific interest and investigation. There is at present a voluminous literature on drug use of various kinds.
    A. ingestion  B. derivatives  C. addiction  D. opiates

20.____

21. Of course, the fact that criminal laws are extremely patterned in definition does not mean that the majority of persons who violate them are dealt with as criminals. Quite the contrary, for a great many forbidden acts are voluntarily engaged in within situations of privacy and go unobserved and unreported.
    A. symbolic  B. casual  C. scientific  D. broad-gauged

21.____

22. The most punitive way to study punishment is to focus attention on the pattern of punitive action: to study how a penalty is applied, too study what is done to or taken from an offender.
    A. characteristic  B. degrading  C. objective  D. distinguished

22.____

23. The most common forms of punishment in times past have been death, physical torture, mutilation, branding, public humiliation, fines, forfeits of property, banishment, transportation, and imprisonment. Although this list is by no means differentiated, practically every form of punishment has had several variations and applications.
    A. specific  B. simple  C. exhaustive  D. characteristic

23.____

24. There is another important line of inference between ordinary and professional criminals, and that is the source from which they are recruited. The professional criminal seems to be drawn from legitimate employment and, in many instances, from parallel vocations or pursuits.
 A. demarcation   B. justification   C. superiority   D. reference

24._____

25. He took the position that the success of the program was insidious on getting additional revenue.
 A. reputed   B. contingent   C. failure   D. indeterminate

25._____

## KEY (CORRECT ANSWERS)

1. A
2. B
3. B
4. C
5. D

6. C
7. D
8. D
9. A
10. C

11. D
12. D
13. A
14. C
15. A

16. C
17. D
18. C
19. D
20. B

21. D
22. C
23. C
24. A
25. B

# TEST 3

DIRECTIONS: Each question or incomplete statement is followed by several suggested answers or completions. Select the one that BEST answers the question or completes the statement. *PRINT THE LETTER OF THE CORRECT ANSWER IN THE SPACE AT THE RIGHT.*

Questions 1-5.

DIRECTIONS: Questions 1 through 5 are to be answered on the basis of the following.

You are a supervising officer in an investigative unit. Earlier in the day, you directed Detectives Tom Dixon and Sal Mayo to investigate a reported assault and robbery in a liquor store within your area of jurisdiction.

Detective Dixon has submitted to you a preliminary investigative report containing the following information:

- At 1630 hours on 2/20, arrived at Joe's Liquor Store at 350 SW Avenue with Detective Mayo to investigate A & R.
- At store interviewed Rob Ladd, store manager, who stated that he and Joe Brown (store owner) had been stuck up about ten minutes prior to our arrival.
- Ladd described the robbers as male whites in their late teens or early twenties. Further stated that one of the robbers displayed what appeared to be an automatic pistol as he entered the store, and said, *Give us the money or we'll kill you.* Ladd stated that Brown then reached under the counter where he kept a loaded .38 caliber pistol. Several shots followed, and Ladd threw himself to the floor.
- The robbers fled, and Ladd didn't know if any money had been taken.
- At this point, Ladd realized that Brown was unconscious on the floor and bleeding from a head wound.
- Ambulance called by Ladd, and Brown was removed by same to General Hospital.
- Personally interviewed John White, 382 Dartmouth Place, who stated he was inside store at the time of occurrence. White states that he hid behind a wine display upon hearing someone say, *Give us the money.* He then heard shots and saw two young men run from the store to a yellow car parked at the curb. White was unable to further describe auto. States the taller of the two men drove the car away while the other sat on passenger side in front.
- Recovered three spent .38 caliber bullets from premises and delivered them to Crime Lab.
- To General Hospital at 1800 hours but unable to interview Brown, who was under sedation and suffering from shock and a laceration of the head.
- Alarm #12487 transmitted for car and occupants.
- Case Active.

Based solely on the contents of the preliminary investigation submitted by Detective Dixon, select one sentence from the following groups of sentences which is MOST accurate and is grammatically correct.

1.  A. Both robbers were armed.
    B. Each of the robbers were described as a male white.
    C. Neither robber was armed.
    D. Mr. Ladd stated that one of the robbers was armed.

    1.____

2.  A. Mr. Brown fired three shots from his revolver.
    B. Mr. Brown was shot in the head by one of the robbers.
    C. Mr. Brown suffered a gunshot wound of the head during the course of the robbery.
    D. Mr. Brown was taken to General Hospital by ambulance.

    2.____

3.  A. Shots were fired after one of the robbers said, *Give us the money or we'll kill you.*
    B. After one of the robbers demanded the money from Mr. Brown, he fired a shot.
    C. The preliminary investigation indicated that although Mr. Brown did not have a license for the gun, he was justified in using deadly physical force.
    D. Mr. Brown was interviewed at General Hospital.

    3.____

4.  A. Each of the witnesses were customers in the store at the time of occurrence.
    B. Neither of the witnesses interviewed was the owner of the liquor store.
    C. Neither of the witnesses interviewed were the owner of the store.
    D. Neither of the witnesses was employed by Mr. Brown.

    4.____

5.  A. Mr. Brown arrived at General Hospital at about 5:00 P.M.
    B. Neither of the robbers was injured during the robbery.
    C. The robbery occurred at 3:30 P.M. on February 10.
    D. One of the witnesses called the ambulance.

    5.____

Questions 6-10.

DIRECTIONS:  Each of Questions 6 through 10 consists of information given in outline form and four sentences labeled A, B, C, and D.  For each question, choose the one sentence which CORRECTLY expresses the information given in outline form and which also displays PROPER English usage.

6.  Client's Name:  Joanna Jones
    Number of Children:  3
    Client's Income:  None
    Client's Marital Status:  Single

    A. Joanna Jones is an unmarried client with three children who have no income.
    B. Joanna Jones, who is single and has no income, a client she has three children.
    C. Joanna Jones, whose three children are clients, is single and has no income.
    D. Joanna Jones, who has three children, is an unmarried client with no income.

    6.____

7. Client's Name:  Bertha Smith
   Number of Children:  2
   Client's Rent:  $1050 per month
   Number of Rooms:  4

   A. Bertha Smith, a client, pays $1050 per month for her four rooms with two children.
   B. Client Bertha Smith has two children and pays $1050 per month for four rooms.
   C. Client Bertha Smith is paying $1050 per month for two children with four rooms.
   D. For four rooms and two children client Bertha Smith pays $1050 per month.

   7._____

8. Name of Employee:  Cynthia Dawes
   Number of Cases Assigned:  9
   Date Cases were Assigned:  12/16
   Number of Assigned Cases Completed:  8

   A. On December 16, employee Cynthia Dawes was assigned nine cases; she has completed eight of these cases.
   B. Cynthia Dawes, employee on December 16, assigned nine cases, completed eight.
   C. Being employed on December 16, Cynthia Dawes completed eight of nine assigned cases.
   D. Employee Cynthia Dawes, she was assigned nine cases and completed eight, on December 16.

   8._____

9. Place of Audit:  Broadway Center
   Names of Auditors:  Paul Cahn, Raymond Perez
   Date of Audit:  11/20
   Number of Cases Audited:  41

   A. On November 20, at the Broadway Center 41 cases was audited by auditors Paul Cahn and Raymond Perez.
   B. Auditors Raymond Perez and Paul Cahn has audited 41 cases at the Broadway Center on November 20.
   C. At the Broadway Center, on November 20, auditors Paul Cahn and Raymond Perez audited 41 cases.
   D. Auditors Paul Cahn and Raymond Perez at the Broadway Center, on November 20, is auditing 41 cases.

   9._____

10. Name of Client:  Barbra Levine
    Client's Monthly Income:  $2100
    Client's Monthly Expenses:  $4520

    A. Barbra Levine is a client, her monthly income is $2100 and her monthly expenses is $4520.
    B. Barbra Levine's monthly income is $2100 and she is a client, with whose monthly expenses are $4520.

    10._____

C. Barbra Levine is a client whose monthly income is $2100 and whose monthly expenses are $4520.
D. Barbra Levine, a client, is with a monthly income which is $2100 and monthly expenses which are $4520.

Questions 11-13.

DIRECTIONS: Questions 11 through 13 involve several statements of fact presented in a very simple way. These statements of fact are followed by 4 choices which attempt to incorporate all of the facts into one logical statement which is properly constructed and grammatically correct.

11. I. Mr. Brown was sweeping the sidewalk in front of his house.
    II. He was sweeping it because it was dirty.
    III. He swept the refuse into the street.
    IV. Police Officer gave him a ticket.

    Which one of the following BEST presents the information given above?
    A. Because his sidewalk was dirty, Mr. Brown received a ticket from Officer Green when he swept the refuse into the street.
    B. Police Officer Green gave Mr. Brown a ticket because his sidewalk was dirty and he swept the refuse into the street.
    C. Police Officer Green gave Mr. Brown a ticket for sweeping refuse into the street because his sidewalk was dirty.
    D. Mr. Brown, who was sweeping refuse from his dirty sidewalk into the street, was given a ticket by Police Officer Green.

11.____

12. I. Sergeant Smith radioed for help.
    II. The sergeant did so because the crowd was getting larger.
    III. It was 10:00 A.M. when he made his call.
    IV. Sergeant Smith was not in uniform at the time of occurrence.

    Which one of the following BEST presents the information given above?
    A. Sergeant Smith, although not on duty at the time, radioed for help at 10 o'clock because the crowd was getting uglier.
    B. Although not in uniform, Sergeant Smith called for help at 10:00 A.M. because the crowd was getting uglier.
    C. Sergeant Smith radioed for help at 10:00 A.M. because the crowd was getting larger.
    D. Although he was not in uniform, Sergeant Smith radioed for help at 10:00 A.M. because the crowd was getting larger.

12.____

13. I. The payroll office is open on Fridays.
    II. Paychecks are distributed from 9:00 A.M. to 12 Noon.
    III. The office is open on Fridays because that's the only day the payroll staff is available.
    IV. It is open for the specified hours in order to permit employees to cash checks at the bank during lunch hour.

13.____

The choice below which MOST clearly and accurately presents the above idea is:
  A. Because the payroll office is open on Fridays from 9:00 A.M. to 12 Noon, employees can cash their checks when the payroll staff is available.
  B. Because the payroll staff is only available on Fridays until noon, employees can cash their checks during their lunch hour.
  C. Because the payroll staff is available only on Fridays, the office is open from 9:00 A.M. to 12 Noon to allow employees to cash their checks.
  D. Because of payroll staff availability, the payroll office is open on Fridays. It is open from 9:00 A.M. to 12 Noon so that distributed paychecks can be cashed at the bank while employees are on their lunch hour.

Questions 14-16.

DIRECTIONS: In each of Questions 14 through 6, the four sentences are from a paragraph in a report. They are not in the right order. Which of the following arrangements is the BEST one?

14. I. An executive may answer a letter by writing his reply on the face of the letter itself instead of having a return letter typed.
    II. This procedure is efficient because it saves the executive's time, the typist's time, and saves office file space.
    III. Copying machines are used in small offices as well as large offices to save time and money in making brief replies to business letters.
    IV. A copy is made on a copy machine to go into the company files, while the original is mailed back to the sender.

    The CORRECT answer is:
    A. I, II, IV, III    B. I, IV, II, III    C. III, I, IV, II    D. III, IV, II, I

14.____

15. I. Most organizations favor one of the types but always include the others to a lesser degree.
    II. However, we can detect a definite trend toward greater use of symbolic control.
    III. We suggest that our local police agencies are today primarily utilizing material control.
    IV. Control can be classified into three types: physical, material, and symbolic.

    The CORRECT answer is:
    A. IV, II, III, I    B. II, I, IV, III    C. III, IV, II, I    D. IV, I, III, II

15.____

16. I. They can and do take advantage of ancient political and geographical boundaries, which often give them sanctuary from effective policy activity.
    II. This country is essentially a country of small police forces, each operating independently within the limits of its jurisdiction.
    III. The boundaries that define and limit police operations do not hinder the movement of criminals, of course.
    IV. The machinery of law enforcement in America is fragmented, complicated, and frequently overlapping.

16.____

The CORRECT answer is:
   A. III, I, IV    B. II, IV, I, III    C. IV, II, III, I    D. IV, III, II, I

17. Examine the following sentence, and then choose from below the words which should be inserted in the blank spaces to produce the best sentence.
The unit has exceeded _____ goals and the employees are satisfied with _____ accomplishments.
   A. their, it's    B. it's; it's    C. its, there    D. its, their

18. Examine the following sentence, and then choose from below the words which should be inserted in the blank spaces to produce the best sentence.
Research indicates that employees who _____ no opportunity for close social relationships often find their work unsatisfying, and this _____ of satisfaction often reflects itself in low production.
   A. have; lack    B. have; excess    C. has; lack    D. has; excess

19. Words in a sentence must be arranged properly to make sure that the intended meaning of the sentence is clear.
The sentence below that does NOT make sense because a clause has been separated from the word on which its meaning depends is:
   A. To be a good writer, clarity is necessary.
   B. To be a good writer, you must write clearly.
   C. You must write clearly to be a good writer.
   D. Clarity is necessary to good writing.

Questions 20-21.

DIRECTIONS: Each of Questions 20 and 21 consists of a statement which contains a word (one of those underlined) that is either incorrectly used because it is not in keeping with the meaning the quotation is evidently intended to convey, or is misspelled. There is only one INCORRECT word in each quotation. Of the four underlined words, determine if the first one should be replaced by the word lettered A, the second one replaced by the word lettered B, the third one replaced by the word lettered C, or the fourth one replaced by the word lettered D.

20. The alleged killer was occasionally permitted to excercise in the corridor.
   A. alledged    B. ocasionally    C. permited    D. exercise

21. Defense counsel stated, in affect, that their conduct was permissible under the First Amendment.
   A. council    B. effect    C. there    D. permissable

Question 22.

DIRECTIONS: Question 22 consists of one sentence. This sentence contains an incorrectly used word. First, decide which is the incorrectly used word. Then, from among the options given, decide which word, when substituted for the incorrectly used word, makes the meaning of the sentence clear.

22. As today's violence has no single cause, so its causes have no single scheme.  22.____
    A. deference   B. cure   C. flaw   D. relevance

23. In the sentence, *A man in a light-grey suit waited thirty-five minutes in the ante-room for the all-important document*, the word IMPROPERLY hyphenated is  23.____
    A. light-grey
    B. thirty-five
    C. ante-room
    D. all-important

24. In the sentence, *The candidate wants to file his application for preference before it is too late*, the word *before* is used as a(n)  24.____
    A. preposition
    B. subordinating conjunction
    C. pronoun
    D. adverb

25. In the sentence, *The perpetrators ran from the scene*, the word *from* is a  25.____
    A. preposition   B. pronoun   C. verb   D. conjunction

## KEY (CORRECT ANSWERS)

| | | | |
|---|---|---|---|
| 1. | D | 11. | D |
| 2. | D | 12. | D |
| 3. | A | 13. | D |
| 4. | B | 14. | C |
| 5. | D | 15. | D |
| 6. | D | 16. | C |
| 7. | B | 17. | D |
| 8. | A | 18. | A |
| 9. | C | 19. | A |
| 10. | C | 20. | D |

21. B
22. B
23. C
24. B
25. A

# PREPARING WRITTEN MATERIAL
## EXAMINATION SECTION
## TEST 1

DIRECTIONS: Each question or incomplete statement is followed by several suggested answers or completions. Select the one that BEST answers the question or completes the statement. *PRINT THE LETTER OF THE CORRECT ANSWER IN THE SPACE AT THE RIGHT.*

Questions 1-4.

DIRECTIONS: Questions 1 through 4 each consist of a sentence which may or may not be an example of good English. The underlined parts of each sentence may be correct or incorrect. Examine each sentence, considering grammar, punctuation, spelling, and capitalization. If the English usage in the underlined parts of the sentence given is better than any of the changes in the underlined words suggested in options B, C, or D, choose option A. If the changes in the underlined words suggested in options B, C, or D would make the sentence correct, choose the correct option. Do not choose an option that will change the meaning of the sentence.

1. This Fall, the office will be closed on Columbus Day, October 9th.  1.____
   A. Correct as is
   B. fall...Columbus Day; October
   C. Fall...columbus day, October
   D. fall...Columbus Day – October

2. There weren't no paper in the supply closet.  2.____
   A. Correct as is
   B. weren't any
   C. wasn't any
   D. wasn't no

3. The alphabet, or A to Z sequence are the basis of most filing systems.  3.____
   A. Correct as is
   B. alphabet, or A to Z sequence, is
   C. alphabet, or A to Z sequence, are
   D. alphabet, or A too Z sequence, is

4. The Office Aide checked the register and finding the date of the meeting.  4.____
   A. Correct as is
   B. regaster and finding
   C. register and found
   D. regaster and found

Questions 5-10.

DIRECTIONS: Questions 5 through 10 consist of sentences which contain examples of correct or incorrect English usage. Examine each sentence with reference to grammar, spelling, punctuation, and capitalization. Chooses one of the following options that would be BEST for correct English usage:

2 (#1)

   A. The sentence is correct
   B. There is one mistake
   C. There are two mistakes
   D. There are three mistakes

5. Mrs. Fitzgerald came to the 59th Precinct to retreive her property which were stolen earlier in the week.    5._____

6. The two officer's responded to the call, only to find that the perpatrator and the victim have left the scene.    6._____

7. Mr. Coleman called the 61st Precinct to report that, upon arriving at his store, he discovered that there was a large hole in the wall and that three boxes of radios were missing.    7._____

8. The Administrative Leiutenant of the 62nd Precinct held a meeting which was attended by all the civilians, assigned to the Precinct.    8._____

9. Three days after the robbery occurred the detective apprahended two suspects and recovered the stolen items.    9._____

10. The Community Affairs Officer of the 64th Precinct is the liaison between the Precinct and the community; he works closely with various community organizations, and elected officials,    10._____

Questions 11-18.

DIRECTIONS: Questions 11 through 18 are to be answered on the basis of the following paragraph, which contains some deliberate errors in spelling and/or grammar and/or punctuation. Each line of the paragraph is preceded by a number. There are 9 lines and 9 numbers.

| Line No. | Paragraph Line |
| --- | --- |
| 1 | The protection of life and proporty are, one of |
| 2 | the oldest and most important functions of a city. |
| 3 | New York City has it's own full-time police Agency. |
| 4 | The police Department has the power an it shall |
| 5 | be there duty to preserve the Public piece, |
| 6 | prevent crime detect and arrest offenders, supress |
| 7 | riots, protect the rites of persons and property, etc. |
| 8 | The maintainance of sound relations with the community they |
| 9 | serve is an important function of law enforcement officers |

11. How many errors are contained in line one?    11._____

12. How many errors are contained in line two?    12._____

13. How many errors are contained in line three?    13._____

14. How many errors are contained in line four?  14._____

15. How many errors are contained in line five?  15._____

16. How many errors are contained in line six?  16._____

17. How many errors are contained in line seven?  17._____

18. How many errors are contained in line eight?  18._____

19. In the sentence, *The candidate wants to file his application for preference before it is too late*, the word *before* is used as a(n)  19._____
    A. preposition
    B. subordinating conjunction
    C. pronoun
    D. adverb

20. The one of the following sentences which is grammatically PREFERABLE to the others is:  20._____
    A. Our engineers will go over your blueprints so that you may have no problems in construction.
    B. For a long time he had been arguing that we, not he, are to blame for the confusion.
    C. I worked on this automobile for two hours and still cannot find out what is wrong with it.
    D. Accustomed to all kinds of hardships, fatigue seldom bothers veteran policemen.

# KEY (CORRECT ANSWERS)

| | | | |
|---|---|---|---|
| 1. | A | 11. | C |
| 2. | C | 12. | D |
| 3. | B | 13. | C |
| 4. | C | 14. | B |
| 5. | C | 15. | C |
| 6. | D | 16. | B |
| 7. | A | 17. | A |
| 8. | C | 18. | A |
| 9. | C | 19. | B |
| 10. | B | 20. | A |

# TEST 2

DIRECTIONS: Each question or incomplete statement is followed by several suggested answers or completions. Select the one that BEST answers the question or completes the statement. *PRINT THE LETTER OF THE CORRECT ANSWER IN THE SPACE AT THE RIGHT.*

1. The plural of
   A. turkey is turkies
   B. cargo is cargoes
   C. bankruptcy is bankruptcys
   D. son-in-law is son-in-laws

   1.____

2. The abbreviation *viz.* means MOST NEARLY
   A. namely   B. for example   C. the following   D. see

   2.____

3. In the sentence, *A man in a light-grey suit waited thirty-five minutes in the ante-room for the all-important document,* the word IMPROPERLY hyphenated is
   A. light-grey   B. thirty-five   C. ante-room   D. all-important

   3.____

4. The MOST accurate of the following sentences is:
   A. The commissioner, as well as his deputy and various bureau heads, were present.
   B. A new organization of employers and employees have been formed.
   C. One or the other of these men have been selected.
   D. The number of pages in the book is enough to discourage a reader.

   4.____

5. The MOST accurate of the following sentences is:
   A. Between you and me, I think he is the better man.
   B. He was believed to be me.
   C. Is it us that you wish to see?
   D. The winners are him and her.

   5.____

Questions 6-13.

DIRECTIONS: The sentences numbered 6 through 13 deal with some phase of police activity. They may be classified most appropriately under one of the following four categories.

   A. Faulty because of incorrect grammar
   B. Faulty because of incorrect punctuation
   C. Faulty because of incorrect use of a word
   D. Correct

Examine each sentence carefully. Then, in the space at the right, print the capital letter preceding the option which is the BEST of the four suggested above. All incorrect sentences contain only one type of error. Consider a sentence correct if it contains none of the types of errors mentioned, even though there may be other correct ways of expressing the same thought.

6. The Department Medal of Honor is awarded to a member of the Police Force who distinguishes himself inconspicuously in the line of police duty by the performance of an act of gallantry.   6.____

7. Members of the Detective Division are charged with the prevention of crime, the detection and arrest of criminals and the recovery of lost or stolen property,   7.____

8. Detectives are selected from the uniformed patrol forces after they have indicated by conduct, aptitude and performance that they are qualified for the more intricate duties of a detective.   8.____

9. The patrolman, pursuing his assailant, exchanged shots with the gunman and immortally wounded him as he fled into a nearby building.   9.____

10. The members of the Traffic Division has to enforce the Vehicle and Traffic Law, the Traffic Regulations and ordinances relating to vehicular and pedestrian traffic.   10.____

11. After firing a shot at the gunman, the crowd dispersed from the patrolman's line of fire.   11.____

12. The efficiency of the Missing Persons Bureau is maintained with a maximum of public personnel due to the specialized training given to its members.   12.____

13. Records of persons arrested for violations of Vehicle and Traffic Regulations are transmitted upon request to precincts, courts and other authorized agencies.   13.____

14. Following are two sentences which may or may not be written in correct English:   14.____
    I. Two clients assaulted the officer.
    II. The van is illegally parked.
    Which one of the following statements is CORRECT?
    A. Only Sentence I is written in correct English.
    B. Only Sentence II is written in correct English.
    C. Sentences I and II are both written in correct English.
    D. Neither Sentence I nor Sentence II is written in correct English.

15. Following are two sentences which may or may not be written in correct English:   15.____
    I. Security Officer Rollo escorted the visitor to the patrolroom.
    II. Two entry were made in the facility logbook.
    Which one of the following statements is CORRECT?
    A. Only Sentence I is written in correct English.
    B. Only Sentence II is written in correct English.
    C. Sentences I and II are both written in correct English.
    D. Neither Sentence I nor Sentence II is written in correct English.

16. Following are two sentences which may or may not be written in correct English:　　16.____
    I. Officer McElroy putted out a small fire in the wastepaper basket.
    II. Special Officer Janssen told the visitor where he could obtained a pass.
    Which one of the following statements is CORRECT?
    A. Only Sentence I is written in correct English.
    B. Only Sentence II is written in correct English.
    C. Sentences I and II are both written in correct English.
    D. Neither Sentence I nor Sentence II is written in correct English.

17. Following are two sentences which may or may not be written in correct English:　　17.____
    I. Security Officer Warren observed a broken window while he was on his post in Hallway C.
    II. The worker reported that two typewriters had been stolen from the office,
    Which one of the following statements is CORRECT?
    A. Only Sentence I is written in correct English.
    B. Only Sentence II is written in correct English.
    C. Sentences I and II are both written in correct English.
    D. Neither Sentence I nor Sentence II is written in correct English,

18. Following are two sentences which may or may not be written in correct English:　　18.____
    I. Special Officer Cleveland was attempting to calm an emotionally disturbed visitor.
    II. The visitor did not stop crying and calling for his wife.
    Which one of the following statements is CORRECT?
    A. Only Sentence I is written in correct English.
    B. Only Sentence II is written in correct English.
    C. Sentences I and II are both written in correct English.
    D. Neither Sentence I nor Sentence II is written in correct English.

19. Following are two sentences that may or may not be written in correct English:　　19.____
    I. While on patrol, I observes a vagrant loitering near the drug dispensary.
    II. I escorted the vagrant out of the building and off the premises.
    Which one of the following statements is CORRECT?
    A. Only Sentence I is written in correct English.
    B. Only Sentence II is written in correct English.
    C. Sentences I and II are both written in correct English.
    D. Neither Sentence I nor Sentence II is written in correct English.

20. Following are two sentences which may or may not be written in correct English:　　20.____
    I. At 4:00 P.M., Sergeant Raymond told me to evacuate the waiting area immediately due to a bomb threat.
    II. Some of the clients did not want to leave the building.
    Which one of the following statements is CORRECT?
    A. Only Sentence I is written in correct English.
    B. Only Sentence II is written in correct English.
    C. Sentences I and II are both written in correct English.
    D. Neither Sentence I nor Sentence II is written in correct English.

## KEY (CORRECT ANSWERS)

| | | | |
|---|---|---|---|
| 1. | B | 11. | A |
| 2. | A | 12. | C |
| 3. | C | 13. | D |
| 4. | D | 14. | C |
| 5. | A | 15. | A |
| 6. | C | 16. | D |
| 7. | B | 17. | A |
| 8. | D | 18. | A |
| 9. | C | 19. | B |
| 10. | A | 20. | C |

# REPORT WRITING

## EXAMINATION SECTION
## TEST 1

DIRECTIONS: Each question or incomplete statement is followed by several suggested answers or completions. Select the one that BEST answers the question or completes the statement. *PRINT THE LETTER OF THE CORRECT ANSWER IN THE SPACE AT THE RIGHT.*

1. Police Officer Johnson responds to the scene of an assault and obtains the following information:
   Time of Occurrence: 8:30 P.M.
   Place of Occurrence: 120-18 119th Avenue, Apt. 2A
   Suspects: John Andrews, victim's ex-husband and unknown white male
   Victim: Susan Andrews
   Injury: Broken right arm
   Officer Johnson is preparing a complaint report on the incident.
   Which one of the following expresses the above information MOST clearly and accurately?

   A. Susan Andrews was assaulted at 120-18 119th Avenue, Apt. 2A. At 8:30 P.M., her ex-husband, John Andrews, and an unknown white male broke her arm.
   B. At 8:30 P.M., Susan Andrews was assaulted at 120-18 119th Avenue, Apt. 2A, by her ex-husband, John Andrews, and an unknown white male. Her right arm was broken.
   C. John Andrews, an unknown white male, and Susan Andrews' ex-husband, assaulted and broke her right arm at 8:30 P.M., at 120-18 119th Avenue, Apt. 2A.
   D. John Andrews, ex-husband of Susan Andrews, broke her right arm with an unknown white male at 120-18 119th Avenue, at 8:30 P.M. in Apt. 2A.

2. While on patrol, Officers Banks and Thompson see a man lying on the ground bleeding. Officer Banks records the following details about the incident:
   Time of Incident: 3:15 P.M.
   Place of Incident: Sidewalk in front of 517 Rock Avenue
   Incident: Tripped and fell
   Name of Injured: John Blake
   Injury: Head wound
   Action Taken: Transported to Merry Hospital
   Officer Banks is completing a report on the incident.
   Which one of the following expresses the above information MOST clearly and accurately?

   A. At 3:15 P.M., Mr. John Blake was transported to Merry Hospital. He tripped and fell, injuring his head on sidewalk in front of 517 Rock Avenue.
   B. Mr. John Blake tripped and fell on the sidewalk at 3:15 P.M. in front of 517 Rock Avenue. He was transported to Merry Hospital while he sustained a head wound.
   C. Mr. John Blake injured his head when he tripped and fell on the sidewalk in front of 517 Rock Avenue at 3:15 P.M. He was transported to Merry Hospital.
   D. A head was wounded on the sidewalk in front of 517 Rock Avenue at 3:15 P.M. Mr. John Blake tripped and fell and was transported to Merry Hospital.

3. When assigned to investigate a complaint, a police officer should
   I. Interview witnesses and obtain facts
   II. Conduct a thorough investigation of circumstances concerning the complaint
   III. Prepare a complaint report
   IV. Determine if the complaint report should be closed or referred for further investigation
   V. Enter complaint report on the Complaint Report Index and obtain a complaint report number at the station house

   While on patrol, Police Officer John is instructed by his supervisor to investigate a complaint by Mr. Stanley Burns, who was assaulted by his brother-in-law, Henry Traub. After interviewing Mr. Burns, Officer John learns that Mr. Traub has been living with Mr. Burns for the past two years. Officer John accompanies Mr. Burns to his apartment but Mr. Traub is not there. Officer John fills out the complaint report and takes the report back to the station house where it is entered on the Complaint Report Index and assigned a complaint report number. Officer John's actions were

   A. *improper,* primarily because he should have stayed at Mr. Burns' apartment and waited for Mr. Traub to return in order to arrest him
   B. *proper,* primarily because after obtaining all the facts, he took the report back to the station house and was assigned a complaint report number
   C. *improper,* primarily because he should have decided whether to close the report or refer it for further investigation
   D. *proper,* primarily because he was instructed by his supervisor to take the report from Mr. Burns even though it involved his brother-in-law

4. Police Officer Waters was the first person at the scene of a fire which may have been the result of arson. He obtained the following information:

   Place of Occurrence:   35 John Street, Apt. 27
   Time of Occurrence:    4:00 P.M.
   Witness:               Daisy Logan
   Incident:              Fire (possible arson)
   Suspect:               Male, white, approximately 18 years old, wearing blue jeans and a plaid shirt, running away from the incident Officer Waters is completing a report on the incident.

   Which one of the following expresses the above information MOST clearly and accurately?

   A. At 4:00 P.M., Daisy Logan saw a white male, approximately 18 years old who was wearing blue jeans and a plaid shirt, running from the scene of a fire at 35 John Street, Apt. 27.
   B. Seeing a fire at 35 John Street, a white male approximately 18 years old, wearing blue jeans and a plaid shirt, was seen running from Apt. 27 at 4:00 P.M. reported Daisy Logan.
   C. Approximately 18 years old and wearing blue jeans and a plaid shirt, Daisy Logan saw a fire and a white male running from 35 John Street, Apt. 27 at 4:00 P.M.
   D. Running from 35 John Street, Apt. 27, the scene of the fire, reported Daisy Logan at 4:00 P.M., was a white male approximately 18 years old and wearing blue jeans and a plaid shirt.

5. Police Officer Sullivan obtained the following information at the scene of a two-car accident:

   Place of Occurrence: 2971 William Street
   Drivers and Vehicles Involved: Mrs. Wilson, driver of blue 2004 Toyota Camry; Mr. Bailey, driver of white 2001 Dodge
   Injuries Sustained: Mr. Bailey had a swollen right eye; Mrs. Wilson had a broken left hand

   Which one of the following expresses the above information MOST clearly and accurately?

   A. Mr. Bailey, owner of a white 2001 Dodge, at 2971 William Street, had a swollen right eye. Mrs. Wilson, with a broken left hand, is the owner of the blue 2004 Toyota Camry. They were in a car accident.
   B. Mrs. Wilson got a broken left hand and Mr. Bailey a swollen right eye at 2971 William Street. The vehicles involved in the car accident were a 2001 Dodge, white, owned by Mr. Bailey, and Mrs. Wilson's blue 2004 Toyota Camry.
   C. Mrs. Wilson, the driver of the blue 2004 Toyota Camry, and Mr. Bailey, the driver of the white 2001 Dodge, were involved in a car accident at 2971 William Street. Mr. Bailey sustained a swollen right eye, and Mrs. Wilson broke her left hand.
   D. Mr. Bailey sustained a swollen right eye and Mrs. Wilson broke her left hand in a car accident at 2971 William Street. They owned a 2001 white Dodge and a 2004 blue Toyota Camry.

6. Officer Johnson has issued a summons to a driver and has obtained the following information:

   Place of Occurrence: Corner of Foster Road and Woodrow Avenue
   Time of Occurrence: 7:10 P.M.
   Driver: William Grant
   Offense: Driving through a red light
   Age of Driver: 42
   Address of Driver: 23 Richmond Avenue

   Officer Johnson is making an entry in his Memo Book regarding the incident.
   Which one of the following expresses the above information MOST clearly and accurately?

   A. William Grant, lives at 23 Richmond Avenue at 7:10 P.M., went through a red light. He was issued a summons at the corner of Foster Road and Woodrow Avenue. The driver is 42 years old.
   B. William Grant, age 42, who lives at 23 Richmond Avenue, was issued a summons for going through a red light at 7:10 P.M. at the corner of Foster Road and Woodrow Avenue.
   C. William Grant, age 42, was issued a summons on the corner of Foster Road and Woodrow Avenue for going through a red light. He lives at 23 Richmond Avenue at 7:10 P.M.
   D. A 42-year-old man who lives at 23 Richmond Avenue was issued a summons at 7:10 P.M. William Grant went through a red light at the corner of Foster Road and Woodrow Avenue.

7. Police Officer Frome has completed investigating a report of a stolen auto and obtained the following information:
   Date of Occurrence:   October 26, 2004
   Place of Occurrence:  51st Street and 8th Avenue
   Time of Occurrence:   3:30 P.M.
   Crime:                Auto theft
   Suspect:              Michael Wadsworth
   Action Taken:         Suspect arrested
   Which one of the following expresses the above information MOST clearly and accurately?

   A. Arrested on October 26, 2004 was a stolen auto at 51st Street and 8th Avenue at 3:30 P.M. driven by Michael Wadsworth.
   B. For driving a stolen auto at 3:30 P.M., Michael Wadsworth was arrested at 51st Street and 8th Avenue on October 26, 2004.
   C. On October 26, 2004 at 3:30 P.M., Michael Wadsworth was arrested at 51st Street and 8th Avenue for driving a stolen auto.
   D. Michael Wadsworth was arrested on October 26, 2004 at 3:30 P.M. for driving at 51st Street and 8th Avenue. The auto was stolen.

7.____

8. Police Officer Wright has finished investigating a report of Grand Larceny and has obtained the following information:
   Time of Occurrence:   Between 1:00 P.M. and 2:00 P.M.
   Place of Occurrence:  In front of victim's home, 85 Montgomery Avenue
   Victim:               Mr. Williams, owner of the vehicle
   Crime:                Automobile broken into
   Property Taken:       Stereo valued at $1,200
   Officer Wright is preparing a report on the incident. Which one of the following expresses the above information MOST clearly and accurately?

   A. While parked in front of his home Mr. Williams states that between 1:00 P.M. and 2:00 P.M. an unknown person broke into his vehicle. Mr. Williams, who lives at 85 Montgomery Avenue, lost his $1,200 stereo.
   B. Mr. Williams, who lives at 85 Montgomery Avenue, states that between 1:00 P.M. and 2:00 P.M. his vehicle was parked in front of his home when an unknown person broke into his car and took his stereo worth $1,200.
   C. Mr. Williams was parked in front of 85 Montgomery Avenue, which is his home, when it was robbed of a $1,200 stereo. When he came out, he observed between 1:00 P.M. and 2:00 P.M. that his car had been broken into by an unknown person.
   D. Mr. Williams states between 1:00 P.M. and 2:00 P.M. that an unknown person broke into his car in front of his home. Mr. Williams further states that he was robbed of a $1,200 stereo at 85 Montgomery Avenue.

8.____

9. Police Officer Fontaine obtained the following details relating to a suspicious package:

Place of Occurrence: Case Bank, 2 Wall Street
Time of Occurrence: 10:30 A.M.
Date of Occurrence: October 10, 2004
Complaint: Suspicious package in doorway
Found By: Emergency Service Unit

Officer Fontaine is preparing a report for department records.
Which one of the following expresses the above information MOST clearly and accurately?

A. At 10:30 A.M., the Emergency Service Unit reported they found a package on October 10, 2004 which appeared suspicious. This occurred in a doorway at 2 Wall Street, Case Bank.
B. A package which appeared suspicious was in the doorway of Case Bank. The Emergency Service Unit reported this at 2 Wall Street at 10:30 A.M. on October 10, 2004 when found.
C. On October 10, 2004 at 10:30 A.M., a suspicious package was found by the Emergency Service Unit in the doorway of Case Bank at 2 Wall Street.
D. The Emergency Service Unit found a package at the Case Bank. It appeared suspicious at 10:30 A.M. in the doorway of 2 Wall Street on October 10, 2004.

10. Police Officer Reardon receives the following information regarding a case of child abuse:

Victim: Joseph Mays
Victim's Age: 10 years old
Victim's Address: Resides with his family at 42 Columbia Street, Apt. 1B
Complainant: Victim's uncle, Kevin Mays
Suspects: Victim's parents

Police Officer Reardon is preparing a report to send to the Department of Social Services.
Which one of the following expresses the above information MOST clearly and accurately?

A. Kevin Mays reported a case of child abuse to his ten-year-old nephew, Joseph Mays, by his parents. He resides with his family at 42 Columbia Street, Apt. 1B.
B. Kevin Mays reported that his ten-year-old nephew, Joseph Mays, has been abused by the child's parents. Joseph Mays resides with his family at 42 Columbia Street, Apt. 1B.
C. Joseph Mays has been abused by his parents. Kevin Mays reported that his nephew resides with his family at 42 Columbia Street, Apt. 1B. He is ten years old.
D. Kevin Mays reported that his nephew is ten years old. Joseph Mays has been abused by his parents. He resides with his family at 42 Columbia Street, Apt. 1B.

11. While on patrol, Police Officer Hawkins was approached by Harry Roland, a store owner, who found a leather bag valued at $200.00 outside his store. Officer Hawkins took the property into custody and removed the following items:

    | | |
    |---|---|
    | 2 Solex watches, each valued at | $500.00 |
    | 4 14-kt. gold necklaces, each valued at | $315.00 |
    | Cash | $519.00 |
    | 1 diamond ring, valued at | $400.00 |

    Officer Hawkins is preparing a report on the found property.
    Which one of the following is the TOTAL value of the property and cash found?

    A. $1,734   B. $3,171   C. $3,179   D. $3,379

12. While on patrol, Police Officer Blake observes a man running from a burning abandoned building. Officer Blake radios the following information:
    Place of Occurrence:   310 Hall Avenue
    Time of Occurrence:   8:30 P.M.
    Type of Building:   Abandoned
    Suspect:   Male, white, about 35 years old
    Crime:   Arson
    Officer Blake is completing a report on the incident.
    Which one of the following expresses the above information MOST clearly and accurately?

    A. An abandoned building located at 310 Hall Avenue was on fire at 8:30 P.M. A white male, approximately 35 years old, was observed fleeing the scene.
    B. A white male, approximately 35 years old, at 8:30 P.M. was observed fleeing 310 Hall Avenue. The fire was set at an abandoned building.
    C. An abandoned building was set on fire. A white male, approximately 35 years old, was observed fleeing the scene at 8:30 P.M. at 310 Hall Avenue.
    D. Observed fleeing a building at 8:30 P.M. was a white male, approximately 35 years old. An abandoned building, located at 310 Hall Avenue, was set on fire.

13. Police Officer Winters responds to a call regarding a report of a missing person. The following information was obtained by the Officer:
    Time of Occurrence:   3:30 P.M.
    Place of Occurrence:   Harrison Park
    Reported By:   Louise Dee - daughter
    Description of Missing
    Person:   Sharon Dee, 70 years old, 5'5", brown eyes, black hair - mother

    Officer Winters is completing a report on the incident. Which one of the following expresses the above information MOST clearly and accurately?

    A. Mrs. Sharon Dee, reported missing by her daughter, Louise, was seen in Harrison Park. The last time she saw her was at 3:30 P.M. She is 70 years old with black hair, brown eyes, and 5'5".
    B. Louise Dee reported that her mother, Sharon Dee, is missing. Sharon Dee is 70 years old, has black hair, brown eyes, and is 5'5". She was last seen at 3:30 P.M. in Harrison Park.
    C. Louise Dee reported Sharon, her 70-year-old mother at 3:30 P.M., to be missing after being seen last at Harrison Park. Described as being 5'5", she has black hair and brown eyes.

D. At 3:30 P.M. Louise Dee's mother was last seen by her daughter in Harrison Park. She has black hair and brown eyes. Louise reported Sharon is 5'5" and 70 years old.

14. While on patrol, Police Officers Mertz and Gallo receive a call from the dispatcher regarding a crime in progress.
When the Officers arrive, they obtain the following information:

Time of Occurrence: 2:00 P.M.
Place of Occurrence: In front of 2124 Bristol Avenue
Crime: Purse snatch
Victim: Maria Nieves
Suspect: Carlos Ortiz
Witness: Jose Perez, who apprehended the subject

The Officers are completing a report on the incident.
Which one of the following expresses the above information MOST clearly and accurately?

14.____

A. At 2:00 P.M., Jose Perez witnessed Maria Nieves. Her purse was snatched. The suspect, Carlos Ortiz, was apprehended in front of 2124 Bristol Avenue.
B. In front of 2124 Bristol Avenue, Carlos Ortiz snatched the purse belonging to Maria Nieves. Carlos Ortiz was apprehended by a witness to the crime after Jose Perez saw the purse snatch at 2:00 P.M.
C. At 2:00 P.M., Carlos Ortiz snatched a purse from Maria Nieves in front of 2124 Bristol Avenue. Carlos Ortiz was apprehended by Jose Perez, a witness to the crime.
D. At 2:00 P.M., Carlos Ortiz was seen snatching the purse of Maria Nieves as seen and apprehended by Jose Perez in front of 2124 Bristol Avenue.

15. Police Officers Willis and James respond to a crime in progress and obtain the following information:

Time of Occurrence: 8:30 A.M.
Place of Occurrence: Corner of Hopkin Avenue and Amboy Place
Crime: Chain snatch
Victim: Mrs. Paula Evans
Witness: Mr. Robert Peters
Suspect: White male

Officers Willis and James are completing a report on the incident.
Which one of the following expresses the above information MOST clearly and accurately?

15.____

A. Mrs. Paula Evans was standing on the corner of Hopkin Avenue and Amboy Place at 8:30 A.M. when a white male snatched her chain. Mr. Robert Peters witnessed the crime.
B. At 8:30 A.M., Mr, Robert Peters witnessed Mrs. Paula Evans and a white male standing on the corner of Hopkin Avenue and Amboy Place. Her chain was snatched.
C. At 8:30 A.M., a white male was standing on the corner of Hopkin Avenue and Amboy Place. Mrs. Paula Evans' chain was snatched, and Mr. Robert Peters witnessed the crime.

D. At 8:30 A.M., Mr. Robert Peters reported he witnessed a white male snatching Mrs. Paula Evans' chain while standing on the corner of Hopkin Avenue and Amboy Place.

16. Police Officers Cleveland and Logan responded to an assault that had recently occurred. The following information was obtained at the scene:

Place of Occurrence: Broadway and Roosevelt Avenue
Time of Occurrence: 1:00 A.M.
Crime: Attempted robbery, assault
Victim: Chuck Brown, suffered a broken tooth
Suspect: Lewis Brown, victim's brother

Officer Logan is completing a report on the incident.
Which one of the following expresses the above information MOST clearly and accurately?

A. Lewis Brown assaulted his brother Chuck on the corner of Broadway and Roosevelt Avenue. Chuck Brown reported his broken tooth during the attempted robbery at 1:00 A.M.
B. Chuck Brown had his tooth broken when he was assaulted at 1:00 A.M. on the corner of Broadway and Roosevelt Avenue by his brother, Lewis Brown, while Lewis was attempting to rob him.
C. An attempt at 1:00 A.M. to rob Chuck Brown turned into an assault at the corner of Broadway and Roosevelt Avenue when his brother Lewis broke his tooth.
D. At 1:00 A.M., Chuck Brown reported that he was assaulted during his brother's attempt to rob him. Lewis Brown broke his tooth. The incident occurred on the corner of Broadway and Roosevelt Avenue.

17. Police Officer Mannix has just completed an investigation regarding a hit-and-run accident which resulted in a pedestrian being injured. Officer Mannix has obtained the following information:

Make and Model of Car: Pontiac, Trans Am
Year and Color of Car: 2006, white
Driver of Car: Male, black
Place of Occurrence: Corner of E. 15th Street and 8th Avenue
Time of Occurrence: 1:00 P.M.

Officer Mannix is completing a report on the accident.
Which one of the following expresses the above information MOST clearly and accurately?

A. At 1:00 P.M., at the corner of E. 15th Street and 8th Avenue, a black male driving a white 2006 Pontiac Trans Am was observed leaving the scene of an accident after injuring a pedestrian with the vehicle.
B. On the corner of E. 15th Street and 8th Avenue, a white Pontiac, driven by a black male, a 2006 Trans Am injured a pedestrian and left the scene of the accident at 1:00 P.M.
C. A black male driving a white 2006 Pontiac Trans Am injured a pedestrian and left with the car while driving on the corner of E. 15th Street and 8th Avenue at 1:00 P.M.
D. At the corner of E. 15th Street and 8th Avenue, a pedestrian was injured by a black male. He fled in his white 2006 Pontiac Trans Am at 1:00 P.M.

18. The following details were obtained by Police Officer Dwight at the scene of a family dispute:

Place of Occurrence: 77 Baruch Drive
Victim: Andrea Valdez, wife of Walker
Violator: Edward Walker
Witness: George Valdez, victim's brother
Crime: Violation of Order of Protection
Action Taken: Violator arrested

Police Officer Dwight is preparing a report on the incident.
Which one of the following expresses the above information MOST clearly and accurately?

   A. George Valdez saw Edward Walker violate his sister's Order of Protection at 77 Baruch Drive. Andrea Valdez's husband was arrested for this violation.
   B. Andrea Valdez's Order of Protection was violated at 77 Baruch Drive. George Valdez saw his brother-in-law violate his sister's Order. Edward Walker was arrested.
   C. Edward Walker was arrested for violating an Order of Protection held by his wife, Andrea Valdez. Andrea's brother, George Valdez, witnessed the violation at 77 Baruch Drive.
   D. An arrest was made at 77 Baruch Drive when an Order of Protection held by Andrea Valdez was violated by her husband. George Valdez, her brother, witnessed Edward Walker.

19. The following details were obtained by Police Officer Jackson at the scene of a robbery:

Place of Occurrence: Chambers Street, northbound A platform
Victim: Mr. John Wells
Suspect: Joseph Miller
Crime: Robbery, armed with knife, wallet taken
Action Taken: Suspect arrested

Officer Jackson is completing a report on the incident.
Which one of the following expresses the above information
MOST clearly and accurately?

   A. At Chambers Street northbound A platform, Joseph Miller used a knife to remove the wallet of John Wells while waiting for the train. Police arrested him.
   B. Mr. John Wells, while waiting for the northbound A train at Chambers Street, had his wallet forcibly removed at knifepoint by Joseph Miller. Joseph Miller was later arrested.
   C. Joseph Miller was arrested for robbery. At Chambers Street, John Wells stated that his wallet was taken. The incident occurred at knifepoint while waiting on a northbound A platform.
   D. At the northbound Chambers Street platform, John Wells was waiting for the A train. Joseph Miller produced a knife and removed his wallet. He was arrested.

20. Police Officer Bellows responds to a report of drugs being sold in the lobby of an apartment building. He obtains the following information at the scene:

Time of Occurrence: 11:30 P.M.
Place of Occurrence: 1010 Bath Avenue
Witnesses: Mary Markham, John Silver
Suspect: Harry Stoner
Crime: Drug sales
Action Taken: Suspect was gone when police arrived

Officer Bellows is completing a report of the incident. Which one of the following expresses the above information MOST clearly and accurately?

A. Mary Markham and John Silver witnessed drugs being sold and the suspect flee at 1010 Bath Avenue. Harry Stoner was conducting his business at 11:30 P.M. before police arrival in the lobby.
B. In the lobby, Mary Markham reported at 11:30 P.M. she saw Harry Stoner, along with John Silver, selling drugs. He ran from the lobby at 1010 Bath Avenue before police arrived.
C. John Silver and Mary Markham reported that they observed Harry Stoner selling drugs in the lobby of 1010 Bath Avenue at 11:30 P.M. The witnesses stated that Stoner fled before police arrived.
D. Before police arrived, witnesses stated that Harry Stoner was selling drugs. At 1010 Bath Avenue, in the lobby, John Silver and Mary Markham said they observed his actions at 11:30 P.M.

21. While on patrol, Police Officer Fox receives a call to respond to a robbery. Upon arriving at the scene, he obtains the following information:

Time of Occurrence: 6:00 P.M.
Place of Occurrence: Sal's Liquor Store at 30 Fordham Road
Victim: Sal Jones
Suspect: White male wearing a beige parka
Description of Crime: Victim was robbed in his store at gunpoint

Officer Fox is completing a report on the incident. Which one of the following expresses the above information MOST clearly and accurately?

A. I was informed at 6:00 P.M. by Sal Jones that an unidentified white male robbed him at gunpoint at 30 Fordham Road while wearing a beige parka at Sal's Liquor Store.
B. At 6:00 P.M., Sal Jones was robbed at gunpoint in his store. An unidentified white male wearing a beige parka came into Sal's Liquor Store at 30 Fordham Road, he told me.
C. I was informed at 6:00 P.M. while wearing a beige parka an unidentified white male robbed Sal Jones at gunpoint at Sal's Liquor Store at 30 Fordham Road.
D. Sal Jones informed me that at 6:00 P.M. he was robbed at gunpoint in his store, Sal's Liquor Store, located at 30 Fordham Road, by an unidentified white male wearing a beige parka.

22. The following details were obtained by Police Officer Connors at the scene of a bank robbery:

Time of Occurrence: 10:21 A.M.
Place of Occurrence: Westbury Savings and Loan
Crime: Bank Robbery
Suspect: Male, dressed in black, wearing a black woolen face mask
Witness: Mary Henderson of 217 Westbury Ave.
Amount Stolen: $6141 U.S. currency

Officer Connors is completing a report on the incident. Which one of the following expresses the above information MOST clearly and accurately?

  A. At 10:21 A.M., the Westbury Savings and Loan was witnessed being robbed by Mary Henderson of 217 Westbury Avenue. The suspect fled dressed in black with a black woolen face mask. He left the bank with $6141 in U.S. currency.
  B. Dressed in black wearing a black woolen face mask, Mary Henderson of 217 Westbury Avenue saw a suspect flee with $6141 in U.S. currency after robbing the Westbury Savings and Loan. The robber was seen at 10:21 A.M.
  C. At 10:21 A.M., Mary Henderson of 217 Westbury Avenue, witness to the robbery of the Westbury Savings and Loan, reports that a male, dressed in black, wearing a black face mask, did rob said bank and fled with $6141 in U.S. currency.
  D. Mary Henderson, of 217 Westbury Avenue, witnessed the robbery of the Westbury Savings and Loan at 10:21 A.M. The suspect, a male, was dressed in black and was wearing a black woolen face mask. He fled with $6141 in U.S. currency.

23. At the scene of a dispute, Police Officer Johnson made an arrest after obtaining the following information:

Place of Occurrence: 940 Baxter Avenue
Time of Occurrence: 3:40 P.M.
Victim: John Mitchell
Suspect: Robert Holden, arrested at scene
Crime: Menacing
Weapon: Knife
Time of Arrest: 4:00 P.M.

Officer Johnson is completing a report of the incident.
Which one of the following expresses the above information MOST clearly and accurately?

  A. John Mitchell was menaced by a knife at 940 Baxter Avenue. Robert Holden, owner of the weapon, was arrested at 4:00 P.M., twenty minutes later, at the scene.
  B. John Mitchell reports at 3:40 P.M. he was menaced at 940 Baxter Avenue by Robert Holden. He threatened him with his knife and was arrested at 4:00 P.M. at the scene.
  C. John Mitchell stated that at 3:40 P.M. at 940 Baxter Avenue he was menaced by Robert Holden, who was carrying a knife. Mr. Holden was arrested at the scene at 4:00 P.M.
  D. With a knife, Robert Holden menaced John Mitchell at 3:40 P.M. The knife belonged to him, and he was arrested at the scene of 940 Baxter Avenue at 4:00 P.M.

24. Officer Nieves obtained the following information after he was called to the scene of a large gathering:
    Time of Occurrence: 2:45 A.M.
    Place of Occurrence: Mulberry Park
    Complaint: Loud music
    Complainant: Mrs. Simpkins, 42 Mulberry Street, Apt. 25
    Action Taken: Police officer dispersed the crowd
    Officer Nieves is completing a report on the incident. Which one of the following expresses the above information MOST clearly and accurately?

    A. Mrs. Simpkins, who lives at 42 Mulberry Street, Apt. 25, called the police to make a complaint. A large crowd of people were playing loud music in Mulberry Park at 2:45 A.M. Officer Nieves responded and dispersed the crowd.
    B. Officer Nieves responded to Mulberry Park because Mrs. Simpkins, the complainant, lives at 42 Mulberry Street, Apt. 25. Due to a large crowd of people who were playing loud music at 2:45 A.M., he immediately dispersed the crowd.
    C. Due to a large crowd of people who were playing loud music in Mulberry Park at 2:45 A.M., Officer Nieves responded and dispersed the crowd. Mrs. Simpkins called the police and complained. She lives at 42 Mulberry Street, Apt. 25.
    D. Responding to a complaint by Mrs. Simpkins, who resides at 42 Mulberry Street, Apt. 25, Officer Nieves dispersed a large crowd in Mulberry Park. They were playing loud music. It was 2:45 A.M.

25. While patroling the subway, Police Officer Clark responds to the scene of a past robbery where he obtains the following information:
    Place of Occurrence: Northbound E train
    Time of Occurrence: 6:30 P.M.
    Victim: Robert Brey
    Crime: Wallet and jewelry taken
    Suspects: 2 male whites armed with knives
    Officer Clark is completing a report on the incident.
    Which one of the following expresses the above information MOST clearly and accurately?

    A. At 6:30 P.M., Robert Brey reported he was robbed of his wallet and jewelry. On the northbound E train, two white males approached Mr. Brey. They threatened him before taking his property with knives.
    B. While riding the E train northbound, two white men approached Robert Brey at 6:30 P.M. They threatened him with knives and took his wallet and jewelry.
    C. Robert Brey was riding the E train at 6:30 P.M. when he was threatened by two whites. The men took his wallet and jewelry as he was traveling northbound.
    D. Robert Brey reports at 6:30 P.M. he lost his wallet to two white men as well as his jewelry. They were carrying knives and threatened him aboard the northbound E train.

## KEY (CORRECT ANSWERS)

1. B
2. C
3. C
4. A
5. C

6. B
7. C
8. B
9. C
10. B

11. D
12. A
13. B
14. C
15. A

16. B
17. A
18. C
19. B
20. C

21. D
22. D
23. C
24. A
25. B

# TEST 2

DIRECTIONS: Each question or incomplete statement is followed by several suggested answers or completions. Select the one that BEST answers the question or completes the statement. *PRINT THE LETTER OF THE CORRECT ANSWER IN THE SPACE AT THE RIGHT.*

1. Police Officer Johnson has just finished investigating a report of a burglary and has obtained the following information:  
   Place of Occurrence: Victim's residence  
   Time of Occurrence: Between 8:13 P.M. and 4:15 A.M.  
   Victim: Paul Mason of 1264 Twentieth Street, Apt. 3D  
   Crime: Burglary  
   Damage: Filed front door lock  
   Officer Johnson is preparing a report of the incident. Which one of the following expresses the above information MOST clearly and accurately?

   A. Paul Mason's residence was burglarized at 1264 Twentieth Street, Apt. 3D, between 8:13 P.M. and 4:15 A.M. by filing the front door lock.
   B. Paul Mason was burglarized by filing the front door lock and he lives at 1264 Twentieth Street, Apt. 3D, between 8:13 P.M. and 4:15 A.M.
   C. Between 8:13 P.M. and 4:15 A.M., the residence of Paul Mason, located at 1264 Twentieth Street, Apt. 3D, was burglarized after the front door lock was filed.
   D. Between 8:13 P.M. and 4:15 A.M., at 1264 Twentieth Street, Apt. 3D, after the front door lock was filed, the residence of Paul Mason was burglarized.

   1.____

2. Police Officer Lowell has just finished investigating a burglary and has received the following information:  
   Place of Occurrence: 117-12 Sutphin Boulevard  
   Time of Occurrence: Between 9:00 A.M. and 5:00 P.M.  
   Victim: Mandee Cotton  
   Suspects: Unknown  
   Officer Lowell is completing a report on this incident.  
   Which one of the following expresses the above information MOST clearly and accurately?

   A. Mandee Cotton reported that her home was burglarized between 9:00 A.M. and 5:00 P.M. Ms. Cotton resides at 117-12 Sutphin Boulevard. Suspects are unknown.
   B. A burglary was committed at 117-12 Sutphin Boulevard reported Mandee Cotton between 9:00 A.M. and 5:00 P.M. Ms. Cotton said unknown suspects burglarized her home.
   C. Unknown suspects burglarized a home at 117-12 Sutphin Boulevard between 9:00 A.M. and 5:00 P.M. Mandee Cotton, homeowner, reported.
   D. Between the hours of 9:00 A.M. and 5:00 P.M., it was reported that 117-12 Sutphin Boulevard was burglarized. Mandee Cotton reported that unknown suspects are responsible.

   2.____

3. Police Officer Dale has just finished investigating a report of attempted theft and has obtained the following information:

Place of Occurrence: In front of 103 W. 105th Street
Time of Occurrence: 11:30 A.M.
Victim: Mary Davis
Crime: Attempted theft
Suspect: Male, black, scar on right side of face
Action Taken: Drove victim around area to locate suspect

Officer Dale is preparing a report on the incident. Which one of the following expresses the above information MOST clearly and accurately?

   A. Mary Davis was standing in front of 103 W. 105th Street when Officer Dale arrived after an attempt to steal her pocketbook failed at 11:30 A.M. Officer Dale canvassed the area looking for a black male with a scar on the right side of his face with Ms. Davis in the patrol car.
   B. Mary Davis stated that, at 11:30 A.M., she was standing in front of 103 W. 105th Street when a black male with a scar on the right side of his face attempted to steal her pocketbook. Officer Dale canvassed the area with Ms. Davis in the patrol car.
   C. Officer Dale canvassed the area by putting Mary Davis in a patrol car looking for a black male with a scar on the right side of his face. At 11:30 A.M. in front of 103 W. 105th Street, she said he attempted to steal her pocketbook.
   D. At 11:30 A.M., in front of 103 W. 105th Street, Officer Dale canvassed the area with Mary Davis in a patrol car who said that a black male with a scar on the right side of his face attempted to steal her pocketbook.

4. While on patrol, Police Officer Santoro received a call to respond to the scene of a shooting. The following details were obtained at the scene:

Time of Occurrence: 4:00 A.M.
Place of Occurrence: 232 Senator Street
Victim: Mike Nisman
Suspect: Howard Conran
Crime: Shooting
Witness: Sheila Norris

Officer Santoro is completing a report on the incident.
Which one of the following expresses the above information MOST clearly and accurately?

   A. Sheila Norris stated at 4:00 A.M. she witnessed a shooting of her neighbor in front of her building. Howard Conran shot Mike Nisman and ran from 232 Senator Street.
   B. Mike Nisman was the victim of a shooting incident seen by his neighbor. At 4:00 A.M., Sheila Norris saw Howard Conran shoot him and run in front of their building. Norris and Nisman reside at 232 Senator Street.
   C. Sheila Norris states that at 4:00 A.M. she witnessed Howard Conran shoot Mike Nisman, her neighbor, in front of their building at 232 Senator Street. She further states she saw the suspect running from the scene.
   D. Mike Nisman was shot by Howard Conran at 4:00 A.M. His neighbor, Sheila Norris, witnessed him run from the scene in front of their building at 232 Senator Street.

5. Police Officer Taylor responds to the scene of a serious traffic accident in which a car struck a telephone pole, and obtains the following information:

Place of Occurrence: Intersection of Rock Street and Amboy Place
Time of Occurrence: 3:27 A.M.
Name of Injured: Carlos Black
Driver of Car: Carlos Black
Action Taken: Injured taken to Beth-El Hospital

Officer Taylor is preparing a report on the accident. Which one of the following expresses the above information MOST clearly and accurately?

- A. At approximately 3:27 A.M., Carlos Black drove his car into a telephone pole located at the intersection of Rock Street and Amboy Place. Mr. Black, who was the only person injured, was taken to Beth-El Hospital.
- B. Carlos Black, injured at the intersection of Rock Street and Amboy Place, hit a telephone pole. He was taken to Beth-El Hospital after the car accident which occurred at 3:27 A.M.
- C. At the intersection of Rock Street and Amboy Place, Carlos Black injured himself and was taken to Beth-El Hospital. His car hit a telephone pole at 3:27 A.M.
- D. At the intersection of Rock Street and Amboy Place at 3:27 A.M., Carlos Black was taken to Beth-El Hospital after injuring himself by driving into a telephone pole.

6. While on patrol in the Jefferson Housing Projects, Police Officer Johnson responds to the scene of a Grand Larceny.

The following information was obtained by Officer Johnson:

Time of Occurrence: 6:00 P.M.
Place of Occurrence: Rear of Building 12A
Victim: Maria Lopez
Crime: Purse snatched
Suspect: Unknown

Officer Johnson is preparing a report on the incident.
Which one of the following expresses the above information MOST clearly and accurately?

- A. At the rear of Building 12A, at 6:00 P.M., by an unknown suspect, Maria Lopez reported her purse snatched in the Jefferson Housing Projects.
- B. Maria Lopez reported that at 6:00 P.M. her purse was snatched by an unknown suspect at the rear of Building 12A in the Jefferson Housing Projects.
- C. At the rear of Building 12A, Maria Lopez reported at 6:00 P.M. that her purse had been snatched by an unknown suspect in the Jefferson Housing Projects.
- D. In the Jefferson Housing Projects, Maria Lopez reported at the rear of Building 12A that her purse had been snatched by an unknown suspect at 6:00 P.M.

7. Criminal Possession of Stolen Property 2nd Degree occurs when a person knowingly possesses stolen property with intent to benefit himself or a person other than the owner, or to prevent its recovery by the owner, and when the
    I. value of the property exceeds two hundred fifty dollars; or
    II. property consists of a credit card; or
    III. person is a pawnbroker or is in the business of buying, selling, or otherwise dealing in property; or
    IV. property consists of one or more firearms, rifles, or shotguns.

    Which one of the following is the BEST example of Criminal Possession of Stolen Property in the Second Degree?

    A. Mary knowingly buys a stolen camera valued at $225 for her mother's birthday.
    B. John finds a wallet containing $100 and various credit cards. John keeps the money and turns the credit cards in at his local precinct.
    C. Mr. Varrone, a pawnbroker, refuses to buy Mr. Cutter's stolen VCR valued at $230.
    D. Mr. Aquista, the owner of a toy store, knowingly buys a crate of stolen water pistols valued at $260.

8. Police Officer Dale has just finished investigating a report of menacing and obtained the following information:

    Time of Occurrence:   10:30 P.M.
    Place of Occurrence:  (Hallway) 77 Hill Street
    Victim:               Grace Jackson
    Suspect:              Susan, white female, 30 years of age
    Crime:                Menacing with a knife

    Officer Dale is preparing a report on the incident.
    Which one of the following expresses the above information MOST clearly and accurately?

    A. At 10:30 P.M., Grace Jackson was stopped in the hallway of 77 Hill Street by a 30-year-old white female known to Grace as Susan. Susan put a knife to Grace's throat and demanded that Grace stay out of the building or Susan would hurt her.
    B. Grace Jackson was stopped in the hallway at knifepoint and threatened to stay away from the building located at 77 Hill Street. The female who is 30 years of age known as Susan by Jackson stopped her at 10:30 P.M.
    C. At 10:30 P.M. in the hallway of 77 Hill Street, Grace Jackson reported a white female 30 years of age put a knife to her throat. She knew her as Susan and demanded she stay away from the building or she would get hurt.
    D. A white female 30 years of age known to Grace Jackson as Susan stopped her in the hallway of 77 Hill Street. She put a knife to her throat and at 10:30 P.M. demanded she stay away from the building or she would get hurt.

9. Police Officer Bennett responds to the scene of a car accident and obtains the following information from the witness:

    Time of Occurrence:   3:00 A.M.
    Victim:               Joe Morris, removed to Methodist Hospital
    Crime:                Struck pedestrian and left the scene of accident
    Description of Auto:  Blue 2008 Pontiac, license plate BOT-3745

    Officer Bennett is preparing an accident report. Which one of the following expresses the above information MOST clearly and accurately?

A. Joe Morris, a pedestrian, was hit at 3:00 A.M. and removed to Methodist Hospital. Also a blue Pontiac, 2008 model left the scene, license plate BOT-3745.
B. A pedestrian was taken to Methodist Hospital after being struck at 3:00 A.M. A blue automobile was seen leaving the scene with license plate BOT-3745. Joe Morris was knocked down by a 2008 Pontiac.
C. At 3:00 A.M., Joe Morris, a pedestrian, was struck by a blue 2008 Pontiac. The automobile, license plate BOT-3745, left the scene. Mr. Morris was taken to Methodist Hospital.
D. Joe Morris, a pedestrian at 3:00 A.M. was struck by a Pontiac. A 2008 model, license plate BOT-3745, blue in color, left the scene and the victim was taken to Methodist Hospital.

10. At 11:30 A.M., Police Officers Newman and Johnson receive a radio call to respond to a reported robbery. The Officers obtained the following information:
Time of Occurrence: 11:20 A.M.
Place of Occurrence: Twenty-four hour newsstand at 2024 86th Street
Victim: Sam Norris, owner
Amount Stolen: $450.00
Suspects: Two male whites
Officer Newman is completing a complaint report on the incident.
Which one of the following expresses the above information MOST clearly and accurately?

A. At 11:20 A.M., it was reported by the newsstand owner that two male whites robbed $450.00 from Sam Norris. The Twenty-four hour newsstand is located at 2024 86th Street.
B. At 11:20 A.M., Sam Norris, the newsstand owner, reported that the Twenty-four hour newsstand located at 2024 86th Street was robbed by two male whites who took $450.00.
C. Sam Norris, the owner of the Twenty-four hour newsstand located at 2024 86th Street, reported that at 11:20 A.M. two white males robbed his newsstand of $450.00.
D. Sam Norris reported at 11:20 A.M. that $450.00 had been taken from the owner of the Twenty-four hour newsstand located at 2024 86th Street by two male whites.

11. While on patrol, Police Officers Carter and Popps receive a call to respond to an assault in progress. Upon arrival, they receive the following information:
Place of Occurrence: 27 Park Avenue
Victim: John Dee
Suspect: Michael Jones
Crime: Stabbing during a fight
Action Taken: Suspect arrested
The Officers are completing a report on the incident.
Which one of the following expresses the above information MOST clearly and accurately?

A. In front of 27 Park Avenue, Michael Jones was arrested for stabbing John Dee during a fight.
B. Michael Jones was arrested for stabbing John Dee during a fight in front of 27 Park Avenue.

C. During a fight, Michael Jones was arrested for stabbing John Dee in front of 27 Park Avenue.
D. John Dee was stabbed by Michael Jones, who was arrested for fighting in front of 27 Park Avenue.

12. Police Officer Gattuso responded to a report of a robbery and obtained the following information regarding the incident:

    Place of Occurrence:       Princess Grocery, 6 Button Place
    Time of Occurrence:        6:00 P.M.
    Crime:                     Robbery of $200
    Victim:                    Sara Davidson, owner of Princess Grocery
    Description of Suspect:    White, female, red hair, blue jeans, and white T-shirt
    Weapon:                    Knife

    Officer Gattuso is preparing a report on the incident.
    Which one of the following expresses the above information MOST clearly and accurately?

    A. Sara Davidson reported at 6:00 P.M. her store Princess Grocery was robbed at knifepoint at 6 Button Place. A white woman with red hair took $200 from her wearing blue jeans and a white T-shirt.
    B. At 6:00 P.M., a red-haired woman took $200 from 6 Button Place at Princess Grocery owned by Sara Davidson, who was robbed by the white woman. She was wearing blue jeans and a white T-shirt and used a knife.
    C. In a robbery that occurred at knifepoint, a red-haired white woman robbed the owner of Princess Grocery. Sara Davidson, the owner of the 6 Button Place store which was robbed of $200, said she was wearing blue jeans and a white T-shirt at 6:00 P.M.
    D. At 6:00 P.M., Sara Davidson, owner of Princess Grocery, located at 6 Button Place, was robbed of $200 at knifepoint. The suspect is a white female with red hair wearing blue jeans and a white T-shirt.

13. Police Officer Martinez responds to a report of an assault and obtains the following information regarding the incident:

    Place of Occurrence:   Corner of Frank and Lincoln Avenues
    Time of Occurrence:    9:40 A.M.
    Crime:                 Assault
    Victim:                Mr. John Adams of 31 20th Street
    Suspect:               Male, white, 5'11", 170 lbs., dressed in gray
    Injury:                Victim suffered a split lip
    Action Taken:          Victim transported to St. Mary's Hospital

    Officer Martinez is completing a report on the incident. Which one of the following expresses the above information MOST clearly and accurately?

    A. At 9:40 A.M., John Adams was assaulted on the corner of Frank and Lincoln Avenues by a white male, 5'11", 170 lbs., dressed in gray, suffering a split lip. Mr. Adams lives at 31 20th Street and was transported to St. Mary's Hospital.
    B. At 9:40 A.M., John Adams was assaulted on the corner of Frank and Lincoln Avenues by a white male, 5'11", 170 lbs., dressed in gray, and lives at 31 20th Street. Mr. Adams suffered a split lip and was transported to St. Mary's Hospital.

C. John Adams, who lives at 31 20th Street, was assaulted at 9:40 A.M. on the corner of Frank and Lincoln Avenues by a white male, 5'11", 170 lbs., dressed in gray. Mr. Adams suffered a split lip and was transported to St. Mary's Hospital.
D. Living at 31 20th Street, Mr. Adams suffered a split lip and was transported to St. Mary's Hospital. At 9:40 A.M., Mr. Adams was assaulted by a white male, 5'11", 170 lbs., dressed in gray.

14. The following information was obtained by Police Officer Adams at the scene of an auto accident:

    Date of Occurrence:    August 7, 2004
    Place of Occurrence:   541 W. Broadway
    Time of Occurrence:    12:45 P.M.
    Drivers:               Mrs. Liz Smith and Mr. John Sharp
    Action Taken:          Summons served to Mrs. Liz Smith

    Officer Adams is completing a report on the accident. Which one of the following expresses the above information MOST clearly and accurately?

    A. At 541 W. Broadway, Mr. John Sharp and Mrs. Liz Smith had an auto accident at 12:45 P.M. Mrs. Smith received a summons on August 7, 2004.
    B. Mrs. Liz Smith received a summons at 12:45 P.M. on August 7, 2004 for an auto accident with Mr. John Sharp at 541 W. Broadway.
    C. Mr. John Sharp and Mrs. Liz Smith were in an auto accident. At 541 W. Broadway on August 7, 2004 at 12:45 P.M., Mrs. Smith received a summons.
    D. On August 7, 2004 at 12:45 P.M. at 541 W. Broadway, Mrs. Liz Smith and Mr. John Sharp were involved in an auto accident. Mrs. Smith received a summons.

14.____

15. Police Officer Gold and his partner were directed by the radio dispatcher to investigate a report of a past burglary. They obtained the following information at the scene:

    Date of Occurrence:    April 2, 2004
    Time of Occurrence:    Between 7:30 A.M. and 6:15 P.M.
    Place of Occurrence:   124 Haring Street, residence of victim
    Victim:                Mr. Gerald Palmer
    Suspect:               Unknown
    Crime:                 Burglary
    Items Stolen:          Assorted jewelry, $150 cash, TV, VCR

    Officer Gold must complete a report on the incident. Which one of the following expresses the above information MOST clearly and accurately?

    A. Mr. Gerald Palmer stated that on April 2, 2004, between 7:30 A.M. and 6:15 P.M., while he was at work, someone broke into his house at 124 Haring Street and removed assorted jewelry, a VCR, $150 cash, and a TV.
    B. Mr. Gerald Palmer stated while he was at work that somebody broke into his house on April 2, 2004 and between 7:30 A.M. and 6:15 P.M. took his VCR, TV, assorted jewelry, and $150 cash. His address is 124 Haring Street.
    C. Between 7:30 A.M. and 6:15 P.M. on April 2, 2004, Mr. Gerald Palmer reported an unknown person at 124 Haring Street took his TV, VCR, $150 cash, and assorted jewelry from his house. Mr. Palmer said he was at work at the time.
    D. An unknown person broke into the house at 124 Haring Street and stole a TV, VCR, assorted jewelry, and $150 cash from Mr. Gerald Palmer. The suspect broke in on April 2, 2004 while he was at work, reported Mr. Palmer between 7:30 A.M. and 6:15 P.M.

15.____

16. While on patrol, Police Officers Morris and Devine receive a call to respond to a reported burglary. The following information relating to the crime was obtained by the Officers:

Time of Occurrence: 2:00 A.M.
Place of Occurrence: 2100 First Avenue
Witness: David Santiago
Victim: John Rivera
Suspect: Joe Ryan
Crime: Burglary, DVD player stolen

The Officers are completing a report on the incident.
Which one of the following expresses the above information MOST clearly and accurately?

    A. David Santiago, the witness reported at 2:00 A.M. he saw Joe Ryan leave 2100 First Avenue, home of John Rivera, with a DVD player.
    B. At 2:00 A.M. David Santiago reported that he had seen Joe Ryan go into 2100 First Avenue and steal a DVD player. John Rivera lives at 2100 First Avenue.
    C. David Santiago stated that Joe Ryan burglarized John Rivera's house at 2100 First Avenue. He saw Joe Ryan leaving his house at 2:00 A.M. with a DVD player.
    D. David Santiago reported that at 2:00 A.M. he saw Joe Ryan leave John Rivera's house, located at 2100 First Avenue, with Mr. Rivera's DVD player.

17. When a police officer responds to an incident involving the victim of an animal bite, the officer should do the following in the order given:
    I. Determine the owner of the animal
    II. Obtain a description of the animal and attempt to locate it for an examination if the owner is unknown
    III. If the animal is located and the owner is unknown, comply with the Care and Disposition of Animal procedure
    IV. Prepare a Department of Health Form 480BAA and deliver it to the Desk Officer with a written report
    V. Notify the Department of Health by telephone if the person has been bitten by an animal other than a dog or cat.

Police Officer Rosario responds to 1225 South Boulevard where someone has been bitten by a dog. He is met by John Miller who informs Officer Rosario that he was bitten by a large German Shepard. Mr. Miller also states that he believes the dog belongs to someone in the neighborhood but does not know who owns it. Officer Rosario searches the area for the dog but is unable to find it.
What should Officer Rosario do NEXT?

    A. Locate the owner of the animal.
    B. Notify the Department of Health by telephone.
    C. Prepare a Department of Health Form 480BAA.
    D. Comply with the Care and Disposition of Animal procedure.

18. The following details were obtained by Police Officer Howard at the scene of a hit-and-run accident:

    Place of Occurrence: Intersection of Brown Street and Front Street
    Time of Occurrence: 11:15 A.M.
    Victim: John Lawrence
    Vehicle: Red Chevrolet, license plate 727PQA
    Crime: Leaving the scene of an accident

    Officer Howard is completing a report on the incident. Which one of the following expresses the above information MOST clearly and accurately?

    A. A red Chevrolet, license plate 727PQA, hit John Lawrence. It left the scene of the accident at 11:15 A.M. at the intersection of Brown and Front Streets.
    B. At 11:15 A.M., John Lawrence was walking at the intersection of Brown Street and Front Street when he was struck by a red Chevrolet, license plate 727PQA, which left the scene.
    C. It was reported at 11:15 A.M. that John Lawrence was struck at the intersection of Brown Street and Front Street. The red Chevrolet, license plate 727PQA, left the scene.
    D. At the intersection of Brown Street and Front Street, John Lawrence was the victim of a car at 11:15 A.M. which struck him and left the scene. It was a red Chevrolet, license plate 727PQA.

19. Police Officer Donnelly has transported an elderly male to Mt. Hope Hospital after finding him lying on the street. At the hospital, Nurse Baker provided Officer Donnelly with the following information:

    Name: Robert Jones
    Address: 1485 E. 97th St.
    Date of Birth: May 13, 1935
    Age: 73 years old
    Type of Ailment: Heart condition

    Officer Donnelly is completing an Aided Report.
    Which one of the following expresses the above information MOST clearly and accurately?

    A. Mr. Robert Jones, who is 73 years old, born on May 13, 1935, collapsed on the street. Mr. Jones, who resides at 1485 E. 97th Street, suffers from a heart condition.
    B. Mr. Robert Jones had a heart condition and collapsed today on the street, and resides at 1485 E. 97th Street. He was 73 years old and born on May 13, 1935.
    C. Mr. Robert Jones, who resides at 1485 E. 97th Street, was born on May 13, 1935, and is 73 years old, was found lying on the street from a heart condition.
    D. Mr. Robert Jones, born on May 13, 1935, suffers from a heart condition at age 73 and was found lying on the street residing at 1485 E. 97th Street.

20. Police officers on patrol are often called to a scene where a response from the Fire Department might be necessary.
    In which one of the following situations would a request to the Fire Department to respond be MOST critical?

A. A film crew has started a small fire in order to shoot a scene on an October evening.
B. Two manhole covers blow off on a September afternoon.
C. Homeless persons are gathered around a trash can fire on a February morning.
D. A fire hydrant has been opened by people in the neighborhood on a July afternoon.

21. Police Officer Johnson arrives at the National Savings Bank five minutes after it has been robbed at gunpoint.
The following are details provided by eyewitnesses: <u>Suspect</u>
Sex: Male
Ethnicity: White
Height: 5'10" to 6'2"
Weight: 180 lbs. to 190 lbs.
Hair Color: Blonde
Clothing: Black jacket, blue dungarees
Weapon: .45 caliber revolver
Officer Johnson is completing a report on the incident.
Which one of the following expresses the above information MOST clearly and accurately?
A white male

A. weighing 180-190 lbs. robbed the National Savings Bank. He was white with a black jacket with blonde hair, is 5'10" to 6'2", and blue dungarees. The robber was armed with a .45 caliber revolver.
B. weighing around 180 or 190 lbs. was wearing a black jacket and blue dungarees. He had blonde hair and had a .45 caliber revolver, and was 5'10" to 6'2". He robbed the National Savings Bank.
C. who was 5'10" to 6'2" and was weighing 180 to 190 lbs., and has blonde hair and wearing blue dungarees and a black jacket with a revolver, robbed the National Savings Bank.
D. armed with a .45 caliber revolver robbed the National Savings Bank. The robber was described as being between 180-190 lbs., 5'10" to 6'2", with blonde hair. He was wearing a black jacket and blue dungarees.

22. While on patrol, Police Officer Rogers is approached by Terry Conyers, a young woman whose pocketbook has been stolen. Ms. Conyers tells Officer Rogers that the following items were in her pocketbook at the time it was taken:
   4 Traveler's checks, each valued at $20.00
   3 Traveler's checks, each valued at $25.00
   Cash of $212.00
   1 wedding band valued at $450.00
Officer Rogers is preparing a Complaint Report on the robbery.
Which one of the following is the TOTAL value of the property and cash taken from Ms. Conyers?

A. $707     B. $807     C. $817     D. $837

23. While on patrol, Police Officer Scott is dispatched to respond to a reported burglary. Two burglars entered the home of Mr. and Mrs. Walker and stole the following items:
    3 watches valued at $65.00 each
    1 amplifier valued at $340.00
    1 television set valued at $420.00
    Officer Scott is preparing a Complaint Report on the burglary.
    Which one of the following is the TOTAL value of the property stolen?

    A. $707   B. $825   C. $920   D. $955

24. While on patrol, Police Officer Smith is dispatched to investigate a grand larceny. Deborah Paisley, a businesswoman, reports that her 2000 Porsche was broken into. The following items were taken:
    1 car stereo system valued at $2,950.00
    1 car phone valued at $1,060.00
    Ms. Paisley's attache case valued at $200.00 was also taken from the car in the incident. The attache case contained two new solid gold pens valued at $970.00 each.
    Officer Smith is completing a Complaint Report.
    Which one of the following is the TOTAL dollar value of the property stolen from Ms. Paisley's car?

    A. $5,180   B. $5,980   C. $6,040   D. $6,150

25. Police Officer Grundig is writing a Complaint Report regarding a burglary and assault case. Officer Grundig has obtained the following facts:
    Place of Occurrence:    2244 Clark Street
    Victim:                 Mrs. Willis
    Suspect:                Mr. Willis, victim's ex-husband
    Complaint:              Unlawful entry; head injury inflicted with a bat
    Officer Grundig is completing a report on the incident. Which one of the following expresses the above information MOST clearly and accurately?

    A. He had no permission or authority to do so and it caused her head injuries, when Mr. Willis entered his ex-wife's premises. Mrs. Willis lives at 2244 Clark Street. He hit her with a bat.
    B. Mr. Willis entered 2244 Clark Street, the premises of his ex-wife. He hit her with a bat, without permission and authority to do so. It caused Mrs. Willis to have head injuries.
    C. After Mr. Willis hit his ex-wife, Mrs. Willis, at 2244 Clark Street, the bat caused her to have head injuries. He had no permission nor authority do so so.
    D. Mr. Willis entered his ex-wife's premises at 2244 Clark Street without her permission or authority. He then struck Mrs. Willis with a bat, causing injuries to her head.

## KEY (CORRECT ANSWERS)

1. C
2. A
3. B
4. C
5. A

6. B
7. D
8. A
9. C
10. C

11. B
12. D
13. C
14. D
15. A

16. D
17. C
18. B
19. A
20. B

21. D
22. C
23. D
24. D
25. D

# WORD MEANING
## EXAMINATION SECTION
## TEST 1

DIRECTIONS: Each question or incomplete statement is followed by several suggested answers or completions. Select the one that BEST answers the question or completes the statement. *PRINT THE LETTER OF THE CORRECT ANSWER IN THE SPACE AT THE RIGHT.*

1. In the sentence, *Malice was immanent in all his remarks*, the word *immanent* means MOST NEARLY

   A. elevated
   B. inherent
   C. threatening
   D. foreign

2. In the sentence, *The extant copies of the document were found in the safe*, the word *extant* means MOST NEARLY

   A. existing
   B. original
   C. forged
   D. duplicate

3. In the sentence, *The recruit was more complaisant after the captain spoke to him*, the word *complaisant* means MOST NEARLY

   A. calm
   B. affable
   C. irritable
   D. confident

4. In the sentence, *The man was captured under highly creditable circumstances*, the word *creditable* means MOST NEARLY

   A. doubtful
   B. believable
   C. praiseworthy
   D. unexpected

5. In the sentence, *His superior officers were more sagacious than he*, the word *sagacious* means MOST NEARLY

   A. shrewd   B. obtuse   C. absurd   D. verbose

6. In the sentence, *He spoke with impunity*, the word *impunity* means MOST NEARLY

   A. rashness
   B. caution
   C. without fear
   D. immunity

7. In the sentence, *The new patrolman displayed unusual temerity during the emergency*, the word *temerity* means MOST NEARLY

   A. fear   B. rashness   C. calmness   D. anxiety

8. In the sentence, *The portions of food were parsimoniously served*, the word *parsimoniously* means MOST NEARLY

   A. stingily
   B. piously
   C. elaborately
   D. generously

9. In the sentence, *Generally the speaker's remarks were sententious,* the word *sententious* means MOST NEARLY

   A. verbose
   B. witty
   C. argumentative
   D. pithy

10. In the sentence, *The prisoner was fractious when brought to the station house,* the word *fractious* means MOST NEARLY

    A. penitent
    B. talkative
    C. irascible
    D. broken-hearted

11. In the sentence, *The judge was implacable when the attorney pleaded for leniency,* the word *implacable* means MOST NEARLY

    A. inexorable
    B. disinterested
    C. inattentive
    D. indifferent

12. In the sentence, *The court ordered the mendacious statements stricken from the record,* the word *mendacious* means MOST NEARLY

    A. begging
    B. lying
    C. threatening
    D. lengthy

13. In the sentence, *The district attorney spoke in a strident voice,* the word *strident* means MOST NEARLY

    A. loud
    B. harsh-sounding
    C. sing-song
    D. low

14. In the sentence, *The speaker had a predilection for long sentences,* the word *predilection* means MOST NEARLY

    A. aversion
    B. talent
    C. propensity
    D. diffidence

15. A section of the Penal Law states that *a morbid propensity to commit prohibited acts.... forms no defense to a prosecution therefor.*
    The word *propensity* as used in this statute means MOST NEARLY

    A. capacity    B. ability    C. tendency    D. aptitude

16. A police department rule provides that a *Chaplain shall have the assimilated rank of Inspector.*
    The word *assimilated* as used in this rule means MOST NEARLY

    A. false
    B. superior
    C. comparable
    D. presumed

17. A police department rule provides that *Pushcarts and derelict automobiles shall be delivered to the Bureau of Incumbrances.*
    The word *derelict* as used in this rule means MOST NEARLY

    A. dilapidated
    B. abandoned
    C. delinquent
    D. contraband

18. A police department rule provides that *when the exigencies of the service shall so require, a captain may assign a patrolman from the outgoing platoon to house duty.*
The word *exigencies* as used in this rule means MOST NEARLY

   A. needs
   B. conveniences
   C. changes
   D. increases

19. A police department rule provides for the award of a Medal for Merit *for an act of outstanding bravery, performed in the line of duty, at imminent personal hazard of life.*
The word *imminent* as used in this rule means MOST NEARLY

   A. impending   B. inherent   C. certain   D. great

20. A police department rule provides that *the Police Commissioner shall have cognizance and control of the government, administration, disposition and discipline of the Police Department.*
The word *cognizance* as used in this rule means MOST NEARLY

   A. responsibility for
   B. jurisdiction over
   C. knowledge of
   D. ability for

21. A police department rule provides that a member of the department shall not communicate with a railroad company *for the purpose of expediting the issue of a transportation pass.*
The word *expediting* as used in this rule means MOST NEARLY

   A. extorting
   B. procuring
   C. demanding
   D. hastening

22. A section of the Penal Law provides, in part, that *whenever the punishment or penalty for an offense is mitigated by any provision of this chapter, such provision may be applied to any sentence or judgment imposed for the offense.*
The word *mitigated* as used in this statute means MOST NEARLY

   A. removed
   B. augmented
   C. changed
   D. decreased

23. A Police Department Manual of Procedure provides that a member of the force who comes into possession of a document containing scurrilous matter will take precautions to safeguard fingerprints thereon.
The word *scurrilous* as used in this regulation means MOST NEARLY

   A. irrelevant
   B. offensive
   C. defamatory
   D. evidentiary

24. Under cases of *Mendicancy* should be listed cases of

   A. loitering
   B. begging
   C. carrying of weapons
   D. injury to property

25. A police department rule states that *the Department Medal of Honor may be awarded to a member of the Force who distinguishes himself by an act of gallantry and intrepidity.*
The word *intrepidity* as used in this rule means MOST NEARLY

   A. chivalry   B. virility   C. fear   D. courage

## KEY (CORRECT ANSWERS)

| | | | |
|---|---|---|---|
| 1. | B | 11. | A |
| 2. | A | 12. | B |
| 3. | B | 13. | B |
| 4. | C | 14. | C |
| 5. | A | 15. | C |
| 6. | D | 16. | C |
| 7. | B | 17. | B |
| 8. | A | 18. | A |
| 9. | D | 19. | A |
| 10. | C | 20. | C |

21. D
22. D
23. B
24. B
25. D

# TEST 2

DIRECTIONS: Each question or incomplete statement is followed by several suggested answers or completions. Select the one that BEST answers the question or completes the statement. *PRINT THE LETTER OF THE CORRECT ANSWER IN THE SPACE AT THE RIGHT.*

1. A foreman who <u>expedites</u> a job
   - A. abolishes it
   - B. makes it bigger
   - C. slows it down
   - D. speeds it up

2. If a man is working at a <u>uniform</u> speed, it means he is working at a speed which is
   - A. changing
   - B. fast
   - C. slow
   - D. steady

3. To say that a caretaker is <u>obstinate</u> means that he is
   - A. cooperative
   - B. patient
   - C. stubborn
   - D. willing

4. To say that a caretaker is <u>negligent</u> means that he is
   - A. careless
   - B. neat
   - C. nervous
   - D. late

5. To say that something is <u>absurd</u> means that it is
   - A. definite
   - B. not clear
   - C. ridiculous
   - D. unfair

6. To say that a foreman is <u>impartial</u> means that he is
   - A. fair
   - B. improving
   - C. in a hurry
   - D. watchful

7. A foreman who is <u>lenient</u> is one who is
   - A. careless
   - B. harsh
   - C. inexperienced
   - D. mild

8. A foreman who is <u>punctual</u> is one who is
   - A. able
   - B. polite
   - C. prompt
   - D. sincere

9. If you think one of your men is too <u>awkward</u> to do a job, it means you think he is too
   - A. clumsy
   - B. lazy
   - C. old
   - D. weak

10. A man who is <u>seldom</u> late is late
    - A. always
    - B. never
    - C. often
    - D. rarely

Questions 11-18.

DIRECTIONS: In Questions 11 through 18, select the choice that is CLOSEST in meaning to the underlined word.

11. A central file eliminates the need to retain duplicate material. 11.____

    A. keep    B. change    C. locate    D. process

12. Filing is a routine office task. 12.____

    A. proper    B. regular    C. simple    D. difficult

13. Sometimes a word, phrase, or sentence must be deleted to correct an error. 13.____

    A. removed    B. added    C. expanded    D. improved

14. Your supervisor will evaluate your work. 14.____

    A. judge    B. list    C. assign    D. explain

15. Railroad Clerks must ascertain the identification of all individuals claiming to be Transit Authority employees. 15.____

    A. observe    B. record    C. challenge    D. verify

16. A Railroad Clerk must not permit anyone to loiter near his booth. 16.____

    A. throw refuse    B. smoke
    C. stand idly    D. make noise

17. The Transit Authority has a program for eliminating graffiti in subway cars. 17.____

    A. noise    B. markings
    C. vandalism    D. debris

18. The Railroad Clerk will deduct the number of tokens she sold from the number of tokens she had in reserve when she started her tour of duty. 18.____

    A. add    B. subtract    C. multiply    D. divide

Questions 19-30.

DIRECTIONS: Questions 19 through 30 contain incorrectly used words which change the meaning of the statement. Identify the word in the statement that is incorrect and select the choice that would make the sentence correct.

19. Lack of employee input in the case of training often exists, but is frequently dealt with in evaluation of the training effort. Failure to deal with as important a factor as this can be ruinous to the training effort. 19.____

    A. Seldom    B. Margin
    C. Ancillary    D. Contributory

3 (#2)

20. It is a fallacy that policies generated at the top of the hierarchy are often not acceptable to those on the lower levels, particularly in the case of blue-collar workers among whom the rewards and sanctions of the union or members of the immediate social group are more impelling than the rewards or sanctions available to management.

    A. Parologism                 B. Truism
    C. Commands               D. Undetermined

20.\_\_\_\_

21. Basically, an organization develops when employees in it have rather free control over their behavior within the organization, when the philosophy of the organization is that maximum interpersonal interplay through a minimum number of hierarchical levels is desirable, and when a person traditionally called a *trainer* performs an integrating function.

    A. Instinctively             B. Total
    C. Flat                       D. Strong

21.\_\_\_\_

22. In gaining cooperation in human relations, the one who would influence must often foster his own ego and fertilize and feed that of the one who is to be influenced.

    A. Lassitude                 B. Emulate
    C. Suppress                  D. Implant

22.\_\_\_\_

23. In the United States, in general, we have been criticized for our emphasis upon physical, materialistic, and economic goals. These are still important, but the trends point toward the more complex, or appreciation of the beautiful, as for example in the architecture of our new factories and colors in the workplaces.

    A. Ephemeral     B. Concrete     C. Prosaic     D. Aesthetic

23.\_\_\_\_

24. Standards of production performance are necessary to reveal the quantities of material, the number of hours of labor, the machine hours, and quantities of service (as, for example, power, steam, etc.) necessary to perform the various production operations. The establishment of such standards is an engineering rather than an accounting task, but it should be emphasized that such standards are needless to the development of the budgetary procedure at least insofar as the budget is to serve as a tool of control. Such standards serve not only in the development of the budget and in measuring efficiency of production performance, but also in developing purchase requirements and in estimating costs.

    A. Manifest                  B. Evaluation
    C. Essential                  D. Function

24.\_\_\_\_

25. Where standard costs are not available or their use is impracticable due to uncertainty of prices, estimates of the costs must be made on the basis of past experience and expected conditions. Ability to use standards largely eliminates the use of the budget for purposes of control of costs but its value remains for purposes of coordination of the program with purchases and finance.

    A. Failure                      B. Current
    C. Culmination            D. Apparent

25.\_\_\_\_

26. While one of the first objectives of the labor budget is to provide the highest practicable degree of regularity of employment, consideration must also be given to the estimating and perdurability of labor cost. Regularity of employment in itself effects some reduction in labor cost, but when carried beyond the point of practicability, it may increase other costs. For example, additional sales effort may be required to expand sales volume or to develop new products for slack periods; the cost of carrying inventories and the dangers of obsolescence and price declines must also be considered. A proper balance must be secured.

    A. Material    B. Control    C. Futures    D. To

26.____

27. The essentials of budgeting perhaps can be summarized in this manner:
    1. Develop a sound business program.
    2. Report on the progress in achieving that program.
    3. Take necessary action as to all variances which are inevitable.
    4. Revise the program to meet the changing conditions as required.

    A. Perfect            B. Plans
    C. Controllable    D. Secure

27.____

28. If a planning and control procedure is considered worthwhile, then it is a syllogism that preparation for the installation should be adequate. Time devoted to this educational aspect ordinarily will prove quite rewarding. The management to be involved with the budget, and particularly the middle management, must have a clear understanding of the budgetary procedure.

    A. Acquired    B. Remedial    C. Monetary    D. Truism

28.____

29. Among the Housing Manager's overall responsibilities in administering a project is the prevention of the development of conditions which might lead to termination of tenancy and eviction of a tenant. Where there appears to be doubt that a tenant is fully aware of his responsibilities and is thus jeopardizing his tenancy, the Housing Manager should acquaint him with these responsibilities. Where a situation involves behavior of a tenant or a member of his family, the Housing Manager should confirm, through discussions and referrals to social agencies, correction of the conditions before they reach a state where there is no alternative but termination proceedings.

    A. Coordinate    B. Identify
    C. Assert          D. Attempt

29.____

30. The one universal administrative complaint is that the budget is inadequate. Between adequacy and inadequacy lie all degrees of adequacy. Further, human wants are modest in relation to human resources. From these two facts we may conclude that the fundamental criterion of administrative decision must be a criterion of efficiency (the degree to which the goals have been reached relative to the available resources) rather than a criterion of adequacy (the degree to which its goals have been reached). The task of the manager is to maximize social values relative to limited resources.

    A. Improve    B. Simple
    C. Limitless    D. Optimize

30.____

## KEY (CORRECT ANSWERS)

| | | | |
|---|---|---|---|
| 1. | D | 16. | C |
| 2. | D | 17. | B |
| 3. | C | 18. | B |
| 4. | A | 19. | A |
| 5. | C | 20. | B |
| 6. | A | 21. | D |
| 7. | D | 22. | C |
| 8. | C | 23. | D |
| 9. | A | 24. | C |
| 10. | D | 25. | B |
| 11. | A | 26. | B |
| 12. | B | 27. | C |
| 13. | A | 28. | D |
| 14. | A | 29. | D |
| 15. | D | 30. | C |

# WORD MEANING

## EXAMINATION SECTION
## TEST 1

DIRECTIONS: Each question or incomplete statement is followed by several suggested answers or completions. Select the one that BEST answers the question or completes the statement. *PRINT THE LETTER OF THE CORRECT ANSWER IN THE SPACE AT THE RIGHT.*

1. Local responsibility for the relief of economic need long having been recognized as inadequate, the state and federal governments have established schemes of *categorical* assistance and social insurance.
   In the preceding sentence, the italicized word means MOST NEARLY

   A. conditional  B. economic
   C. pecuniary   D. classified

   1.____

2. When a person *vicariously* lives out his own problems in novels and plays, he is engaging in an experience that is, in terms of the italicized word in this sentence,

   A. dynamic      B. monastic
   C. substituted  D. dignified

   2.____

3. The Alcoholics Anonymous program, which in essence amounts to a *therapeutic* procedure, is codified into twelve steps. The italicized word in the preceding sentence means MOST NEARLY

   A. compensatory  B. curative
   C. sequential    D. volitional

   3.____

4. The professor developed a different central theme during every *semester.*
   The italicized word in the preceding sentence means MOST NEARLY

   A. bi-annual period of instruction
   B. orientation period
   C. slide demonstration
   D. weekly lecture series

   4.____

5. To say that the Community Chest movement seems to have been *indigenous* to the North American continent describes this movement, in terms of the italicized word in this sentence, MOST NEARLY as

   A. imported  B. essential
   C. native    D. homogeneous

   5.____

6. There should be no *opprobrium* attached to the term "second-hand housing" since every house is second-hand after the first occupancy.
   The italicized word in the preceding sentence means MOST NEARLY

   A. stigma   B. honor   C. rank   D. credit

   6.____

7. Clinics are now seeing many people who complain of seriously disturbed feelings and other symptoms relating to *traumatic* war experiences.
   In the preceding sentence, the italicized word means MOST NEARLY

   A. recent
   B. worldwide
   C. prodigious
   D. shocking

8. The nature of the *pathology* underlying the compulsion is obscure.
   In the preceding sentence, the italicized word means MOST NEARLY

   A. drive
   B. disease
   C. deterioration
   D. development

9. If the interests of a social welfare agency are concerned with bringing opportunities for self-help to underprivileged *ethnic* groups, its activities involve MOST NEARLY, in terms of the italicized word in this sentence,

   A. racial factors
   B. minority units
   C. religious affiliations
   D. economic conditions

10. Increased facilities for medical care (though interrupted to some extent by the *exigencies* of wartime) will safeguard the health of many children who in previous generations would have been doomed to an early death or to physical disability.
    In the preceding sentence, the MOST NEARLY CORRECT equivalent of the italicized word is

    A. obstacles
    B. occurrences
    C. extenuations
    D. exactions

11. He described a hypothetical situation to illustrate his point.
    In the preceding sentence, the word *hypothetical* means MOST NEARLY

    A. actual
    B. theoretical
    C. typical
    D. unusual

12. I gave tacit approval to my partner's proposed business changes.
    In the preceding sentence, the word *tacit* means MOST NEARLY

    A. enthusiastic
    B. partial
    C. silent
    D. written

13. Jones was considered an astute lawyer by the members of his profession.
    In the preceding sentence, the word *astute* means MOST NEARLY

    A. clever
    B. persevering
    C. poorly trained
    D. unethical

14. There were intimations even in early days of the way in which he would go.
    In the preceding sentence, the word *intimations* means MOST NEARLY

    A. hints
    B. patterns
    C. plans
    D. purposes

15. His last book was published posthumously.
    In the preceding sentence, the word *posthumously* means MOST NEARLY

    A. after the death of the author
    B. printed free by the publisher
    C. without a dedication
    D. without royalties

16. When he was challenged, he used every known subterfuge. In the preceding sentence, the word *subterfuge* means MOST NEARLY

    A. evasion to justify one's conduct
    B. means of attack to defend one's self
    C. medical device
    D. unconscious thought

17. His partner suggested a course of action that would alleviate the difficulties which confronted him.
    In the preceding sentence, the word *alleviate* means MOST NEARLY

    A. correct   B. lessen   C. remove   D. solve

18. Among the applicants for the new apartment, white collar workers were preponderant.
    In the preceding sentence, the word *preponderant* means MOST NEARLY

    A. considered not eligible   B. in evidence
    C. superior in number   D. the first to apply

19. The captain gave a lucid explanation of his plans for the coming campaign.
    In the preceding sentence, the word *lucid* means MOST NEARLY

    A. clear   B. graphic
    C. interesting   D. thorough

20. He led a sedentary life.
    In the preceding sentence, the word *sedentary* means MOST NEARLY

    A. aimless   B. exciting   C. full   D. inactive

21. His plan for the next campaign was very plausible.
    In the preceding sentence, the word *plausible* means MOST NEARLY

    A. appropriate   B. believable
    C. usable   D. valuable

22. The office manager thought it advisable to mollify his subordinate.
    The word *mollify*, as used in this sentence, means MOST NEARLY

    A. reprimand   B. caution   C. calm   D. question

23. The bureau chief adopted a dilatory policy.
    The word *dilatory*, as used in this sentence, means MOST NEARLY

    A. tending to cause delay
    B. acceptable to all affected
    C. severe but fair
    D. prepared with great care

24. He complained about the paucity of requests.
    The word *paucity*, as used in this sentence, means MOST NEARLY

    A. great variety   B. unreasonableness
    C. unexpected increase   D. scarcity

25. To say that an event is *imminent* means MOST NEARLY that it is

   A. near at hand
   B. unpredictable
   C. favorable or happy
   D. very significant

26. The general manager delivered a laudatory speech.
    The word *laudatory*, as used in this sentence, means MOST NEARLY

   A. clear and emphatic
   B. lengthy
   C. introductory
   D. expressing praise

27. We all knew of his aversion for performing statistical work.
    The word *aversion*, as used in this sentence, means MOST NEARLY

   A. training
   B. dislike
   C. incentive
   D. lack of preparation

28. The engineer was circumspect in making his recommendations.
    The word *circumspect*, as used in this sentence, means MOST NEARLY

   A. hostile   B. outspoken   C. biased   D. cautious

29. To say that certain clerical operations were *obviated* means MOST NEARLY that these operations were

   A. extremely distasteful
   B. easily understood
   C. made unnecessary
   D. very complicated

30. The interviewer was impressed with the client's demeanor. The word *demeanor*, as used in this sentence, means MOST NEARLY

   A. outward manner
   B. plan of action
   C. fluent speech
   D. extensive knowledge

31. To say that the information was *gratuitous* means MOST NEARLY that it was

   A. given freely
   B. deeply appreciated
   C. brief
   D. valuable

32. She considered the supervisor's action to be arbitrary. The word *arbitrary*, as used in this sentence, means MOST NEARLY

   A. inconsistent
   B. justifiable
   C. appeasing
   D. dictatorial

33. He sent the irate employee to the personnel manager. The word *irate* means MOST NEARLY

   A. irresponsible
   B. untidy
   C. insubordinate
   D. angry

34. An *ambiguous* statement is one which is

   A. forceful and convincing
   B. capable of being understood in more than one sense
   C. based upon good judgment and sound reasoning processes
   D. uninteresting and too lengthy

35. To *extol* means MOST NEARLY to

   A. summon    B. praise    C. reject    D. withdraw

36. The word *proximity* means MOST NEARLY

   A. similarity        B. exactness
   C. harmony           D. nearness

37. His friends had a detrimental influence on him.
    The word *detrimental* means MOST NEARLY

   A. favorable    B. lasting
   C. harmful      D. short-lived

38. The chief inspector relied upon the veracity of his inspectors.
    The word *veracity* means MOST NEARLY

   A. speed        B. assistance
   C. shrewdness   D. truthfulness

39. There was much diversity in the suggestions submitted.
    The word *diversity* means MOST NEARLY

   A. similarity   B. value
   C. triviality   D. variety

40. The survey was concerned with the problem of indigence.
    The word *indigence* means MOST NEARLY

   A. poverty      B. corruption
   C. intolerance  D. morale

41. The investigator considered this evidence to be extraneous.
    The word *extraneous* means MOST NEARLY

   A. significant    B. pertinent but unobtainable
   C. not essential  D. inadequate

42. He was surprised at the temerity of the new employee.
    The word *temerity* means MOST NEARLY

   A. shyness     B. enthusiasm
   C. rashness    D. self-control

43. The term *ex officio* means MOST NEARLY

   A. expelled from office
   B. a former holder of a high office
   C. without official approval
   D. by virtue of office or position

44. The aims of the students and the aims of the faculty often coincide.
    The word *coincide* means MOST NEARLY

   A. agree      B. are ignored
   C. conflict   D. are misinterpreted

45. The secretary of the department was responsible for setting up an index of relevant magazine articles.
The word *relevant* means MOST NEARLY

   A. applicable
   B. controversial
   C. miscellaneous
   D. recent

46. One of the secretary's duties consisted of sorting and filing facsimiles of student term papers.
The word *facsimiles* means MOST NEARLY

   A. bibliographical listings
   B. exact copies
   C. summaries
   D. supporting documentation

47. Stringent requirements for advanced physics courses often result in small class sizes.
The word *stringent* means MOST NEARLY

   A. lengthy
   B. remarkable
   C. rigid
   D. vague

48. The professor explained that the report was too verbose to be submitted.
The word *verbose* means MOST NEARLY

   A. brief    B. specific    C. general    D. wordy

49. The faculty meeting pre-empted the conference room in the Dean's office.
The word *pre-empted* means MOST NEARLY

   A. appropriated
   B. emptied
   C. filled
   D. reserved

50. The professor's credentials became a subject of controversy.
The word *controversy* means MOST NEARLY

   A. annoyance    B. debate    C. envy    D. review

## KEY (CORRECT ANSWERS)

| | | | | |
|---|---|---|---|---|
| 1. D | 11. B | 21. B | 31. A | 41. C |
| 2. C | 12. C | 22. C | 32. D | 42. C |
| 3. B | 13. A | 23. A | 33. D | 43. D |
| 4. A | 14. A | 24. D | 34. B | 44. A |
| 5. C | 15. A | 25. A | 35. B | 45. A |
| 6. A | 16. A | 26. D | 36. D | 46. B |
| 7. D | 17. B | 27. B | 37. C | 47. C |
| 8. B | 18. C | 28. D | 38. D | 48. D |
| 9. A | 19. A | 29. C | 39. D | 49. A |
| 10. D | 20. D | 30. A | 40. A | 50. B |

# TEST 2

DIRECTIONS: Each question or incomplete statement is followed by several suggested answers or completions. Select the one that BEST answers the question or completes the statement. *PRINT THE LETTER OF THE CORRECT ANSWER IN THE SPACE AT THE RIGHT.*

1. The suspect was detained until a witness proved he could not have committed the crime. 1.____
   As used in this sentence, the word *detained* means MOST NEARLY

   A. suspected     B. accused     C. held     D. observed

2. The fireman's equilibrium improved shortly after he had stumbled out of the smoke-filled building. 2.____
   As used in this sentence, the word *equilibrium* means MOST NEARLY

   A. breathing     B. balance     C. vision     D. vigor

3. The water supply in the tank began to dwindle soon after the pumps were turned on. 3.____
   As used in this sentence, the word *dwindle* means MOST NEARLY

   A. grow smaller     B. whirl about
   C. become muddy    D. overflow

4. They thought his illness was feigned. 4.____
   As used in this sentence, the word *feigned* means MOST NEARLY

   A. hereditary     B. contagious
   C. pretended      D. incurable

5. The officer corroborated the information given by the fireman. 5.____
   As used in this sentence, the word *corroborated* means MOST NEARLY

   A. questioned     B. confirmed
   C. corrected      D. accepted

6. Only after an inspection were they even able to surmise what caused the fire. 6.____
   As used in this sentence, the word *surmise* means MOST NEARLY

   A. guess     B. discover     C. prove     D. isolate

7. Officers shall report all flagrant violations of regulations or laws by subordinates. 7.____
   As used in this sentence, the word *flagrant* means MOST NEARLY

   A. glaring      B. accidental
   C. habitual     D. minor

8. The man was cajoled into signing the contract. 8.____
   As used in this sentence, the word *cajoled* means MOST NEARLY

   A. bribed     B. coaxed     C. confused     D. forced

9. The announcement was met with general derision. 9.____
   As used in this sentence, the word *derision* means MOST NEARLY

   A. anger     B. applause     C. disbelief     D. ridicule

10. The speaker's words were moving but irrelevant.
    As used in this sentence, the word *irrelevant* means MOST NEARLY

    A. insincere
    B. not based upon facts
    C. not bearing upon the subject under discussion
    D. self-contradictory

11. The breakdown of the machine was due to a defective gasket.
    As used in this sentence, the word *gasket* means MOST NEARLY

    A. filter           B. piston
    C. sealer           D. transmission

12. The noise of the pneumatic drill disturbed the teacher.
    As used in this sentence, the word *pneumatic* means MOST NEARLY

    A. air pressure          B. electricity
    C. internal combustion   D. water pressure

13. He exercised the prerogatives of his office with moderation.
    As used in this sentence, the word *prerogatives* means MOST NEARLY

    A. burdens          B. duties
    C. opportunities    D. privileges

14. He made his decisions after a cursory examination of the facts.
    As used in this sentence, the word *cursory* means MOST NEARLY

    A. biased           B. critical
    C. exhaustive       D. hasty

15. John was appointed provisional chairman of the arrange-ments committee.
    As used in this sentence, the word *provisional* means MOST NEARLY

    A. official         B. permanent
    C. temporary        D. unofficial

16. After the bush is planted, the ground around it should be tamped.
    As used in this sentence, the word *tamped* means MOST NEARLY

    A. loosened    B. packed    C. raked    D. watered

17. The volcano was dormant during the time I visited the island.
    As used in this sentence, the word *dormant* means MOST NEARLY

    A. erupting         B. extinct
    C. inactive         D. threatening

18. A starter's gun is not considered to be a lethal weapon.
    As used in this sentence, the word *lethal* means MOST NEARLY

    A. criminal    B. deadly    C. offensive    D. reliable

19. At the crucial moment, the seismograph failed to function. As used in this sentence, the word *seismograph* means MOST NEARLY an instrument for measuring

    A. earthquakes      B. heartbeats
    C. humidity         D. nuclear radiation

20. The supervisor's instructions were terse.
    As used in this sentence, the word *terse* means MOST NEARLY

    A. detailed    B. harsh    C. vague    D. concise

21. He did not wish to evade these issues.
    As used in this sentence, the word *evade* means MOST NEARLY

    A. avoid    B. examine    C. settle    D. discuss

22. The prospects for an early settlement were dubious.
    As used in this sentence, the word *dubious* means MOST NEARLY

    A. strengthened    B. uncertain
    C. weakened    D. cheerful

23. The visitor was morose.
    As used in this sentence, the word *morose* means MOST NEARLY

    A. curious    B. gloomy    C. impatient    D. timid

24. He was unwilling to impede the work of his unit.
    As used in this sentence, the word *impede* means MOST NEARLY

    A. carry out    B. criticize    C. praise    D. hinder

25. The remuneration was unsatisfactory.
    As used in this sentence, the word *remuneration* means MOST NEARLY

    A. payment    B. summary
    C. explanation    D. estimate

26. A *recurring* problem is one that

    A. replaces a problem that existed previously
    B. is unexpected
    C. has long been overlooked
    D. comes up from time to time

27. His subordinates were aware of this magnanimous act. As used in this sentence, the word *magnanimous* means MOST NEARLY

    A. insolent    B. shrewd
    C. unselfish    D. threatening

28. The new employee is a zealous worker.
    As used in this sentence, the word *zealous* means MOST NEARLY

    A. awkward    B. untrustworthy
    C. enthusiastic    D. skillful

29. To *impair* means MOST NEARLY to

    A. weaken    B. conceal    C. improve    D. expose

30. The unit head was in a quandary.
    As used in this sentence, the word *quandary* means MOST NEARLY

    A. violent dispute    B. puzzling predicament
    C. angry mood    D. strong position

31. His actions were judicious.
    As used in this sentence, the word *judicious* means MOST NEARLY

    A. wise        B. biased        C. final        D. limited

32. His report contained many irrelevant statements.
    As used in this sentence, the word *irrelevant* means MOST NEARLY

    A. unproven                B. not pertinent
    C. hard to understand      D. insincere

33. He was not present at the inception of the program.
    As used in this sentence, the word *inception* means MOST NEARLY

    A. beginning        B. discussion
    C. conclusion       D. rejection

34. The word *solicitude* means MOST NEARLY

    A. request          B. isolation
    C. seriousness      D. concern

35. He was asked to pacify the visitor.
    As used in this sentence, the word *pacify* means MOST NEARLY

    A. escort        B. interview        C. calm        D. detain

36. To say that a certain document is *authentic* means MOST NEARLY that it is

    A. fictitious       B. well written
    C. priceless        D. genuine

37. A clerk who is *meticulous* in performing his work is one who is

    A. alert to improved techniques
    B. likely to be erratic and unpredictable
    C. excessively careful of small details
    D. slovenly and inaccurate

38. A pamphlet which is *replete* with charts and graphs is one which

    A. deals with the construction of charts and graphs
    B. is full of charts and graphs
    C. substitutes illustrations for tabulated data
    D. is in need of charts and graphs

39. His former secretary was diligent in carrying out her duties.
    The word *diligent* means MOST NEARLY

    A. incompetent      B. cheerful
    C. careless         D. industrious

40. To *supersede* means MOST NEARLY to

    A. take the place of        B. come before
    C. be in charge of          D. divide into equal parts

41. A person is a *tyro* if he is MOST NEARLY a

    A. charlatan
    B. novice
    C. scholar
    D. talebearer

42. A tenant who is *adamant* in his complaints about the noise emanating from the neighboring apartment is MOST NEARLY

    A. belligerent
    B. justified
    C. petty
    D. unyielding

43. The assistant, according to his supervisor's report, had performed his tasks assiduously. The word *assiduously* means MOST NEARLY

    A. diligently
    B. expertly
    C. inefficiently
    D. reluctantly

44. The current exigency of affairs at the Authority was given as the reason for the decision. The word *exigency* means MOST NEARLY

    A. conduct
    B. investigation
    C. trend
    D. urgency

45. The discovery of the defalcation was made by the manager. The word *defalcation* means MOST NEARLY

    A. damage
    B. error
    C. fraud
    D. theft

46. The halcyon days that followed could not have been predicted. The word *halcyon* means MOST NEARLY

    A. eventful
    B. festive
    C. frenzied
    D. untroubled

47. The assistant submitted a sententious report after he had made his investigation. The word *sententious* means MOST NEARLY

    A. laudatory
    B. pithy
    C. tentative
    D. unfavorable

48. An assistant should be characterized as *saturnine* if he is MOST NEARLY

    A. apathetic
    B. enigmatic
    C. gloomy
    D. sarcastic

49. A situation arising at a project is *anomalous* if the situation is MOST NEARLY

    A. irritating
    B. perplexing
    C. recurrent
    D. unusual

50. The Housing Authority did what it could to palliate the condition about which the tenants had complained. The word *palliate* means MOST NEARLY

    A. reconsider
    B. rectify
    C. relieve
    D. remedy

## KEY (CORRECT ANSWERS)

| | | | | |
|---|---|---|---|---|
| 1. C | 11. C | 21. A | 31. A | 41. B |
| 2. B | 12. A | 22. B | 32. B | 42. D |
| 3. A | 13. D | 23. B | 33. A | 43. A |
| 4. C | 14. D | 24. D | 34. D | 44. D |
| 5. B | 15. C | 25. A | 35. C | 45. D |
| 6. A | 16. B | 26. D | 36. D | 46. D |
| 7. A | 17. C | 27. C | 37. C | 47. B |
| 8. B | 18. B | 28. C | 38. B | 48. C |
| 9. D | 19. A | 29. A | 39. D | 49. D |
| 10. C | 20. D | 30. B | 40. A | 50. C |

# TEST 3

DIRECTIONS: Each question or incomplete statement is followed by several suggested answers or completions. Select the one that BEST answers the question or completes the statement. *PRINT THE LETTER OF THE CORRECT ANSWER IN THE SPACE AT THE RIGHT.*

1. The employees were skeptical about the usefulness of the new procedure.
   The word *skeptical,* as used in this sentence, means MOST NEARLY

   A. enthusiastic
   B. indifferent
   C. doubtful
   D. misinformed

2. He presented abstruse reasons in defense of his proposal.
   The word *abstruse,* as used in this sentence, means MOST NEARLY

   A. unnecessary under the circumstances
   B. apparently without merit or value
   C. hard to be understood
   D. obviously sound

3. A program of austerity is in effect in many countries. The word *austerity,* as used in this sentence, means MOST NEARLY

   A. rigorous self-restraint
   B. military censorship
   C. rugged individualism
   D. self-indulgence

4. The terms of the contract were abrogated at the last meeting of the board.
   The word *abrogated,* as used in this sentence, means MOST NEARLY

   A. discussed
   B. summarized
   C. agreed upon
   D. annulled

5. The enforcement of stringent regulations is a difficult task.
   The word *stringent,* as used in this sentence, means MOST NEARLY

   A. unreasonable
   B. strict
   C. unpopular
   D. obscure

6. You should not disparage the value of his suggestions. The word *disparage,* as used in this sentence, means MOST NEARLY

   A. ignore
   B. exaggerate
   C. belittle
   D. reveal

7. The employee's conduct was considered reprehensible by his superior.
   The word *reprehensible,* as used in this sentence, means MOST NEARLY

   A. worthy of reward or honor
   B. in accordance with rules and regulations
   C. detrimental to efficiency and morale
   D. deserving of censure or rebuke

8. He said he would emulate the persistence of his co-workers. The word *emulate,* as used in this sentence, means MOST NEARLY

   A. strive to equal
   B. acknowledge
   C. encourage
   D. attach no significance to

261

9. The revised regulations on discipline contained several mitigating provisions.
   The word *mitigating*, as used in this sentence, means MOST NEARLY

   A. making more effective
   B. containing contradictions
   C. rendering less harsh
   D. producing much criticism

10. The arrival of the inspector at the office on that day was fortuitous.
    The word *fortuitous*, as used in this sentence, means MOST NEARLY

    A. accidental
    B. unfortunate
    C. prearranged
    D. desirable

11. The development of the program received its real impetus in the recent action of the commissioner.
    The word *impetus*, as used in this sentence, means MOST NEARLY

    A. formulation
    B. impediment
    C. implementation
    D. stimulus

12. However, the purpose is not to be pedantic but to be practical.
    The word *pedantic*, as used in this sentence, means MOST NEARLY

    A. affected
    B. philosophical
    C. progressive
    D. scientific

13. There is much just criticism of the dilatoriness with which many large organizations perform their work and the red tape that is required in the discharge of official duties.
    The word *dilatoriness*, as used in this sentence, means MOST NEARLY

    A. complications
    B. delay
    C. dilations
    D. splendor

14. If it appears that this report moves occasionally into the general field of administrative problems, your indulgence is asked, since it seems to us that voices should be heard wherever possible in behalf of sound, scientific public administration.
    The word *indulgence*, as used in this sentence, means MOST NEARLY

    A. criticism
    B. assistance
    C. forbearance
    D. concentration

15. The supervisor's chief functions as leader are to develop the individuals under him and to integrate them into a cooperative team.
    The word *integrate*, as used in this sentence, means MOST NEARLY

    A. develop
    B. mold
    C. unify
    D. work

16. The impression is widespread that it is inherently impossible to secure the same efficiency and economy in the administration of public affairs that can be secured in the conduct of private undertakings.
    The word *inherently*, as used in this sentence, means MOST NEARLY

    A. admittedly
    B. internally
    C. naturally
    D. practically

17. The production manager had followed an opportunistic policy and had met new requirements as they appeared.
    The word *opportunistic,* as used in this sentence, means MOST NEARLY

    A. efficient  B. expedient
    C. farsighted  D. important

18. Therein is epitomized the agricultural revolution which, hand in hand with the industrial revolution, is rebuilding the country and our social life.
    The word *epitomized,* as used in this sentence, means MOST NEARLY

    A. annotated  B. described
    C. expatriated  D. summarized

19. A periodic appraisal of the method of effectuating decisions is important.
    The word *effectuating,* as used in this sentence, means MOST NEARLY

    A. affecting  B. developing
    C. fulfilling  D. making

20. The classifications of filing material in this office are, then, artificial and overlapping, and are designed for transient convenience.
    The word *transient,* as used in this sentence, means MOST NEARLY

    A. basic  B. local  C. operating  D. temporary

21. From a research standpoint, there is hardly a paucity of material for us to consider.
    The word *paucity,* as used in this sentence, means MOST NEARLY

    A. abundance  B. adequate amount
    C. insufficiency  D. unsatisfactory quality

22. This assignment was handled expeditiously.
    The word *expeditiously* means MOST NEARLY

    A. clumsily  B. without preparation
    C. speedily  D. on a trial basis

23. Miss Lind is scrupulous in performing her duties.
    The word *scrupulous* means MOST NEARLY

    A. slow  B. conscientious
    C. careless  D. gracious

24. To *apprise* means MOST NEARLY to

    A. award  B. inform
    C. dispossess  D. discover

25. His report on this matter is opportune.
    The word *opportune* means MOST NEARLY

    A. timely  B. biased  C. hostile  D. hopeful

26. His actions had a deleterious effect on the other employees.
The word *deleterious* means MOST NEARLY

   A. restraining
   B. highly pleasing
   C. harmful
   D. misleading

27. The size of the staff was increased, and the gain in output was commensurate.
The word *commensurate* means MOST NEARLY

   A. praiseworthy
   B. enormous
   C. of equal extent
   D. trivial in proportion

28. Miss Hunter is assiduous in keeping these records.
The word *assiduous* means MOST NEARLY

   A. negligent
   B. untrained
   C. unrestricted
   D. diligent

29. His bookkeeper said that our account was dormant.
The word *dormant* means MOST NEARLY

   A. inadequate
   B. transferred
   C. inactive
   D. overdrawn

30. The supervisor's criticisms were caustic.
The word *caustic* means MOST NEARLY

   A. sarcastic and severe
   B. unfair and undeserved
   C. ominous but justified
   D. fitful and unsteady

31. The word *impediment* means MOST NEARLY

   A. hindrance
   B. trick or deception
   C. insinuation
   D. urgent matter

32. This procedure did not preclude errors in judgment.
The word *preclude* means MOST NEARLY

   A. arise from
   B. prevent
   C. account for
   D. define

33. The statements made at the initial conference were retracted at a subsequent meeting.
The word *retracted* means MOST NEARLY

   A. developed
   B. criticized
   C. endorsed
   D. withdrawn

34. He was unwilling to supplant his immediate superior.
The word *supplant* means MOST NEARLY

   A. fill the needs of
   B. request aid from
   C. take the place of
   D. withhold support for

35. Miss Olin has a prepossessing manner.
The word *prepossessing* means MOST NEARLY

   A. authoritative
   B. likable
   C. apologetic
   D. deceiving

36. The methods used to solve these critical problems were analogous.
    The word *analogous* means MOST NEARLY

    A. similar
    B. unconventional
    C. clever
    D. unsound

37. This letter appears to have been written by some indigent person.
    The word *indigent,* as used in this sentence, means MOST NEARLY

    A. foreign-born
    B. needy
    C. uneducated
    D. angry

38. The conference began under auspicious circumstances.
    The word *auspicious,* as used in this sentence, means MOST NEARLY

    A. favorable
    B. chaotic
    C. questionable
    D. threatening

39. An inordinate amount of work was assigned to the newly appointed clerk.
    The word *inordinate,* as used in this sentence, means MOST NEARLY

    A. unanticipated
    B. adequate
    C. inexcusable
    D. excessive

40. The report which was obtained surreptitiously was very detailed and fully documented.
    The word *surreptitiously,* as used in this sentence, means MOST NEARLY

    A. stealthily
    B. a short time ago
    C. with great difficulty
    D. unexpectedly

41. We all knew him to be a man of probity.
    The word *probity,* as used in this sentence, means MOST NEARLY

    A. culture
    B. proven ability
    C. integrity
    D. dignity and poise

42. He made a cursory study of the problem before starting on the assignment.
    The word *cursory,* as used in this sentence, means MOST NEARLY

    A. detailed
    B. secret
    C. hasty
    D. methodical

43. The regulation had a salutary effect upon the members of the staff.
    The word *salutary,* as used in this sentence, means MOST NEARLY

    A. disturbing
    B. beneficial
    C. confusing
    D. premature

44. The solicitous supervisor discussed the employee's grievances with them.
    The word *solicitous,* as used in this sentence, means MOST NEARLY

    A. concerned
    B. impartial
    C. wise
    D. experienced

45. The employee categorically denied all responsibility for the error.
    The word *categorically,* as used in this sentence, means MOST NEARLY

    A. repeatedly
    B. loudly
    C. hesitantly
    D. absolutely

46. No stipend was specified in the agreement.     46.____
    The word *stipend,* as used in this sentence, means MOST NEARLY

    A. statement of working conditions
    B. receipt for payment
    C. compensation for services
    D. delivery date

47. The supervisor pointed out that the focus of the study was not clear.     47.____
    The word *focus,* as used in this sentence, means MOST NEARLY

    A. end      B. objective      C. follow-up      D. location

48. The faculty of the department agreed that the departmental program was deficient.     48.____
    The word *deficient,* as used in this sentence, means MOST NEARLY

    A. excellent      B. inadequate
    C. demanding      D. sufficient

49. The secretary was asked to type a rough draft of a college course syllabus.     49.____
    The word *syllabus,* as used in this sentence, means MOST NEARLY

    A. directory of departments and services
    B. examination schedule
    C. outline of a course of study
    D. rules and regulations

50. The college offered a variety of seminars to upperclassmen.     50.____
    The word *seminars,* as used in this sentence, means MOST NEARLY

    A. reading courses with no formal supervision
    B. study courses for small groups of students engaged in research under a teacher
    C. guidance conferences with grade advisors
    D. work experiences in different occupational fields

# KEY (CORRECT ANSWERS)

| | | | | |
|---|---|---|---|---|
| 1. C | 11. D | 21. C | 31. A | 41. C |
| 2. C | 12. A | 22. C | 32. B | 42. C |
| 3. A | 13. B | 23. B | 33. D | 43. B |
| 4. D | 14. C | 24. B | 34. C | 44. A |
| 5. B | 15. C | 25. A | 35. B | 45. D |
| 6. C | 16. C | 26. C | 36. A | 46. C |
| 7. D | 17. B | 27. C | 37. B | 47. B |
| 8. A | 18. D | 28. D | 38. A | 48. B |
| 9. C | 19. C | 29. C | 39. D | 49. C |
| 10. A | 20. D | 30. A | 40. A | 50. B |

# WORD MEANING
## EXAMINATION SECTION
## TEST 1

DIRECTIONS: Each question or incomplete statement is followed by several suggested answers or completions. Select the one that BEST answers the question or completes the statement. *PRINT THE LETTER OF THE CORRECT ANSWER IN THE SPACE AT THE RIGHT.*

1. Rules must be applied with discretion.
   As used in this sentence, the word *discretion* means MOST NEARLY

   A. impartiality  B. judgment
   C. severity      D. patience

2. The officer and his men ascended the stairs as rapidly as they could.
   As used in this sentence, the word *ascended* means MOST NEARLY

   A. went up     B. washed down
   C. chopped     D. shored up

3. The store's refusal to accept delivery of the merchandise was a violation of the express provisions of the contract. As used in this sentence, the word *express* means MOST NEARLY

   A. clear   B. implied   C. penalty   D. disputed

4. He needed public assistance because he was incapacitated. As used in this sentence, the word *incapacitated* means MOST NEARLY

   A. uneducated     B. disabled
   C. uncooperative  D. discharged

5. The worker explained to the client that signing the document was compulsory.
   As used in this sentence, the word *compulsory* means MOST NEARLY

   A. temporary   B. required
   C. different   D. comprehensive

6. The woman's actions did not jeopardize her eligibility for benefits.
   As used in this sentence, the word *jeopardize* means MOST NEARLY

   A. delay   B. reinforce   C. determine   D. endanger

7. The cause of the emergency was a defective gas flue.
   As used in this sentence, the word *flue* means MOST NEARLY

   A. burner   B. duct   C. jet   D. supply

8. The crux of the matter is finding the right man for the job.
   As used in this sentence, the word *crux* means MOST NEARLY

   A. obvious solution       B. neglected consideration
   C. final step             D. decisive point

9. His assistance in this project was invaluable.
   As used in this sentence, the word *invaluable* means MOST NEARLY

   A. worthless
   B. priceless
   C. inconspicuous
   D. difficult to evaluate

10. There are many facets to this problem.
    As used in this sentence, the word *facets* means MOST NEARLY

    A. alternatives
    B. aspects
    C. difficulties
    D. solutions

11. The map clearly indicated the contour of the lake.
    As used in this sentence, the word *contour* means MOST NEARLY

    A. composition
    B. location
    C. outline
    D. source

12. The hot weather made him lethargic.
    As used in this sentence, the word *lethargic* means MOST NEARLY

    A. drowsy    B. perspire    C. tense    D. thirsty

13. The arrangements for the meeting were haphazard.
    As used in this sentence, the word *haphazard* means MOST NEARLY

    A. according to a plan
    B. determined by mere chance
    C. overly detailed
    D. disregarded

14. The committee could not agree on an agenda for the conference.
    As used in this sentence, the word *agenda* means MOST NEARLY

    A. rules of procedure
    B. meeting place
    C. qualifications of delegates
    D. things to be done

15. The recipient of the money checked the total amount.
    As used in this sentence, the word *recipient* means MOST NEARLY

    A. receiver    B. carrier    C. borrower    D. giver

16. Mr. Warren could not attend the luncheon because he had a prior appointment.
    As used in this sentence, the word *prior* means MOST NEARLY

    A. conflicting
    B. official
    C. previous
    D. important

17. The time allowed to complete the task was not adequate.
    As used in this sentence, the word *adequate* means MOST NEARLY

    A. long    B. enough    C. excessive    D. required

18. The investigation unit began an extensive search for the information.
    As used in this sentence, the word *extensive* means MOST NEARLY

    A. complicated
    B. superficial
    C. thorough
    D. leisurely

19. The secretary answered the telephone in a courteous manner.
    As used in this sentence, the word *courteous* means MOST NEARLY

    A. businesslike  B. friendly
    C. formal        D. polite

20. Every good office worker needs basic skills.
    As used in this sentence, the word *basic* means MOST NEARLY

    A. fundamental  B. advanced
    C. unusual      D. outstanding

21. He turned out to be a good instructor.
    As used in this sentence, the word *instructor* means MOST NEARLY

    A. student   B. worker   C. typist   D. teacher

22. The quantity of work in the office was under study.
    As used in this sentence, the word *quantity* means MOST NEARLY

    A. amount       B. flow
    C. supervision  D. type

23. The morning was spent examining the time records.
    As used in this sentence, the word *examining* means MOST NEARLY

    A. distributing  B. collecting
    C. checking      D. filing

24. The candidate filled in the proper spaces on the form.
    As used in this sentence, the word *proper* means MOST NEARLY

    A. blank  B. appropriate
    C. many   D. remaining

25. Employees who can produce a considerable amount of good work are very valuable.
    As used in this sentence, the word *considerable* means MOST NEARLY

    A. large   B. potential   C. necessary   D. frequent

26. No person should assume that he knows more than anyone else.
    As used in this sentence, the word *assume* means MOST NEARLY

    A. verify   B. hope   C. suppose   D. argue

27. The parties decided to negotiate through the night.
    As used in this sentence, the word *negotiate* means MOST NEARLY

    A. suffer   B. play   C. think   D. bargain

28. Employees who have severe emotional problems may create problems at work.
    As used in this sentence, the word *severe* means MOST NEARLY

    A. serious   B. surprising
    C. several   D. common

29. Supervisors should try to be as objective as possible when dealing with subordinates. As used in this sentence, the word *objective* means MOST NEARLY

    A. pleasant   B. courteous   C. fair   D. strict

30. He advocated a new course of action. As used in this sentence, the word *advocated* means MOST NEARLY

    A. described
    B. refused to discuss
    C. argued against
    D. supported

31. A clerk who is assigned to make a *facsimile* of a report should make a copy which is

    A. exact   B. larger   C. smaller   D. edited

32. An employee must be a person of integrity. As used in this sentence, the word *integrity* means MOST NEARLY

    A. intelligence
    B. competence
    C. honesty
    D. keenness

33. A person who displays *apathy* is

    A. irritated
    B. confused
    C. indifferent
    D. insubordinate

34. The supervisor admonished the clerk for his tardiness. As used in this sentence, the word *admonished* means MOST NEARLY

    A. reproved
    B. excused
    C. transferred
    D. punished

35. A *lucrative* business is one which is

    A. unprofitable
    B. gainful
    C. unlawful
    D. speculative

36. To say that the work is *tedious* means MOST NEARLY that it is

    A. technical
    B. interesting
    C. tiresome
    D. confidential

37. A *vivacious* person is one who is

    A. kind
    B. talkative
    C. lively
    D. well-dressed

38. An *innocuous* statement is one which is

    A. forceful   B. harmless   C. offensive   D. brief

39. To say that the order was *rescinded* means MOST NEARLY that it was

    A. revised
    B. canceled
    C. misinterpreted
    D. confirmed

40. To say that the administrator *amplified* his remarks means MOST NEARLY that the remarks were

    A. shouted
    B. expanded
    C. carefully analyzed
    D. summarized briefly

41. Peremptory commands will be resented in any office.  41.____
    As used in this sentence, the word *peremptory* means MOST NEARLY

    A. unexpected          B. unreasonable
    C. military            D. dictatorial

42. A clerk should know that the word *sporadic* means MOST NEARLY  42.____

    A. occurring regularly  B. sudden
    C. scattered            D. disturbing

43. To *vacillate* means MOST NEARLY to  43.____

    A. lubricate    B. waver
    C. decide       D. investigate

44. A *homogeneous* group of persons is characterized by its  44.____

    A. similarity    B. teamwork
    C. discontent    D. differences

45. A *vindictive* person is one who is  45.____

    A. prejudiced    B. unpopular
    C. petty         D. revengeful

Questions 46-48.

DIRECTIONS: Each of Questions 46 through 48 consists of a capitalized word followed by four suggested meanings of the word. Select the word or phrase which means MOST NEARLY the same as the capitalized word.

46. EQUILIBRIUM  46.____

    A. horse drawn      B. unequal
    C. kind of library  D. balance

47. RECIPROCATE  47.____

    A. to overcome      B. to avenge
    C. to interchange   D. to mix

48. REFRACTION  48.____

    A. increase    B. refutation
    C. bending     D. uniting

49. The surface of the metal was embossed.  49.____
    As used in this sentence, the word *embossed* means MOST NEARLY

    A. polished    B. rough    C. raised    D. painted

50. Stoppage of water flow is often caused by dirt accumulating in an elbow.  50.____
    As used in this sentence, the word *accumulating* means MOST NEARLY

    A. clogging    B. collecting
    C. rusting     D. confined

## KEY (CORRECT ANSWERS)

| | | | | |
|---|---|---|---|---|
| 1. B | 11. C | 21. D | 31. A | 41. D |
| 2. A | 12. A | 22. A | 32. C | 42. C |
| 3. A | 13. B | 23. C | 33. C | 43. B |
| 4. B | 14. D | 24. B | 34. A | 44. A |
| 5. B | 15. A | 25. A | 35. B | 45. D |
| 6. D | 16. C | 26. C | 36. C | 46. D |
| 7. B | 17. B | 27. D | 37. C | 47. C |
| 8. D | 18. C | 28. A | 38. B | 48. C |
| 9. B | 19. D | 29. C | 39. B | 49. C |
| 10. B | 20. A | 30. D | 40. B | 50. B |

# TEST 2

DIRECTIONS: Each question or incomplete statement is followed by several suggested answers or completions. Select the one that BEST answers the question or completes the statement. *PRINT THE LETTER OF THE CORRECT ANSWER IN THE SPACE AT THE RIGHT.*

1. Employees are responsible for the good care, proper maintenance and serviceable condition of property issued or assigned to their use.
   As used in the above sentence, the words *serviceable condition* means MOST NEARLY

   A. capable of being repaired
   B. fit for use
   C. ease of handling
   D. minimum cost

2. An employee shall be on the alert constantly for potential accident hazards.
   As used in the above sentence, the word *potential* means MOST NEARLY

   A. dangerous   B. careless   C. possible   D. frequent

3. The foreman is the keyman in safety in any working group.
   As used in the above sentence, the word *keyman* means MOST NEARLY

   A. watchman
   B. most important man
   C. man to whom to bring problems
   D. man who issues safety tools

4. It is best to find small defects before they can do great damage.
   As used in the above sentence, the word *defects* means MOST NEARLY

   A. faults   B. shorts   C. bearings   D. dangers

5. It is easier and cheaper to maintain equipment than to repair the equipment when it is too late.
   As used in the above sentence, the word *maintain* means MOST NEARLY

   A. buy good                B. use up
   C. keep in good condition  D. throw away

6. Where the length of roadway pavement is less than 100 lineal feet, the requirement of cores may be waived. As used in the above sentence, the word *waived* means MOST NEARLY

   A. eliminated   B. enforced
   C. considered   D. postponed

7. Where only part of the sidewalk is to be relaid, the concrete shall match the predominant color of the existing sidewalk.
   As used in the above sentence, the word *predominant* means MOST NEARLY

   A. lightest   B. darkest
   C. main       D. contrasting

8. All stands must be substantially built so as not to create any hazard to passersby or other persons.
   As used in the above sentence, the word *hazard* means MOST NEARLY

   A. delay
   B. danger
   C. obstruction
   D. inconvenience

9. The lights shall be lighted and remain lighted every night during the hours prescribed.
   As used in the above sentence, the word *prescribed* means MOST NEARLY

   A. required
   B. not needed
   C. before midnight
   D. of darkness

10. The department in its discretion may direct that certain regulations be waived.
    As used in the above sentence, the word *discretion* means MOST NEARLY

    A. jurisdiction
    B. operation
    C. organization
    D. judgment

11. All canopy permits shall be posted in a conspicuous place at the entrance for which the permit is issued.
    As used in the above sentence, the word *conspicuous* means MOST NEARLY

    A. well known
    B. inaccessible
    C. easily observed
    D. obscure

12. Where a street opening is made by a licensed plumber, a plumber's bond may be filed in lieu of a street obstruction bond.
    As used in the above sentence, the words *in lieu of* means MOST NEARLY

    A. in addition to
    B. instead of
    C. immediately as
    D. appurtenant to

13. A solvent will also assist the paint in the penetration of porous surfaces.
    As used in the above sentence, the word *penetration* means MOST NEARLY

    A. covering
    B. protection
    C. cleaning
    D. entering

14. A painter should make sure he has sufficient paint to do the job.
    As used in the above sentence, the word *sufficient* means MOST NEARLY

    A. enough
    B. the right kind of
    C. the proper color of
    D. mixed

15. Religious bigotry is repugnant to all true democrats. As used in the above sentence, the word *repugnant* means MOST NEARLY

    A. dangerous
    B. distasteful
    C. revealing
    D. surprising

16. To obtain durability, exposed brickwork should be built of well-burned bricks.
    As used in the above sentence, the word *durability* means MOST NEARLY

    A. beauty
    B. water resistance
    C. strength
    D. long life

Questions 17-19.

DIRECTIONS: Each of Questions 17 through 19 consists of a capitalized word followed by four suggested meanings of the word. Select the word or phrase which means MOST NEARLY the same as the capitalized word.

17. CONDUIT

    A. easy   B. behavior   C. channel   D. puzzle

18. CATALYSIS

    A. catacomb   B. charge
    C. fumigation   D. activation

19. INCREMENT

    A. accusation   B. expense
    C. addition   D. discrepancy

20. The machinist is machining a bearing housing of conventional design.
    As used in the above sentence, the word *conventional* means MOST NEARLY

    A. complicated   B. superior
    C. new   D. common

21. When turning a piece of tenacious metal on a lathe, a lubricant is used to prevent excessive friction by conducting the heat away.
    As used in the above sentence, the word *tenacious* means MOST NEARLY

    A. annealed   B. soft   C. tough   D. coarse

22. In a particular shop, a machinist is assigned to the task of coordinating various machining operations.
    As used in the above sentence, the word *coordinating* means MOST NEARLY

    A. repairing   B. replacing
    C. testing   D. scheduling

23. The employee made an insignificant error.
    As used in the above statement, the word *insignificant* means MOST NEARLY

    A. serious   B. accidental
    C. minor   D. hidden

24. Work areas must be kept clear of accumulations of equipment, materials, and rubbish.
    As used in the above sentence, the word *accumulations* means MOST NEARLY

    A. different kinds   B. piles
    C. interference   D. seldom used

25. All material in bags or bundles which are stored in tiers must be stacked and blocked so as to produce a stable pile.
    As used in the above sentence, the word *tiers* means MOST NEARLY

    A. groups   B. rooms   C. layers   D. sheds

26. Men must report all accidents, no matter how trivial. As used in the above sentence, the word *trivial* means MOST NEARLY

    A. often
    B. treated
    C. caused
    D. insignificant

27. The water level in the gage glass was dormant during the peak load conditions. As used in the above sentence, The word *dormant* means MOST NEARLY

    A. fluctuating
    B. inactive
    C. clean
    D. foaming

28. The instructor's words were understood but irrelevant. As used in the above sentence, the word *irrelevant* means MOST NEARLY

    A. unchallenging to the audience
    B. unconvincing to the audience
    C. not bearing upon the subject under discussion
    D. not based upon facts

29. An employee who is *zealous* in his work is one who is MOST NEARLY

    A. enthusiastic
    B. envious
    C. courteous
    D. patient

30. It is not the revolutions that destroy machinery, but the friction. As used in the above sentence, the word *friction* means MOST NEARLY

    A. rotation
    B. speed
    C. evolution
    D. resistance

31. A worker who makes a *significant* error makes one which is MOST NEARLY

    A. important
    B. accidental
    C. meaningless
    D. doubtful

32. A worker who is given *explicit* directions is given directions which are MOST NEARLY

    A. forceful
    B. erroneous
    C. confusing
    D. definite

33. If a supervisor gives *concise* instructions to his men daily, this means that his instructions are

    A. brief     B. wordy     C. changed     D. lengthy

34. If a foreman makes an *intricate* sketch of the bearing assembly, this means that the sketch is

    A. evident     B. obvious     C. clear     D. involved

35. *Gradual decrease in the width of an elongated object* is called a

    A. bevel     B. slope     C. spiral     D. taper

36. The worker showed great resentment towards his supervisor. As used in the above sentence, the word *resentment* means MOST NEARLY

    A. fear     B. dislike     C. affection     D. regard

37. Lubrication is an essential part of preventive maintenance.
    As used in the above sentence, the word *essential* means MOST NEARLY

    A. frequent
    B. useful
    C. required
    D. indispensable

38. Grader brakes are adequate for low speed working conditions.
    As used in the above sentence, the word *adequate* means MOST NEARLY

    A. good    B. strong    C. built    D. sufficient

39. The frame of a caterpillar grader consists of two cross braced members which converge to form a single arched beam.
    As used in the above sentence, the word *converge* means MOST NEARLY

    A. come together
    B. are welded
    C. operate as a unit
    D. are used

40. Mud is an impediment to work in many ways.
    As used in the above sentence, the word *impediment* means MOST NEARLY

    A. detriment    B. nuisance    C. hindrance    D. problem

41. *To make rows of small holes through a substance* defines the word

    A. penetrate    B. perforate    C. permeate    D. pulsate

42. A specification for electric work states: The Contractor, when performing work inside of the existing building, shall take all requisite measures to protect the furniture, shades, woodwork, plaster, and other items from any possible damage.
    As used in the above sentence, the word *requisite* means MOST NEARLY

    A. usual    B. requested    C. specified    D. necessary

43. When many statements in a worker's report are *redundant*, they are MOST NEARLY

    A. brief    B. wordy    C. adequate    D. regular

44. When an inspector's report is *concise*, it is MOST NEARLY

    A. rambling
    B. unclear
    C. to the point
    D. drawn out

45. An employee who is *dilatory* in his work is one who is MOST NEARLY

    A. expeditious
    B. inconsistent
    C. inaccurate
    D. slow

46. *To swing backward and forward* defines the word

    A. alternate
    B. gesticulate
    C. oscillate
    D. procrastinate

47. *A situation involving choices between equally unsatisfactory alternatives* is called a

    A. crisis    B. deadlock    C. dilemma    D. farce

48. A statement of self-evident truth is called a(n)  48._____

   A. adage
   B. axiom
   C. hypothesis
   D. theory

Questions 49-50.

DIRECTIONS: Questions 49 and 50 are to be answered on the basis of the following paragraph.

   Extraneous noises developed by the system as installed in the building shall not be perceptible when the system is operating 6 db (sound volume) above the average operating level of the sound system.

49. The word *extraneous*, as used in the above paragraph, means MOST NEARLY  49._____

   A. meaningless
   B. foreign
   C. odd
   D. loud

50. The word *perceptible*, as used in the above paragraph, means MOST NEARLY  50._____

   A. receivable
   B. acceptable
   C. vibrating
   D. audible

## KEY (CORRECT ANSWERS)

| | | | | |
|---|---|---|---|---|
| 1. B | 11. C | 21. C | 31. A | 41. B |
| 2. C | 12. B | 22. D | 32. D | 42. D |
| 3. B | 13. D | 23. C | 33. A | 43. B |
| 4. A | 14. A | 24. B | 34. D | 44. C |
| 5. C | 15. B | 25. C | 35. D | 45. D |
| 6. A | 16. D | 26. D | 36. B | 46. C |
| 7. C | 17. C | 27. B | 37. D | 47. C |
| 8. B | 18. D | 28. C | 38. D | 48. B |
| 9. A | 19. C | 29. A | 39. A | 49. B |
| 10. D | 20. D | 30. D | 40. C | 50. D |

# EXAMINATION SECTION
## TEST 1

DIRECTIONS: Each question or incomplete statement is followed by several suggested answers or completions. Select the one that BEST answers the question or completes the statement. *PRINT THE LETTER OF THE CORRECT ANSWER IN THE SPACE AT THE RIGHT.*

Questions 1-50.

DIRECTIONS: Each of Questions 1 through 50 consists of a word in capital letters followed by four suggested meanings of the word. For each question, choose the word or phrase which means MOST NEARLY the same as the word in capital letters.

1. ABUT
    A. abandon   B. assist   C. border on   D. renounce

2. ABSCOND
    A. draw in   B. give up
    C. refrain from   D. deal off

3. BEQUEATH
    A. deaden   B. hand down   C. make sad   D. scold

4. BOGUS
    A. sad   B. false   C. shocking   D. stolen

5. CALAMITY
    A. disaster   B. female   C. insanity   D. patriot

6. COMPULSORY
    A. binding   B. ordinary   C. protected   D. ruling

7. CONSIGN
    A. agree with   B. benefit
    C. commit   D. drive down

8. DEBILITY
    A. failure   B. legality
    C. quality   D. weakness

9. DEFRAUD
    A. cheat   B. deny
    C. reveal   D. tie

10. DEPOSITION
    A. absence   B. publication
    C. removal   D. testimony

11. DOMICILE
    A. anger   B. dwelling
    C. tame   D. willing

2 (#1)

12. HEARSAY
    A. selfish  B. serious  C. rumor  D. unlikely

13. HOMOGENEOUS
    A. human  B. racial  C. similar  D. unwise

14. ILLICIT
    A. understood  B. uneven  C. unkind  D. unlawful

15. LEDGER
    A. book of accounts  B. editor
    C. periodical  D. shelf

16. NARRATIVE
    A. gossip  B. natural  C. negative  D. story

17. PLAUSIBLE
    A. reasonable  B. respectful  C. responsible  D. rightful

18. RECIPIENT
    A. absentee  B. receiver  C. speaker  D. substitute

19. SUBSTANTIATE
    A. appear for  B. arrange
    C. confirm  D. combine

20. SURMISE
    A. aim  B. break  C. guess  D. order

21. ALTER EGO
    A. business partner  B. confidential friend
    C. guide  D. subconscious conflict

22. FOURTH ESTATE
    A. the aristocracy  B. the clergy
    C. the judiciary  D. the newspapers

23. IMPEACH
    A. accuse  B. find guilty
    C. remove  D. try

24. PROPENSITY
    A. dislike  B. helpfulness
    C. inclination  D. supervision

25. SPLENETIC
    A. charming  B. peevish  C. shining  D. sluggish

26. SUBORN
    A. bribe someone to commit perjury
    B. demote someone several levels in rank
    C. deride
    D. substitute

27. TALISMAN
    A. charm
    B. juror
    C. prayer shawl
    D. native

28. VITREOUS
    A. corroding
    B. glassy
    C. nourishing
    D. sticky

29. WRY
    A. comic
    B. grained
    C. resilient
    D. twisted

30. SIGNATORY
    A. lawyer who draws up a legal document
    B. document that must be signed by a judge
    C. person who signs a document
    D. true copy of a signature

31. RETAINER
    A. fee paid to a lawyer for his services
    B. document held by a third party
    C. court decision to send a prisoner back to custody pending trial
    D. legal requirement to keep certain types of files

32. BEQUEATH
    A. to receive assistance from a charitable organization
    B. to give personal property by will to another
    C. to transfer real property from one person to another
    D. to receive an inheritance upon the death of a relative

33. RATIFY
    A. approve and sanction
    B. forego
    C. produce evidence
    D. summarize

34. CODICIL
    A. document introduced in evidence in a civil action
    B. subsection of a law
    C. type of legal action that can be brought by a plaintiff
    D. supplement or an addition to a will

35. ALIAS
    A. assumed name
    B. in favor of
    C. against
    D. a writ

36. PROXY
    A. a phony document in a real estate transaction
    B. an opinion by a judge of a civil court
    C. a document containing appointment of an agent
    D. a summons in a lawsuit

37. ALLEGED
    A. innocent
    B. asserted
    C. guilty
    D. called upon

38. EXECUTE
    A. to complete a legal document by signing it
    B. to set requirements
    C. to render services to a duly elected executive of a municipality
    D. to initiate legal action such as a lawsuit

38.____

39. NOTARY PUBLIC
    A. lawyer who is running for public office
    B. judge who hears minor cases
    C. public officer, one of whose functions is to administer oaths
    D. lawyer who gives free legal services to persons unable to pay

39.____

40. WAIVE
    A. to disturb a calm state of affairs
    B. to knowingly renounce a right or claim
    C. to pardon someone for a minor fault
    D. to purposely mislead a person during an investigation

40.____

41. ARRAIGN
    A. to prevent an escape
    B. to defend a prisoner
    C. to verify a document
    D. to accuse in a court of law

41.____

42. VOLUNTARY
    A. by free choice      B. necessary
    C. important           D. by design

42.____

43. INJUNCTION
    A. act of prohibiting      B. process of inserting
    C. means of arbitrating    D. freedom of action

43.____

44. AMICABLE
    A. compelled       B. friendly
    C. unimportant     D. insignificant

44.____

45. CLOSED SHOP
    A. one that employs only members of a union
    B. one that employs union members and unaffiliated employees
    C. one that employs only employees with previous experience
    D. one that employs skilled and unskilled workers

45.____

46. ABDUCT
    A. lead     B. kidnap     C. sudden     D. worthless

46.____

47. BIAS
    A. ability     B. envy     C. prejudice     D. privilege

47.____

48. COERCE
    A. cancel     B. force     C. rescind     D. rugged

48.____

49. CONDONE
    A. combine    B. pardon    C. revive    D. spice

50. CONSISTENCY
    A. bravery        B. readiness
    C. strain         D. uniformity

## KEY (CORRECT ANSWERS)

| | | | | |
|---|---|---|---|---|
| 1. C | 11. B | 21. B | 31. A | 41. D |
| 2. D | 12. C | 22. D | 32. B | 42. A |
| 3. B | 13. C | 23. A | 33. A | 43. A |
| 4. B | 14. D | 24. C | 34. D | 44. B |
| 5. A | 15. A | 25. B | 35. A | 45. A |
| 6. A | 16. D | 26. A | 36. C | 46. B |
| 7. C | 17. A | 27. A | 37. B | 47. C |
| 8. D | 18. B | 28. B | 38. A | 48. B |
| 9. A | 19. C | 29. D | 39. C | 49. B |
| 10. D | 20. C | 30. C | 40. B | 50. D |

# TEST 2

DIRECTIONS: Each question or incomplete statement is followed by several suggested answers or completions. Select the one that BEST answers the question or completes the statement. *PRINT THE LETTER OF THE CORRECT ANSWER IN THE SPACE AT THE RIGHT.*

1. In the sentence, *The prisoner was fractious when brought to the station house*, the word *fractious* means MOST NEARLY
   A. penitent
   B. talkative
   C. irascible
   D. broken-hearted

   1.___

2. In the sentence, *The judge was implacable when the attorney pleaded for leniency*, the word *implacable* means MOST NEARLY
   A. inexorable
   B. disinterested
   C. inattentive
   D. indifferent

   2.___

3. In the sentence, *The court ordered the mendacious statements stricken from the record*, the word *mendacious* means MOST NEARLY
   A. begging
   B. lying
   C. threatening
   D. lengthy

   3.___

4. In the sentence, *The district attorney spoke in a strident voice*, the word *strident* means MOST NEARLY
   A. loud
   B. harsh-sounding
   C. sing-song
   D. low

   4.___

5. In the sentence, *The speaker had a predilection for long sentences*, the word *predilection* means MOST NEARLY
   A. aversion
   B. talent
   C. propensity
   D. diffidence

   5.___

6. A person who has an uncontrollable desire to steal without need is called a
   A. dipsomaniac
   B. kleptomaniac
   C. monomaniac
   D. pyromaniac

   6.___

7. In the sentence, *Malice was immanent in all his remarks*, the word *immanent* means MOST NEARLY
   A. elevated
   B. inherent
   C. threatening
   D. foreign

   7.___

8. In the sentence, *The extant copies of the document were found in the safe*, the word *extant* means MOST NEARLY
   A. existing
   B. original
   C. forged
   D. duplicate

   8.___

9. In the sentence, *The recruit was more complaisant after the captain spoke to him*, the word *complaisant* means MOST NEARLY
   A. calm
   B. affable
   C. irritable
   D. confident

   9.___

10. In the sentence, *The man was captured under highly creditable circumstances*, the word *creditable* means MOST NEARLY
    A. doubtful
    B. believable
    C. praiseworthy
    D. unexpected

11. In the sentence, *His superior officers were more sagacious than he*, the word *sagacious* means MOST NEARLY
    A. shrewd
    B. obtuse
    C. absurd
    D. verbose

12. In the sentence, *He spoke with impunity*, the word *impunity* means MOST NEARLY
    A. rashness
    B. caution
    C. without fear
    D. immunity

13. In the sentence, *The new officer displayed unusual temerity during the emergency*, the word *temerity* means MOST NEARLY
    A. fear
    B. rashness
    C. calmness
    D. anxiety

14. In the sentence, *The portions of food were parsimoniously served*, the word *parsimoniously* means MOST NEARLY
    A. stingily
    B. piously
    C. elaborately
    D. generously

15. In the sentence, *Generally the speaker's remarks were sententious*, the word *sententious* means MOST NEARLY
    A. verbose
    B. witty
    C. argumentative
    D. pithy

Questions 16-20.

DIRECTIONS: Next to the number which corresponds with the number of each item in Column I, place the letter preceding the adjective in Column II which BEST describes the persons in Column I.

| COLUMN I | | COLUMN II |
| --- | --- | --- |
| 16. Talkative woman | A. | abstemious |
| 17. Person on a reducing diet | B. | pompous |
| 18. Scholarly professor | C. | erudite |
| 19. Man who seldom speaks | D. | benevolent |
| 20. Charitable person | E. | docile |
| | F. | loquacious |
| | G. | indefatigable |
| | H. | taciturn |

Questions 21-25.

DIRECTIONS: Next to the number which corresponds with the number preceding each profession in Column I, place the letter preceding the word in Column II which BEST explains the subject matter of that profession.

| COLUMN I | COLUMN II | |
|---|---|---|
| 21. Geologist | A. animals | 21.___ |
| 22. Oculist | B. eyes | 22.___ |
| 23. Podiatrist | C. feet | 23.___ |
| 24. Palmist | D. fortune-telling | 24.___ |
| 25. Zoologist | E. language | 25.___ |
| | F. rocks | |
| | G. stamps | |
| | H. woman | |

Questions 26-30.

DIRECTIONS: Next to the number corresponding to the number of each of the words in Column I, place the letter preceding the word in Column II that is MOST NEARLY OPPOSITE to it in meaning.

| COLUMN I | COLUMN II | |
|---|---|---|
| 26. comely | A. beautiful | 26.___ |
| 27. eminent | B. cowardly | 27.___ |
| 28. frugal | C. kind | 28.___ |
| 29. gullible | D. sedate | 29.___ |
| 30. valiant | E. shrewd | 30.___ |
| | F. ugly | |
| | G. unknown | |
| | H. wasteful | |

## KEY (CORRECT ANSWERS)

| | | |
|---|---|---|
| 1. C | 11. A | 21. F |
| 2. A | 12. D | 22. B |
| 3. B | 13. B | 23. C |
| 4. B | 14. A | 24. D |
| 5. C | 15. D | 25. A |
| 6. B | 16. F | 26. F |
| 7. B | 17. A | 27. G |
| 8. A | 18. C | 28. H |
| 9. B | 19. H | 29. E |
| 10. C | 20. D | 30. B |

# POLICE VOCABULARY

Police officers are expected to understand and use many specialized words. Some of the words that are presented here will appear in the exam. You should know what the words mean before *you* take the test. If you have any doubt about the meaning of any of the words listed below or any other words contained in this booklet, check the definitions in a dictionary before taking the exam.

| | | | |
|---|---|---|---|
| abandon | abet | accessory | accomplice |
| accordance | accurate | acknowledge | acquaintance |
| acquittal | adjacent | adjoining | admissible |
| advise | aid | alias | alibi |
| allege | allocate | altercation | annul |
| apparently | appearance | apprehend | apprehension |
| appropriate | arson | articulate | ascertain |
| assailant | assume | bludgeon | boisterous |
| burglary | circumstances | commission | commit |
| complexion | competent | complaint | complainant |
| compliance | conceal | condone | confinement |
| confirm | confiscate | conjunction | constitutional |
| contraband | controversy | credible | corroborate |
| corruptible | counsel | culpable | curfew |
| cursory | custody | defendant | defraud |
| delinquent | deploy | detain | detriment |
| diagonally | discreet | discretion | discriminate |
| discriminatory | dispatch | dispatcher | disperse |
| disturbance | directive | dispute | divulge |
| duress | dwelling | effect | embezzlement |
| evacuation | excessive | exclude | extensive |
| facility | feasible | felony | frisk |
| fugitive | gallant | gratuities | guardian |
| harass | homicide | hysterical | identical |
| incapacitate | incarcerate | incite | incident |
| incriminate | indicate | indigence | influence |
| insufficient | interrogate | interrogation | intersecting |
| investigation | investigative | impede | implements |
| implicate | judgment | justifiable | justification |
| jurisdiction | juvenile | lapse | legality |
| loiter | malevolent | mandatory | mediate |
| minor | misdemeanor | mitigating | negligence |
| negotiation | obstruct | obtain | occupant |
| occupation | occurrence | offender | offense |
| operator | pedestrian | perpetrate | perpetrator |
| personnel | pertinent | potential | precedence |
| preceding | precinct | preliminary | premeditate |
| premises | presence | preserve | primary |
| prior | priority | procedure | processing |
| prosecute | prosecution | prosecutor | protection |
| provocation | provoke | pursuant | pursuit |
| recovered | reinforcements | relinquish | render |
| request | requirement | residence | resident |
| respond | robbery | ruse | secure |
| security | seize | sequence | spontaneous |
| submit | subordinate | subsequent | substantial |
| sufficient | suspect | suspicious | suppress |
| technicality | technique | testify | theft |
| thwart | transport | vandalism | vehicle |
| vehicular | verify | vicinity | violate |
| violation | warrant | | |

In the test, you will be given questions like the sample questions below. For each question, you are to pick the word or phrase closest in meaning to the word or phrase in capital letters.

SAMPLE QUESTIONS

1. DIVULGE

    A. tell
    B. vomit
    C. give
    D. take

2. EXCLUDE

    A. leave out
    B. erase
    C. give to
    D. add

3. OCCUPANT

    A. job
    B. resident
    C. take over
    D. owner

# KEY (CORRECT ANSWERS)

1. A
2. A
3. B

# SPELLING

# EXAMINATION SECTION

# TEST 1

DIRECTIONS: Each question or incomplete statement is followed by several suggested answers or completions. Select the one that BEST answers the question or completes the statement. *PRINT THE LETTER OF THE CORRECT ANSWER IN THE SPACE AT THE RIGHT.*

Questions 1-5.

DIRECTIONS: Questions 1 through 5 consist of four words. Indicate the letter of the word that is CORRECTLY spelled.

1. A. harassment  B. harrasment  1.____
   C. harasment   D. harrassment

2. A. maintainance  B. maintenence  2.____
   C. maintainence  D. maintenance

3. A. comparable  B. comprable  3.____
   C. comparible  D. commparable

4. A. suficient  B. sufficiant  4.____
   C. sufficient  D. suficiant

5. A. fairly   B. fairley   C. farely   D. fairlie   5.____

Questions 6-10.

DIRECTIONS: Questions 6 through 10 consist of four words. Indicate the letter of the word that is INCORRECTLY spelled.

6. A. pallor  B. ballid  C. ballet  D. pallid  6.____

7. A. urbane  B. surburbane  7.____
   C. interurban  D. urban

8. A. facial  B. physical  C. fiscle  D. muscle  8.____

9. A. interceed  B. benefited  9.____
   C. analogous  D. altogether

10. A. seizure  B. irrelevant  10.____
    C. inordinate  D. dissapproved

## KEY (CORRECT ANSWERS)

1. A  6. B
2. D  7. B
3. A  8. C
4. C  9. A
5. A  10. D

# TEST 2

DIRECTIONS: Each of Questions 1 through 15 consists of two words preceded by the letters A and B. In each question, one of the words may be spelled INCORRECTLY or both words may be spelled CORRECTLY. If one of the words in a question is spelled INCORRECTLY, print in the space at the right the capital letter preceding the INCORRECTLY spelled word. If both words are spelled CORRECTLY, print the letter C.

1. A. easely          B. readily          1.____
2. A. pursue          B. decend           2.____
3. A. measure         B. laboratory       3.____
4. A. exausted        B. traffic          4.____
5. A. discussion      B. unpleasant       5.____
6. A. campaign        B. murmer           6.____
7. A. guarantee       B. sanatary         7.____
8. A. communication   B. safty            8.____
9. A. numerus         B. celebration      9.____
10. A. nourish        B. begining         10.____
11. A. courious       B. witness          11.____
12. A. undoubtedly    B. thoroughly       12.____
13. A. accessible     B. artifical        13.____
14. A. feild          B. arranged         14.____
15. A. admittence     B. hastily          15.____

## KEY (CORRECT ANSWERS)

1. A    6. B    11. A
2. B    7. B    12. C
3. C    8. B    13. B
4. A    9. A    14. A
5. C    10. B   15. A

# TEST 3

DIRECTIONS: In each of the following sentences, one word is misspelled. Following each sentence is a list of four words taken from the sentence. Indicate the letter of the word which is MISSPELLED in the sentence. *PRINT THE LETTER OF THE CORRECT ANSWER IN THE SPACE AT THE RIGHT.*

1. The placing of any inflammable substance in any building, or the placing of any device or contrivance capable of producing fire, for the purpose of causing a fire is an attempt to burn.
   - A. inflammable
   - B. substance
   - C. device
   - D. contrivence

   1._____

2. The word *break* also means obtaining an entrance into a building by any artifice used for that purpose, or by collussion with any person therein.
   - A. obtaining
   - B. entrance
   - C. artifice
   - D. colussion

   2._____

3. Any person who with intent to provoke a breech of the peace causes a disturbance or is offensive to others may be deemed to have committed disorderly conduct.
   - A. breech
   - B. disturbance
   - C. offensive
   - D. committed

   3._____

4. When the offender inflicts a grevious harm upon the person from whose possession, or in whose presence, property is taken, he is guilty of robbery.
   - A. offender
   - B. grevious
   - C. possession
   - D. presence

   4._____

5. A person who wilfuly encourages or advises another person in attempting to take the latter's life is guilty of a felony.
   - A. wilfuly
   - B. encourages
   - C. advises
   - D. attempting

   5._____

6. He maliciously demurred to an ajournment of the proceedings.
   - A. maliciously
   - B. demurred
   - C. ajournment
   - D. proceedings

   6._____

7. His innocence at that time is irrelevant in view of his more recent villianous demeanor.
   - A. innocence
   - B. irrelevant
   - C. villianous
   - D. demeanor

   7._____

8. The mischievous boys aggrevated the annoyance of their neighbor.
   - A. mischievous
   - B. aggrevated
   - C. annoyance
   - D. neighbor

   8._____

9. While his perseverence was commendable, his judgment was debatable.    9.____
   A. perseverence         B. commendable
   C. judgment             D. debatable

10. He was hoping the appeal would facilitate his aquittal.    10.____
    A. hoping              B. appeal
    C. facilitate          D. aquittal

11. It would be preferable for them to persue separate courses.    11.____
    A. preferable          B. persue
    C. separate            D. courses

12. The litigant was complimented on his persistance and achievement.    12.____
    A. litigant            B. complimented
    C. persistance         D. achievement

13. Ocassionally there are discrepancies in the descriptions of miscellaneous items.    13.____
    A. ocassionally        B. discrepancies
    C. descriptions        D. miscellaneous

14. The councilmanic seargent-at-arms enforced the prohibition.    14.____
    A. councilmanic        B. seargeant-at-arms
    C. enforced            D. prohibition

15. The teacher had an ingenious device for maintaining attendance.    15.____
    A. ingenious           B. device
    C. maintaning          D. attendance

16. A worrysome situation has developed as a result of the assessment that absenteeism is increasing despite our conscientious efforts.    16.____
    A. worrysome           B. assessment
    C. absenteeism         D. conscientious

17. I concurred with the credit manager that it was practicable to charge purchases on a biennial basis, and the company agreed to adhere to this policy.    17.____
    A. concurred           B. practicable
    C. biennial            D. adhear

18. The pastor was chagrined and embarassed by the irreverent conduct of one of his parishioners.    18.____
    A. chagrined           B. embarassed
    C. irreverent          D. parishioners

19. His inate seriousness was belied by his flippant demeanor.    19.____
    A. inate               B. belied
    C. flippant            D. demeanor

20. It was exceedingly regrettable that the excessive number of challenges in the court delayed the start of the trial.
    A. exceedingly
    B. regrettable
    C. excessive
    D. challanges

20.____

## KEY (CORRECT ANSWERS)

| | | | |
|---|---|---|---|
| 1. | D | 11. | B |
| 2. | D | 12. | C |
| 3. | A | 13. | A |
| 4. | B | 14. | B |
| 5. | A | 15. | C |
| 6. | C | 16. | A |
| 7. | C | 17. | D |
| 8. | B | 18. | B |
| 9. | A | 19. | A |
| 10. | D | 20. | D |

# TEST 4

Questions 1-11.

DIRECTIONS: Each question consists of three words in each question, one of the words may be spelled incorrectly or all three may be spelled correctly. For each question if one of the words is spelled INCORRECTLY, write the letter of the incorrect word in the space at the right. If all three words are spelled CORRECTLY, write the letter D in the space at the right.

SAMPLE I: (A) guide   (B) departmint   (C) stranger
SAMPLE II: (A) comply   (B) valuable   (C) window
In Sample I, departmint is incorrect. It should be spelled department.
Therefore, B is the answer.
In Sample II, all three words are spelled correctly. Therefore, D is the answer.

| | | | | | |
|---|---|---|---|---|---|
| 1. | A. argument | B. reciept | C. complain | | 1.___ |
| 2. | A. sufficient | B. postpone | C. visible | | 2.___ |
| 3. | A. expirience | B. dissatisly | C. alternate | | 3.___ |
| 4. | A. occurred | B. noticable | C. appendix | | 4.___ |
| 5. | A. anxious | B. guarantee | C. calendar | | 5.___ |
| 6. | A. sincerely | B. affectionately | C. truly | | 6.___ |
| 7. | A. excellant | B. verify | C. important | | 7.___ |
| 8. | A. error | B. quality | C. enviroment | | 8.___ |
| 9. | A. exercise | B. advance | C. pressure | | 9.___ |
| 10. | A. citizen | B. expence | C. memory | | 10.___ |
| 11. | A. flexable | B. focus | C. forward | | 11.___ |

Questions 12-15.

DIRECTIONS: Each of Questions 12 through 15 consists of a group of four words. Examine each group carefully; then in the space at the right, indicate
A. if only one word in the group is spelled correctly
B. if two words in the group are spelled correctly
C. if three words in the group are spelled correctly
D. if all four words in the group are spelled correctly

12. Wendsday, particular, similar, hunderd                    12.___

297

13. realize, judgment, opportunities, consistent      13.____

14. equel, principle, assistense, committee      14.____

15. simultaneous, privilege, advise, ocassionaly      15.____

---

## KEY (CORRECT ANSWERS)

| | | |
|---|---|---|
| 1. B | 6. D | 11. A |
| 2. D | 7. A | 12. B |
| 3. A | 8. C | 13. D |
| 4. B | 9. D | 14. A |
| 5. C | 10. B | 15. C |

# TEST 5

DIRECTIONS: Each of Questions 1 through 15 consists of two words preceded by the letters A and B. In each item, one of the words may be spelled INCORRECTLY or both words may be spelled CORRECTLY. If one of the words in a question is spelled INCORRECTLY, print in the space at the right the letter preceding the INCORRECTLY spelled word. If bot words are spelled CORRECTLY, print the letter C.

1. A. justified    B. offering        1.____
2. A. predjudice   B. license         2.____
3. A. label        B. pamphlet        3.____
4. A. bulletin     B. physical        4.____
5. A. assure       B. exceed          5.____
6. A. advantagous  B. evident         6.____
7. A. benefit      B. occured         7.____
8. A. acquire      B. graditude       8.____
9. A. amenable     B. boundry         9.____
10. A. deceive     B. voluntary       10.____
11. A. imunity     B. conciliate      11.____
12. A. acknoledge  B. presume         12.____
13. A. substitute  B. prespiration    13.____
14. A. reputable   B. announce        14.____
15. A. luncheon    B. wretched        15.____

## KEY (CORRECT ANSWERS)

1. C     6. A     11. A
2. A     7. B     12. A
3. C     8. B     13. B
4. C     9. B     14. A
5. C     10. C    15. C

299

# TEST 6

DIRECTIONS: Questions 1 through 15 contain lists of words, one of which is misspelled. Indicate the MISSPELLED word in each group. *PRINT THE LETTER OF THE CORRECT ANSWER IN THE SPACE AT THE RIGHT.*

1. A. felony          B. lacerate        1.____
   C. cancellation    D. seperate

2. A. batallion       B. beneficial      2.____
   C. miscellaneous   D. secretary

3. A. camouflage      B. changeable      3.____
   C. embarrass       D. inoculate

4. A. beneficial      B. disasterous     4.____
   C. incredible      D. miniature

5. A. auxilliary      B. hypocrisy       5.____
   C. phlegm          D. vengeance

6. A. aisle           B. cemetary        6.____
   C. courtesy        D. extraordinary

7. A. crystallize     B. innoculate      7.____
   C. eminent         D. symmetrical

8. A. judgment        B. maintainance    8.____
   C. bouillon        D. eery

9. A. isosceles       B. ukulele         9.____
   C. mayonaise       D. iridescent

10. A. remembrance    B. occurence       10.____
    C. correspondence D. countenance

11. A. corpuscles     B. mischievous     11.____
    C. batchelor      D. bulletin

12. A. terrace        B. banister        12.____
    C. concrete       D. masonery

13. A. balluster      B. gutter          13.____
    C. latch          D. bridging

14. A. personnell     B. navel           14.____
    C. therefor       D. emigrant

15. A. committee B. submiting 15._____
    C. amendment D. electorate

## KEY (CORRECT ANSWERS)

| | | | | | |
|---|---|---|---|---|---|
| 1. | D | 6. | B | 11. | C |
| 2. | A | 7. | B | 12. | D |
| 3. | C | 8. | B | 13. | A |
| 4. | B | 9. | C | 14. | A |
| 5. | A | 10. | B | 15. | B |

# TEST 7

Questions 1-5.

DIRECTIONS: Questions 1 through 5 consist of groups of four words. Select answer
A if only one word is spelled correctly in a group
B if TWO words are spelled correctly in a group
C if THREE words are spelled correctly in a group
D if all FOUR words are spelled correctly in a group.

1. counterfeit, embarass, panicky, supercede           1._____

2. benefited, personnel, questionnaire, unparalelled   2._____

3. bankruptcy, describable, proceed, vacuum            3._____

4. handicapped, mispell, offerred, pilgrimmage         4._____

5. corduroy, interfere, privilege, separator           5._____

Questions 6-10.

DIRECTIONS: Questions 6 through 10 consist of four pairs of words each. Some of the words are spelled correctly; others are spelled incorrectly. For each question, indicate in the space at the right the letter preceding that pair of words in which BOTH words are spelled CORRECTLY.

6. A. hygienic, inviegle       B. omniscience, pittance       6._____
   C. plagarize, nullify       D. seargent, perilous

7. A. auxilary, existence      B. pronounciation, accordance  7._____
   C. ignominy, indegence      D. suable, baccalaureate

8. A. discreet, inaudible      B. hypocrisy, currupt          8._____
   C. liquidate, maintainance  D. transparancy, onerous

9. A. facility; stimulent      B. frugel, sanitary            9._____
   C. monetary, prefatory      D. punctileous, credentials

10. A. bankruptsy, perceptible  B. disuade, resilient         10._____
    C. exhilerate, expectancy   D. panegyric, disparate

Questions 11-15.

DIRECTIONS: Each question or incomplete statement is followed by several suggested answers or completions. Select the one that BEST answers the question or completes the statement. PRINT THE LETTER OF THE CORRECT ANSWER IN THE SPACE AT THE RIGHT.

11. The silent *e* must be retained when the suffix *–able* is added to the word       11.____
    A. argue        B. love        C. move        D. notice

12. The CORRECTLY spelled word in the choices below is       12.____
    A. kindergarden          B. zylophone
    C. hemorrhage            D. mayonaise

13. Of the following words, the one spelled CORRECTLY is       13.____
    A. begger                B. cemetary
    C. embarassed            D. coyote

14.
    A. dandilion    B. wiry        C. sieze       D. rythmic       14.____

15. A. beligerent             B. anihilation
    C. facetious              D. adversery

# KEY (CORRECT ANSWERS)

| | | | | | |
|---|---|---|---|---|---|
| 1. | B | 6. | B | 11. | D |
| 2. | C | 7. | D | 12. | C |
| 3. | D | 8. | A | 13. | D |
| 4. | A | 9. | C | 14. | B |
| 5. | D | 10. | D | 15. | C |

# TEST 8

DIRECTIONS: In each of the following sentences, one word is misspelled. Following each sentence is a list of four words taken from the sentence. Indicate the letter of the word which is MISSPELLED. *PRINT THE LETTER OF THE CORRECT ANSWER IN THE SPACE AT THE RIGHT.*

1. If the administrator attempts to withold information, there is a good likelihood that there will be serious repercussions.
   A. administrator
   B. withold
   C. likelihood
   D. repercussions

   1.____

2. He condescended to apologize, but we felt that a beligerent person should not occupy an influential position.
   A. condescended
   B. apologize
   C. beligerent
   D. influential

   2.____

3. Despite the sporadic delinquent payments of his indebtedness, Mr. Johnson has been an exemplery customer.
   A. sporadic
   B. delinquent
   C. indebtedness
   D. exemplery

   3.____

4. He was appreciative of the support he consistantly acquired, but he felt that he had waited an inordinate length of time for it.
   A. appreciative
   B. consistantly
   C. acquired
   D. inordinate

   4.____

5. Undeniably they benefited from the establishment of a receivership, but the question of statutary limitations remained unresolved.
   A. undeniably
   B. benefited
   C. receivership
   D. statutary

   5.____

6. Mr. Smith profered his hand as an indication that he considered it a viable contract, but Mr. Nelson alluded to the fact that his colleagues had not been consulted.
   A. profered
   B. viable
   C. alluded
   D. colleagues

   6.____

7. The treatments were beneficial according to the optomotrists, and the consensus was that minimal improvement could be expected.
   A. beneficial
   B. optomotrists
   C. consensus
   D. minimal

   7.____

8. Her frivolous manner was unbecoming because the air of solemnity at the cemetery was pervasive.
   A. frivalous
   B. solemnity
   C. cemetery
   D. pervasive

   8.____

9. The clandestine meetings were designed to make the two adversaries more amicable, but they served only to intensify their emnity.
    A. clandestine
    B. adversaries
    C. amicable
    D. emnity

10. Do you think that his innovative ideas and financial acumen will help stabalize the fluctuations of the stock market?
    A. innovative
    B. acumen
    C. stabalize
    D. fluctuations

11. In order to keep a perpetual inventory, you will have to keep an uninterrupted surveillance of all the miscellanious stock.
    A. perpetual
    B. uninterrupted
    C. surveillance
    D. miscellanious

12. She used the art of pursuasion on the children because she found that caustic remarks had no perceptible effect on their behavior.
    A. pursuasion
    B. caustic
    C. perceptible
    D. effect

13. His sacreligious outbursts offended his constituents, and he was summarily removed from office by the City Council.
    A. sacreligious
    B. constituents
    C. summarily
    D. Council

14. They exhorted the contestants to greater efforts, but the exhorbitant costs in terms of energy expended resulted in a feeling of lethargy.
    A. exhorted
    B. contestants
    C. exhorbitant
    D. lethargy

15. Since he was knowledgable about illicit drugs, he was served with a subpoena to appear for the prosecution.
    A. knowledgable
    B. illicit
    C. subpoena
    D. prosecution

16. In spite of his lucid statements, they denigrated his report and decided it should be succintly paraphrased.
    A. lucid
    B. denigrated
    C. succintly
    D. paraphrased

17. The discussion was not germane to the contraversy, but the indicted man's insistence on further talk was allowed.
    A. germane
    B. contraversy
    C. indicted
    D. insistence

18. The legislators were enervated by the distances they had traveled during the election year to fullfil their speaking engagements.
    A. legislators
    B. enervated
    C. traveled
    D. fullfil

19. The plaintiffs' attornies charge the defendant in the case with felonious assault.  19.____
    A. plaintiffs'  B. attornies
    C. defendant  D. felonious

20. It is symptomatic of the times that we try to placate all, but a proposal for new forms of disciplinery action was promulgated by the staff.  20.____
    A. symptomatic  B. placate
    C. disciplinery  D. promulgated

## KEY (CORRECT ANSWERS)

| | | | |
|---|---|---|---|
| 1. | B | 11. | D |
| 2. | C | 12. | A |
| 3. | D | 13. | A |
| 4. | B | 14. | C |
| 5. | D | 15. | A |
| 6. | A | 16. | C |
| 7. | B | 17. | B |
| 8. | A | 18. | D |
| 9. | D | 19. | B |
| 10. | C | 20. | C |

# TEST 9

DIRECTIONS: Each of Questions 1 through 15 consists of a single word which is spelled either correctly or incorrectly. If the word is spelled CORRECTLY, you are to print the letter C (Correct) in the space at the right. If the word is spelled INCORRECTL, you are to print the letter W (Wrong).

1. pospone            1._____
2. diffrent           2._____
3. height             3._____
4. carefully          4._____
5. ability            5._____
6. temper             6._____
7. deslike            7._____
8. seldem             8._____
9. alcohol            9._____
10. expense           10._____
11. vegatable         11._____
12. dispensary        12._____
13. specemin          13._____
14. allowance         14._____
15. exersise          15._____

## KEY (CORRECT ANSWERS)

| | | |
|---|---|---|
| 1. W | 6. C | 11. W |
| 2. W | 7. W | 12. C |
| 3. C | 8. W | 13. W |
| 4. C | 9. C | 14. C |
| 5. C | 10. C | 15. W |

# TEST 10

DIRECTIONS: Each of Questions 1 through 10 consists of four words, one of which may be spelled incorrectly or all four words may be spelled correctly. If one of the words in a question is spelled incorrectly, print in the space at the right the capital letter preceding the word which is spelled INCORRECTLY. If all four words are spelled CORRECTLY, print the letter E.

1. A. dismissal     B. collateral     1.____
   C. leisure     D. proffession

2. A. subsidary     B. outrageous     2.____
   C. liaison     D. assessed

3. A. already     B. changeable     3.____
   C. mischevous     D. cylinder

4. A. supersede     B. deceit     4.____
   C. dissension     D. imminent

5. A. arguing     B. contagious     5.____
   C. comparitive     D. accessible

6. A. indelible     B. existance     6.____
   C. presumptuous     D. mileage

7. A. extention     B. aggregate     7.____
   C. sustenance     D. gratuitous

8. A. interrogate     B. exaggeration     8.____
   C. vacillate     D. moreover

9. A. parallel     B. derogatory     9.____
   C. admissible     D. appellate

10. A. safety     B. cumalative     10.____
    C. disappear     D. usable

## KEY (CORRECT ANSWERS)

| | | | |
|---|---|---|---|
| 1. | D | 6. | B |
| 2. | A | 7. | A |
| 3. | C | 8. | E |
| 4. | E | 9. | C |
| 5. | C | 10. | B |

# TEST 11

DIRECTIONS: Each of questions 1 through 10 consists of four words, one of which may be spelled incorrectly or all four words may be spelled correctly. If one of the words in a question is spelled INCORRECTLY, print in the space at the right the capital letter preceding the word which is spelled incorrectly. If all four words are spelled CORRECTLY, print the letter E.

1. A. vehicular B. gesticulate  
   C. manageable D. fullfil                          1.____

2. A. inovation B. onerous  
   C. chastise D. irresistible                        2.____

3. A. familiarize B. dissolution  
   C. oscillate D. superflous                         3.____

4. A. census B. defender  
   C. adherence D. inconceivable                      4.____

5. A. voluminous B. liberalize  
   C. bankrupcy D. conversion                         5.____

6. A. justifiable B. executor  
   C. perpatrate D. dispelled                         6.____

7. A. boycott B. abeyence  
   C. enterprise D. circular                          7.____

8. A. spontaineous B. dubious  
   C. analyze D. premonition                          8.____

9. A. intelligible B. apparently  
   C. genuine D. crucial                              9.____

10. A. plentiful B. ascertain  
    C. carreer D. preliminary                         10.____

## KEY (CORRECT ANSWERS)

| | | | |
|---|---|---|---|
| 1. | D | 6. | C |
| 2. | A | 7. | B |
| 3. | D | 8. | A |
| 4. | E | 9. | E |
| 5. | C | 10. | C |

# TEST 12

DIRECTIONS: Each of questions 1 through 25 consists of four words, one of which may be spelled incorrectly or all four words may be spelled correctly. If one of the words in a question is spelled INCORRECTLY, print in the space at the right the capital letter preceding the word which is spelled incorrectly. If all four words are spelled CORRECTLY, print the letter E.

1. A. temporary  B. existance  C. complimentary  D. altogether  1._____

2. A. privilege  B. changeable  C. jeopardize  D. commitment  2._____

3. A. grievous  B. alloted  C. outrageous  D. mortgage  3._____

4. A. tempermental  B. accommodating  C. bookkeeping  D. panicky  4._____

5. A. auxiliary  B. indispensable  C. ecstasy  D. fiery  5._____

6. A. dissappear  B. buoyant  C. imminent  D. parallel  6._____

7. A. loosly  B. medicine  C. schedule  D. defendant  7._____

8. A. endeavor  B. persuade  C. retroactive  D. desparate  8._____

9. A. usage  B. servicable  C. disadvantageous  D. remittance  9._____

10. A. beneficary  B. receipt  C. excitable  D. implement  10._____

11. A. accompanying  B. intangible  C. offerred  D. movable  11._____

12. A. controlling  B. seize  C. repetitious  D. miscellaneous  12._____

13. A. installation  B. accommodation  C. consistant  D. illuminate  13._____

14. A. incidentaly  B. privilege  C. apparent  D. chargeable  14._____

310

2 (#12)

15. A. prevalent B. serial 15.____
C. briefly D. disatisfied

16. A. reciprocal B. concurrence 16.____
C. persistence D. withold

17. A. deferred B. suing 17.____
C. fulfilled D. pursuant

18. A. questionable B. omission 18.____
C. acknowledgment D. insistent

19. A. guarantee B. committment 19.____
C. mitigate D. publicly

20. A. prerogative B. apprise 20.____
C. extrordinary D. continual

21. A. arrogant B. handicapped 21.____
C. judicious D. perennial

22. A. permissable B. deceive 22.____
C. innumerable D. retrieve

23. A. notable B. allegiance 23.____
C. reimburse D. illegal

24. A. wholly B. disbursement 24.____
C. hindrance D. conciliatory

25. A. guidance B. condemn 25.____
C. publically D. coercion

## KEY (CORRECT ANSWERS)

| | | | |
|---|---|---|---|
| 1. | B | 11. | C |
| 2. | E | 12. | E |
| 3. | B | 13. | C |
| 4. | A | 14. | A |
| 5. | E | 15. | D |
| | | | |
| 6. | A | 16. | D |
| 7. | A | 17. | E |
| 8. | D | 18. | A |
| 9. | B | 19. | B |
| 10. | A | 20. | C |

| | |
|---|---|
| 21. | E |
| 22. | A |
| 23. | E |
| 24. | E |
| 25. | C |

# TESTS IN SPELLING

# EXAMINATION SECTION
## TEST 1

DIRECTIONS: In each question of the following tests, select the letter of the one MIS-SPELLED word in each of the listed groups of five (5) words. *PRINT THE LETTER OF THE CORRECT ANSWER IN THE SPACE AT THE RIGHT.*

1. A. barely        B. assigned     C. mechanical  D. concequently   E. lovingly      1.____
2. A. obedient      B. elaborate    C. disgust     D. bearing        E. ambasador    2.____
3. A. awkward       B. charitable   C. typhoid     D. compitition    E. ruffle        3.____
4. A. concervatory  B. ninth        C. morsel      D. squirrels      E. luxury        4.____
5. A. loyalty       B. occasional   C. hosiery     D. bungalow       E. undicided     5.____
6. A. efficient     B. suberb       C. achievement D. bored          E. specimen      6.____
7. A. adaquate      B. salaries     C. utilize     D. alcohol        E. colonel       7.____
8. A. forcibly      B. guardian     C. preceeding  D. quartile       E. quizzes       8.____
9. A. seiges        B. unanimous    C. ridiculous  D. everlasting    E. omissions     9.____
10. A. itemized     B. ignoramus    C. adige       D. adieu          E. nickel       10.____
11. A. resources    B. fileal       C. nervous     D. logical        E. certificate  11.____
12. A. wiring       B. turkeys      C. morass      D. obvious        E. bigimmy      12.____
13. A. affirmitive  B. noisy        C. clothe      D. carnage        E. perceive     13.____
14. A. ignorant     B. literally    C. humerists   D. business       E. awkward      14.____
15. A. thermometer  B. tragady      C. partisan    D. kinsman        E. grandiose    15.____
16. A. fundamental  B. herald       C. delinquent  D. kindergarden   E. ascertain    16.____
17. A. apropriation B. year's       C. vacancy     D. enthusiastic   E. dormitory    17.____
18. A. crochet      B. courtesies   C. troup       D. occasionally   E. spirits      18.____
19. A. typewriting  B. inadequate   C. legitimate  D. fuelless       E. restarant    19.____
20. A. tabloux      B. cooperage    C. wrapped     D. tenant         E. referring    20.____

## KEY (CORRECT ANSWERS)

1. D. consequently
2. E. ambassador
3. D. competition
4. A. conservatory
5. E. undecided
6. B. suburb
7. A. adequate
8. C. preceding OR proceeding
9. A. sieges
10. C. adage
11. B. filial
12. E. bigamy
13. A. affirmative
14. C. humorists
15. B. tragedy
16. D. kindergarten
17. A. appropriation
18. C. troop OR troupe
19. E. restaurant
20. A. tableaux OR tableaus

# TEST 2

DIRECTIONS: In each question of the following tests, select the letter of the one MISSPELLED word in each of the listed groups of five (5) words. *PRINT THE LETTER OF THE CORRECT ANSWER IN THE SPACE AT THE RIGHT.*

1. A. loot  B. surgery  C. breif  D. talcum  E. Christmas  1.____
2. A. commenced  B. congenial  C. fatal  D. politician  E. standerd  2.____
3. A. unbarable  B. physician  C. potato  D. wiring  E. adorable  3.____
4. A. error  B. regretted  C. instetute  D. typhoid  E. we're  4.____
5. A. merly  B. opportunity  C. patterns  D. unctious  E. righteous  5.____
6. A. luxury  B. forty  C. control  D. originally  E. intemate  6.____
7. A. plague  B. ignorance  C. poltrey  D. hence  E. bruise  7.____
8. A. athletic  B. exebition  C. leased  D. interrupt  E. spirits  8.____
9. A. destruction  B. prairie  C. quartet  D. status  E. competators  9.____
10. A. triumph  B. utility  C. loyalty  D. antisapte  E. crochet  10.____
11. A. lieutenant  B. recrute  C. thermometer  D. quantities  E. usefulness  11.____
12. A. wholly  B. sitting  C. probably  D. criticism  E. lynche  12.____
13. A. anteque  B. galvanized  C. mercantile  D. academy  E. defense  13.____
14. A. kinsman  B. declaration  C. absurd  D. dispach  E. patience  14.____
15. A. opportune  B. abbuting  C. warranted  D. refrigerator  E. raisin  15.____
16. A. deffered  B. principalship  C. lovable  D. athletic  E. conveniently  16.____
17. A. mislaid  B. receipted  C. skedule  D. mission  E. whereabouts  17.____
18. A. tuition  B. unnatural  C. remodel  D. consequence  E. misdameanor  18.____
19. A. assessment  B. advises  C. embassys  D. border  E. leased  19.____
20. A. morale  B. legitemate  C. infamy  D. indebtedness  E. technical  20.____

## KEY (CORRECT ANSWERS)

1. C. brief
2. E. standard
3. A. unbearable
4. C. institute
5. A. merely
6. E. intimate
7. C. poultry OR paltry
8. B. exhibition
9. E. competition
10. D. anticipate
11. B. recruit
12. E. lynch
13. A. antique
14. D. dispatch
15. B. abutting
16. A. deferred OR differed
17. C. schedule
18. E. misdemeanor
19. C. embassies
20. B. legitimate

# TEST 3

DIRECTIONS: In each question of the following tests, select the letter of the one MISSPELLED word in each of the listed groups of five (5) words. *PRINT THE LETTER OF THE CORRECT ANSWER IN THE SPACE AT THE RIGHT.*

1. A. stepfather B. fireman C. loot D. conclusivly E. commodity 1.____
2. A. mislaid B. roommate C. religous D. thesis E. temporary 2.____
3. A. statutes B. malice C. unbridled D. aisle E. cavelry 3.____
4. A. aknowledge B. immensely C. quantities D. erratic E. postponed 4.____
5. A. people's B. foreign C. obsticles D. opportunity E. cordially 5.____
6. A. fragrance B. burgaleries C. clothe D. twins E. herculean 6.____
7. A. warranted B. yoke C. democrat D. parashute E. Bible 7.____
8. A. existance B. enthusiasm C. medal D. sandwiches E. dunce 8.____
9. A. loyalty B. eternal C. chanceler D. psychology E. assessment 9.____
10. A. bungalow B. mutilate C. forcible D. ridiculous E. cawcus 10.____
11. A. lieutenant B. abandoned C. successor D. phisycal E. inquiries 11.____
12. A. nuisance B. coranation C. voluntary D. faculties E. awe 12.____
13. A. indipendance B. notwithstanding C. tariff D. opportune E. accompanying 13.____
14. A. statutes B. rhubarb C. corset D. prurient E. subsedy 14.____
15. A. partisan B. initiate C. colonel D. ilness E. errant 15.____
16. A. acquired B. wrapped C. propriater D. screech E. dune 16.____
17. A. sufrage B. countenance C. fraternally D. undo E. fireman 17.____
18. A. ladies B. chef C. spirituelist D. Sabbath E. itemized 18.____
19. A. ere B. interests C. cheesecloth D. paridoxical E. garish 19.____
20. A. bulletin B. neutral C. porttiere D. discretion E. inconvenienced 20.____

## KEY (CORRECT ANSWERS)

1. D. conclusively
2. C. religious
3. E. cavalry
4. A. acknowledge
5. C. obstacles
6. B. burglaries
7. D. parachute
8. A. existence
9. C. chancellor
10. E. caucus
11. D. physical
12. B. coronation
13. A. independence
14. E. subsidy
15. D. illness
16. C. proprietor
17. A. suffrage
18. C. spiritualist
19. D. paradoxical
20. C. portiere

# TEST 4

DIRECTIONS: In each question of the following tests, select the letter of the one MISSPELLED word in each of the listed groups of five (5) words. *PRINT THE LETTER OF THE CORRECT ANSWER IN THE SPACE AT THE RIGHT.*

1. A. I'd  B. premises  C. hysterics  D. aparantly  E. faculties  1.____
2. A. discipline  B. ajurnment  C. bachelor  D. lose  E. wrapped  2.____
3. A. simular  B. bulletin  C. lovable  D. bored  E. quizzes  3.____
4. A. attendance  B. preparation  C. refrigerator  D. cafateria  E. twelfth  4.____
5. A. inconvenienced  B. courtesies  C. raisin  D. hosiery  E. politicean  5.____
6. A. reccommendation  B. colonel  C. sandwiches  D. women's  E. undoubtedly  6.____
7. A. technical  B. imediately  C. temporarily  D. dormitory  E. voluntary  7.____
8. A. salaries  B. abandoned  C. consistent  D. unconcious  E. herald  8.____
9. A. duly  B. leer  C. emphasise  D. vacant  E. requisition  9.____
10. A. melancholy  B. citrus  C. omissions  D. bazaar  E. derigable  10.____
11. A. acquired  B. mercury  C. stetistics  D. thought  E. vassal  11.____
12. A. tempature  B. calendar  C. series  D. gout  E. alcohol  12.____
13. A. important  B. foreigner  C. Australia  D. leggend  E. rhythm  13.____
14. A. height  B. achevement  C. monarchial  D. axle  E. fertile  14.____
15. A. falsity  B. prestige  C. conquer  D. arketecture  E. Jerusalem  15.____
16. A. magnifecent  B. bacteria  C. holly  D. diseases  E. cellar  16.____
17. A. medicine  B. grievous  C. beaker  D. benefits  E. attendents  17.____
18. A. military  B. vacancy  C. weird  D. feudalism  E. hybird  18.____
19. A. adopted  B. agrigate  C. Renaissance  D. tournament  E. colonies  19.____
20. A. vivisection  B. penitentiary  C. candadacy  D. seer  E. Sabbath  20.____

## KEY (CORRECT ANSWERS)

1. D. apparently
2. B. adjournment
3. A. similar
4. D. cafeteria
5. E. politician
6. A. recommendation
7. B. immediately
8. D. unconscious
9. C. emphasizes or emphasis
10. E. dirigible
11. C. statistics
12. A. temperature
13. D. legend
14. B. achievement
15. D. architecture
16. A. magnificent
17. E. attendants
18. E. hybrid
19. B. aggregate
20. C. candidacy

# TEST 5

DIRECTIONS: In each question of the following tests, select the letter of the one MISSPELLED word in each of the listed groups of five (5) words. *PRINT THE LETTER OF THE CORRECT ANSWER IN THE SPACE AT THE RIGHT.*

1. A. acknowledging  B. deligate  C. foliage  D. staid  E. loot  1.____
2. A. gandar  B. losing  C. notwithstanding  D. worlds  E. torrent  2.____
3. A. medal  B. utilize  C. efficiency  D. apricot  E. soliceting  3.____
4. A. museum  B. Christian  C. possesion  D. occasional  E. bored  4.____
5. A. capitol  B. sieze  C. premises  D. fragrance  E. tonnage  5.____
6. A. requisition  B. faculties  C. canon  D. chaufur  E. stomach  6.____
7. A. solemn  B. ascertain  C. I'll  D. chef  E. delinquant  7.____
8. A. parliments  B. distributor  C. voluntary  D. lovable  E. counsel  8.____
9. A. morale  B. democrat  C. rhumatism  D. dormitory  E. leased  9.____
10. A. screech  B. missapropriating  C. courtesies  D. wraith  E. furlough  10.____
11. A. tryst  B. tarriff  C. visible  D. accent  E. contraries  11.____
12. A. dizzy  B. leggings  C. steak  D. compaine  E. interior  12.____
13. A. profit  B. tiranny  C. shocked  D. response  E. innocent  13.____
14. A. freshman  B. vague  C. larsiny  D. ignorant  E. worrying  14.____
15. A. disatesfied  B. jealous  C. unfortunately  D. economical  E. lettuce  15.____
16. A. based  B. primarily  C. condemned  D. accompanied  E. dupped  16.____
17. A. superntendant  B. veil  C. congenial  D. quantities  E. ere  17.____
18. A. unanimous  B. dessert  C. undoubtedly  D. kolera  E. nuisance  18.____
19. A. woman's  B. bolero  C. 'tis  D. Pullman  E. envellop  19.____
20. A. initiate  B. grist  C. pagent  D. mention  E. adieu  20.____

## KEY (CORRECT ANSWERS)

1. B. delegate
2. A. gander
3. E. soliciting
4. C. possession
5. B. seize
6. D. chauffeur
7. E. delinquent
8. A. parliaments
9. C. rheumatism
10. B. misappropriating
11. B. tariff
12. D. campaign
13. B. tyranny
14. C. larceny
15. A. dissatisfied
16. E. duped
17. A. superintendent
18. D. cholera
19. E. envelope
20. C. pageant

# TEST 6

DIRECTIONS: In each question of the following tests, select the letter of the one MISSPELLED word in each of the listed groups of five (5) words. *PRINT THE LETTER OF THE CORRECT ANSWER IN THE SPACE AT THE RIGHT.*

1. A. attach  B. voucher  C. twins  D. assistence  E. cordial  1.____
2. A. faculties  B. people's  C. indetedness  D. ignorant  E. resource  2.____
3. A. wholly  B. apitite  C. twelfth  D. unauthorized  E. embroider  3.____
4. A. certified  B. attorneys  C. foggy  D. potato  E. extravigent  4.____
5. A. hysterics  B. simelar  C. intelligent  D. label  E. salaries  5.____
6. A. apponants  B. we're  C. finely  D. herald  E. continuous  6.____
7. A. cancellation  B. athletic  C. perminant  D. preference  E. utilize  7.____
8. A. urns  B. zephyr  C. tuition  D. incidentally  E. aquisition  8.____
9. A. kinsaan  B. bazaar  C. foliage  D. wretched  E. asassination  9.____
10. A. insignia  B. bimonthly  C. typewriting  D. notariety  E. psychology  10.____
11. A. continually  B. guild  C. vegtable  D. vague  E. patience  11.____
12. A. desease  B. parole  C. gallery  D. awkward  E. you'd  12.____
13. A. border  B. warrant  C. operated  D. economics  E. ilegal  13.____
14. A. fatal  B. agatation  C. obliged  D. studying  E. resignation  14.____
15. A. ammendment  B. promptness  C. glimpse  D. canon  E. tract  15.____
16. A. wholly  B. apricot  C. destruction  D. pappal  E. leisure  16.____
17. A. issuing  B. rabbid  C. unusual  D. parasite  E. khaki  17.____
18. A. nowadays  B. courtesies  C. negotiate  D. gaurdian  E. derrick  18.____
19. A. partisan  B. seanse  C. vacancy  D. fragrance  E. corps  19.____
20. A. equipped  B. nuisance  C. phrenology  D. foriegn  E. insignia  20.____

## KEY (CORRECT ANSWERS)

1. D. assistance
2. C. indebtedness
3. B. appetite
4. E. extravagant
5. B. similar
6. A. opponents
7. C. permanent
8. E. acquisition
9. E. assassination
10. D. notoriety
11. C. vegetable
12. A. disease
13. E. illegal
14. B. agitation
15. A. amendment
16. D. papal
17. B. rabid
18. D. guardian
19. B. eance
20. D. foreign

---

# TEST 7

DIRECTIONS: In each question of the following tests, select the letter of the one MIS-SPELLED word in each of the listed groups of five (5) words. *PRINT THE LETTER OF THE CORRECT ANSWER IN THE SPACE AT THE RIGHT.*

1. A. frightfully   B. mantain       C. post office    D. specific    E. bachelor      1._____
2. A. cease         B. turkeys       C. woman's        D. hustling    E. weild         2._____
3. A. expidition    B. valuing       C. typhoid        D. grapevines  E. advice        3._____
4. A. balance       B. visible       C. correspondant  D. etc.        E. arctic        4._____
5. A. benefit       B. arkives       C. classified     D. inasmuch    E. sincerity     5._____
6. A. obedient      B. vengeance     C. plague         D. fascinate   E. contageous    6._____
7. A. desicion      B. partner       C. economy        D. piece       E. arrogant      7._____
8. A. dyeing        B. lightning     C. millenary      D. undulate    E. embarrass     8._____
9. A. strenuous     B. isicle        C. panel          D. suburb      E. luxury        9._____
10. A. aisle        B. proffer       C. people's       D. condemed    E. morale        10._____
11. A. advising     B. recognizing   C. seize          D. supply      E. tradegy       11._____
12. A. intensive    B. stationary    C. benifit        D. equipped    E. preferring    12._____
13. A. predjudice   B. pervade       C. excel          D. capitol     E. chimera       13._____
14. A. all right    B. ninty         C. cronies        D. nervous     E. separate      14._____
15. A. atheletic    B. queue         C. schedule       D. furl        E. credible      15._____
16. A. inevitable   B. sincerly      C. monkeys        D. definite    E. cynical       16._____
17. A. niece        B. accommodate   C. loveliness     D. reciept     E. forcibly      17._____
18. A. cancel       B. chagrined     C. allies         D. playwright  E. liutenant     18._____
19. A. pageant      B. alcohol       C. villian        D. Odyssey     E. criticize     19._____
20. A. acknowledge  B. article       C. contemptible   D. taciturn    E. sovregin      20._____

## KEY (CORRECT ANSWERS)

1. B. maintain
2. E. wield
3. A. expedition
4. C. correspondent
5. B. archives
6. E. contagious
7. A. decision
8. C. millinery
9. B. icicle
10. D. condemned
11. E. tragedy
12. C. benefit
13. A. prejudice
14. B. ninety
15. A. athletic
16. B. sincerely
17. D. receipt
18. E. lieutenant
19. C. villain
20. E. sovereign

# TEST 8

DIRECTIONS: In each question of the following tests, select the letter of the one MISSPELLED word in each of the listed groups of five (5) words. *PRINT THE LETTER OF THE CORRECT ANSWER IN THE SPACE AT THE RIGHT.*

| | | | | | | | | | | |
|---|---|---|---|---|---|---|---|---|---|---|
| 1. | A. | incurred | B. | cieling | C. | strengthen | D. | carnage | E. | typical | 1.____ |
| 2. | A. | twins | B. | year's | C. | acutely | D. | changible | E. | facility | 2.____ |
| 3. | A. | deliscious | B. | enormous | C. | likeness | D. | witnesses | E. | commodity | 3.____ |
| 4. | A. | scenes | B. | enlargement | C. | discretion | D. | acknowledging | E. | sesion | 4.____ |
| 5. | A. | annum | B. | strenuous | C. | tretchery | D. | infamy | E. | opportune | 5.____ |
| 6. | A. | marmelade | B. | loot | C. | kinsman | D. | crochet | E. | hawser | 6.____ |
| 7. | A. | sophmore | B. | duly | C. | across | D. | lovable | E. | propaganda | 7.____ |
| 8. | A. | quantities | B. | rickety | C. | roommate | D. | penetentiary | E. | lose | 8.____ |
| 9. | A. | interrupt | B. | cauldron | C. | convienient | D. | successor | E. | apiece | 9.____ |
| 10. | A. | acquire | B. | incesent | C. | forfeit | D. | typewritten | E. | dysentery | 10.____ |
| 11. | A. | inferred | B. | whisle | C. | jovial | D. | conscript | E. | gracious | 11.____ |
| 12. | A. | tantalizing | B. | ominous | C. | conductor | D. | duchess | E. | telegram | 12.____ |
| 13. | A. | reconcile | B. | primitive | C. | sausy | D. | quinine | E. | cede | 13.____ |
| 14. | A. | immagine | B. | viaduct | C. | chisel | D. | Saturn | E. | currant | 14.____ |
| 15. | A. | amplify | B. | greace | C. | cholera | D. | perilous | E. | theology | 15.____ |
| 16. | A. | pursevere | B. | deodorize | C. | ligament | D. | illuminate | E. | dropsy | 16.____ |
| 17. | A. | cavalier | B. | transparent | C. | perjury | D. | vicinaty | E. | navigate | 17.____ |
| 18. | A. | postpone | B. | dictaphone | C. | corral | D. | alligator | E. | arteficial | 18.____ |
| 19. | A. | cannon | B. | hospital | C. | distilliry | D. | righteous | E. | secession | 19.____ |
| 20. | A. | matrimony | B. | digestable | C. | scrutiny | D. | artisan | E. | mediocre | 20.____ |

## KEY (CORRECT ANSWERS)

1. B. ceiling
2. D. changeable
3. A. delicious
4. E. session
5. C. treachery
6. A. marmalade
7. A. sophomore
8. D. penitentiary
9. C. convenient
10. B. incessant
11. B. whistle
12. E. telegram
13. C. saucy
14. A. imagine
15. B. grease
16. A. persevere
17. D. vicinity
18. E. artificial
19. C. distillery
20. B. digestible

# TEST 9

DIRECTIONS: In each question of the following tests, select the letter of the one MISSPELLED word in each of the listed groups of five (5) words. *PRINT THE LETTER OF THE CORRECT ANSWER IN THE SPACE AT THE RIGHT.*

1. A. feirce B. ascent C. allies D. doctor E. coming 1.____
2. A. hopeless B. absense C. foretell D. certain E. similar 2.____
3. A. advise B. muscle C. manual D. provocation E. copywright 3.____
4. A. behooves B. reservoir C. frostbiten D. squalor E. ambuscade 4.____
5. A. systematic B. precious C. tremendos D. insulation E. brilliant 5.____
6. A. significant B. jurisdiction C. libel D. monkies E. legacy 6.____
7. A. dual B. authentic C. serenety D. mechanism E. suburban 7.____
8. A. candel B. dissolution C. laceration D. portend E. pigeon 8.____
9. A. loyalty B. periodic C. presume D. led E. suprano 9.____
10. A. mania B. medicinal C. dungarees D. overwelming E. masquerade 10.____
11. A. pitiful B. latter C. ommitted D. agreement E. reconcile 11.____
12. A. bananna B. routine C. likewise D. indecent E. habitually 12.____
13. A. relieve B. copys C. ninety D. crowded E. electoral 13.____
14. A. adviseable B. illustrative C. financial D. nevertheless E. chimneys 14.____
15. A. prisioner B. immediate C. statistics D. surgeon E. abscond 15.____
16. A. option B. extradite C. comparitive D. jealousy E. illusion 16.____
17. A. handicaped B. assurance C. sympathy D. speech E. dining 17.____
18. A. recommend B. carraige C. disapprove D. independent E. mortgage 18.____
19. A. systematic B. ingenuity C. tenet D. uncanny E. intrigueing 19.____
20. A. arduous B. hideous C. fervant D. companies E. breach 20.____

## KEY (CORRECT ANSWERS)

1. A. fierce
2. B. absence
3. E. copyright
4. C. frostbitten
5. C. tremendous
6. D. monkeys
7. C. serenity
8. A. candle
9. E. soprano
10. D. overwhelming
11. C. omitted
12. A. banana
13. B. copies
14. A. advisable
15. A. prisoner
16. C. comparative
17. A. handicapped
18. B. carriage
19. E. intriguing
20. C. fervent

# TEST 10

DIRECTIONS: In each question of the following tests, select the letter of the one MIS-SPELLED word in each of the listed groups of five (5) words. *PRINT THE LETTER OF THE CORRECT ANSWER IN THE SPACE AT THE RIGHT.*

1. A. together  B. attempt  C. loyality  D. innocent  E. rinse  1.____
2. A. argueing  B. emergency  C. kindergarten  D. religious  E. schedule  2.____
3. A. society  B. anticipate  C. dissatisfy  D. responsable  E. temporary  3.____
4. A. chaufeur  B. grammar  C. planned  D. dining room  E. accurate  4.____
5. A. confidence  B. maturity  C. aspirations  D. evasion  E. insurence  5.____
6. A. unnecessary  B. dirigible  C. transparant  D. similar  E. appetite  6.____
7. A. treachery  B. comedian  C. arrest  D. recollect  E. mistep  7.____
8. A. falsify  B. blight  C. flexible  D. drasticaly  E. meddlesome  8.____
9. A. congestion  B. publickly  C. receipts  D. academic  E. paralyze  9.____
10. A. possibilities  B. undergoes  C. consistant  D. aggression  E. pledge  10.____
11. A. wrist  B. welfare  C. necessity  D. scenery  E. tendancy  11.____
12. A. commiting  B. accusation  C. endurance  D. agreeable  E. excitable  12.____
13. A. despair  B. surgury  C. privilege  D. appreciation  E. journeying  13.____
14. A. cameos  B. propaganda  C. delicious  D. heathen  E. interupt  14.____
15. A. relieve  B. disappear  C. development  D. matress  E. ninety-nine  15.____
16. A. finally  B. bullitin  C. doctor  D. desirable  E. sincerely  16.____
17. A. wrest  B. array  C. auspices  D. sacrafice  E. generations  17.____
18. A. liquid  B. vegetable  C. silence  D. familiar  E. fasinate  18.____
19. A. tomato  B. suspence  C. leisure  D. license  E. permanent  19.____
20. A. characteristic  B. soliciting  C. repitious  D. immediately  E. extravagant  20.____

## KEY (CORRECT ANSWERS)

1. C. loyalty
2. A. arguing
3. D. responsible
4. A. chauffeur
5. E. insurance
6. C. transparent
7. E. misstep
8. D. drastically
9. B. publicly
10. C. consistent
11. E. tendency
12. A. committing
13. B. surgery
14. E. interrupt
15. D. mattress
16. B. bulletin
17. D. sacrifice
18. E. fascinate
19. B. suspense
20. C. repetitious

www.ingramcontent.com/pod-product-compliance
Lightning Source LLC
Chambersburg PA
CBHW081756300426
44116CB00014B/2140